FIRST GENERATION: AN AUTOBIOGRAPHY

First Generation

An Autobiography

ERNEST SIRLUCK

UNIVERSITY OF TORONTO PRESS
Toronto Buffalo London

© University of Toronto Press Incorporated 1996
Toronto Buffalo London
Printed in Canada
Reprinted in 2018

ISBN 0-8020-0793-7 (cloth)
ISBN 978-1-4875-8206-7 (paper)

Printed on acid-free paper

Canadian Cataloguing in Publication Data

Sirluck, Ernest, 1918–
   First generation : an autobiography

   Includes index.
   ISBN 0-8020-0793-7

1. Sirluck, Ernest, 1918– . 2. University of Chicago – Biography. 3. University of Toronto – Biography. 4. University of Manitoba – Biography. 5. College teachers – Canada – Biography. 6. College administrators – Canada – Biography. I. Title.

LA2325.S57A3 1996   378.1'2'092   C95-932837-8

University of Toronto Press acknowledges the financial assistance to its publishing program of the Canada Council and the Ontario Arts Council.

To Lesley, Robert, and Kate

Contents

PREFACE ix

Chapter One: Winkler, 1918–1935   3

Chapter Two: Winnipeg, 1935–1940   30

Chapter Three: Toronto, 1940–1942   67

Chapter Four: Canadian Army, 1942–1945   99

Chapter Five: Toronto, 1945–1947   145

Chapter Six: Chicago, 1947–1962   165

Chapter Seven: Toronto, 1962–1970   219

Chapter Eight: Winnipeg, 1970–1976   304

Chapter Nine: Toronto, 1976–   381

INDEX 399

Preface

Some of the unpublished material referred to in the text is available in the University of Toronto Archives, catalogued under my name or under the names of the relevant University of Toronto bodies; some remains in my possession. The account of my army experience is in part based on letters which I wrote to my wife at the time and which she has kept.

I thank the following persons who read all or part of my manuscript and made helpful suggestions, but are not responsible for any errors: Lesley Sirluck, Robert Sirluck, Katherine Ann Sirluck, Ian Montagnes, the late John M. Robson, and Bert Bruser.

Maternal grandparents, Yosel and Freyda Nitikman, and their children: (*left to right*) Mike, Hannah, Aaron, Sam (*front*), and Rose, with Rose's husband, Isaac Sirluck, and their daughter, Gertrude. Winkler, 1910.

Grandfather Usher Zelig Sirluck. Winkler, ca 1910.

Grandmother Bella Sirluck, with her daughter, Goldy, and a niece. Winkler, ca 1912.

Isaac and Rose Sirluck with their children: (*from left*) Gladys, Gertrude, and Hilda. Winkler, 1916.

Ernest Sirluck as an undergraduate at the University of Manitoba, 1937.

Ernest and Lesley Sirluck after their wedding at Hart House, University of Toronto; Claude Bissell and Macushla Pritchard in background. 1942.

Robert (Bert) Sirluck on completing RCAF training. Winnipeg, 1942.

E.S. in the field with Fourth Canadian Armoured Division. France, 1944.

During a divisional rest and rehabilitation break. Holland, 1944.

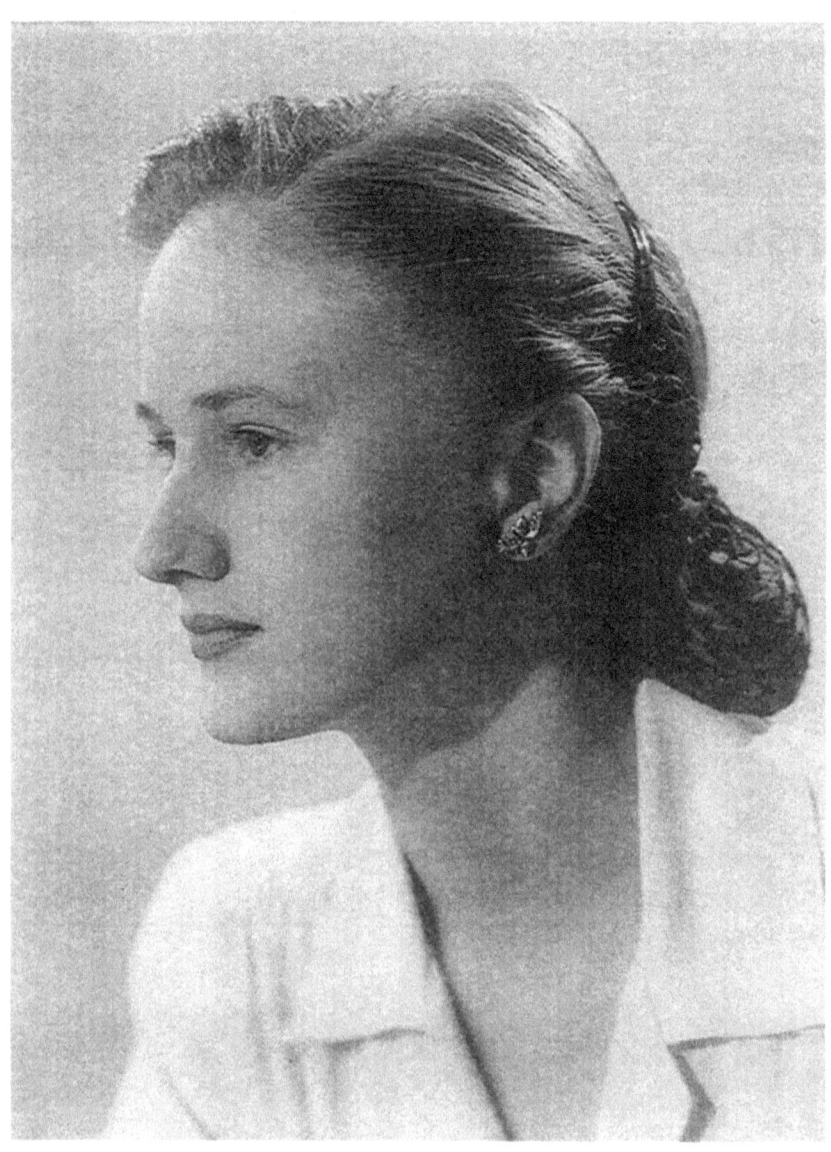

Lesley. Toronto, 1945. (Photo by John Steele)

MBE investiture by Governor General Field Marshal Lord Alexander. Convocation Hall, University of Toronto, 1946. (Canadian Army Photo)

With Isaac Sirluck. University of Chicago, 1950.

With George Steiner, Director of English Studies, Churchill College, Cambridge, and Henry Moore, at the installation of the sculpture Moore gave the College. 1966.

With Sir John Cockcroft, Master of Churchill College, and David Scott, Chairman of the Physics Department, University of Toronto. Massey College, 1967.

Lesley on the roof of University College, making the drawing of the University of Toronto campus that was to be that year's Sirluck Christmas card. 1968.

With Lesley, Kate, and Robert in the president's house, University of Manitoba. Winnipeg, 1970.

Being congratulated by Claude Bissell at installation as president of the University of Manitoba. Ft Garry, 1970.

With Bora Laskin, who was receiving an honorary degree shortly before becoming Chief Justice of Canada. Ft Garry, 1972.

Confronting strike demonstrators. Ft Garry, 1974.

Addressing University of Toronto convocation after receiving honorary degree. Platform party: (*front row, left to right*) John Kelly, Harry Eastman, Carl Goldenberg (also getting an honorary degree), Sidney Hermant, Claude Bissell, Chancellor Pauline McGibbon, President John Evans; leaning forward at right of third row: Marshall McLuhan. 1974. (Photo by Robert Lonsdale)

University of Manitoba farewell reception for the Sirlucks: W.J. Condo, chairman of the Universities Grants Commission, and Hugh Saunderson, E.S.'s predecessor as president of the University (*centre*). Ft Garry, 1976.

FIRST GENERATION: AN AUTOBIOGRAPHY

CHAPTER ONE

Winkler, 1918–1935

I was born on 25 April 1918, in Winkler, Manitoba, a predominantly German-speaking village of four or five hundred people. The doctor, the bank manager, the station-agent, and the druggist were of British descent; there were eight or nine German Lutheran and as many Russian Jewish families; the rest were Mennonites, who had homesteaded in the area about forty years earlier. These were descendants of German and Dutch Anabaptists who had gone to Russia in the mid-eighteenth century on invitation from the Empress Catherine, who gave them extensive special privileges, including religious and cultural autonomy and exemption from military service. In the 1870s, however, Tsar Alexander II's policy of 'Russification' ended these privileges and caused about a third of the Russian Mennonites to emigrate; about seven thousand came to southern Manitoba under an arrangement with the federal government, which set aside two large blocks of free land for them (the East Reserve, centred in Steinbach east of the Red River, and the West Reserve, which later became centred in Winkler), exempted them from military service and, by a secret order-in-council which later caused trouble because it encroached upon provincial jurisdiction, declared that they could educate their children in private as they saw fit. It was an arrangement which would draw considerable criticism, particularly during both world wars, but for the settling of the empty prairies (as well as other reasons) it was a good bargain. The semi-arid, treeless, windswept plain would defeat a considerable proportion of the numerous attempts to farm it, but the Mennonites were well prepared by a century of farming the geologically similar Russian steppe, and they brought with them farming and housing techniques, together with supplies of well-adapted Russian hard red seed wheat, which enabled them to survive the first harsh years and become firmly established.

Although the district was pioneered by the Mennonites, the village was not. During their centuries of religious persecution in Europe, the Mennonites had developed a defensive strategy they called *stelle em Laund* (quiet in the land). When the Canadian Pacific Railway, whose branch-line through southwestern Manitoba had opened a decade earlier, decided in 1892 to build a station on the West Reserve, the Mennonite church pressed Isaac Wiens, the farmer on whose homestead the station would be located, to trade holdings with Valentine Winkler, a non-Mennonite some miles away, so that the community could remain detached from the town they foresaw. This suspicion of towns created an opportunity for others to enter what had been a closed, homogeneous district, an opportunity much more attractive to German and Jewish immigrants than to anglophones, since business with the surrounding farmers had to be transacted in German, to which Yiddish is closely related. Accordingly, German Lutherans, Jews, and a few others established businesses in Winkler, which became the chief trading centre of the district. Arke Nitikman, the first member of my mother's family to reach Winkler, arrived in 1892, about the same time as Aaron Cohen, a fellow-townsman of my father's. By the time I was born the appeal of town life had in part overcome the Mennonites' initial suspicion and there were more Mennonite businesses than others.

When I began school in 1923 the language of the classroom was English, but the language of the playground, as of almost everything else in the village, was *Plattdeutsch* (*Plautdietsch*, as the Mennonites pronounced it), Low German. All the teachers were Mennonite, but most had been born in Canada, so that while English was not their first language it was usually a fairly comfortable second.

In our family the linguistic situation was complicated. My parents spoke Yiddish to each other, but as their years in Canada lengthened and their children grew more numerous and more determinedly English-speaking they gradually increased the proportion of English they spoke at table and in other family situations. We children spoke Yiddish when we visited our grandparents or the other older Jewish immigrants, while speaking English with their children. Prayers at home and religious services in the little two-room synagogue were in Hebrew, but the affairs of the synagogue were conducted in Yiddish. At business we spoke whatever the customer preferred, which was usually German; there were a few Polish and Ukrainian customers to whom my father spoke in their own languages. My mother, who was still in her teens when she reached Canada, had picked up English fairly easily and spoke it with little accent, but the education of girls in the Russian–Jewish *shtetl* did not include literacy and, although she had taught herself to manage a Jewish newspaper, she never learnt to read English. My father was in his mid-twenties when he arrived and his English was therefore more heavily accented, but he could read and write it.

My maternal grandparents, Yosel and Freyda Nitikman, and their five children, of whom Ruchel, my mother, was the eldest, came to Winkler from Vishgorod in Ukraine in stages between 1899 and 1901, part of the great Jewish flight from increasingly grim Russian repression and persecution. My father, Isaac Sirluck, came in 1906; he was performing his compulsory military service when war broke out with Japan in 1904 and intensified the already savage official and unofficial abuse Jewish soldiers suffered in the Russian army. He managed to escape without resorting to the self-inflicted wounds then so common; at Liverpool the Jewish Immigration Aid Society steered him toward work as a harvester in Argentina, where he stooked and pitched for a year and a half, saving enough money to come to Winkler, where he knew Aaron Cohen, like himself from Teofipol' in Ukraine. He and Ruchel (her name by then anglicized to 'Rose') were married about a year after his arrival.

Their first years were hard. My father got started in business as a pedlar with horse and wagon and was developing a promising customer base in the surrounding farm villages when his horse was startled and bolted, the wagon tipped and fell across his leg, and he was put out of business, and into bed for months. He then worked for, and later became a partner in, the general store run by my mother's father and brother, which was renamed the Nitikmans Sirluck Company. His most urgent priority was to get his parents and three sisters out of Russia, which he managed within two or three years of his arrival. My eldest sister, Gertrude, was born in 1908, and Hilda and Gladys came in the next five years. For some years the household had to practise stringent economy as well as the hard work my parents thought natural. However, by the time my birth made it necessary to move out of their small, crowded house, they were able to buy a four-bedroom house at the corner of Sixth (or 'Shady') Street and Mountain Avenue (so named despite the dozen miles that separated it from the nearest small rise, the Pembina Hills). This was the more desirable part of town, boasting most of its trees – tall, fast-growing, short-lived cottonwoods – and with some struggling grass in its front yards behind picket fences.

For several years (1923–30) the Jewish population of Winkler was large enough to maintain a synagogue and *chazan* (cantor), who doubled as *melamed* (teacher) and *shochet* (butcher). The first one I remember was much the best, a humane, civilized man; regrettably, I had not got very far in my Jewish studies before he moved to Winnipeg and was succeeded by much poorer teachers who turned what should have been interesting studies into wearisome chores. The lessons consisted of learning enough Hebrew to read the prayer-book and translate selections from the Hebrew Bible and the Talmud into Yiddish, writing little commentaries on them in Yiddish, and generally preparing for the bar mitzvah; postbiblical Jewish history was left untouched. *Cheder* (school) started just after four o'clock, when the public-school day ended and other schoolchildren played baseball or hockey – or so I contended, although my parents argued that most of them did chores – so that the dullness and oppression of the study-room, the witless pedagogy, and the person and manners of the last of the *melamdim* combined with my resentment at being deprived of games and free time to bring me near to rebellion. My parents urged me to stick it out until my bar mitzvah, and I suppose I'd have done so, but a year or so before that event the *melamed* got into trouble (he was living alone in Winkler, his family still in Russia, and he made some advance to a local girl, which was rejected and reported) and was sent packing the same day; by that time the Jewish community had so dwindled that it could not attract a replacement, and my final preparations for the bar mitzvah were directed by my father.

In contrast to this dreariness, the actual services had some liveliness. Just before sundown on Friday evenings the congregation, all male, the adults freshly shaven and dressed in suit and tie and led by the *chazan*, would recite the *Mincha* (afternoon service) and then chat a little until it was clear the sun had set, whereupon it would recite the *Maariv* (evening service), exchange sabbath greetings, and hurry home, where the ritual candles, wine, and *challah* (braided egg-bread), with their several prayers, were followed by the best meal of the week (usually chicken) on the best tablecloth in the house, accompanied in the luckier families, of which ours was one, by unhurried and agreeable conversation. Saturday-morning service was more ragged, with faces wearing a stubble that would last at least until the sabbath sundown and expressions already beginning to reflect the business concerns to which most of the congregation would hurry when the service was over; but one or two elders could usually be counted on to linger and dispute with the *chazan* and each other the subtleties of the week's biblical and prophetic readings.

On the high holy days, Rosh Hashanah and Yom Kippur, females were admitted to the synagogue – to the second room, of course, where it was supposed that they would not distract the males. Each holy day had its own character, usually strengthened by an element of theatre; my favourite was *Simchath Torah*, the day on which the prescribed annual reading of the Bible was completed and begun anew. Tradition commands that this service be joyously celebrated, with food and wine; all the males, including boys below the age of confirmation, had a turn at carrying the heavy *torah* scroll around the room; when the ceremony was over, there would be a serving of biscuits and tiny glasses of *schnapps* in the synagogue, and then visitations to all the Jewish houses in turn, where food and drink would be laid out in whatever variety and abundance the family could afford. Everyone took some drink and sang and danced the ancient Hebrew composition; the congregation, not ordinarily the gayest of companions, talked louder and laughed harder as it progressed from house to house; and at least old man Danzker and old man Fleischman could be counted on to get a little drunk.

I was a little more than five years old when I started school (there was, of course, no kindergarten in the town). There was no problem about getting up on time: the cowherd who went along Mountain Avenue at seven every morning collecting cows for the day's pasturing always sounded his bugle just under my window. On the first morning, my slightly older cousin Herb Nitikman and I were taken to the schoolyard two blocks west along Mountain Avenue by one of our mothers or sisters, and left at the door. I was busy reconnoitring the crowd of children playing and talking a language I recognized but did not yet understand when Herb grabbed my arm and said, close to tears, 'Let's go home.' I shook him off and he ran down the street, to the jeers of the milling children. I could understand his feelings – our reception had not been friendly – but not his action; and indeed, it haunted him. He came back that afternoon, firmly escorted by his mother, but the damage had been done; for the few remaining years that he lived in Winkler he was treated as a sissy.

I don't know whether that day was my first exposure to crowd antisemitism, but it's the first I remember. The children surrounded me and, switching to English for my benefit, repeatedly explained that I was a dirty Jew who had killed Christ. Wearying of words, several of the boys illustrated the point with blows, and one or two of the girls helped out with a pinch or a tug at my longish hair. I struck out at those I could reach but it didn't have much effect. The baiting was stopped but not rebuked by the appearance of the teacher. I learnt more than I realized in that five-minute demonstration. Nor did things change a great deal as I was growing up, except superficially: there was always someone willing to defend Christianity, and indeed racial purity, by hitting a smaller Jew, and since I was more lightly built and less developed by hard physical labour than these sturdy Mennonites and Lutherans, most of these encounters ended with my taking more and harder blows than I was able to give, and then wiping the stain from my honour (along with the blood from my nose) by analysing at the top of my voice the moral and intellectual defects of my gloating antagonist. My younger brother, Bert, when his turn came, found this kind of exchange unsatisfactory; he sent off to the Charles Atlas Company for their course in body-building and devoted many hours to it. He therefore didn't get much reading done, but the great day came when he was ready for the worst of the school bullies; he was never picked on again while he lived in Winkler.

The first four grades of school were in a single room. This meant that each class received instruction only about a quarter of the time and pupils got almost no individual attention. A slight temporary compensation was that in the lower grades one could listen to what was being said in the higher ones, which was stimulating at first. By the time I got to Grade Four and had to spend much of my time listening to lessons I'd already endured, I'd developed a method to escape boredom: illicit reading. I constantly smuggled magazines and books into class and read them under cover of doing lessons. I was often caught and sometimes punished, but not deterred, since the work of the class was not enough to keep me occupied. I had learnt to read early, but not in school: my sisters read and talked about books, had accumulated a little library at home, and helped me get started. At first I read the children's stories they got for me, and I remained interested when they introduced me to *Boys' Own Annual* and *Chums* (which began my almost lifelong anglophilia), but I soon distressed them by becoming an addict of *Wild West Weekly* and similar publications. As time went on I also read the novels they were reading and liked to discuss these with them, and they were puzzled that I could like these novels and cowboy trash simultaneously. I think it was partly because the western pulps were about as far away from Jewish stereotypes as one could get, and identifying with their heroes allowed me some surcease from the self-hatred that endemic anti-semitism can induce.

When I was eight or nine my uncle Michael, who had apparently played the violin quite well before contracting encephalitis during an outbreak some years earlier, died, leaving his violin to me – or so I was told. A smaller instrument was acquired to serve until I would be big enough for the legacy, and I was put to lessons under a large, dour, and formidable man named Penner, who was also the schoolteacher in charge of Grade Six. Penner was as off-putting a violin teacher as I later found him to be a schoolteacher, and I think not much better as a musician. I wanted to do well and discharge the obligation of family sentiment, but I was not very musical and, besides, Penner seemed interested only in fingering, bowing, and scales. I therefore scanted on practice, and to my astonishment was strapped on the hands. Penner kept in his desk a strap of a peculiarly painful nature, thick but very flexible, with one smooth and one corrugated side; I now think he must have cut it from a thresher-belt. Perhaps I worked a little harder for a while, but that didn't save me from the strap, which he clearly liked using. When, at the age of ten, I reached Grade Six, I was familiar with the strap and with Penner and should have been cautious, but he turned out to be so dogmatic and authoritarian in the classroom that I couldn't refrain from questioning him and sometimes disagreeing. That, I soon learnt, was unsafe; and now when he hit me it was always with the corrugated side and very hard. I had few means of combating these humiliations but I did crawl in the window once after school and cut his strap up with my Scout knife; the next morning, when no one admitted to the deed, he assumed I had done it and strapped me with his belt until both my hands bled. I don't think I challenged him overtly again, but at least I got my parents to agree that I could drop the violin in favour of the piano, which I studied under a less punitive female teacher for three years, but to no great avail.

The teacher in charge of Grade Eight, on the other hand, a fat, white-haired, bespectacled man named P.H. Siemens, favoured a rope and would slaver while using it, first on the buttocks of the bent-over subject, then on the legs. He particularly loved to make the victim cry in front of the class and promise to be good, which was an available escape for those of secure status but not for the lone Jew, always conscious of a need to prove myself to peers only too ready to find cause to bait me. I collected a number of such public ropings, most of which ended only when Siemens tired or reluctantly concluded that he was going dangerously far.

Not all the teachers were sadists, of course; most were decent people carrying out their jobs as they'd been taught to do them. But there was a strong tradition of physical discipline in the community which naturally pervaded the school, and even the gentler women teachers in charge of the lower grades routinely brought rulers forcefully down on knuckles for small infractions, using the edge rather than the flat if they thought it deserved, and sending the worst culprits to the principal's office for strapping or roping.

The school was not a good one and I was contemptuous of it; it took me some years to realize that the continuing influence of the original settlers, with their conviction that education (especially in a language other than *Plautdietsch*) was a dangerous opening for the outside world to get at their children, made it very difficult for the school. For centuries the sect had isolated itself, convinced that it possessed the immediate word of God and distrustful of human reason and society. It had come to Canada on the understanding that it would be allowed to continue this defensive strategy, but in 1916 the Manitoba School Amendment Act, put through by the Norris Liberal government, whose minister of agriculture was the same Valentine Winkler whose fortune rose out of the land exchange which the Mennonite church pressed upon Isaac Wiens, had made attendance at public schools compulsory (English had already been made the sole language of instruction in the schools in 1890). During the First World War considerable resentment of the Mennonites had developed in the English-speaking towns to the west and north of Winkler; it was complained that they spoke the language of the enemy and were exempt from military service while the sons of other people were being killed by other Germans. This led in 1917 to their disenfranchisement as conscientious objectors, and shortly after the war ended they also lost their exemption from military service, and further Mennonite immigration was prohibited. As a result, there was a large Mennonite emigration in 1922-3 to Mexico and Central and South America, where they regained the exemptions they had lost in Canada.

To my grandfather Sirluck, who had been an overseer on an agricultural estate in Ukraine, this came as an opportunity to farm for himself, which Jews had not been permitted to do in Russia, and he bought a farm at Niemberg, some seven miles south of Winkler, which he worked with the help of a hired man. My father and the Nitikmans formed a partnership to buy a number of additional quarter-sections which the continuing emigration made available in Niemberg and Chortitz, about four miles southwest of Winkler. My father supervised the work on the farms, some of it done with hired help, some on a crop-sharing rental. He was now harvesting considerable grain, and decided to avoid the extortionate commissions charged by the grain companies by building his own elevator, confident that by charging less he could secure enough business to make it pay. At first the CPR agreed informally to let him build on the siding where the other grain elevators were, but those companies put pressure on the railway, which rescinded its promise. My father thereupon bought a large lot near the bottom of Mountain Avenue, between Third and Fourth Streets, two blocks from the railway, brought in a disused windmill from Reinfeld, a few miles away, and, to the general derision of the town and district, converted it into what may have been the only prairie grain elevator not on a railway siding. The CPR, being a common carrier, could not refuse him boxcars; these were filled by means of a loader of the type farmers used for moving grain from wagon to bin, and the loader was fed by horse-drawn wagons which hauled the grain from the elevator. It was an awkward, time-consuming, and labour-intensive procedure, but my father was soon getting more grain than any of the larger, more efficient elevators because he charged lower commissions, gave better grades, deducted less for screenings, and generally avoided the tricks that made the large grain companies so disliked.

He now had a great deal to attend to, and a motor car became necessary. In the summer and fall he would rise at five, drive to Chortitz and sometimes to Niemberg to consult with the farm workers about that day's operations, open the store at seven o'clock, come home, a block away, for breakfast, check on the elevator and the rail-side loader, spend the rest of the morning in the store, take his main meal at noon, work in the store until closing time at six, have supper, and then often go back to Chortitz for a final check-up. Often I went with him, and on those empty rutted country roads he taught me to drive, using Eaton's catalogues and newspapers to make me sit higher (indeed, when I first began these lessons I was small enough to stand between his legs). Sometimes when he had no need to go to the farm in the morning I would be sent to get the milk from our Chortitz farm, and occasionally to take or bring a message, before telephones came to Manitoba farms. During seeding and harvesting he would spend a great deal of time on the farm, and I went with him whenever I could. On these occasions I would sometimes do something agricultural and gradually became convinced that I could look after a horse, so I pestered him until he let me have one, to be relinquished during seeding and harvesting times. Stabling the horse was no problem, since the barn which came with the house had been left unchanged when the car replaced the buggy; the stable was now regarded as my responsibility. I welcomed that, and was at first undaunted by the prospect of feeding, watering, mucking out, and exercising 'my' horse, regarding it as evidence that I was almost grown up (I was about ten). Then I received an invitation from my mother's sister Aunt Hannah Silver, in Winnipeg, to spend a week at her house visiting with my cousin Wilfred. I was eager to go; my parents agreed in principle, but my father asked what was to become of the horse while I was away. I had just assumed that it would go back to the farm, but my father pointed out that it would be a burden on the farmer and I'd have to make arrangements, either with him or some other way. I bargained with the farmer, using some of the money I'd saved for the Winnipeg sojourn, and the problem was soon solved, but my father's objective had been achieved: I had learnt that privilege can limit as well as enlarge freedom. Having been granted my wish I was now its servant.

My pride, too, was now engaged. I had envisioned a saddle-horse, but of course there was none on the farm. I was given the smallest workhorse, which was much taller than I and broad in proportion. It would have to be ridden bareback because there was no saddle; and the work-bridle had neither curb nor snaffle – if the horse took the straight bit between its teeth my juvenile tugging would not impress it. The advisability of the undertaking seemed suddenly in doubt, but backing off would have been a terrible humiliation. Over the next few days and with some help from my father I overcame most of my nervousness; a week or two later my father brought a used saddle home from Winnipeg, and soon I was riding about, trying to look nonchalant. I must have seemed an odd figure in a village where horses were associated with work, not pleasure, and Jews with indoor activities, not solitary excursions in fields and on country roads, but to myself I seemed to be coming nearer my *beau idéal*, the cowboy.

What was missing was a gun, and I began to agitate for that. A revolver was too much to hope for at first, so I asked for a .22 rifle, what was known locally as a gopher rifle. My mother was against it: nice Jewish boys didn't go around with guns. That was part of the point, for me, but I think I was too prudent to make it. Her second argument was that it was dangerous: I might hurt myself or others. But my father, who'd been a soldier in Russia, said that since it appeared that I would be using a rifle sometime soon whatever my parents said, it was best for me to learn to use it properly. They compromised on an air rifle, a BB gun, and Dad taught me to use it. A year or so later I graduated to a single-shot .22 rifle, but I was not allowed to take it when I went riding; I'm sure this was sound, and I think even then I recognized that, but it blocked my progress to the compleat cowboy. It had the merit, however, of causing me to go on long walks to shoot gophers, then a plague around Winkler, and brought on a friendship with two other rifle enthusiasts a little older than I was, Harold Kellough, the station-agent's son, and Nelson Funk, son of a local farmer. Until the station-agent was transferred a few years later, the three of us went shooting in all weathers; afterward, Nelson and I went alone. We became pretty good shots, which led to what in retrospect seems incredible risk-taking. Using live ammunition, we played a game we called 'Indian Wars': we would crawl forward using what slight contouring the prairie offered, shooting just over each other's head. On one occasion Nelson and I were cleaning our rifles in the stable (the horse was at the farm); full of hubris, I tossed a cake of saddle-soap to him and dared him to put it on his head for me to shoot off; he did; I shot it off; then I put it on my head and he shot it off – all this with cheap .22s whose inaccuracies we each thought we understood and could compensate for. I think, however, that the soap escapade had a sobering effect; I can't recall any equally rash gun games after that.

I had progressed well beyond the BB gun by then, but hadn't quite finished with it. I had done something to displease my brother, Bert – probably hit him – and he decided to retaliate. When I was going to school after lunch, he hid behind the woodpile and shot me in the bottom with the BB gun as I passed. Fortunately, it was cold weather and I was wearing heavy clothes; it hurt nevertheless, and I was going to punish him, but by the time I caught him I realized that he'd only evened the score and that ended it. We both told the story for years afterward (although he, alas, had far fewer years in which to tell it); it is my son's favourite anecdote about me.

It took a long time before I realized my ambition to own a pistol, and by then I was no longer interested in cowboys. During the 1930s there were many echoes of German Nazism in Winkler, and I persuaded my father that we ought to have some protection in the store. At that time it was legal to have a pistol in a place of business, and he acquired a second-hand Smith & Wesson .32, which we kept unloaded in the safe, along with ammunition. It was not an elegant or powerful gun, but I practised with it until I could use it rather well.

By this time there had been substantial changes in Winkler. As land thereabouts became harder to get, some Mennonites who wanted to farm moved farther west, especially to Swift Current, in Saskatchewan, and the Peace River district, in Alberta. At about the same time large numbers of new Mennonite immigrants arrived from the Soviet Union (the ban on their immigration was lifted in 1923). These were families who had stayed in Russia during the emigration of the 1870s and 1880s despite the 'Russification' program; some had been substantial landowners and most of the rest prosperous business and professional people; all had suffered from the Russian Revolution and had endured years of hardship before being allowed to emigrate. They were naturally embittered, and hated and feared anything that they thought tended toward communism. Unlike their forerunners, few looked to farming; they settled in Mennonite towns, were more political than the original settlers (by now called 'Old Coloniers,' as distinguished from 'Immigrants'), with whom they soon began to vie for dominance, and in general introduced a sharper and more aggressive tone to the community.

As the Mennonite community grew, the Jewish shrank. My grandfather Sirluck died when I was still a little boy; I remember him as more approachable than the other elders, affably pulling Herb and me on a sleigh, but there were rumours of a strong temper and of youthful exploits (years later his younger brother in Pittsburgh told me of a haughty Russian landowner on horseback who had struck Grandfather with his whip and had been pulled down and beaten). A few years later, the Nitikman families moved to Winnipeg, followed not long after by my grandmother Sirluck. Non-agricultural immigrants not of British or American stock were effectively banned in 1931, and as the Depression deepened and more Jews fled Germany the avowedly antisemitic director of the Immigration Service, F.C. Blair, with the open support of the Quebec Liberal caucus in Parliament, had administered the regulations with increasing harshness toward them. Mere assurance of employment on a Canadian farm ceased to be enough; a binding, long-term legal contract was sometimes successful. Blair knew that very few Canadian Jews were able to give such guarantees, but my father was, and after more than a year of negotiating he was able to bring out a family of distant relatives, who remained on the farm in Chortitz for a number of years.

But in Winkler itself there was, by the time I left for university, only one other Jewish family, and there was a coolness between them and us. After my cousin Herb left, therefore, there were no Jewish boys of my own age in Winkler whom I cared to associate with, and this intensified my need for non-Jewish companionship.

I usually found it, but it was always precarious. When I was a little boy, apparently friendly games often turned nasty and I became a dirty Jew, a Christ-killer. By the time I reached high school such incidents grew rarer, but they were correspondingly more violent. When I was in Grade Nine, for example, Peter Doerksen, the son of the local Ford dealer, a large youth in Grade Ten with whom I had exchanged some words about Jews, came to my seat during recess, where I had thought to outwait his anger, and choked me until I lost consciousness; we were four or five yards from the teacher, who throughout the scuffle sat at his desk with his head down. A year later Victor Unruh, the son of a preacher recently arrived from Russia, some years older and much larger than I, spoke about Jews in such a way that, although I knew he was deliberately goading me into it, I had to fight him; he beat me gleefully and savagely. I went to my room when I got home, trying to keep my father from seeing me, but he asked why I wasn't at supper, came up, saw the marks of the beating, and demanded to know who had done it. I feared to tell him but had to; I implored him to do nothing, but he wouldn't listen; he took me to Unruh's house, showed my bruises to the father, and demanded that Victor be punished. I groaned inwardly, knowing what this would mean; the next day Victor caught me in the schoolyard and tortured me for a quarter-hour in ways that wouldn't show (Unruh, who joined the local Nazis not long after, was later conscripted into the Canadian army and killed in action against Germany – an irony not lost on Winkler people). But these punishments for being Jewish were becoming infrequent events; I had become reasonably good at baseball and hockey, rather better than that at tennis, had a reputation for being the classroom critic, hung around at the very few places of resort (the Chinese café, the pool hall, the skating-rink hut), was a mighty hunter of gophers, rabbits, and crows, and generally made myself too much a part of the community to be really lonely.

It was my mother who suffered most because of the departure of the other Jewish families. She was very close to her parents and siblings; now that they had left, as had the other Jewish women, and one after another her own three daughters, she found herself too much alone. Her husband was busy at work, her sons at school and play, and she was on companionable terms with very few Winkler women, whose social lives were centred in their church and who were immersed in their huge families. She would dearly have loved to move to Winnipeg, but even if my father had wanted to he could not then have disengaged from the land: the Depression had begun and there was no market for agricultural land; just keeping it in the face of operating costs, mortgage payments, and taxes was getting harder all the time (in the end he did have to let some of it go). I don't know whether she urged him to arrange matters so that we could move, but I know she wanted to go. However, I never heard her complain, and although I know she was lonely and bored (made worse by her inability to read English), she maintained an air of cheerfulness on which we depended more than I realized; I often heard her singing at work in the kitchen. She went to visit her kin in Winnipeg when she could, but we three males were not an easy lot to leave to our own devices and her visits were fewer and shorter than I now wish they'd been.

Her great occasions were the visits we got from the Winnipeg families; sometimes these involved three or four carloads of people. Those of my sisters who were within driving distance would come back for these events, and for days beforehand there would be incessant preparations: chickens or ducks taken to the *shochet* for slaughter; great sheets of dough rolled out for *lokshen* (noodles) and smaller ones for pastry; heaps of apples, plums, peaches, rhubarb, or gooseberries for pies; much baking of white and rye bread, cinnamon buns, cookies, strudel, *kmishbrot*, cakes; my father fetching up his home-made grape or blueberry wine from the cellar; Bert and I bringing in firewood and water and going to cut ice from under the sawdust in the small ice house behind the store; and my mother everywhere, doing endless things and tired but breaking out frequently in snatches of song. The meals were central to these visits, my parents' (and particularly my mother's) opportunity to show how much they were valued. We all, regardless of age, had wine for the opening prayer; it was remarkable how few people asked for a second glass; this was no reflection on my father's wine, which was good of its kind, but liberal drinking was not part of our family culture. Liberal eating, however, was, at least on these occasions, and people who ordinarily seemed the soul of moderation drew out these meals – partly with talk – until the youngsters, interested as they were, grew restless. Then there would be walks or drives to the farm and trips to the store for goods at cost to take back to Winnipeg, and about mid-afternoon I would be set to cranking the heavy ice-cream maker. When the guests left Sunday evening I always felt an attenuation of my connection with the world at large, a resurgence of my sense of isolation, or at best remoteness.

Other family occasions took place elsewhere. One or other of the Winnipeg families would take a cottage for a month at Winnipeg Beach or Gimli, on Lake Winnipeg, and we would share it with them for one or two weeks; several summers we took a cottage for a fortnight at Lake Manitou, near Watrous, Saskatchewan, where the mineral salts were widely thought to be therapeutic, and would be joined by some of the Winnipeg people. These joint undertakings kept me in touch with my cousins as we were growing up, and I became particularly friendly with Wilfred Silver, who was about a year older than I and who shared many tastes with me. As a result I was invited several times to spend a week visiting the Silvers, and these were high points of the year; I had a large appetite for the city and its resources (I didn't understand how limited Winnipeg's then were), and the week would pass in excited exploration, although much of the afternoon would go to western movies. Perhaps the most satisfying bit of technology Winnipeg offered me was the garden hose: coming as I did from a dry-farming area utterly dependent upon rain and usually suffering some degree of drought, I thought the ability to summon forth as much water as was wanted by a turn of the valve, and then smell the gratitude of the grass as the stream hit the ground, represented true power over nature, and I spent a good deal of time watering the Silvers' lawn. Wilfred sometimes came to spend a week or two with us in Winkler, and these reciprocal visits helped us become good friends.

The Great Depression which followed the Crash of 1929 hit the Canadian West much harder than it did central Canada. For one thing, it was accompanied by a succession of natural disasters: we were part of the great dust bowl of the Dirty Thirties, when summer dust-storms often blotted from view houses or barns a hundred yards away; there were successive years of heavy grasshopper infestation; wheat rust was a recurrent plague (resistant wheat varieties had not yet been developed); hail levelled promising crops, ruinous in the days before crop insurance. A second factor was that, except for some of the grain companies, all the major institutions with which the farmer dealt – the banks and loan companies, the railways, the implement and supply companies – were based in the East; so was the federal government; neither group was much influenced by western needs. The prices of things prairie farmers sold fell fast and far, those of things they bought or services they used fell much more slowly and not nearly so far; land and implement foreclosures were prompt and bankruptcies became widespread. A third factor was that, with the partial exception of the few cities, the Prairies were, in those days before oil was found, a one-industry economy; when agriculture was depressed, everything else became depressed. Unemployment grew to levels never known in Canada before or since; farms were abandoned; families moved fruitlessly in search of work. This was before unemployment insurance and modern welfare; 'relief' was on a shared municipal–provincial basis, was considered charity, and was as meagre as it was thought demeaning. Hunger was a palpable reality.

In the Winkler area, sturdy independent farmers were driven to mortgage their land just to keep going; villagers mortgaged their homes; as the bad years continued, nearly everyone became sunk in debt. People ate less, wore patched clothes, did not replace equipment as it wore out; many a car became a 'Bennett Buggy' (engine replaced by a horse; named after the Conservative prime minister who refused to acknowledge any federal responsibility for economic stimulus, or even assistance, to those rendered helpless by the general economic collapse).

In these circumstances Winkler proved a fertile ground for Nazi propaganda. The cultural and emotional attachment to Germany prepared the way for it, the obsessive fear and hatred of anything that could be associated with 'communism' furthered it, the shared language facilitated it, and the long and virulent tradition of Christian hatred of Jews partnered it. The churches and Sunday schools of Winkler probably did not teach the Nazi racial creed, but they did not dispute it, and they taught the story put forward in the New Testament and used throughout the centuries to justify so many massacres, that 'the Jews' had insisted to a reluctant Pilate that Jesus be crucified; a favourite verse in Winkler, as in so much of Christendom, was Matthew 27:25, 'His blood be on us, and on our children.' As the Depression deepened and hope waned, people increasingly felt that the political and economic systems – representative democracy and capitalism – had failed, and that the real choice lay between socialism and fascism. In Winkler, 'socialism' meant the horrors of the Bolshevik Revolution; few would choose it. A number of Winkler people, particularly after Hitler became chancellor of Germany in 1933, subscribed to German Nazi publications; the Graefers, a Lutheran family who operated the telephone exchange, pasted sheets of *Der Stürmer* and *Völkischer Beobachter*, two of the most extreme Nazi papers, in the windows fronting Main Street where I, or whoever was getting the store's mail from the post office, had to pass twice a day (I sometimes made it an ostentatious point to stop and study the hideous cartoons of hook-nosed, thick-lipped, skullcapped Jews, but it was too upsetting a thing to do often); the telephone system belonged to the Manitoba government, which voiced no objection to these displays. William Whittaker's Canadian Nationalist Party, which wore brown shirts and swastikas and had links with Adrien Arcand's militant Blue Shirts in Quebec, held well-attended meetings in Winkler and formed a flourishing branch there.

The evening of the day I learnt that a Winkler branch had been established, I was putting on my skates next to an older friend, Jack Funk, on whose other side sat a tall, thin young man named Ed Penner and aptly nicknamed *der Schlang* (the Snake); I said in what was intended to be a detached tone, 'Jack, have you heard that Whittaker's Nationalist Party has established a branch here and that the Snake is its secretary?' 'Is that right?' replied Funk (Penner was silent); 'I'm the president.' I tried to appear unmoved, but I doubt that I succeeded. Funk, a brother of my shooting companion Nelson, had, despite our age difference, spent a good deal of time with me, talking about, among other things, political and economic problems, on which he had taken a socialistic position; I liked and trusted him, and it had seemed that he reciprocated. I was badly shaken by what he said, managed an ironic 'Congratulations,' and skated off. He caught up with me and said, 'There's nothing personal in it, and I hope we can stay friends.' Although my heart ached, I replied, 'If you believe Jews to be what the Nazis say, you can't be friends with one; if you don't and have joined the Nazis anyway, knowing what they're doing in Germany and want to do here, you're worse than they are.' I never spoke to him again; I never fully got over the pain of the betrayal; it was one of the sharpest and most hurtful lessons I ever received about how precarious the friendship of a Gentile for a Jew can be.

In order not to expose myself to another such shock, I cut relations with the other people who had been part of my association with Funk. I did this without explanation, largely because I feared they would also turn out to belong to the Nazis or to sympathize with them, and I didn't want to confront it. In this I was wrong, and paid for my error as I realized in time that the man whom, next to Funk, I saw most, Peter Bueckert, kept aloof from the Nazis while continuing to see Funk; but by the time this became clear I was too ashamed to approach him, and so lost another friend, this time to my overdefensiveness. Nelson Funk came to tell me that he didn't share Jack's views; I appreciated this and continued to see something of him, but our interests were diverging; in any case, when he finished school he left for Chicago, where he found work not available in Winkler. We never saw each other after he left; he was killed serving in the American air force during the war.

As news of Nazi atrocities began to filter out, and as meetings in Winkler of the Canadian Nationalist Party became more frequent, I decided that it would have a small salutary effect for me to be seen target-practising. I explained to my parents that, if Canadian Nazis assumed that Canadian Jews would be as unresisting as German Jews, it was important that in our small, isolated, and German-oriented area this assumption be countered; Winkler seemed a likely place for an experimental pogrom, and it should be locally understood that such an undertaking would prove costly. Whatever his thoughts on the subject, my father agreed that I could set up a target behind the store, where half the village passed daily, and I was out there as often as I could manage. As targets for my .22 I used kitchen matches stuck upright in a board, and for the revolver, empty cans, and I kept at it until I rarely missed. Everyone in town knew that I had two guns, liked using them, and usually hit what I aimed at. I tried to reinforce the desired impression by frequently quoting a piece of doggerel that had formed part of the nineteenth-century advertising campaign accompanying the introduction of the Colt revolver, something like:

When faced with foes of greater size,
Fear not; call on me, and I will equalize.

I referred to the Smith & Wesson as my 'Equalizer.'

Unfortunately, the clarity of my purpose was a little obscured, at least temporarily, when one day Nelson Funk and I walked along the railway track and, finding no gophers, shot insulators off a number of telegraph poles. We were observed, and shortly after I got home Jack Felde, the town constable, came for me. I spent a very educational night in the tiny town lock-up, where my father brought me chicken soup; by next morning, when I was sent home, I had developed a much keener sense of property rights, even when the hated CPR was the owner, than I'd had the day before. (Curiously, Nelson was not even questioned.)

The Depression affected our family less than most in Winkler: there was no longer a mortgage on the house nor, so far as I know, on the store or elevator; we never went short of food, shelter, or clothing. But income from my father's businesses shrank to less than costs; he was unable to keep up payments on all the land and had to reduce his holdings. To avoid putting people out of work, he postponed his planned switch from horses to tractors; then, when his renters could not make ends meet out of their share of the crops, he felt obliged to keep them going on credit. In the store, too, most business was on credit, to be paid (naturally without interest charges) when the crop was in; but crops year after year were very disappointing, and prices low, so that many customers didn't pay their bills for years on end, some never. His available funds steadily shrank; he switched to the cheapest, and surely the worst, car made in North America, the Whippet, which he bought at a discount (but not at a bargain, since it was always under repair); indulgences such as vacations and new clothes were given up, everything that could be recycled was, everyone watched carefully to prevent waste. I don't remember that any of this troubled me much (although I hated that miserable car); indeed, it would have been much worse had we continued to enjoy our previous standard of living amidst so much want and misery.

But one thing did matter. I had always assumed that, like my sisters, I would go to university when I finished high school, but when I graduated in 1934 my father did not have enough money to send me. He suggested that I stay in the Winkler school for the optional Grade Twelve, which would admit me to second-year standing at the University of Manitoba, by which time things might be better; but I could not face another year of that school, which had only a handful of books in its 'library,' where the only foreign language offered was German, and where the only competent upper-level teacher was a Nazi sympathizer. I therefore offered to work in the store for a year, save my pay, and come back to Winkler to work during summers; he said we would try it that way, although he could not really promise to have the money the following year.

I don't think I minded working; I was learning quite a lot and came to do a few things on my own (like organizing what I called our 'Third-of-a-Century Sale,' which did pretty well for those depressed times). Most of the customers treated me with a mixture of amused indulgence and cautious friendliness, and seemed to enjoy giving me practice in *Plautdietsch* and watching me struggle with their hundred-pound sacks of flour and sugar, which I learned to manage reasonably well onto wagons, buggies, and cars, but had trouble loading onto the much higher truck-beds of the time.

The Winkler area was a great producer of babies. It was not uncommon for a Mennonite couple to marry young, have eight or ten children in rapid succession, and then for the wife, worn out by this productivity and by heavy labour in house, barn, garden, and sometimes field, to die, young in years but old and sagging in body, whereupon the widower would remarry and have several more children. (This situation was epitomized by the characteristic family procession of the area farmers come to town – man walking in front, wife in loose floor-length skirt covering lapsed belly next, and the three or four youngest children who had helped to break her body trailing behind.) There was only one doctor in Winkler, C.W. Wiebe, and no hospital; much of his practice consisted of delivering babies in the outlying farms and villages, requiring a good deal of night driving, which during the winter was over very uncertain roads.

One day when I was loitering over a Coke at the drugstore where Wiebe had his office, he asked me to come with him on such a call; it was unexpected, but I went home for warmer clothes (cars didn't yet have heaters) and a book and went with him. It was the middle of the night before the delivery was over; Wiebe got into the passenger seat and slept while I negotiated our way home. I did this a number of times; he once offered to pay me, but I knew that he wasn't at the time getting paid very often himself, and declined. Many years later, when I was being installed as president of the University of Manitoba, I invited Dr Wiebe to the reception; he stood there beaming while I greeted him and introduced him to my wife, children, and colleagues; all the while he refused to say a word, not even 'hello.' I think the situation affected him and he distrusted his voice. Four years later, while I was on an official visit to China, our son, Robert, who was spending the summer in a tent on the Winkler farm working some acres of potatoes he'd asked to have, came down with bronchitis and went to see Dr Wiebe, who promptly clapped him into his new hospital, jacked up his legs to drain the infection, and gave him frequent lectures on the damage done by smoking, interspersed with the occasional anecdote about me as a youth.

Before the Second World War there was a periodic exercise called the 'Imperial Debates.' Teams of recent graduates of British universities would travel through what was still called 'the British Empire,' debating against teams from local universities (also usually graduates) on set topics of general interest. In 1934 there was such an exercise, and the topic in Manitoba was 'Resolved that this house must follow the Moscow road,' with the home team upholding the negative. One of the Manitobans, Sam Freedman, later chief justice of the Manitoba Court of Appeal (the other was Andrew Stewart, later president of the University of Alberta), was a friend of my sister Gladys, and she took me to the debate. I was fascinated. Each side presented what seemed to me highly organized logical structures and then, in rebuttal, thrust in telling criticisms; all four speaking styles were accomplished; but the visitors seemed to me to have a lighter, gayer finish to serious argumentation. I was particularly entranced with their easy way with language; I still recall one of them, a short, plump, balding, Welsh lawyer, saying, 'My opponent calls me a communist; I am not a communist; I'm an unemployed cap-i-tal-ist,' with the accent on the second syllable. For a youngster anxious to get his English right in a community where English was either a second language or not spoken at all, this deliberate waywardness suggested an easy linguistic authority which I instantly envied.

I drove back to Winkler that night reflecting on the arguments I'd heard and thinking that I'd learnt more in those two hours than in any number of lessons at school; accordingly, I went to the school principal and suggested that the school sponsor a similar debate on the same topic. I'm now a little surprised that he agreed, but he did. The difficulty came in getting anyone to take the affirmative; in Winkler, saying anything favourable about 'the Moscow road' was tantamount to declaring oneself an atheistic communist revolutionary, a Bolshevik killer. Finally, the principal told me that unless I could arrange for an affirmative team there could be no debate. I decided, not altogether reluctantly, to take the affirmative myself and found a partner in Peter Bueckert, an independent young man in his twenties who, as the second son of Winkler's almost perpetual mayor, had a somewhat anti-establishment attitude, and with whom I'd had many talks about, *inter alia*, politics and economics (this was before the incident with Jack Funk). I don't remember who was on the opposing team or who got the decision, but we drew quite a large audience and the debate became the subject of a good deal of gossip; for many it seemed to confirm the alleged link between Jews and communists. I was becoming, so far as I understood the term, a 'social democrat' and was strongly opposed to revolutionary communism and to Stalinist

Russia, but this was a distinction which most Winklerites rejected as unreal. I fear that this debate, together with my rather swaggering behaviour with guns, gave me at sixteen or seventeen a small reputation as a dangerous radical.

That year I got a lot of reading done. Released from the platitudes of the school curriculum, I was free to cast about for matter. There was no library in Winkler, and although the local stationer had a small book section it was largely German; but there were then two widely available and useful publishers' series: Dent's Everyman's Library, from England, sold for thirty-five cents a volume, and Random House's Modern Library, from the United States, for ninety-five cents. Each published its list, and these, eked out with occasional reviews of current books in the Winnipeg newspapers, formed my basic bibliography before I knew what the word meant. Every trip to Winnipeg included time spent in one of its very few bookshops, particularly those which carried a fair stock of Everyman's titles; Modern Library volumes, being more expensive (equal at the time to about four bushels of wheat delivered to the elevator) had to be bought more sparingly. I would take home these volumes, which would have been thought pretty commonplace by someone from a more literate environment, with much the same excitement as I was later to feel when I uncovered some sixteenth- or seventeenth-century rarity in a London bookshop. I often read very late into the night, which might lead to two remonstrations, one from my father as he came down to stoke the small furnace which could not go through a cold night without attention, another from my mother if it were a Monday or Thursday night, when she would come down to knead her twice-weekly bread dough in those days before quick-rising yeast; they feared for my health, but their objections grew fewer as they perceived them to be ineffectual and it began to occur to them that I could be engaged in worse activities.

I did the banking for the store, which put me into daily contact with the teller and the accountant, two unmarried young men who lived in a flat above the bank. Bill Uhrich was of a Winkler Lutheran family; Dick Fulton was of British descent and came from Portage-la-Prairie, about a hundred miles away. Although both were considerably older than I, we became friendly, and soon I was playing poker with them and one or two others in their apartment. I lost a little money at first, but the company and the excitement were more than worth it, and after a while I came to hold my own with them. Bill decided to use his vacation the following summer tenting at Clear Lake, in Riding Mountain National Park, a couple of hundred miles northwest of Winkler, and invited me to come with him. My parents were dubious about the wisdom of allowing a seventeen-year-old to go off with a bachelor in his mid-twenties known as something of a gay blade (in the old-fashioned sense), but I was determined to go, and they could not reasonably argue that it was economically unmanageable: Bill had a Ford Model A roadster, the most stylish car in town, and a tent; he would provide transportation and shelter, and we would share other costs.

Their doubts would have been intensified had they known that Bill, who was engaged to a nurse at the Ninette Provincial Sanatorium, intended to stop there overnight and had offered to get his fiancée to bring along a friend for me. Puritanical Winkler was not an easy place for anyone to mature sexually; for a Jew the sectarian, racist, separatist character of the community made matters a great deal harder. One could chat with girls one had known at school, skate with them, play tennis with them, but that was almost all; there were no movies, dances were very rare and banned by many families, and walking out was regarded as a prelude to courtship, and since marriage to a Jew was unthinkable, parents were not eager for their daughters to walk out with one. On the few occasions when I did walk out with girls I had the sense that they anticipated parental rebuke. Sometimes I formed part of a mixed party, but I felt that I was seen as an alien presence for whom room was being tolerantly made. At one such party there was a fairly clear expectation that matters would progress, but the girls in this particular group revealed a crude side I had not suspected; they must have been disgusted by my resultant backwardness.

When the great day for our trip arrived I was more than ready. We got to Ninette, pitched our tent in a clearing in the woods, picked the girls up at the sanatorium, returned to camp, made and ate dinner, talked and sang over the fire. If B. was surprised at my youth (she was in her twenties), she didn't say anything; when Bill and his fiancée retired we talked for a while, continued to find each other acceptable, and went to bed. I can't recall ever parting with anything so gladly as I did that night with my virginity. The next day when we went on to Clear Lake I was in a wonderful glow and the holiday was a great success, as unlike Winkler as it could be.

The Depression continued to deepen; to make matters worse, the crop in the Winkler area was very poor in 1935. Reluctantly, my father informed me that he had no more money than he'd had the previous year; could I wait another year? This was unthinkable to me; I had been eagerly counting the weeks until registration day at the university, and the notion of a further postponement, and another year in a Winkler so distant from the great world of intellect, culture, and affairs, was intolerable. A related issue was the course I would take. I wanted to take Arts, but my parents, who had not objected to that for my sisters, said times were now harder and if I were to go to university I'd have to take something that would help me earn a living, like Law or Medicine. There were stormy discussions for several days; finally a compromise was reached. The first two years of Arts were a law-school prerequisite; I would take them, as pre-Law, and I could go when planned, but would have to stay with my aunt and uncle Nitikman. I was assured that it would not be charity: room and board would be paid, and all three of my sisters had stayed with relatives when they were at university. I was not pleased but agreed, resolving that I'd make other arrangements for my second year.

CHAPTER TWO

Winnipeg, 1935–1940

I

In 1935 all the universities in Canada were experiencing difficulties, but those of the University of Manitoba were probably the most severe. The province had been hit as shatteringly by the combination of the Great Depression and the Great Drought as the other Prairie provinces; in addition the university suffered from what was locally called the 'Great Defalcation': the chairman of its board of governors, J.A. Machray, who was also its bursar and investment agent, had fraudulently dissipated its entire endowment. (He was impartial: he did the same with the endowments of the Anglican Diocese of Rupert's Land and St John's College, of both of which he was chancellor.) The provincial government, whose finances had been badly weakened, cut the university's grant severely several years in succession, and the university, under extreme pressure, made staff reductions, placed the faculty on one-year appointments, made three successive salary cuts, all serious, and for some years virtually eliminated such non-salary expenses as library acquisitions, laboratory supplies, and building maintenance.

In Arts and Science all this was made worse by a physical split. It had been intended to move the faculty to new buildings at Ft Garry, seven miles beyond the city limits, but the Depression and some other factors caused a compromise: the senior division, with most of the support facilities, went to Ft Garry, while the junior division (the first two years) remained in 'temporary' buildings at Broadway and Osborne Street in the centre of the city. First- and second-year students were thus spared the long, slow streetcar ride to the new campus, but in every other respect they were disadvantaged: cut off from the society and influence of senior students and, most of the time, senior faculty, limited to a divisional library with few books, fewer journals, and almost no study space, and to laboratories capable at most of rudimentary demonstrations, with no local athletic or recreational facilities, and with literally no residential presence (Ft Garry had some residential places but they were reserved for students at that site).

While not oblivious of all this, I was undismayed by it. I was intoxicated by my escape from my special environment in Winkler – a tiny religious and linguistic minority within another religious and linguistic minority, both puritanical, both habituated to persecution and therefore habitually defensive in orientation – into what seemed to me the wonderful freedom and vitality of a large city (Winnipeg's population was then about a quarter-million). The U of M was to be the centre of my life for some years, and I was aware that it was not the rich cultural institution a university ought to be, but it and the city were such an advance on what I'd known that I was in no mood to complain.

My domestic situation was less satisfactory. The Nitikman house on Glenwood Crescent in Kildonan was comfortable enough, but it had no extra rooms and I was put into my cousin Herb's room, which placed me at a moral disadvantage, for although we had both lost our privacy, his had been forfeited to me. The family received me warmly and treated me well, but Auntie Annie, a classic manager, or *balibusta*, seemed to feel that she had some quasi-maternal responsibility for me and freely offered the kind of advice and guidance that my own parents had forgone for some time. Inviting anyone home to undergo her matriarchal scrutiny was out of the question.

Saturdays I usually took lunch a few houses up the street, with Grandmother Nitikman. Grandfather had died some years earlier, but Grandmother continued to maintain what amounted to family headquarters in her house on the east bank of the Red River. Her unmarried son, Sam, lived with her and made it a point to be home for Saturday lunch. My parents would come when they visited Winnipeg, as would my sister Gertrude, recently married and living in Altona, another Mennonite town some twenty miles east of Winkler. Auntie Hannah had died suddenly in the early summer, and Uncle Sol and his children would often come. It was, in the months following Hannah's death, a sad gathering, but that was not its inherent nature, and in later years it was often lively and stimulating, although Grandmother, for whom further blows were in store, remained permanently subdued. The food was always prepared before the sabbath, overcooked, then reheated, but when the family was not mourning the inertness of the food was more than compensated for by the animation of the conversation.

At the university I soon found that although antisemitism was not as crude and overt as in Winkler it was nevertheless widespread and institutionalized. In the medical school and hospitals there was, as my cousin Shlomo Mitchell later demonstrated in a widely publicized investigation, an increasingly strict hidden quota for Jewish students, interns, and residents. It was difficult for a Jew to enter Engineering. Law was somewhat different: Jewish students seemed to find no special difficulty getting into the school but on graduation they were almost never able to article except with a Jewish firm, so that the practice of law in the province was largely segregated. There were no Jews on the university faculty (at that time Law and Medicine depended heavily upon the unpaid part-time teaching contributions of practising members of the professions, and I do not know whether any Jews were among them). The student fraternities and sororities were segregated. Jews participated freely in official student activities but the social life of the university was largely segregated, and even in the classroom there were in effect two groups.

I found this situation very uncomfortable and was determined not to go along with it. I joined a Jewish fraternity, Sigma Alpha Mu, and another Jewish organization, the Menorah Society (a discussion group), but in classroom, library, common-room, locker-room, corridor, and off campus, I attempted to hold a balance between Jewish and other associates. Since this was somewhat unusual it created a degree of suspicion on both sides, especially as Nazi and Fascist successes in Europe and the growth of similar movements closer to home brought out latent hostility among Gentiles and made Jews more worried and defensive. More than once during my undergraduate years I was asked by one or other Jewish student whether I knew where I belonged. I thought I did, and it was not in a self-imposed ghetto.

But my approach could lead to embarrassment. I had become friendly with another first-year student whom I will call John; once a group of us were chatting and he looked to the other side of the common-room, where some Jewish students were being a little noisy, and said, 'God, how I hate those bloody Jews! I could bite their throats with pleasure.' It took me a minute or two to decide what to do, then I got up and walked out. He came running after me and apologized in a confused way. I don't remember just what I said but I avoided him in the following days; then his mother phoned and asked me to Sunday tea, and I didn't think I could refuse. During tea she and John's older sister made a great thing of our 'friendship,' about which they said John often spoke, and in showing me out John mumbled something about hoping to outgrow some youthful prejudices. Since I knew that it was not his sentiment but only his failure to recognize that I was Jewish that made his outburst unusual, I decided not to insist on a break.

One Saturday afternoon some weeks after the beginning of term I was at a movie when a young man got up from where he was sitting and slipped into the seat next to mine. 'I recognized you by your laugh,' he said. He was a student named Alan Adamson who was in the same section of English 101 as I. After the movie we went for a beer and talked; it was the beginning of a close friendship. A few weeks later Alan brought along to lunch a student with whom he shared another course, Ogden Turner, a pleasant fellow who shared many of our interests, and we gradually became a kind of trio; in second term we contrived to be in the same sections of most of our courses and did many things together. Like me, Ogden was a country boy living in lodgings (he was from Saskatchewan), and Alan, knowing that I wanted to live away from family, suggested that Ogden and I get an apartment together for the following academic year. Both principals had some reservations, but the promoter kept at it and in time the idea became established. We found a rooming-house on Broadway just steps from the university, with two furnished rooms and rudimentary light-housekeeping facilities; the larger room was on the ground floor and the other on the third, so because it was such a rambling 'apartment,' we called it 'The Rambler.' We engaged the rooms for September and put down a modest deposit, although I didn't think the time ripe to discuss it with my parents.

The curriculum of first year was somewhat disappointing. It was really the equivalent of Grade Twelve, and was given at the university only because many of the province's high schools didn't go beyond Grade Eleven. During my year out of school I had read rather a lot and was eager to follow my developing interests, but instead I had to spread my work over five disparate courses. I would have taken English and history in any case; I approved of the requirement of a foreign language and would have liked to take French, but since the Winkler school taught only German that was the only language for which I had the prerequisite standing; taking mathematics made sense, although I don't think I would have had it not been compulsory; I had at the time no interest in science and chose botany from the prescribed group as closest to my country background and because the professor had an international reputation and had published two clever limericks on relativity. My hopes to take philosophy and psychology (which in Manitoba constituted a single subject at the time) and economics had to be deferred until second year, and I never did manage to fit political science in.

I had not developed methodical study habits, and my work varied greatly with my interest in the subject and the quality of the instruction. Professor A.H.R. Buller, the versifying botanist, one of the six original professors appointed when the university became a teaching institution in 1904, gave his lectures in a large theatre with numbered seats to which he assigned students in alphabetical order so that he could take the attendance easily. 'S' was so far back that Buller's tired voice barely reached me as he read, from frayed and yellowed notes, material that was almost entirely taxonomic in nature and ceased to interest me about the second week, after which I attended his classes only often enough to ward off suspension, and when I did attend usually read some novel or worked on an exercise for some other class. I did the assigned exercises, crammed a little for the exam, and got a passing grade, after which I closed my mind to science until its increasing impact upon ordinary life awakened my curiosity.

My instructor in German Authors was Professor J.H. Heinzelman, who had been appointed in 1913 when the university began to teach non-science subjects. His interest in German literature seemed genuine and although his classes were rather unstructured, they were *gemütlich*. For German Grammar, however, we had a thick-set, youngish man named Anton Bürzle, brought in that year from Germany as an exchange teacher. I have no direct evidence that he was a Nazi, but it is highly unlikely that in 1935 anyone would be sent out as a cultural emissary of the New Germany who was not a Party member, as Heinzelman and the university should have known. Bürzle's manner was authoritarian and his pedagogy heavily Germanic, which got my back up from the first. Soon he began experimentally to harass the few recognizably Jewish students in the class, gathering boldness from some favourable feedback from the majority group. At first I wasn't sure what he was doing; then, one day about the third or fourth week of term, he fastened upon a timid and flustered girl who was having the usual Jewish difficulty with the pronunciation of German words which had entered unaltered into Yiddish and there acquired slightly different vowel or consonant values. 'Not *icccch*; *ich*,' he yelled after her fourth or fifth unsuccessful attempt to render the sound he demanded; 'What's wrong with you?' The girl was on the point of tears, and some of the more unsympathetic members of the class were tittering in delight; I could take no more and stood up (standing was not customary). 'Why don't you ask me?' I said; 'I have the same trouble.' (It wasn't true.) He was startled, hesitated, then said, 'No, you haven't.' I then produced the most exaggerated *icccch* I could and followed it with similarly affected *dicccch*, *sicccch*, and *micccch*, and said, 'Why don't you ask me what's wrong with me?' He stared and didn't answer. I said, 'Is it only Jewish mispronunciations that bother you? Members of the class have been saying *itch, ditch, sitch, mitch* for weeks, and you've politely helped them, but you act personally affronted when there's an echo of Yiddish in a pronunciation.' Bürzle denied this, I sat down, and the hour was finished with no further disruption. For the rest of the year I was alert and challenging, but I could never draw him into another confrontation. The incident became widely known, but it was a time of growing Nazi influence and there may have been as much sympathy for Bürzle as for me, perhaps more. At the end of the year I got a good mark in Authors and a poor one in Grammar, so my combined standing in German was only fair.

When war broke out in 1939, Bürzle, as a German national and suspected Nazi, was interned. Many years later I encountered him at a meeting of the Modern Languages Association in New York. He did a double-take, hesitated for a second, then put down his head and hurried away. I checked the German section of the program: he was giving a paper and was a professor in an American university.

An amiable and engaging young Scot named William Lawson was my instructor in mathematics. Within limits I enjoyed the course but knew I wouldn't pursue math beyond the required first year and didn't invest much time in it; I got a middling grade.

My professor in history was a middle-aged Nova Scotian named Joseph Howe. At first I thought it quite exciting to study with a descendant of the famous opponent of Confederation, but I very soon found that he had none of his ancestor's brilliance. It was a survey course in the whole of European history, and perhaps Howe cannot justly be blamed for its barebone dryness; still, his contribution was eccentric and not very articulate. He often felt a need to assert, with gestures, the historical importance of the short Roman sword, to which he attributed Roman military success and which he called the most lethal weapon in the history of warfare – this to students some of whose fathers had been at Ypres and Vimy Ridge! Still, despite Howe's shortcomings and the dreariness of the textbooks, the formal study of history was too exciting to be quite spoilt and I did reasonably well.

English was the subject I had most looked forward to. My

instructors were a middle-aged professor named Clark Hopper and a younger associate professor named Lloyd Wheeler, both of whom seemed decent, modest, rather dull men. I retained that impression of the former, but as the weeks went by I revised my opinion of Wheeler. He was shy and insecure, and his classroom manner was very low-key (he tended to speak down, toward his desk, rather than outward, to the students), but he was committed to literature and interested in encouraging students to engage with it. When students expressed opinions he seemed not to regard them as challenges, as some other professors did, but rather as matters for discussion, and I soon began to look forward to his classes. My essays and the Christmas exam got high grades, but the final exam brought out the worst of my youthful arrogance. The first question, which was compulsory and valued at 20 per cent of the whole, was on Wordsworth; I was at the time reading and identifying with the kind of criticism which disparaged Wordsworth and heaped contempt upon his admirers; and my complete answer to the question was: 'Wordsworth bores me.' The next day Wheeler intercepted me and asked me why I'd answered as I had, and I said because it was true. He shook his head and said, 'I hope saying so was worth the scholarship you threw away.' This was momentarily sobering, but I reflected on my likely grades in botany, German, and mathematics, and decided the self-indulgence had not been as expensive as Wheeler thought, although it was as foolish.

In fact, I was not interested in a scholarship, although, considering the family's financial situation, I should have been. The university offered so many opportunities for activities for which I'd been starved that I threw myself into them without much regard for the effect on my grades. I took part in debates and became president of the Arts Junior Division Debating Society; I joined the Dramatic Society and played the protagonist in Eugene O'Neill's *The Rope*; I attended fraternity meetings and performed the burdensome, time-consuming duties of a pledge and later of an initiate; I attended meetings of the Menorah Society; I was meeting new people all the time; I went out with girls; and I read insatiably: news, current affairs, literature, criticism. I also became involved in student politics. Student government started at the faculty or school level with councils, each of which sent a representative to the central governing body, the University of Manitoba Students Union. I became a member of the Junior Division Arts Council in first term with my election as president of the Debating Society, and found the council meetings interesting enough to make me decide in second term to run for the position of junior representative to UMSU. I didn't make any promises but I made some speeches about the needs of the junior division, particularly in the library, and I was elected.

Also in second term, I got a small foretaste of what I did not yet know was to be my future profession. Two of the fraternity's pledges of the previous year had failed in English and therefore could not, according to the fraternity's rather unusual rule, be initiated; if they failed in a second try they'd have to be dropped. I was assigned to get them through the course. I think they expected to be coached only in examination technique (for which I was soon to demonstrate such disregard) but I insisted on tutoring them in the course material itself. It was more work than they had expected and once or twice they rebelled, but since they were both wilful, headstrong, and noisy sons of rich men I was not reluctant to bully them a little for their own good and my satisfaction. To their great relief they got acceptable grades, their families and the fraternity were pleased, and I learnt that teaching came easily to me and gave pleasure.

In August 1936, my mother entered a Winnipeg hospital for abdominal surgery. I visited her there a few days after the operation and remember still her radiant smile when I came into her room; in those days I didn't often see her looking happy. We had a longer and better conversation than in years, and I left feeling very relieved and quite confident. She continued to make a good recovery and a week or so later was discharged; on her way from the hospital to Grandmother's house she suffered an embolism and lapsed into unconsciousness. Early the next morning my father, who was with her, phoned me in Winkler, where I was spending the summer working in the store, and told me to get a car and come at once, bringing my brother, Bert. She was still in a coma when we arrived and died without regaining consciousness.

Jewish burial is swift but *shiva* is long: a week during which the immediate family does not leave the house and other mourners come morning and evening for prayers. It was my grandmother's house, and she had now lost three children, two in less than a year; inevitably, she set the tone for the gathering.

At the end of that claustrophobic week my father, Bert, and I returned to Winkler. A local woman was engaged to help with the housekeeping, but that arrangement was clearly unsatisfactory and I was concerned about how things would go when I left for the beginning of term. As that approached I felt increasingly guilty about abandoning my father and Bert, and offered to delay my return to school for a year. My father declined my offer, which greatly relieved me, if not my guilt.

Before school started, however, I took the bus to Kansas City, Missouri, where the fraternity was holding a regional convention. The most memorable part of the trip was the bus ride home, when for a good part of the way I was seated beside a burly man who turned out to belong to the German-American *Bund* and was vehement in support of Hitler and of sympathizer movements in the United States. He insisted that *The Protocols of the Elders of Zion* was authentic; that Franklin D. Roosevelt, who was then campaigning for a second presidential term, was a Jew; and that Germany was destined to sweep aside the decrepit empires of yesteryear – Britain, France, and Russia – and install a new world order. This was an aspect of the United States that I had read about, but I was not fully prepared for the reality, especially when it weighed seventy pounds more than I and couldn't be walked away from. I thought later that what made it different for me from its counterpart in Canada was that the latter, at least in English-speaking Canada, had perforce to profess a certain tenderness for the British interest, which was a kind of limitation on its menace, or so at least it seemed to my patriotic imagination.

II

Turner and I moved as planned into The Rambler and I registered for courses in English, history, philosophy, and economics. Academically, second year was much more interesting than first. It was the point at which genuine university-level work began, and it was the first year in which I took only subjects I wanted to.

In English I had E.K. Brown, who had arrived in Manitoba the previous year as the new head of the department and caused much stir. He was very un-Manitoban: only twenty-nine when appointed head, very suave and self-assured but without trace of arrogance or *hauteur*, with an easy smiling manner, already somewhat corpulent and looking as if he'd never been a boy, and with a considerable reputation for both scholarship and critical acumen; his special distinction in our eyes was that he wrote on Canadian literature as well as more usual literary topics. Not everyone was then convinced that there was a Canadian literature, and it seemed especially wonderful to me that the serious and reasoned arguments for it were being advanced not by deprived and resentful Prairie and Pacific writers isolated from the mainstream but by a Torontonian whose doctorate was from the Sorbonne and whose other publications were on established literary figures.

His lectures were both illuminating and stimulating, and I eagerly joined in the discussions, but I had still not developed systematic work habits and on the day our first essay was due I arrived at the university empty-handed. I knew that Brown, whose class was not until after lunch, did not accept late essays, so I took the whole morning, skipping one or two other classes. I ignored secondary sources and wrote fast for about three hours; then I attached a note explaining the lack of apparatus as a consequence of my delinquency, and handed my essay in. Brown's comments were a judicious balance of appreciation for the essay's merits with rebuke for its formal shortcomings and made me realize that being late in one's assignments was childish; my remaining essays for him were on time and observed all the formalities. In the second term I was invited, along with some others, to tea at his place, where I met his wife, Peggy, an attractive young woman who was cutting her own considerable swath in Winnipeg society (she was an American with money and knowledge of how to use it).

What was most un-Manitoban about Brown was that he was not in the least apologetic about being a teacher of English. It was not merely that he was free of the general depression that hung over the Manitoba faculty because of bad times and the local financial disaster; even more important, he was equally free of the feeling of uncertainty, and even inferiority, that most Humanities faculty members displayed in that unpolished, impoverished, largely immigrant society in which pioneer values and attitudes lingered. He was not defensive about cultural values: he took them for granted; and it was clear that he thought the intellectual quality of his discipline the equal of any, despite the higher value placed on the sciences and professions by the local society. I had already begun to contemplate an academic career, and Brown's example greatly encouraged me. It came as a sad blow when we learnt in second term that he was returning to the University of Toronto; I told him so, and he suggested that I let him know from time to time how things were with me.

Lloyd Wheeler had organized an English club, usually referred to by its members as 'The Morons,' for selected senior students, and Adamson, Turner, and I were delighted to be invited to join it while still in second year. It met about once a month to give and discuss papers, usually on living writers or current literary movements, and generally for the mutual support of travellers in what was, in Manitoba, lonely terrain. Occasionally we'd have a paper by a faculty member, and that year we had the first of two or three visits by a short professor of chemistry who read from a work in progress subsequently published as *Sarah Binks*; it added greatly to my pleasure in this funny work that Paul Hiebert was a Mennonite born in Pilot Mound, some fifty miles west of Winkler. Many years later I nominated him for an honorary degree and had the pleasure of presenting him for it.

In history I had H. Noel Fieldhouse, a tall Englishman of imposing presence, physique, and accent, whose lectures were usually crowded and much discussed. Fieldhouse purported to be a scholar, spoke learnedly of recondite matters like Bolingbroke's activities in the Irish College in Paris at the beginning of the eighteenth century, and made much of the need to use primary source material (speaking in flowing English while looking at an open book, he would say parenthetically, 'translating at sight from the

Russian [or French, or whatever],' until we were able to count half a dozen or more languages in which he was at such ease, only to learn from older students that he had been translating the same passages 'at sight' for years and that the translations were pencilled in). However, he had published little except newspaper articles and had far more the temperament of a performer than a scholar; indeed, he was a rhetorician in the Quintilian sense, where appearance, bearing, gesture, voice, and diction are carefully calculated for effect, and the organizing principle is persuasion rather than analysis or demonstration. (Perhaps this was why Marshall McLuhan found him the 'most inspiring' teacher he had ever studied under.)* I found Fieldhouse fascinating but dangerous; I didn't think him a fascist, but some others did, and in the circumstances of 1937 some of his positions raised the question. He poured scorn on the idea of a Czechoslovakian state and was sympathetic to the position of the *Volksdeutsche* both there and in Danzig, was contemptuous of Leon Blum's Popular Front government in France, disclaimed Mosley's British Fascist Movement but supported some of its goals, and spoke ambiguously about Jews, whose treatment in various parts of Europe was being increasingly reported in the press.

He was a very clever debater, one of whose techniques was to throw out subordinate positions bound to be challenged by liberals or leftists, and then to outflank the challenger's argument with hitherto unmentioned material advanced with magisterial authority. I was wary of challenging him at first, and was always polite and respectful when I did, but it was inevitable that I would argue with him, and I sometimes met his enfilading fire with some reserve material of my own (I was reading a lot of current-affairs journals). He later went to McGill, where he subsequently became dean of arts; I saw him at an academic conference shortly after my return to Canada in the 1960s, and although his manner was not much changed it was clear that the student movement had badly shaken his self-assurance.

* Letter to Fieldhouse, 4 February 1970; cited in Philip Marchand, *Marshall McLuhan: The Medium and the Messenger* (Toronto: Random House, 1989), p. 15

The sole professor of philosophy was Rupert C. Lodge, another Englishman but a marked contrast with Fieldhouse: a small man with a small voice and precise manner who published voluminously, analysing everything into idealism, realism, and pragmatism, and affected to despise popularity. (His relations with Fieldhouse were poor: they were reported to bait each other in faculty meetings, were frequently at odds when seen on the streetcar to the campus, and made cutting remarks about each other in class. No one knew the cause, but I suspected that it was social: Lodge was a nephew of Sir Oliver Lodge, the well-known occultist, and belonged to a social class which Fieldhouse emulated and wanted people to think was his own, and Lodge, like so many Englishmen in the colonies – Canada was still a Dominion, if not strictly a colony – seems to have thought it his duty to keep his countryman in his proper English social place.) The course was an introduction to logic, which I found interesting and instructive, although Lodge, whose ego was as large as his physique was small, asserted his intellectual superiority by teaching it as from a great height. The class was not large and I participated quite actively in discussion.

The other half of the course, an introduction to psychology, ought to have been interesting but wasn't. Perhaps my expectations were unreasonable, but the approach taken by the professor, a long, dry man named H.W. Wright, was disappointing. I became convinced that amateur psychology was more fun and didn't pursue the subject beyond that year.

Another exaggerated expectation that was to be disappointed was in economics. W.J. Waines, a stocky, affable man whom I liked, was probably a good economist and a good guide for senior students, but he didn't make the subject interesting to the beginner, and despite my recognition of its importance I dropped it too at the end of the year. Although I didn't pursue economics, Bill Waines and I were on friendly terms and, when my wife and I paid our regular Christmas-vacation visits to Winnipeg in the late 1940s and 1950s, he would invite us to his locally celebrated bring-your-own-bottle New Year's Eve parties. In the 1960s, when he was a senior administrator, I used to meet him quite often at academic conferences, and once in quite funny circumstances in London: after the day's sessions during my first Commonwealth Universities conference in 1963 I stayed late at a pub with him and several other Manitobans, and when we returned to our temporary quarters I found that I'd misplaced my door key and had to scramble to get in; the next afternoon, at a garden party in Buckingham Palace and with a considerable audience, Waines and Douglas Chevrier, the U of M registrar, handed me, with a great flourish, what they called 'the key of the kingdom,' which they'd somehow managed to recover that morning while I was at a business session.

Sharing quarters with Ogden Turner was satisfactory for the time being but I didn't think the arrangement should be extended beyond the academic year, and so began persuading the fraternity to acquire a house (we had been using a downtown office for meetings and the homes of members for social occasions). The question was whether we could expect enough paying residents to finance a suitable house, and I therefore urged that we accept as residents a few older persons who were not members. This was agreed in principle and we located a fairly large house at the corner of Stradbrooke Avenue and Wellington Crescent, next to Premier John Bracken's house and one door away from one of the leading Gentile fraternities. A lot of work was needed to finish arrangements and get the house in order for the coming term, and my cousin Wilfred and I were among the most active workers. At the end of term I was elected first house chairman, thus exposing me to an unending series of financial and disciplinary problems which may have been good training for my later administrative duties but which I didn't at all enjoy.

Before the end of term I received something of a shock. My father asked me to go to an address on Selkirk Avenue to meet a Mrs Chasanoff; he didn't say why. I was greeted by a stocky, worn woman in her mid-fifties, soft-spoken, anxious to please, and obviously nervous. She had been widowed early, had come to Canada and struggled to raise two boys; now that her sons were well established she had given up her job. As we chatted and her uneasiness lessened, it became clear that she was a very pleasant, decent person. The next day my father came to Winnipeg and asked what I thought of her. I said I liked her. He asked what I would think if he married her. I ought not to have been surprised but I was; I had thought perhaps he was considering engaging her as a housekeeper. It seemed to me a very short time since my mother had died and I couldn't help feeling hurt on her account, but I knew how hard it was for my father to live alone and raise a fourteen-year-old son in Winkler, and I managed to avoid a destructive pause before saying that I would think well of it. My father's tension eased somewhat and he said, 'Then tell your sisters and Bert.'

This was a heavy assignment but I carried it out, beginning with Gertrude in Winnipeg and proceeding, by telephone, to Hilda and Gladys in New York. In each case I was met with shocked disbelief and something approaching hysteria, and in each case I emphasized Mrs Chasanoff's grandmotherliness and Father's need, especially respecting Bert, talking until the reaction wore down and ending only when each agreed to tell Father that it would be all right. With Bert, who was most directly affected, I had an easier time, explaining to him that we had to help Father over a big hump; he was upset, but he agreed to conceal it from Father.

When I reported all this to my father, he said, 'Now tell Sam.' This proved a difficult mission, with an unfortunate outcome. After his anger was partly dissipated, Sam said he didn't think Grandmother should be told. I was appalled, but he insisted that it would reawaken her grief and that she'd been through enough, so I agreed to pass his opinion on. My father was upset by it but after much consideration he decided to yield to it, on the ground that Sam lived with his mother and probably knew best. This was a bad decision and a precedent for a worse.

A month or so after the marriage Gertrude and I went by bus to New York to visit Hilda and Gladys, who had not yet met Mrs Sirluck and were eager to be briefed. I spent the week discovering New York, rushing about to as many of the places I'd read about as I could, thus preventing any of them from registering strongly but gathering a cumulative impression of economic power and cultural riches. I went home reverberating with excitement and determined to come again as soon as possible.

That summer in Winkler was a fairly delicate balancing act.

There was quite a lot to do helping Mrs Sirluck get settled in, although she made no demands. Bert was uneasy with the new situation and needed quite a lot of comforting and reassurance, and even Father needed occasionally to be told that it was all working out well. When September came I was guiltily glad to escape to Winnipeg, a feeling distinct from and additional to my ordinary eagerness to return to the university.

III

The Depression had begun to ease a little, the grasshoppers and wheat rust had abated somewhat, and there was needed rain that summer, so I was able to persuade my father that I should get a BA before entering Law. I even brought forward the possibility of a career as an academic, which he heard with sceptical indulgence. How many Jewish professors were there at the University of Manitoba? I admitted that there were none. Were there any in other Canadian universities? I didn't know. (In fact, as shown in a suppressed contemporary report of the Canadian Jewish Congress which has since come to light, there were none.)* What made me think I could get a job? Somebody had to be first, I replied, not knowing that in English it would be I. He remained unconvinced, but there were two years to graduation (I didn't tell him that I'd begun to think of the five-year honours program) and time enough for mature reflection.

Third year meant senior division and the Ft Garry campus, a change which I welcomed despite the long, slow ride on the infre-

---

* In 1989, Irving Abella summarized the still-unpublished report: 'Banks, insurance companies, department stores and large industrial and commercial interests did not hire Jews. Jewish doctors could not get hospital appointments. There was not one Jewish judge in the entire country. Law firms rarely hired Jews. Not only did universities and professional schools devise quotas against Jewish students, they did not hire Jewish faculty. There was not one Jewish professor at any Canadian university, though the University of Toronto did appoint Jacob Finkelman as a lecturer in law. There were no Jewish school principals, very few teachers, and almost no Jewish engineers, architects, or nurses': 'The Making of a Chief Justice: Bora Laskin, the Early Years' (Cambridge: Cambridge Lecture Series of the Canadian Institute of Advanced Legal Studies, 1989), pp. 4–5. See also Abella, *A Coat of Many Colours* (Toronto: Lester and Orpen Dennys, 1990), p. 181.

quent streetcar – a serious nuisance at best and a hardship in winter – because it took us out of the disheartening temporary Broadway buildings and into our new building, with what seemed to me at the time its good library. The architecture of the new Arts and Science buildings was ludicrous: college Gothic in pale Manitoba limestone, dropped into a campus of prairie Palladian done in red stone; even my untrained and inexperienced eye was jolted by the grotesque mismatch every time I entered the campus. But our anachronistic Gothic fortress was free of the smell of decay, had cleanable stone floors, rooms in which small classes were not lost, lockers in the basement away from the classrooms, and above all the library. There were comfortable common-rooms (sexually segregated), and as a student officer I had access to a small office for the student council. In the two months or so before Manitoba's iron winter demonstrated the true isolation of that campus it seemed a decent-enough place to work, although even in September and October one noticed that everybody left the campus as soon as their assignments for the day were over, and the professors fastest of all.

I registered for two courses in English and one each in history and philosophy, and Adamson and Turner did the same. We were all intensely curious about the man who was succeeding Brown as head of the English department, Roy Daniells. He too arrived from Toronto, where he had done his graduate work and was teaching, but he was born in England and grew up in British Columbia, where he did his undergraduate work, and his attitude toward Toronto was ironic. He was thirty-five, unmarried, whimsically moustachioed, always appearing harried and on the verge of despair, hurrying along at a kind of restrained lope, but consciously elegant in dress, manner, and speech. His initial lectures won our immediate approval. They were studied performances, but the persona they presented was very attractive: superficially self-deprecating, humorously humble, irreverent about monuments and institutions, but absolutely serious about poetry and criticism (other literary forms were important too, but his passion was poetry; we did not at once learn that he was himself a poet). His critical views were very heavily influenced by Eliot, Richards, Empson, and

Leavis, but in 1937 that was not yet commonplace, at least not in Manitoba, and he gave us a sensitive and exciting introduction to Donne and the Metaphysicals. In view of his critical allegiance he was somewhat ambivalent about Milton, whom he presented to us largely as a contrast with his beloved Metaphysicals; but despite his temperamental dislike of the epic posture he attempted to be fair, which, as I later found to be usual in such cases, meant emphasizing the minor poems. His family had been fervent Plymouth Brethren; breaking from that fundamentalist millenarian sect so troubled his conscience that at nineteen he spent an expiatory year working in a leper colony; and he always had difficulty separating Milton's Puritanism from these personal traumas.

Without family or friends in Winnipeg, and surrounded by what throughout his dozen years there he regarded as an uncongenial, even inimical society, Daniells formed closer relationships with students than was usual, and I benefited greatly from his friendship; in and out of the classroom, he helped me widen my horizons, sharpen my perceptions, and above all discipline and modulate my responses. It was only slowly and reluctantly that I came to realize that he was much poorer at dealing with peers than with juniors; quite soon tensions developed with Wheeler, whom he at first accepted as his closest colleague. This syndrome got its fullest expression later at the University of British Columbia, where, as head of the department, he got into a towering battle with his old friend and fellow-poet Earle Birney, so extreme and bitter that their friends all across Canada had virtually to choose sides (I refused, valuing them both, and I think each felt that I'd let him down).

But, while it was a pleasure to study under Daniells, I had three other professors of English that year. Aaron J. Perry, who taught Old and Middle English, was a special burden to me. He had taught all three of my sisters, had treated them each in turn as a favourite, had spoken at the Winkler school and dined at our house, where as a boy I'd helped him on with his galoshes (he was physically handicapped), and he now looked to continue his relationship with the newest of the Sirlucks. I was bored beyond measure by his teaching, which was totally unleavened by any research more recent than a quarter-century. To escape, I concocted a scheme: I told him (untruthfully) that for financial reasons I'd had to take a part-time job which unfortunately clashed with his class times, and asked whether he'd give me a reading list and let me write the exam on the basis of home study. He agreed, expressing regret that I would not be in his class, which I pretended to share. My conscience troubled me, but the alternative was to skip classes without saying anything, which would have been humiliating to the old man.

Fletcher Argue, who taught the Romantic poets, was a trial of another sort: he was excitable, voluble, and believed in 'dynamic' teaching; that is, he would read 'with feeling' and even act out the poems he was presenting. I still feel a rush of embarrassment when I recall his rendition of Burns's 'To a Mouse': he got on top of his desk (he was a large man), adopted what he thought the posture of a 'wee, sleeket, cowran, tim'rous beastie,' and recited the poem with a twang that might have caused Burns to reach for a claymore. It was most inadvisable to disagree with him; he would throw a fatherly arm around your shoulder and babble incomprehensibly. When I returned to the university several decades later I was amazed to find that a building had been named after him.

Doris Saunders, on the other hand, was sober, hard-working, and responsible, even doing some scholarship when her heavy teaching duties permitted, but to my youthful mind she seemed plodding and dull. She was aware that I took her course in eighteenth-century literature because it was required, but I observed the amenities: I attended her class most of the time (she knew I didn't attend Perry's and skipped many of Argue's) and occasionally participated in discussion, although not very keenly.

Third-year history was Canadian, taught by R.O. MacFarlane, a rather gruff Ontarian who emphasized working with primary sources (I recall the pain of having to buy the Government Printing Office's four-volume set of the Grey–Elgin Papers). The class was so small that we met in his office, which meant that we worked largely by discussion, and it soon became clear to me that I knew much less about Canadian history than did my city-bred classmates; this was at least partly because, in Winkler, French was an unknown language and Quebec an unknown territory. I enjoyed and benefited from this course, although I was a little put off to find that MacFarlane belonged to the Native Sons of Canada, a somewhat xenophobic organization with some antisemitic connections.

Lodge, the professor of philosophy, was away on sabbatical and was replaced for the year by Marcus Long, a young man not long out of Ireland and fresh from his PhD at Northwestern. We were taken with his jovial manner and quickly became friendly; our introduction to the study of philosophy under him was extremely relaxed, which was enjoyable at first, but after a while I began to think that he was not serious about his subject and grew somewhat discontent. He seemed to evade all hard questions, tried to agree with every view put forward in class, and pursued popularity and publicity by all means available. During the war I ran into him once or twice in London, but the initial attraction had long gone. He later became a professor at the University of Toronto, popular with non-specializing undergraduates and radio audiences.

My extracurricular activities were, if anything, even more numerous than in second year. I again served on the two student councils and some of their committees, and found enough satisfaction in it to decide, in the second term, to run for the position of senior arts representative to UMSU; Adamson and Turner also ran for office, and all three of us won our contests. After the election I therefore moved from the Junior to the Senior Arts Council and stayed on UMSU, where I was given several committee assignments.

I never missed a meeting of the English Club, and spent a good deal of time that year doing a paper for it on William Faulkner. I read everything of his I could get my hands on, and I fear that I tried to get a little of every work into my paper, displaying early a bias toward inclusiveness that I've never entirely overcome. My fellow-Morons may have felt that they could have done with a little less (which I think may also have been true of some of my later audiences), but there was considerable discussion and I learnt a good deal from the undertaking.

That year I had another experience of coaching: two Roman Catholic nuns were repeating third-year English and seemed fated to fail it again, and Wheeler asked whether I'd help them. They were as meek as my earlier charges were fractious, which was harder on me; I spent more hours with them than I'd expected; they offered to pay me, but I got the impression it would have to come out of their meagre personal allowances and declined, whereupon they announced that they would pray for me daily for three years. I don't think they intended any irony. It was a great relief to everyone when they scraped through the exam.

The job of house chairman at the fraternity was very time-consuming and rather troublesome. Finding a housekeeper and supervising her work was part of it; riding herd on the residents and arbitrating their differences over the use of the house and its facilities was another part; but the worst was collecting the rents and trying to pay the bills. The undergraduates were, in this respect if not in others, less difficult than the older men who were not members of the fraternity but whom we needed to engender revenue. Often these men couldn't – or said they couldn't – pay their rents, and I became very tired of going after them. They knew we needed them and doubted that we'd turn them out. Many times I had to borrow from the chapter treasurer, himself often pressed, to pay the house bills. Finally, in exasperation, and knowing that we might lose not only tenants but any prospect of collecting back rent, I confronted the delinquents with an ultimatum. Over the next few weeks they all paid down their debts in instalments and thereafter paid their rents more or less on time; but by then my tenure as house chairman was drawing to an end, so that most of the benefit of the confrontation was reaped by my successor. I was then elected president, which meant that in the following academic year I would again have to give much time to the fraternity.

German rearmament and aggressiveness had been a growing worry; then, in March 1938, Hitler's army entered Austria to wild acclaim, followed the next month by the formal *Anschluss*. Once again, as when Hitler remilitarized the Rhineland, Britain and France did nothing; the Soviet Union limited itself to words. The German threat was obviously growing, and the likelihood that it would be stopped in good time was diminishing. I was worried, but even so I did not understand the extent of the danger; I did not think that France, which was bound by treaty to defend Czechoslovakia, and Britain, pledged to support France if she intervened, or the Soviet Union, would be equally inert when Czechoslovakia, with its unwilling and non-Germanic population, democratic government, trained army, and large arms industry, was at stake. Nevertheless, my faith in Britain and France was severely shaken. In the circles within which I moved, reactions were very diverse. In the fraternity, as in my family, dismay and alarm predominated, with some anger and disillusionment. On campus, most people other than Germans and Jews saw the event as rather distant and not a major concern; those who did see it as a threat usually ranked it well below Mussolini's adventurism in Africa, which seemed to menace Britain's Empire more directly. In Winkler it was better understood, since many people subscribed to German newspapers and magazines and had correspondents in Germany, and therefore knew something of Hitler's objectives. There was a good deal of ambivalence: Mennonite pacifism was made uneasy by the use of military force, while German ancestry responded to the 'unification of the German people.' The considerable number of Nazi sympathizers in Winkler were thrilled by the success of the *Anschluss*, which they openly interpreted as an omen.

That spring I won my first scholarship, which helped me prepare my father for the notion of a five-year program. The financial pressure on him was diminishing as normal moisture conditions on the land began to return and the acuteness of the Depression eased, locally as well as internationally, so he was willing to entertain the idea, although not yet to commit to it.

Life in Winkler was not very agreeable for me that summer. Superficially things at the store, the elevator and farm, the tennis court, and on the street were largely unchanged, but sooner or later everyone I encountered asked what I thought about the *Anschluss*, and few impressed me as wholly open when they in turn said what they felt; the truth was usually unspoken but discernible. The National Socialists, of course, strutted about with increasing cockiness, which grew more pronounced as the summer wore on and Hitler's pressure on Czechoslovakia increased. Bert and I resumed our public target-practice and he intensified his muscle-building; I joined him for long morning runs. I did not make things better for myself; since the night years earlier when Jack Funk, whom I'd thought my friend, had told me he was president of the local branch of the Nazi Party, I'd withdrawn from any contact with his other friends, some of whom had also been mine; in the uncertainty of the current climate I withdrew even further, although even then I wondered whether I was doing right, and now think I wasn't. Most of my closer friends were gone; Bill Uhrich had been transferred to Flin Flon and Dick Fulton to Portage-la-Prairie; Nelson Funk and Harold Kellough had left years earlier; the people who were available were for the most part ones whose attitudes I'd begun to question and was therefore no longer comfortable with.

Throughout the summer German pressure on Czechoslovakia grew, with contrived incidents in the Sudetenland, soon imitated by Hungary and Poland in the regions with corresponding ethnic minorities. Canadian and American newspapers were reporting the news relatively straightforwardly, but increasingly the British papers closest to the government were moving toward the German viewpoint, until in early September *The Times* of London, in a leading article widely believed to have been inspired by Prime Minister Chamberlain, who had been talking of 'self-determination' for Czechoslovakia's minorities, suggested that in the interests of peace and 'a more homogeneous Czechoslovakia' the 'minority areas' should be ceded. About the time I returned to Winnipeg to register for my fourth year, events began to move very fast: the Nuremberg Rally of the Nazi Party swelled to a very threatening crescendo; Chamberlain went to see Hitler at Berchtesgaden and agreed that the Czech Sudetenland should be ceded to Germany; Poland and Hungary made their respective demands on Czechoslovakia; France and Britain pressed Czechoslovakia into ceding the Sudetenland; Chamberlain went to Berchtesgaden again to present Hitler with this gift, only to have it rejected and to receive a new demand: immediate German military occupation of the Sudetenland, which Chamberlain was unable to sell to his cabinet; there was mobilization in Czechoslovakia and partial mobilization in France and Britain; Hitler, Mussolini, Chamberlain, and Daladier met at Munich.

By this time I hardly knew what to hope for, or rather what was most to be feared. I knew that Hitler should be stopped before it was too late, but most sources – including the British papers commonly received in Canada – insisted that it was already too late to do it without war, that Britain and France were not in a state to take on rearmed Germany, whether it was joined by Italy or not, and that no help should be expected from the Soviet Union, which couldn't be trusted, or the United States, where isolationism had returned to dominance. As for a will to resist, the dreadful blood-lettings of the Great War of 1914–18 were still the dominating experiences of Britain and France, leading to very widespread pacifist sentiment; the Oxford Union resolved that 'This House will not fight for King or country,' and when Chamberlain announced in the Commons that Hitler had invited him to Munich the House broke into a frenzy of cheering. Mackenzie King, the prime minister of Canada, who had previously visited and praised Hitler, congratulated Chamberlain on his work for peace. French Canada's sympathies were more with Roman Catholic and Fascist Italy and Spain than with the Allies, and in any case it was isolationist, as was the Co-operative Commonwealth Federation and many other Canadians, although there was still a substantial base of British loyalism in the country. I had myself imbibed endless pacifist literature, of which Beverly Nichols's *Cry Havoc* was an influential example, and was persuaded of the horror, waste, and futility of most wars, although I retained sufficient detachment to think that some wars might have to be fought.

On 30 September, a number of us gathered at Adamson's house to listen to the broadcast of Chamberlain's Commons speech on the results of the Munich Conference. Most of us were males of military age; all of us were tense and worried. As Chamberlain's disagreeable voice pronounced the preliminary sentences the suspense increased; when he said that it had been agreed that the German army would occupy the Sudetenland and that the Czech government would not resist there was a moment of utter stillness; and when he declared that he had 'brought back peace with honour,' that there would be 'peace in our time,' there was a surge of relief, and cheers to echo the applause in the Commons. To my shame I shared in the relief, but I did not cheer; I knew that Czechoslovakia had been shamefully betrayed, and I feared that worse would come, but I also feared war and tried to console myself with the thought that the democracies, having been so close to war, would now get their forces into readiness to meet another crisis in better shape, and that such readiness would deter Hitler from further adventures. Whatever my rationalizations, the fact is that I shared in the relief general in that room and in the country – that I was glad of that dishonourable 'peace with honour' even though I didn't believe it meant 'peace in our time' – and a half-century later I am still ashamed of that.

IV

The prescription for the honours program was two courses in each of two subjects in the fourth year and four courses in a single subject in the fifth. Not wanting to drop either history or philosophy, Adamson and I (Turner did not intend to do a fifth year) persuaded the registrar and the departments to allow us to take one of each in the fourth year, along with two in English. Thus I had another experience of Lodge, returned from his sabbatical having written another of his formula books. He began the year with the Olympian attitude we were familiar with; but this time the subject was philosophy, not logic, and the class numbered only eight or ten, so there was a good deal of discussion and some downright argument, which gradually brought him down from his heights and into the arena. At the last meeting of the class, he did something which deeply shocked me: he gave oral appraisals of each of us in turn, starting from the one he ranked lowest. Since that was a horse-loving friend with whom I still sometimes rode, a pleasant, unintellectual, athletic girl whom Lodge described as unsuited for philosophical studies, the hour was painful for me from the outset. He proceeded with deadly deliberation through the whole class, setting out what he saw as each person's academic strengths and weaknesses. I was the last; I need not repeat his positive comment, but his criticism showed how he had reacted to my class participation: 'The trouble with Mr Sirluck is that he thinks all the good professors are in other universities and that he has nothing to learn from anyone here.' In a lifetime spent in universities I never saw anything better calculated to set students against each other than this vain and cruel procedure.

For history I had William L. Morton, recently returned from a Rhodes scholarship with, if not exactly an Oxford accent, what was thought an Oxford manner of barely opening his lips while speaking; since he also usually kept his pipe in his mouth, he was not easy to follow. He was to become a leading historian of Canada, but the course he offered that year was Nineteenth-Century British History. I learnt a good deal from it, particularly from what was my first substantial research assignment, the first decade of *Punch*. Morton made no suggestions as to what to look for or how to go about it, which was not very helpful; perhaps he thought I knew more about research method than I did. The only holding of the opening years of *Punch* in Manitoba was in the Legislative Library; I spent many days in its basement stacks, hardly ever seeing another user – an early exposure to a situation I've often encountered since: expensive and virtually unused resources in the libraries of governments which deny similar resources to their universities, although the latter constitute the true user community. In those days one often heard people say, '*Punch* isn't what it used to be,' and then the smart retort: 'It never was.' I found that it had been, in its opening years, not only mordantly satirical but passionately reformist, almost revolutionary, with the most vivid and searing accounts I'd seen of mid-nineteenth-century British lower-class living and working conditions and of political corruption, but that it softened markedly toward the end of its first decade.

In English I studied with Daniells and Wheeler. I could no longer derive from them the stimulus of a fresh sensibility or viewpoint, but we were covering subject-matter and skills new to me and I was satisfied.

That year I edited the annual literary supplement of *The Manitoban*, the student newspaper. One of my innovations was to offer cash prizes – small, but not derisory in the money values of those days, and not easy for me to raise – for the best original poem, short-story, and essay submitted for publication. I've forgotten who won the short-story award. The best essay was by Leonard Woodbury, who later became a professor of Classics at University College, Toronto, where we became friends and I sometimes surprised new members of High Table by asserting that I was his first publisher. I was also the first publisher of the student who won the poetry prize, Fredelle Bruser, who would later become related to me through my sister Gladys's marriage. Her submission was not a single poem but such a sheaf of them as almost to overwhelm me; most could be safely set aside, but in the end I winnowed one out – one of the shortest – and printed it. I did not meet her because she was at the Broadway site; when we finally met many years later she had been pretty widely published, particularly in the popular press.

The chancellor of the university was John W. Dafoe, the editor of *The Manitoba Free Press* and a power in the land. I admired his editorials and thought it would be appropriate and helpful if Canada's most distinguished journalist wrote something for the literary supplement. He received me in his dark, old-fashioned office with the reserve of one accustomed to too many demands on his time. I don't remember the arguments I used, but he agreed to my request; indeed, he gave me a small sum to help with the costs of the supplement. Years later I would serve on the board of the foundation named after him.

Early in the session two students proposed to me that the Arts Council sponsor a magazine devoted to humanistic studies. The university did not publish a journal, perhaps in part because so few of the faculty wrote for publication; as we discussed the situation we came to think that the contents should be predominantly faculty-written. That, at any rate, was the proposal I took to Council, where it was forcefully pointed out that I was asking it to do with student money what should be done on the university budget. I conceded the point but said that there was no chance of the university doing it without stimulus, and undertook that, if Council would pay for the first year, we would sell enough subscriptions and advertising to pay for most of the second year, and Council agreed. The initiators got out a first number, but were discouraged by its reception and the financial commitment from continuing, and I agreed to edit *The Manitoba Arts Review* in its second year, observing the terms of my undertaking.

At the fraternity I was gradually learning something about being in charge of an organization. Some of the lessons came easily: conducting meetings, formulating goals and plans, delegating tasks. Some things were harder to learn: putting up with nonsense, disguising distaste; and some things which I should have learnt then, such as holding back, not dominating, took me many years, perhaps decades, to learn, and then imperfectly. My chief concern that year was recruitment and the treatment of pledges. We secured a pretty good intake, but there was a general tradition on the campus, shared by our fraternity, of making pledges pass through demeaning and humiliating tasks before being recommended for initiation, on the grounds that this would test their resolution and be good for their character. The real reason, I thought, was that it had been done to the fraters and they wanted their turn at playing master. Furthermore, there would usually be someone who professed dissatisfaction with how a pledge carried out an order and would exercise his 'right' to paddle him as correction. After almost an academic year of such treatment, pledges who received the chapter's approval would go through the ceremony of initiation, which combined a last session of mistreatment with a final ritual of affirmation and brotherhood. The whole thing was almost as distasteful to me then as it had been when I was a pledge, and I set out to reform it, much to the anger of those who enjoyed inflicting humiliation and pain. Some of the members supported my reforms and we had some success, at the cost of several stormy meetings. As president, I headed the chapter's delegation to the annual convention of the International, held that year in St Louis, where I experienced some difficulty in reconciling the endless rhetoric about noble purposes with what I had learnt about the operations of both my own and other fraternities. By spring, when I handed the gavel to my successor, I was ready substantially to reduce my fraternity activities.

Roy Daniells had become friends with Robert ('Pete') McQueen, the head of the economics department, and they sometimes invited me to join them for tea at the Winter Club or for a drink at Daniells's apartment. McQueen was on the board of the Bank of Canada, which meant frequent flights to Ottawa for meetings; in the isolation of Winnipeg winters, the resultant injections of news and gossip about larger affairs was invigorating. McQueen was one of the best collectors of bawdy jokes I've known; his large grin and slightly conspiratorial air made the jokes even better, and the inexhaustible supply led to a steadily widening circle who would exchange the latest McQueen stories almost as a ritual, much as people at the University of Toronto later exchanged Marshall McLuhan stories. A few years later a Trans-Canada Airlines' plane carrying Pete back from a bank meeting crashed and he was killed. Once when he was complaining about the university I asked him why he stayed (his reputation made me confident that he could get a job elsewhere); he replied that in the current local market he'd be unable to sell the house he'd incautiously bought when he arrived in Winnipeg. This helped to make me more hesitant to buy than I would otherwise have been during my early university appointments; fortunately I set the caution aside before the housing market became hopelessly inflated.

In the spring of 1939 most of my classmates, being in the General Course, graduated. Farewells in the Winnipeg of those days, a place of limited opportunity, stood a high chance of being permanent: people rapidly dispersed throughout the country and abroad in pursuit of careers; there was a special thrust toward Ottawa, where the 'Manitoba Mafia' was very visible. Awareness of the odds made us a shade more sentimental at parting than we would otherwise have been. In fact, although I was later to spend some additional years in Winnipeg, there were many of my classmates whom I never saw again, some of whom I valued highly.

My desire to become a professor of English had grown into resolve, so I wrote to a number of American universities for their graduate-school calendars, from which it became clear that I'd need to know a Romance language; I therefore made arrangements to take French in summer school. At this point Wheeler renewed in a more deliberate fashion a cautionary note he had sounded before: would I be able to find a university job? There were no Jewish professors of English in Canada; he didn't know whether there were any in the United States, but he had taken his PhD in Wisconsin, then reputedly the most liberal university in the States, where, despite the considerable number of Jewish graduate students in English, the head had made it clear there would be none on the faculty. A few years earlier a talented Jewish student of his had gone to Minnesota for his PhD but then had been unable to get a teaching post in either country and had had to go into business. Perhaps I should get advice before committing myself? I knew Wheeler was speaking in friendship and I took him seriously, but I never seriously considered changing my mind. I was not blind to the risk, nor was I sure that I could overcome it, but I was determined to try.

For summer school I decided to economize and to escape the dreary long streetcar ride from the city by living in the Ft Garry student residence, an uncomfortable and depressing dormitory occupied during the summer largely by farm youths taking the practical course in Agriculture. The instructor in French was a Welshman named Meredith Jones who was so devoted to his acquired Oxbridge accent that he used it for French as well, which was rather confusing. However, there were few distractions, and the course served its purpose, which was to give me academic standing in French. A bonus was that two of the more interesting members of the faculty of United College, an affiliate of the university, were teaching in the summer school. Arthur Phelps had made a local reputation with his radio broadcasts and newspaper pieces on literary subjects, Arthur Lower a somewhat wider reputation for his aggressive nationalist interpretation of Canadian history. I was glad to meet them both, and occasionally chatted with them in the cafeteria or elsewhere. Thirty years later Lower wrote to congratulate me on moving graduate education in Ontario in what he mistakenly thought a Canadian-nationalist direction.

I spent what was left of the summer in Winkler, where I found my brother increasingly restless and my father worried about him. Bert was uneasy living with a stepmother, however discreet and unassertive. He was unhappy at school, where the teachers expected him to do as well as his siblings; but Bert was not bookish or academic. Antisemitism in Winkler had become more virulent and menacing with the example of *Kristallnacht*, 9 November 1938, the state-organized, Germany-wide pogrom, and Bert's sensitivity to the worsening local atmosphere made him withdraw from some associates, much as I had, but unlike me he found little compensation in reading. I did what I could to be helpful, and fortunately I was still there when school started in the fall and he got into trouble. Some altercation caused the principal, an athletic type, to lay hands on him; Bert, although only sixteen, had been faithful to Charles Atlas, his blood was up, and he struck the principal. An hour or two later I got a call from Dr Wiebe, who was chairman of the school board; he told me that Bert would be expelled, but that it would take a day before the board could meet to do it. I took the hint, called my fellow-Moron Stan Jackson, a master at St John's College School, explained the situation to him, and asked whether Bert could be enrolled there at once, in which case he could simply leave the Winkler school and the board would not have to take any action, leaving his record clean (I relied on Dr Wiebe and the aggrieved principal, Mr Wolkoff, with whom our family had good relations, to make my assertion good, which in the event they did). Jackson consulted the headmaster and got back to me in minutes: yes. I then explained my proposal to Bert and my father, and had Bert packed and in the car in not much more than an hour, and registered at St John's before the office closed for the day.

It was not a magic solution to all Bert's troubles. He was the only Jewish boy in a church-run boarding-school at a time when Christian teaching laid responsibility for the death of Jesus on 'the Jews,' in the language of the more hostile gospels (in other places, 'the people'), and most church services, particularly those of Good Friday, inculcated abhorrence of Jews. Besides, Bert arrived a little late in the term, after the initial groupings had taken place, and so was doubly an outsider. There was some attempted bullying, which led to a confrontation; the athletics master, Andrew Currie, who knew me a little, put the antagonists into the ring with boxing gloves and himself refereed; it was a hard fight without a declared winner, but Bert was never bullied again in the school. When the hockey season opened he came into his own, making the first team each year and becoming close friends with some others on the team. His grades were not high but they were adequate, and he enjoyed school. The fees may have presented my father with a bit of a problem, but he never said so.

V

Once again tension was building on the international scene, after its misleading reduction at Munich. After all his solemn assurances that all he wanted of Czechoslovakia was the Sudetenland, Hitler in March had sent his troops into Bohemia and Moravia, which he declared occupied territory, and into Slovakia, where he set up a puppet regime; he also invited Hungary to take Ruthenia, which it promptly did; and Czechoslovakia, the only genuine democracy in Middle Europe, ceased to exist. Constrained by public opinion, Britain and France lodged protests, and Chamberlain went on the air to say that Hitler had deceived him and that, if Poland were invaded, Britain and France would fight. In April Mussolini invaded Albania, and Britain and France guaranteed the borders of endangered Greece and Romania. Litvinov, the foreign secretary of the Soviet Union and a champion of collective security and the League of Nations, proposed a triple pact of mutual assistance among Britain, France, and the Soviet Union; the Allies rejected this and, in May, Litvinov was ousted and replaced by the more nationalistic Molotov. Three days later, on 6 May, Germany and Italy announced their military alliance. Then, like a bombshell, at 11:00 P.M. on 22 August 1939, German radio announced the Hitler–Stalin Pact, whose secret protocol, not hard to guess, divided up Poland and gave the Soviet Union a free hand in the eastern Baltic and Bessarabia. On the same day Britain announced that it would fight if Poland were attacked, and on 26 August the Anglo–Polish treaty was signed. On 1 September Germany invaded Poland, and Britain and France delivered their ultimatum; it was ignored, and on 3 September they declared war on Germany. A German submarine immediately torpedoed the British passenger ship *Athenia*, with the loss of 112 civilians.

Hitler now had the chance he lusted for to demonstrate *Blitzkrieg*, lightning war. Poland's antiquated air force was destroyed in two days, leaving the *Luftwaffe* free to work at will; Polish cities as well as the Polish army were heavily bombed and strafed; the Polish horse cavalry was crushed by tank divisions; Cracow and Warsaw fell in a week, and by 17 September the Polish army was bottled up and helpless. On that day, at Hitler's invitation, Stalin invaded Poland from the east, and at the end of the month the lines of partition of Poland were agreed and the Baltic states fell into the Soviet sphere of influence.

Having struck terror into the stunned Allies, who had done nothing to help although a massive French army sat still while its ally was destroyed, Hitler now lulled them into a false sense of security: *Sitzkrieg* followed *Blitzkrieg*, while feelers were sent out that Hitler was ready for peace. Only some naval actions interrupted the quiet of what was promptly dubbed the 'phony war.'

In Canada the reaction to the invasion of Poland and the Allies' declaration of war was very subdued. Mackenzie King, the prime minister, wanted to make a point about Canada's independence, so he allowed a week to go by before Canada's separate declaration of war on 10 September. His government let it be understood that Canada's role would be mainly supportive and logistical, which, together with an explicit declaration that there would be no conscription, reduced French-Canadian resistance to Canada's participation. (In addition to Adrien Arcand's openly fascist Blue Shirts, some mainstream French-Canadian leaders, including Camillien Houde, the long-time mayor of Montreal, were proclaiming that Quebec's natural affinities were with Roman Catholic Italy and Spain rather than with *les maudits Anglais* and 'communistic' France.) Mobilization was very half-hearted; the 1st Canadian Division was formed from the small Permanent Force, some part-strength militia units, and volunteers drawn largely from relief camps and the unemployed.

In this atmosphere of strangely mixed fear and inertia, most people went nervously on with their current activities; none of my classmates enlisted, although a few joined the Canadian Officers Training Corps on the campus or one or other of the reserve militia or naval units. I did not. Had Britain and France gone to war in defence of Czechoslovakia the previous year, I believe that, although frightened, I would have enlisted, but the appeasements and betrayals of the intervening twelve months had destroyed my faith in their governments and particularly their leaders. As for Poland, while I shuddered at its destruction and feared the consequence, I felt no attachment to it: it was no democracy, and its reactionary government had continued the country's long history of cruel antisemitism. Its independence had been important to me primarily as an element in the stabilizing balance of power in Europe, now irretrievably upset. Now, with all hope of support from the east shattered by the Hitler–Stalin Pact, there was a phony war, managed by the double-dealing appeasers Chamberlain and Daladier, which might well end in another concocted settlement. Canada's participation was certainly very limited, very consistent with the phoniness of the war. In these circumstances I felt no need to abandon my education in order to enlist, or even to adopt the protective colouration of joining the COTC.

I registered for my final year, all my courses being in English, all with Daniells and Wheeler. For my graduating essay I undertook *The Criterion*, the journal founded by T.S. Eliot in 1922 whose final number had just appeared, announcing its termination because of a 'depression of spirits' induced by 'the present state of public affairs.' It was a fascinating study, from which I learnt a great deal about the culture and politics of between-the-wars Europe, some of it quite new to me, but it left me in no doubt that Eliot, who had been a major influence on me, disliked democracy, had a distaste for Jews, and was drawn to the politer, more ecclesiastical forms of totalitarianism (he thought the sole choice for Europe was between communism and theocracy). For some years Eliot's poetry continued to hold its grip on me, but my study of *The Criterion* helped me little by little to disengage from his criticism, a process much aided by my subsequent study of Milton; by the time I met Eliot (in Chicago and London in the early 1950s) I was sufficiently detached to engage in some disputation with him.

I was no longer serving on any student councils and my role at the fraternity was much reduced; my only significant extra-curricular commitment was *The Manitoba Arts Review*. Adamson was my associate editor, and he rounded up a group of bright first-year people to help, especially with the business side. Pat and Peggy Murray, twins who lived across the road from Adamson (Pat later married George Ford, the Dickens scholar), and their friends Jean Edmonds, who became one of the first women to achieve senior status in the Canadian civil service, and Jean Tweed, who later cofounded a Canadiana bookstore in Toronto, made an effective and agreeable work force. For my assistant editor I chose Bill Anderson, a third-year student who could carry over into the following year, when in fact he became the next editor; he later became a justice in the Supreme Court of Ontario. I solicited articles from the faculty and got enough for two numbers, learning something in the process about the very relaxed academic view of a deadline (actually collecting some of these articles reminded me strongly of collecting the rent in the fraternity house). We procured enough advertising and subscription revenue to fulfil my undertaking to the Arts Council, which made little difficulty about putting up the small balance needed, and I took a copy of each number to the university president, Sidney Smith, the second number with a strong suggestion that the university ought now to take over responsibility for the *Review* or for something like it. He did not disagree but nothing came of it, and the *Review* remained a student enterprise for the dozen or so years it lasted.

In spring the phony war came to an abrupt end. One after another, the neutral countries of northwest Europe either submitted to Hitler or were conquered. In April Denmark submitted to a surprise ultimatum. Norway refused and was conquered in two months, involving some significant German naval losses to the British. In May Belgium, the Netherlands, and Luxembourg were invaded without warning; after four days, which included the bombing of Rotterdam, the Dutch surrendered; the Belgians fought on for two further weeks, when King Leopold, against advice, surrendered. The left flank of the Franco–British front was thus exposed; the Germans had already broken through at Sedan in the centre and now encircled the whole British force and a good part of the French. From 27 May to 5 June there ensued the wonderful evacuation of the British army from Dunkirk – still an army but, without arms and equipment, not a fighting force. With France almost paralysed, Italy attacked it from the south without making headway, but the Germans were advancing everywhere and the new president, Marshal Pétain, surrendered on 22 June.

In three months apparent stalemate had turned into general

catastrophe. Now German propaganda once again said that all German aims had been met, and offered Britain peace. Churchill, the new prime minister, said no, but few politicians in Europe or Asia believed that Britain could fight on for long, and they freely advised Churchill to accept Hitler's offer while he could. Even in the United States, where President Roosevelt's sympathies were clearly with Britain, the strong isolationist tradition proved a fertile field for German propaganda, with the popular hero Colonel Charles Lindbergh, who had recently accepted Germany's second-highest decoration, urging U.S. collaboration with Germany in a 'New Order,' and predicting that Britain would be unable to withstand the attack of the *Luftwaffe*.

I had applied to the Yale graduate school and been accepted, but it now seemed questionable whether I should leave the country. I wrote to E.K. Brown and explained my feelings; he suggested that I come to the University of Toronto for my graduate work. I applied and was accepted.

Graduation was a subdued affair. Everyone was frightened by the turn the war had taken; no one could have confidence in his own plans. For me there was also a sense of anticlimax: most of the students I'd known had been in the four-year program and had graduated the previous year. I got together some books I thought I should read before entering graduate school and withdrew to Winkler for the summer.

After five years in the university I thought I knew its shortcomings. In fact, however, my relations with a few good and generous teachers, together with my initial eagerness to find and adopt a more congenial environment than Winkler, spread a thinning but persistent film of glamour over the institution, which obscured for me its real nature. This lack of clarity was a factor, thirty years later, in a regrettable decision of great importance.

CHAPTER THREE

Toronto, 1940–1942

I

The German conquests of the spring of 1940 were succeeded by an ominous calm reminiscent of the phony war, which the Soviet seizure of the Baltic states hardly disturbed, since there was no resistance. The newspapers were full of anxious speculation that Britain, its land forces disarmed, would soon be invaded – a prospect which some in Winkler anticipated with unconcealed glee, although most of those whose hearts were with Germany thought it prudent to retain their protective colouration a while longer. When, on 19 July, Hitler offered Britain 'peace,' Canadian opinion was very divided; in Winkler the offer was seized upon by the ambivalent majority as providing the perfect solution for their conflicting loyalties, and even the open Nazis welcomed it because they knew acceptance would lead to vassalage. When Britain's rejection of the offer was followed in mid-August by the *Luftwaffe*'s first massive assault, many in Winkler said that the British had brought it on themselves by their stubbornness and wouldn't last long. The latter opinion, at least, became increasingly widespread in Canada as the Battle of Britain continued week after week.

Before it reached its peak I left for Toronto, deeply troubled and fearful of the outcome. During the two-day train trip along the north shore of Lake Superior and deep into the Laurentian Shield my mind was sometimes diverted from the war by the spectacular beauty of the landscape, which I had previously known only in reproductions of Group of Seven paintings, but about the time of my arrival in Toronto the *Luftwaffe* switched its nightly attacks from Royal Air Force bases and installations to London itself, and every day the radio and newspapers told us that all London was burning. A week of this climaxed on 15 September in a huge daylight assault, which we did not know at the time was the turning-point in the Battle of Britain: the RAF had recovered enough in the week of its relative respite to inflict unacceptable punishment on the raiders. The nightly bombing of London continued until early November, but by switching targets the *Luftwaffe* had forfeited its almost successful effort to destroy the RAF and gain control of the skies over Britain; it therefore had to abandon large-scale daylight attacks, and the planned invasion of Britain could not take place. Before the end of the month there was a clear indication that the war would become something more than a struggle of European powers and that the focus would shift away from Britain: Japan joined Germany and Italy in the Axis Pact.

In this agitated atmosphere I wondered whether I should drop all my plans and enlist. I had some feeling that I ought to, but almost none of my classmates had done so, the pacifist environment in which I'd grown up retained much of its hold on me, and the Canadian government was not yet recruiting seriously. Moreover, antisemitism in Canada had grown stronger and more open, partly because of professional, mostly German-financed, organization and propaganda, and partly in reaction against the proposal to admit Jewish refugees from Nazi and Fascist Europe; I was aware that there was a good deal of it in the armed forces, which was not a welcoming prospect. All this combined with my eagerness for graduate study to persuade me to continue with my plans, albeit with an uneasy conscience, which I partially appeased by enrolling in the COTC, reasoning that nothing I could do would be in time to affect the Battle of Britain, and if that were won my training would enable me to contribute to what would clearly have to be a long fight back.

We trained three times a week, at first in civilian clothes and later in uniform. The syllabus included basic infantry training and an introduction to officer training, but the directing staff was for the most part militia, with a very few reserve officers of First World War vintage, and the instruction was therefore uneven and often uncertain. My company consisted of graduates and presented a diversity of occupations and aptitudes; I fear we advanced slowly through the syllabus. I had some advantages bestowed by a country background: I could shoot, walk far, and utilize contours, but the first of these qualifications served me poorly that year. The company commander, an overweight assistant school principal, noticed my score on the rifle range; he fancied himself a marksman and challenged me in front of the company to a contest. Not knowing anything about the military, and not thinking, I accepted. At the next parade we repaired to the rifle range, where he declared that we would shoot for ten dollars (not then a trifling sum); he had brought his own rifle, while I drew one from the rack. After our first shots he studied both targets through binoculars (I could discern with the naked eye that I was outer circle right); we shot again, and he repeated his inspection (I was inner left); after the third shot he viewed the targets (I had a marginal bull) and loudly lamented that 'the bugger is correcting.' It began to occur to me that more might be at stake than the ten dollars. I still had a chance to escape with no worse loss than the money, but he had made the contest so public that I didn't take it. My two final shots were bulls, and my fellow-cadets didn't help matters by cheering. The plump captain said nothing about the ten dollars; he put his rifle and binoculars into their cases and stalked away, followed by his lieutenants, one of whom stopped to congratulate me with what I thought a commiserating look. Shortly thereafter a number of cadets were promoted to corporal and sergeant; I wasn't, nor would I be while in that company, and I could almost always count on getting the joe-jobs.

There were some positive offsets to the wasted time and botched and incompetent training that marked my service in the COTC. I had at last taken a step which would lead into the army and I could stop agonizing about my duty, particularly since I was now surrounded by men who had adopted the same timing and method. The graduate training company included a much wider variety of backgrounds and occupations than could be found in Manitoba, and conversations with my fellow-trainees often showed me new facets of a more developed society. There was also fun in the rueful banter of men doing something they didn't like and which they knew would lead to much worse (among others, Johnny Weingarten and Frank Shuster competed for our laughter and were often funnier, and certainly fresher, than later on TV as Wayne and Shuster). And I was making friends, three of whom in particular I would see a lot of: Paul Corbett, a recent graduate working in a publishing house; Kenneth McNaught, a fourth-year student of history in the undergraduate training company; and, in my second year of training, Claude Bissell, brought back to an appointment in his undergraduate university from an instructorship at Cornell. Bissell, in his *Halfway Up Parnassus*, has written of these early days of our friendship, concentrating, as suits the nature of his book, on our institutional and literary associations, but we probably saw more of each other in the COTC that year than elsewhere.

I found a rooming-house on St George Street, then in effect the western border of the campus, a Victorian–Edwardian street made beautiful by its red maples. I had come a week before registration day, thinking to get settled before classes began. Had I known the university's attitude toward graduate studies I'd have registered by mail and stayed in Winkler to garner at least another fortnight's pay: graduate classes would wait until undergraduate work was well under way. In my innocence I had thought of graduate studies as the crown of a university's curriculum; so it was in some foreign universities, but certainly not in Toronto, where its marginal status was accurately reflected in this subordination to undergraduate work.

E.K. Brown introduced me to his close friend and colleague A.S.P. Woodhouse, a heavy-set man of medium height, large head, and aquiline features, physically somewhat clumsy and untidy, with a lurching walk, an elaborate and emphatic manner of speech, a sense of humour at once sly and robust, and a very keen mind, who immediately made a strongly favourable impression on me. Since I was anxious to get my courses settled and start reading for them, and other professors were not yet seeing graduate students, I took advice from Brown and Woodhouse which led to a rather unusual MA program: two courses from Woodhouse (Milton; Origins of Romanticism) and one from Brown (Method in the Novel); there was also a required non-credit short course in bibliography given by Norman Endicott. All my work was thus to be within University College – no accident, since Brown and Woodhouse regarded the federated colleges' contribution to graduate work as marginal, and I was quite willing to be counselled away from church colleges. With such a start, it turned out that in my entire graduate program I never did a credit course outside University College. Fortunately the narrowness of this base was in part compensated for by some other relationships.

In the fortnight before graduate classes began I spent a good deal of time in the library, whose collection seemed to me, accustomed only to Manitoba's meagreness, quite rich – an impression which was to last only until I began actual research. After browsing through the book stacks I usually went to the periodical room, and there I often saw a short old man with a bushy white walrus moustache who came in every afternoon to read the *The New York Times.* Eventually we spoke, and I learnt that he was the famous W.J. Alexander. I also learnt, not from him, that he had been the first full-time professorial appointment in English in Canada (at Dalhousie in 1884) and the first holder of the Chair of English Language and Literature at Toronto (created in 1889, when Sir Daniel Wilson, the university's first president, gave up the English half of his combined professorship); had remained head until his retirement in 1926; and had largely shaped the department, as well as decisively influencing the teaching of the subject in Ontario schools. This made me realize how new English was as an academic discipline in Canada; at the same time, it gave me a sense of the continuity of the department, strengthened soon after when I met Malcolm Wallace and learnt that he had been the next person appointed after Alexander, had succeeded him as head, and held that position still.

I was already familiar with Brown's classroom manner and found the same urbanity and wit, but greater intimacy, in his conduct of his graduate seminar, which numbered five or six students. The course was a critical examination of structure and function in the novel; the literature of the subject was then still scanty, and secondary reading did not figure heavily. Brown demonstrated his method by leading us through selected novels by a limited number of authors, after which we each in turn reported on other novels by the same authors (I did *Emma* and *Henry Esmond* in first term and *Middlemarch* and *The Ambassadors* in second). The work did not seem to me very different from the practical criticism we had done in fourth and fifth year at Manitoba, except that much more time was being devoted to single works and detail was correspondingly emphasized. I found the method congenial and Brown's subtlety, penetration, and scope of reference enriching.

My double exposure to Woodhouse was like a crash course in the history of ideas (or, as he sometimes said in order to avoid conflict with the Department of Philosophy, of opinion). His seminars were much larger than Brown's (fifteen or twenty students in each), perhaps because they related more closely to school and college curricula. His procedure for the first few weeks seemed better suited to the undergraduate classroom than to the graduate seminar: spread out at his desk and consciously emulating Samuel Johnson, whose portrait hung just behind his head, he lectured us mercilessly for two hours at a stretch, reading from what he called 'notes' (in fact fully written lectures, interlineated and interleaved with the revisions of the years). It was a method of teaching that would seem perfectly designed to bore students; the reason it didn't was the intellectual energy, the passion, and the wit that characterized both the written lectures and the frequent digressions.

In each course Woodhouse had a set development he wanted to cover and a specific program of topics for student reports; the only choice students had was within a list of assigned topics, each with the date on which it was to be given. In the Origins of Romanticism course the list was presented at the second meeting, long before we knew what the various topics entailed. The first report was to be on Shaftesbury's *Characteristics*, and Woodhouse asked who wanted it. Silence. If no one wanted it, was anyone nevertheless willing to take it? More silence. It was clear not only that no one knew anything about Shaftesbury (I knew only that Locke had been his tutor) but that no one wanted to be first to perform before the formidable professor. The wait became embarrassing; I raised my hand, and Woodhouse went on to parcel out the other topics. I had about a month to prepare my paper; meanwhile, Woodhouse in his weekly lectures set out the framework of ideas on which the course was built. He did this with such power and authority that the conclusions seemed to come on their own (although he never failed to draw them, emphatically and in full form – to 'nail them down,' as he said). It was intoxicating, and seemed an invitation to emulate him.

If so, it was a dangerous one to accept. I found Shaftesbury full of interest and, not content with analysing his work, set him against his formative influences and followed him in his controversies, allowing myself a full ration of sweeping generalizations. Following instructions, I designed my paper to take about forty minutes to read. I got through a page or two before Woodhouse's first question came, and it was followed by a discourse of several minutes on some point I'd missed or conclusion I'd not fully documented. I resumed reading, and soon there was another question and discourse, then another, and the two-hour session ended with half my paper still unread. I thought it would have to remain unread, but Woodhouse said we'd take the rest up at the next meeting. I wondered about his carefully prepared timetable and resolved to get through what was left as quickly as was decent, but the next week the same thing happened: the whole meeting went to my paper and his commentary (except that by this time one or two students were emboldened to raise questions too). It was one of the most educative experiences of my life, introducing me to much more rigorous standards of scholarship than I'd previously encountered and illuminating the intellectual risks of the plausibility which came rather easily to me. When the paper was finished, Woodhouse praised it and explained that he'd allocated the extra session to it because it had raised so many of the points he wanted to cover, but that future papers would have to be limited to about forty minutes. After the class he told me that another reason he'd allowed the extra time was that he thought the disputation between us instructive to the others; I said I was flattered but wondered whether he'd have felt the same had I been winning. I think that was the first time I heard the huge belly-laugh so well known to his intimates but so surprising to those who mistook his intellectual austerity for temperamental severity.

The Milton course, very different in outline from the Origins of Romanticism, was not very different in flavour. Necessarily, biographical matters entered it more deeply, and at set points Woodhouse paid his dues to aesthetics (he liked establishing what he called 'aesthetic patterning'); but it was always the ideas and the ways in which they informed the individual works that counted. Theology and church history, not at that time fashionable components of secular academic study, were frequent preoccupations; other aspects of politics received less attention, despite their importance for the subject. Woodhouse, a Conservative and monarchist who thought of himself almost as an English Tory in the Dominions and once described himself to me as 'like a flying buttress: the best support the Anglican Church can have, but outside,' had so possessed himself of Milton the republican revolutionary, defender of regicide, and radical sectarian that he was able to present his thought and feeling from the inside, a feat I knew how to admire, being a Jew increasingly concentrating on the emphatically Christian literature of the English Renaissance.

My seminar paper was on Milton's political thought, and I did so much work on it that Woodhouse encouraged me to develop it as my MA thesis, with himself as supervisor, and Arthur Barker, of Trinity College, the second reader. Barker, a Toronto graduate, was thirty years old and had taken his PhD at the University of London just three years earlier; he was now turning his thesis into the book shortly to be published as *Milton and the Puritan Dilemma*, and he took a much more active role in the direction of my thesis than was customary for a second reader. He felt that his own book, together with Woodhouse's *Puritanism and Liberty*, which had prepared the way for it, and the work of two or three scholars elsewhere, had covered the major influence on Milton's political thought – religion – and that what remained to be studied was the minor influence – classical republicanism; if, as I had begun to think, I would do my PhD on Milton's thought, that was the direction my master's thesis ought to take. Woodhouse concurred, although with less conviction. I didn't altogether like the idea of working on a 'minor' influence, but I liked the prospect of learning more about classical political thought. A difficulty occurred to me: I knew neither Greek nor Latin. This caused some consternation: how had I got into the graduate program, which, they thought, required the equivalent of the Toronto Honours BA in English, of which Latin was part? In fact it didn't, requiring for the MA any departmentally approved foreign language from a short list, and a second for the PhD; I intended to satisfy the requirements with German and French, respectively. They then concluded that virtually everything I'd need would be available in translation in one or other of my three modern languages, and I could learn enough Latin on my own for what was left over; Greek was dispensable. It was unsound advice, but I was very willing to accept it, and the title of my thesis became 'Milton's Political Thought: A Survey Preliminary to the Investigation of the Classical Influence.'

I had hoped that the course in bibliography would introduce me to the mysterious new discipline I'd begun to hear about, sometimes called 'descriptive bibliography,' but it was just a rather random one-term program to familiarize students who were graduates of other universities with the U of T Library and introduce them to the major reference works and other aids to study. Endicott, a tall, gaunt, high-strung man who knew a lot about books, sensed the disappointment which I tried to conceal and was a little apologetic, remarking to me once that some in the group needed this sort of help. He read more contemporary literature than anyone else in the UC department and pushed to get some of it into the curriculum, but was for years thwarted by the local view that living authors should rarely if ever be taught. He had a wry humour but was embittered by lack of advancement, which he attributed to Woodhouse's influence, and had suffered a disappointment which was at that time still unusual: invited to join an American university at a higher rank and much better pay, he'd been barred from the

United States because he'd been born in China (of missionary parents). It seemed an odd reason; perhaps the fact that his brother was a well-known member of the Communist Party of Canada and he was himself a socialist was a contributing factor.

The Graduate English Club met about once a month during term in the house occupied by the School of Graduate Studies, on Hoskin Avenue at Devonshire Place, the site now of Massey College. There I met the other members of the UC English department: Malcolm Wallace, who was also principal of the college, R.S. Knox, W.H. Clawson, J.F. Macdonald, J.R. McGillivray, and Earle Birney; and those members of the federated-college departments who were interested in graduate work: John Robins, E.J. Pratt, and Northrop Frye from Victoria, Barker from Trinity, and L.K. Shook from St Michael's. Most papers were given by graduate students, but occasionally a faculty member or visiting scholar gave one. At the first or second meeting of the year Brown suggested that for the next meeting I give a paper, and although I thought it too soon and myself too junior, I had little option. I adapted my *Criterion* essay of the previous spring, and had the satisfaction of stirring up quite animated debate; indeed, lines of division among the members that might ordinarily not show at all, or only faintly, were opened wide that night among conservative, liberal, and radical; traditionalist and modernist; religious and secular; and I think I got something of a reputation for seeking out issues.

Brown and Pratt were close friends, which may have been why Pratt first included me in his famous York Club lunches and dinners. Ned, his face flushed with food, drink, and enthusiasm, would preside boisterously over the symposium, where, under the influence of our host and his excellent provisions, serious opinion about literature combined with anecdote, shop talk, and humour to form a bond of fellowship. At the first of these occasions that I attended the other guests included Brown, Pelham Edgar, Northrop Frye, and perhaps one or two others. I may not have formed a very just opinion of Edgar, recently retired and determined to dominate the proceedings, calling the discussion back when it got away from him by unearthing and reading out a letter from Edith Wharton or some other prominent writer, or narrating some encounter he'd had with the great or near-great, but my initial very favourable impressions of Pratt and Frye were about right.

I was beginning to meet people in other departments. One of the most interesting was Frank Underhill, whose journalistic writings about Canadian history and politics I admired. McNaught invited me to a meeting of the History Club which was to be addressed by Arnold Toynbee, whose *A Study of History* was, volume by volume, developing its enormous reputation. I listened with mixed feelings, impressed by Toynbee's scope and passion but put off by the slickness of his theory of challenge and response and worried by his emphasis on religion as civilization's essential survival technique. When he had finished there was an almost reverential hush; then from the back row a voice said, 'I admire the elegance of your presentation, Professor Toynbee, but what has it got to do with history?' Startled and trying to suppress his indignation, Toynbee turned to deal with the questioner; then, when he saw him, his expression changed. 'Ah, Underhill,' he said, as if that explained everything; 'well, perhaps you're right'; and they began exchanging opposing definitions of history as they apparently had done when they were fellow-students at Oxford. Underhill, one of the founders of the CCF, was at this time under attack in the Toronto press and in the university's board of governors, which was attempting to fire him, ostensibly because he was, during wartime, suggesting in public that the British Empire was in decline. I was not a member of the CCF but I had a good deal of sympathy with its criticism of Canadian society, and when after the lecture McNaught introduced me to Underhill, I expressed my support for his positions with respect to both Toynbee and the board. In time we became friends (he liked being with young people) and often talked about society and literature; one of his enthusiasms was Shaw, and I recall with particular pleasure one occasion when he, Frye (a fellow-editor with Underhill of *The Canadian Forum*), Claude Bissell (a Shaw specialist), and I sat long over beer in the King Cole Room of the Park Plaza Hotel discussing Shaw, society, and the difficult emergence of a Canadian literature.

I went to ask the graduate-school examiner for German, Barker Fairley, what kind of exam it would be and how best to prepare for it. Fairley, who was also head of the department at a time when that implied considerable discretionary powers, said that first he'd better get some idea of how much German I knew; he picked up a volume of German poetry and asked me to read and translate, but by the time I'd read out a stanza he said translating wouldn't be necessary, since the meaning was coming through quite clearly. He then took a critical journal off the shelf and I performed again, though not as comfortably because of the unfamiliar technical jargon. Then he asked me to tell him in German something about my background and plans, and after a brief conversation he said that would do: I was certified. This non-exam has since served as my ideal of a language examination, in part because it presupposes a certain relationship between faculty and graduate students.

Just at this point his colleague Hermann Boeschenstein came into the office; Fairley introduced me as that rarity, a graduate student in English who might actually use German in his studies (to my shame, that prophecy proved only marginally correct). Both men became my friends. Fairley, a Yorkshireman of strong leftist convictions, may have made more of the social-democratic views I expressed than I intended; in any case, he invited me to his home, where his wife engaged me in a very aggressive political discussion. It came to me later, when I learnt that she was an officer in the Communist Party of Canada, that she'd probably been trying to recruit me and must have been sorely disappointed. My remissness, however, seemed not to erect any barriers between Fairley and myself; he continued to stop and chat whenever we met in the college. Boeschenstein, a gentle-mannered Swiss who, on behalf of the Red Cross, made periodic visits to the enemy alien internment centres across Canada, told me that he'd met Bürzle in one of them and that some colleague at Manitoba had sent Bürzle, whether innocently or otherwise, Hardy's *Far from the Madding Crowd* (I learnt later that it had been Daniells and that he had, of course, been conscious of the irony).

During the winter term, Brown announced that he had accepted appointment as chairman of the Cornell English department and would be leaving in the summer. I was saddened at the prospect of his second withdrawal as my teacher, but it was not to be complete. He did not stay at Cornell long, soon being summoned to Ottawa as special wartime assistant to Prime Minister Mackenzie King. He visited Toronto often and usually called me for a meal; his conversation continued to open vistas for me, but the university seemed narrower and poorer without him.

As I worked through Milton's prose, I was surprised by the degree of inconsistency I encountered in his political thought, for which the scholarship of the day had not prepared me. Barker's book, which would explore the subject, was not yet finished; at his request, I would read and criticize the manuscript, but that was not until the following year. Nevertheless, his views as second reader influenced my thesis. Staggered by the many turns and contradictions in Milton's thought, I accepted Barker's view that it was the result of a confusion natural to an idealistic poet flung into nit-picking controversy. Woodhouse, who was in a general sense familiar with the problem, had not made a special study of it and was inclined to defer to Barker's opinion about it. My thesis then became a detailed chronological survey of the movement of the political thought, highlighting its shifts and 'confusions'; but I did retain enough of the original plan to relate the concepts and principles to classical political philosophy.

Finishing the thesis in time to graduate that spring was heavy work (I did the typing myself, in quadruplicate), but the alternative was to leave the degree in suspense at a time when one couldn't securely plan even months ahead. I therefore withdrew for a time from nearly all social activity and got it done, so that at the June convocation I was in a front row watching the ancient chancellor, Sir William Mulock, who was reputed to drink a forty-ounce bottle of whisky every day, drop his slumbering head on the shoulder of Lady Eaton, there to receive an honorary degree, while the president, Canon Cody, worked his highly rhetorical way through his convocation address. My enjoyment of the occasion was greatly enhanced by the announcement a day or two earlier that I'd been awarded one of the two fellowships available to the Humanities and Social Sciences division of the graduate school. The dollar amount of the fellowship would seem very meagre by today's standards, but at 1941 prices it would cover fees and about half a year's room and board, and looked wonderful to me.

Immediately following convocation the COTC went to Niagara-on-the-Lake for a two-week camp which was to complete our year's training. There the weakness of the directing staff and the amateurishness of the whole enterprise were even more evident than in the part-time training during the school year. It was not surprising – Canada's small Permanent Force and trained reserve were needed as a core for the active forces, and the COTC had to depend for its cadre on a few 'retreads' from the First World War and some younger people who knew little more about the army than we did – but it was discouraging. When they had exhausted their meagre stock of obsolete lectures and tactical exercises and didn't know what to do with us they sent us on route marches or to the rifle ranges or the drill square, from which we returned little the wiser in the arts of battle or command. There was good company, though; my tent included McNaught, Corbett, and Mavor Moore, already active in theatre, and heard more literary and political discussion than could have been usual. At the end of camp we were told that very few officers were being recruited into the active army and that we should dispose of our summer as we saw fit; those who wished would be welcome in the senior battalion the following academic session.

I went home to Winkler to an unsettled situation. The family had an understanding that, since I was pursuing an academic career, Bert would succeed Father in the management of the farm and business; accordingly, he had enrolled in Agriculture at the University of Manitoba. Now, at the end of his first year, he had exaggerated his age by about six months and joined the air force. The National Resources Mobilization Act had been amended in April to make service for home defence compulsory, but it provided that one son could be exempted to look after a family's business, and Father raised the matter, but Bert and I dissuaded him from pursuing it.

Since the failure of the *Luftwaffe*'s assault the previous fall the danger to Britain had grown less immediate; indeed, the British had since then severely mauled the Italian navy and destroyed

Italy's African army; but now Germany, having conquered Yugoslavia and Greece, was advancing in Libya and things once again were looking worse. Canada's own posture continued to be ambiguous; it was now recruiting actively in the English-speaking provinces but very cautiously in Quebec, using a combination of voluntary enlistment for unrestricted service and conscription for home service only. It had built up a considerable overseas force which was sitting unused in Britain, whence stories of low morale and some disturbances seeped out.

Shortly after I got home the whole complexion of the war changed: on 22 June 1941, Germany attacked its treaty partner, the Soviet Union. To many in Winkler, perhaps most, this was confirmation that Hitler's war was against the communism they hated, and they rejoiced without much concealment over every German advance on the Eastern front. Although I tried to avoid argument in the store it was sometimes impossible, and I probably reinforced for some customers the belief that Jews favoured communism by saying that the invasion of the Soviet Union had shifted the balance of forces in our favour and made the defeat of Germany more likely.

II

I returned to Toronto in the fall and found a boarding-house on Madison Avenue north of Bloor Street, still within easy walking distance of the university. A puzzling thing happened when I went to the School of Graduate Studies to register for the PhD. I had been awarded the Reuben Wells Leonard Fellowship, but now the documentation on my file showed that I'd been given the other fellowship, the Open. I asked the secretary why the change; she seemed embarrassed and gave no explanation, but pointed out that the stipends were about equal. Her evasiveness heightened my curiosity and I asked Woodhouse about it; he said he didn't know the reason but that it didn't matter. It was not until I came to Toronto as associate dean in 1962 that I found what I believe to be the explanation. Many student awards in the university were restricted by ethnic or religious clauses, and the Leonard fellowship and scholarships were restricted to 'white, Protestant, Christian, British Canadian students.' I deduced that the reason I had been thought eligible was that when I registered in the school I had written 'none' in the space for 'religion,' but that some time after the announcement of the award someone must have informed the school that I was Jewish and, since the winner of the Open was a Protestant Christian of British descent, the awards were switched. Some twenty years after this event I moved in the senate that the university negotiate with donors of existing awards the removal of all restrictive clauses, withdraw any awards that could not be so negotiated, and decline any new ones with such restrictions, and told of my experience and what I thought was the explanation; the motion passed without opposition, and in due course most such negotiations were successfully completed, but the Leonard Foundation refused to comply and, in 1982, after another twenty years of fruitless negotiation, the university dropped the foundation's awards.

I had entered 'none' under 'religion' partly because I thought the question improper and potentially discriminatory, but partly because by that time I had none. I had never taken seriously the mystic and supernatural aspects of the Judaism I'd been brought up in (the creation myth and all the other divine interventions and miracle stories had always seemed poetic explanations of what was thought unknowable, and I had valued them only as a people's poetry); the spiritual and moral structure of the religion was more compelling, but even there I hadn't liked all of it. By the time of my bar mitzvah I felt free to pick and choose what I would observe, and thought my morality none the less serious for being selective. Later in my teens I came to think there was much to be learnt and valued in other religions as well – in Christianity, of which I knew a little, and the other world religions, of which I'd read a smattering but knew less than I supposed. I thought that some values were universal and underlay all major religions, and that although the religions were not 'true' in the literal sense, they were useful, perhaps even necessary, as frameworks and sanctions for these values and the moral codes that rose out of them; but in the light of events abroad I was having increasing difficulty with the theological problem of evil. Then I became immersed in Eliot and *The Cri-*

terion, and found that, for many prominent Christian intellectuals, it was not the values that made the dogmas acceptable but the dogmas alone that validated the values. This provided the material for a fascinating absolutist intellectual game, but since I couldn't take the dogmas seriously it made religion itself more remote and irrelevant than ever; and so I had put 'none' in the space for 'religion.'

I had not, however, been consistent: when I went to enroll in the COTC and again wrote 'none' for 'religion,' the officer in charge said, 'You have to have a religion; we have to know how to bury you.' Considering the army's business, that made sense; but casualties were not always fatal, and if I should fall into German hands alive it wouldn't be pleasant to have 'Jew' on my name-tag. Seeing me hesitate, the registering officer said that if it didn't matter to me, why not put down 'C of E,' which would simplify matters like compulsory church parade? I agreed, and have often wondered how many other Jews were registered in the Canadian armed forces as 'Church of England' or the less specific 'Protestant.'

At that time the Toronto PhD in English required six year-long courses beyond the MA, one being Middle English and another an extra-departmental minor, as well as a comprehensive examination and a publishable thesis. I enrolled for three courses for credit: Knox's Shakespeare, Middle English Language (Clawson) and Literature (Birney), and my minor, classical political philosophy with G.S. Brett. At Woodhouse's suggestion I also took a non-credit reading course in Milton's prose with Barker and audited Woodhouse's Milton seminar (he planned somewhat different coverage from the previous year). I was also attempting to define the topic of my PhD thesis, which I hoped to get registered before I entered the army. It was a heavy program – when the COTC was added, too heavy. The clearest penalty I paid was in Middle English Language. The matter itself was uncertain: the differentiation of regional dialects on the basis of very fragmentary evidence, and the tracing of their development toward modern English. The method was generally philological, but it seemed to me that much of the data was suppositional. The real problem, however, was that I found Clawson unendurably boring. I liked problems to be defined so that they could be solved; he held onto their perplexities and uncertainties as though he was afraid of clarifications. The only other member of the seminar was Murdoch McKinnon, a graduate of Victoria College who had had the real advantage of studying with Robins while I was evading Perry, and I have no doubt he got more out of the seminar than I did, but he too found it boring. It was morally impossible for both of us to be away at the same time – Clawson would have been too hurt; we frequently agreed in advance who would attend, and I was away the oftener. I learnt almost nothing in that class, and got much the lowest mark of my graduate career.

By contrast, the literature half of the course was full of interest. Birney, tall, lean, red-headed, and from time to time red-bearded, was a Trotskyite from British Columbia who'd had a hard time getting an academic post and still seemed somewhat marginal in the department. His academic specialty was Chaucer, but his real interests were modern poetry, including his own, and politics. We spent a respectable amount of time on pre-Chaucerian literature in English, but I was also interested in early English ideas of the source and nature of authority in the state, and he allowed me to do my paper on John of Salisbury, whose Latin I had to read in translation. He thought well of the paper and suggested I submit it for publication; I was flattered but reluctant, not feeling secure about working from translations, whereupon he suggested I let him show it to G.G. Coulton, the famous and combative medieval historian who had taken refuge in Toronto from the Blitz. The old man gave me tea in his rented rooms and was kind about my paper; he too thought I should prepare it for publication and gave me some bibliographical references, but I didn't pursue the project, continuing to feel the same insecurity, besides having more than enough on my hands. Birney gave me a mark high enough to prevent my combined grade for the two half-courses from disgracing me. (*David*, Birney's first book of poems, won the Governor-General's Award the following year, which was both a pleasure and a relief to me, since he had been a little edgy about Pratt, who had in 1940 won his second Governor-General's Award – for *Brébeuf and His Brethren* – and was sometimes discussed as if he were the university's only poet.)

The Shakespeare course was another pleasure. Knox, short, intense, with a very Aberdonian accent, introduced us to the major scholarly and critical approaches but spent most of his time on the direct examination of the plays. I was disappointed that he said almost nothing about the textual problem, and I thought it odd that, with Wilson Knight teaching at Trinity and staging Shakespeare at Hart House, there was no reference to him (Knight was seen as an eccentric in the department); but these criticisms did not interfere with my appreciation of Knox's insights, his passion, and his humour, sometimes pawky but more often explosive. I was quite indignant when, as we were coming out of a public lecture Knox had given, Mavor Moore said, 'When can we expect professors of English to be able to speak English?'

Brett met me weekly in his office for an hour, to discuss my reading of the previous week and assign more for the coming week, after the manner of his Alma Mater, Oxford. This was extraordinarily kind, since he was not only a busy and productive scholar and teacher but also an administrator, being head of the Philosophy department and dean of the School of Graduate Studies (an office which, I was later to learn, he did not allow to consume too much of his time). He was a little surprised at the view of Milton's political thought that I put forward, and continued to treat it with some reserve, but he organized my reading of Graeco–Roman philosophy to assist in my approach and from time to time would ask how my work on Milton was progressing and whether I was finding the relations with classical thought I'd anticipated, and I thought that he was growing less sceptical. We met at 11:00 A.M., and several times when we were finished he took me to lunch at the Faculty Club, then occupying the Gallery Dining-Room at Hart House. I recall one such occasion when the room was full and we had to wait some minutes for a table; he stood beside the control desk and surveyed the scene morosely, then said, 'This university is growing too large; it's at the limits of collegiality, if it hasn't already passed them.' Total enrolment in the university was then about six or seven thousand; when, some thirty years later, I resigned the office he had held in the School of Graduate Studies, the school's enrolment alone was about that, and the struggle to preserve some collegiality was unceasing. Once when he took me to lunch he spotted Harold Innis about to sit down and got him to join us; Brett may well have suspected that he was lunching with one of his successors as graduate dean; he couldn't have thought it was with two.

My reading course with Barker also took the form of a weekly meeting in his office, when I would report on a group of Milton's prose works and he would suggest works by other contemporary writers which were relevant to an analysis of Milton's position. This approach soon taught me the limits of our library. Woodhouse encouraged me to submit suggested titles for acquisition, but in wartime conditions rare or out-of-print materials were difficult to buy and not easy to get microfilmed. Besides, Stewart Wallace, the chief librarian, was a historian with a parsimonious view of his narrow budget and sceptical of the judgment of a graduate student in English who was asking for materials more suited, he thought, to a historian; I think that was why a number of the orders Woodhouse authorized for me weren't filled. The university library system had many college and departmental units, some very independent of the central library, and there was not then a union catalogue, so I spent a great deal of time trudging from one library to another searching for the few seventeenth-century political pamphlets they contained; Knox College had the most, and I therefore came to know more about the Presbyterian position than those farther left, for which I had to rely largely on such reprint materials as were available.

Barker was spending a lot of time with me and I was very grateful, but a degree of tension began to develop. My reading in classical philosophy, particularly the Stoics, was making me increasingly interested in the role of natural law in Milton's thought, but Barker thought it was largely negated by the theological limits Milton put on it. Also, I wanted to relate the movement of Milton's thought to the revolutionary currents of his day; Barker, probably feeling that he had satisfied that need in his forthcoming book, thought I should instead relate it to the major republican models available to Milton (when Zera Fink's *The Classical Republicans* was published a few years later, Barker told me that was the book I should have written). In addition to these and other differences of focus was the question of who would be my thesis supervisor. I had never doubted that I would be working under Woodhouse; it was troubling and embarrassing to me to sense that Barker thought he ought to direct my thesis. This expectation emerged gradually, particularly when we were discussing the manuscript of his book, which he asked me to read before it went to press and on which I made some comments which he said were useful. I told Woodhouse of my concern, and he said it was my choice to make; I then told Barker that I intended to work with Woodhouse and hoped he would act as second reader. He said he would, and we papered over the difficulty, but I think he was disappointed and there remained a perceptible strain in our relations.

Auditing Woodhouse's Milton course kept me in touch with him and helped me move toward a definition of thesis topic. The chief difference from the previous year was that he managed to reach the late poems soon enough to be able to devote some time to *Paradise Regained* and *Samson Agonistes*. My pleasure in this was a little qualified, however, when he found that he had to be away for one seminar and asked me to take it. It was to be on *Samson*, and he said I wouldn't have any difficulty: he would give me his notes, which I was to read to the class. There was the manuscript, with the annotations of successive years, and it took me much of the two-hour period to read it out. In the discussion afterwards I had to be very discreet in distinguishing between Woodhouse's views and my own. Later, when he thanked me, he said he'd been told that I'd not once contradicted him but had indicated there was considerable room for other opinions, and asked whether I'd thought of going into the diplomatic service.

I had been elected president of the Graduate English Club and had to arrange the year's papers. Herbert Davis, then president of Smith College, was to return to Toronto, where he had been a leading member of the department, to give the Alexander Lectures that year; I wrote asking him to address the club, and he kindly agreed. The evening he was to speak to us I arrived at the graduate school to find it dark, with a knot of people waiting to be let in: someone had blundered. It was fortunate that the weather was mild because it took me some time to find a caretaker to unlock the door. Davis graciously made a joke of it and eased our embarrassment. The next day was his final lecture; his topic was Swift and Stella, and throughout the series he had carefully assembled the evidence identifying Stella as Esther Johnson and describing Swift's relations with her. The university president, Canon Cody, who had attended all the lectures but peacefully slept through much of them, was now seated on the platform because he was to thank his fellow-president; unfortunately, he again slept, and in his flowery thanks spoke of what he called the 'enduring mystery' of Stella: who was she and what was she to Swift?

Beyond the English department my acquaintance with the faculty, particularly of University College, was broadening, and with it my education. Croft Chapter House, the university's original chemistry laboratory, was at that time the college's senior common-room, where tea and biscuits were served from 3:30 every afternoon. Woodhouse sometimes took me there, and would introduce me to whoever happened to be sitting nearby. Gilbert Norwood, the renowned historian of the Greek drama, was a trifle remote, but his colleague Charles Cochrane, later to be equally renowned for his *Christianity and Classical Culture*, was eager to talk. I came to realize that he felt somewhat isolated in his department, which was why he would stand in the cloister outside his office hand-rolling cigarettes and hoping to intercept someone interesting to talk to; it was in that setting that he made me understand something of St Augustine. Indeed, the hundred feet or so of the West Cloister was for me the true Philosopher's Walk of the university, not the sylvan path of that name a few hundred yards to the northeast. Several members of the smaller departments, lacking the intellectual company offered by the larger departments, used it much as Cochrane did. There Reid McCallum, tall, lean, and shy, would sometimes try out parts of his difficult theory of aesthetics on me; there too his colleague Fulton Anderson, also tall but neither lean nor shy, would talk very sparingly about Bacon and copiously about how much better he could run the Philosophy department than Brett did. Fairley and Boeschenstein hung out there, separately or together always a pleasure to talk to. But the cloister, for all its opportunity, had its hazards too; Theophile Meek waylaid people on whom he could unload his grievances: he never stopped working, he said, except for two hours on Christmas Day, but when a new head was required for the Near Eastern department it was W.R. Taylor who was chosen.

Various small literary chores were coming my way. Some theatrical group was going to produce a Shakespeare play and Knox asked me to speak to them about it; I did, but all I got was thanks. Macmillan of Canada sent me several poetry manuscripts; I took considerable pains with them, and my favourable opinion of the first two or three seemed to satisfy the editor, since he published the books, but I was astonished at the niggardly fee. Finally I was sent a manuscript which I disliked and carefully detailed my reasons for a negative recommendation; the book was published anyway and I was never sent another manuscript. A few years later John Gray, by then editor of Macmillan but on leave to the army, was attached to my division in France and we became friends; I told him of this incident and he offered amends with a bottle of cognac.

From time to time I would see Kenneth McNaught at the library, and on one occasion he suggested we have a more leisurely evening at his home, preferably with our respective girlfriends. I liked the idea and invited the young woman I was seeing. A day or two before the date fixed she came down with a heavy cold and I called McNaught to explain; he suggested that, rather than forgoing the plan, he might ask his sister to join us, and I agreed. Thus, on 19 January 1942, I met Lesley, and could hardly believe my luck. She was beautiful but behaved as if she didn't know it. She had a lovely voice but said little that evening, the other three of us being addicted talkers and giving her little opportunity; she sat there drawing things on a pad and occasionally making observations which shrewdly deflated our excesses. I asked to see what she had drawn and was enchanted; life emanated from the page. I invited her out for dinner the following week; we met first in her studio on Grenville Street, where I saw some of her paintings and dry-point etchings and realized that she was a talented and dedicated artist. My interest steadily grew; I immediately stopped seeing the woman

I'd been dating and Lesley broke off with her boyfriend in the air force; we soon became necessary to each other.

At the end of term I was appointed teaching fellow in the department for the following year. This did not confer faculty status but it did, I believe, make me the first Jew to be appointed to teach English in a Canadian university. In accepting the appointment I explained to Malcolm Wallace that I was likely to be in the army before the end of the coming session; he said he'd take the chance.

The method of choosing officer cadets for the active army involved circulating a list of eligible candidates to the various mobilized units, who then chose as many as they needed to fill vacancies. Candidates not thus chosen faced an uncertain prospect: they might continue to be passed over and enjoy an indefinite period of civilian life; they might be sent for unattached officer training; or they might be conscripted as private soldiers. Conscription had begun the previous year, but for home service only; the increased demand for manpower overseas finally led a reluctant government, in April 1942, to hold a plebiscite to release it from this limitation. The vote was strongly affirmative on a Canada-wide basis but dramatically displayed the French–English division in the country: Quebec voted 73 per cent No, the other eight provinces 80 per cent Yes. The legislation was amended and it became legal to send conscripts overseas. We could not then know that the King government would not invoke the amendment until November 1944; its power to do so increased the desirability of quickly finding a place with a mobilized unit. With this motive added to my reluctance to shorten the uncertain time I would have with Lesley, I decided to stay in Toronto, where I could pursue the search for a posting, rather than return to Winkler for what would remain of the summer after training camp. I explained this to Woodhouse and asked whether I could use my time to satisfy one of the three remaining course requirements; there was no graduate teaching in the summer, but he arranged for me to do a reading course with him on nineteenth-century British thought.

Birney's wife and child were going to Vancouver for two months and he asked whether I'd like to rent the empty room in his apartment on Hazelton Avenue during their absence, for the same price as I was currently paying, and I accepted. The evening before the COTC was to leave for summer camp at Niagara-on-the-Lake a party was given by three young women who had for some time conducted a kind of intellectual salon. I had been there before, usually encountering faculty members, including Birney, Bissell, Brough MacPherson, and others. On this evening those of us who were to be at the barracks at six the next morning left the party early, and I went to bed. An hour or two later, Birney burst into my room, accompanied by A.J.M. Smith, who was spending the summer in Toronto working on what was to become *The Book of Canadian Poetry* and whom Birney had taken along to the party. There had been trouble: one of the young women was very attractive and drew men like a magnet; Smith had been drawn; an anthropologist named Steve Hart, probably in his cups, had apparently resented the competition and insulted Smith; Birney, not overly sober, had leapt to the defence of his guest; many strong words and one or two academic blows were exchanged; and now Birney was demanding that I act as his second, go back to the party, and arrange for him to fight Hart in the morning. It took me the better part of what was left of the night to calm him down, and I was not the smartest cadet on parade at Camp Niagara in the morning.

This time the camp was much better organized and more constructive than the year before, both the directing staff and many of the cadets having had an additional year of training. The lectures and demonstrations had been brought more nearly up-to-date and some of the exercises were quite realistic, the fortnight's work culminating in a large-scale mock attack with considerable equipment and elaborate pyrotechnics. Each corporal was put in charge of a tent; one of the trainees in mine was Clawson's son, just graduating, who contended that the academic life was lazy, using his father's example to deny my protestation that the teaching schedule was heavily supplemented by time-consuming research. Bissell and I were in the same tent, and Corbett was in charge of another nearby, so we were able to spend a good deal of time together. Fred Winnett, the most agreeable member of the Near Eastern department and older than the rest of us, was there; a surprise to me was that Arthur Barker was in a tent farther down the line – he had not trained with the battalion during the year and I could not imagine his entering the army (in the event, he didn't).

At the end of camp most of us passed the tests and were certified as officer-cadets, and during the following weeks Bissell and I made several efforts to find a posting. Malcolm Wallace's son William was an officer in naval Intelligence in Ottawa, which seemed to Bissell a pleasant way to spend the war, so he suggested we go to see him. I was not enamoured of the navy but agreed to the expedition; we took the train, were assigned seats in the rear coach, and about half-way there went forward to the dining-car for lunch. It was a good lunch, and we took our time; when the train stopped in Brockville, where there was a training camp, a considerable number of soldiers disembarked, formed up, shouldered their luggage, and marched off, all of which we watched with what we thought expert eyes, mildly surprised that the train stopped so long. When at length we finished our coffee and went back to resume our seats, there was no coach there: the train had divided at Brockville, with the rear car going to Ottawa and the rest to Montreal. I was horrified because my suitcase contained the manuscript of Art Smith's anthology, which he had asked me to criticize; I was sure it wasn't the only copy, but in those pre-photocopying days the only way to replace a lost carbon was to retype it, an enormous task for *The Book of Canadian Poetry*. With much effort and perhaps a little stridency, I prevailed upon the conductor to wire the stationmaster at Ottawa to hold our luggage; we got off at the first stop, Cornwall, waited until evening for a bus to Ottawa, found our luggage at the station with the typescript safe inside, and reached our hotel in the middle of the night.

The rest of our mission was as successful as the beginning: Wallace seated us across from himself at his desk, behind which was a large uncovered map with many coloured pins, presumably showing the location of ships of various navies. As soon as I realized what they probably were I averted my eyes and decided that I didn't want to belong to Canadian naval Intelligence; of course we weren't asked. Before returning to Toronto I managed a reunion with Alan Adamson, now part of the substantial Manitoba contingent in John Grierson's new National Film Board. Alan had become a committed Marxist; I felt my old affection for him but could see that our common ground had shrunk and that each had entered upon new territory where the other was unlikely to follow.

Another expedition was to a regimental camp not far from Lindsay, where we were interviewed at some length by the commanding officer, who sat at his desk swatting flies throughout the interview. He appeared to think well of us, since at the end he said, 'You're just the kind of officers we want, not like those pesky Jews who keep trying to get in.'

Lesley, perhaps influenced by her brother's recent marriage, began to wonder what our future was. Sitting in Sherwood Park, I explained at length why we couldn't get married: I would soon be in the army and had to consider the possibility of death or disablement, and it would be unfair to place such a load on her. Nor would an engagement be fair in the circumstances: we couldn't know how long we'd be separated and what changes one or the other of us might undergo. If I got back in one piece we could see whether we still suited each other and decide then. Lesley said she agreed. I spent a restless night, then phoned her in the morning and asked her to meet me at the Savarin restaurant at noon. There I asked her to wait while I went across the street to Trans-Canada Airlines. Where was I intending to fly? To Winnipeg. Why? To tell my father that we were getting married – that is, if she wanted to. Yes, she wanted to. By the time I got back with my ticket, she discovered that despite her distaste for beer she'd drunk the one I'd left standing, and has liked beer ever since.

My father was, as I knew he would be, disturbed that I was marrying out of the faith, that I would not ask Lesley to convert, and that there was no arrangement about religious upbringing for any children we might have; but he could tell that I would be inflexible and didn't want a divisive issue. He therefore seized upon the fact that Lesley was an artist, which he thought very favourable, and said he would come to Toronto to meet her and her family. I had not anticipated this but was delighted. When I told Gertrude, my only sibling then in Winnipeg, of my intention, she raised the question of my grandmother. Gertrude was sure the news would upset her greatly.

I discussed it with Sam, who thought the same. He was not distressed on his own account, he said, and he wished us well, but he didn't think Grandmother should be told. It was the same view he'd put forward five years earlier, on different grounds, regarding my father's remarriage; my concurrence then, however reluctant, weakened my position now. I doubted that my grandmother would find the news as upsetting as Sam and Gertrude imagined, and I thought concealing it from her would be demeaning and, in the end, ineffectual; but those who sought to protect her were closer to her than I and might know better, and I didn't want to put more strain on family solidarity than necessary. I knew that Lesley would find this concealment strange and perhaps hurtful, but I didn't doubt that she would concur if I asked, so I agreed. For years thereafter, when we visited Winnipeg, I would go alone to call on Grandmother; our conversations would range widely, but despite my advancing years and her strong family feelings she never asked whether I was thinking of marriage, a sign, I thought, that she knew the situation but was playing the role assigned to her (at least one of my aunts, an enthusiastic gossip, seems almost certain to have told her about the two Mrs Sirlucks a block away). Lesley never complained about this and said it didn't trouble her, but it troubled me, and still does.

When I got back to Toronto, Lesley reported that she had told her parents of our engagement and that they were pleased. There appeared to be no religious difficulty: Carlton McNaught had been brought up a Baptist but had long since rebelled and become an agnostic; Eleanor, brought up a Presbyterian, now had a very generalized belief in a divine being, some interest in Christian Science, and a kind of detached affection for the Anglican Church. Lesley and I were both surprised, therefore, when she vetoed our idea of a civil ceremony and insisted upon a church wedding.

When my father arrived a day or two later he took at once to Lesley and her family and they to him; within a day all signs of guardedness on both sides had disappeared. He declared himself very content that we should marry; but he had his own demand: a Jewish wedding.

After some discussion, Lesley and I proposed that there be two wedding ceremonies, and this was agreed in principle. There remained the problem of securing agreement from a rabbi and a minister. The McNaughts had a friend named John Davidson who was an Anglican minister; he agreed to be a witness at a Jewish marriage service and then to conduct a service in which he would confirm our marriage. My father and I suspected that it would be more difficult to get a rabbi to cooperate; we went to see Rabbi David Monson because he was an army chaplain. He said that before he could conduct a Jewish wedding Lesley would have to convert to Judaism. I said that was out of the question. He asked whether she had refused, and I said I wouldn't ask her. My father then sent me out of the room and talked with the rabbi alone for some ten minutes; when he came out he said the rabbi had dropped his demand. I've often wondered what Dad's argument was – presumably something having to do with special wartime circumstances and the certainty that we would marry, with or without a Jewish ceremony, so that having one would facilitate the retention of some Jewish connection. It was years before I told Lesley of the rabbi's initial demand and our response.

The first ceremony took place in the rabbi's house a few days later; besides my father and Lesley's immediate family, there were the Reverend Davidson and Claude Bissell, the best man. My father did not stay for the Christian service, which was a week later. I had not been comfortable with the thought of an actual church and suggested the university's Hart House Chapel, which was theoretically non-denominational, although apparently used only by Christians; the McNaughts agreed, and the smallness of the chapel allowed us to be constructively selective about the guest list. After the service, which was conducted with great sensitivity by Reverend Davidson and included an almost stagey search through his pockets for the ring by Bissell, the university carillonneur, whom Carlton McNaught knew, rang peal after peal through a startled Toronto Sunday afternoon. There was a very pleasant reception in the McNaught home, where it was much remarked how unlike Toronto it was for all this to happen on a Sunday. Our honeymoon consisted of two days with the telephone disconnected in the apartment we'd found half-way up the hill on Avenue Road; on the third day I had to drill a COTC company (I was now a sergeant).

The evening before the confirming ceremony, some friends held a stag party for me which, in the opinion of Sandra Djwa, had a significant consequence. In a paper read at a conference, 'The Legacy of Northrop Frye,' held at Victoria College in October 1992, Professor Djwa quoted from the entry for 15 August 1942 in Frye's diary: 'Stag at Earle Birney's for Sirluck. Ned [Pratt] read us a new poem ['The Truant']: general theme of the conflict of Orc and Urizen. Swell poem too, infinitely better than a silly fantasia on Hitler's nightmare he'd been discussing with me.' Djwa shows that Frye had been having much trouble finding an overall pattern for his book on Blake, and argues that ' "The Truant" 's indictment of Locke's universe provides a paradigm for what becomes "The Case against Locke," the opening chapter of *Fearful Symmetry*.'

The COTC, which used its graduates of the preceding year as directing staff, was making more demands on my time than I'd anticipated, and getting married and setting up house also took time; I therefore got less reading done in my course with Woodhouse than I'd planned, and although he was sympathetic he noticed. We didn't meet often, and there was less harmony in our views of the nineteenth century than of the seventeenth and eighteenth: we argued vehemently about one of his heroes, Carlyle, whom I thought a kind of forerunner of fascism; fortunately we agreed better about another, Matthew Arnold. Although pressed for time and with my mind not fully engaged, I did manage to work up a tentative thesis proposal which he and Barker approved, and it was registered in the graduate school as 'Milton and the Law of Nature.'

I then turned to the preparation of my teaching assignment for the fall term. Being inexperienced, I did far more work on it than was necessary. I had been assigned the first year of the Pass Course, which consisted of very diverse selections with little coherence or continuity; the theory was, I believe, that of representative sampling. This meant, I thought, that each work needed an introductory lecture on period, genre, tradition, author's concerns, and so forth, before the text itself was analysed. It was a ridiculously ambitious undertaking for a teaching fellow and for such a course, but I was excited by my first professional assignment and brushed aside thoughts of proportional time allocation. When I met my first class I was so exhilarated that the bell marking the end of the hour took me quite by surprise.

Several weeks into term I was offered a posting to the Algonquin Regiment, with the prospect of an early call to officers' training camp; I accepted, and was told to report the following morning for my physical examination. As it happened, my cousin Wilfred called that evening; he was in Toronto briefly on business and was eager to meet Lesley, so we invited him for lunch with the warning that I might be late. I was, the physical being a typical case of army hurry-up-and-wait logistics; when I finally got home Lesley naturally wanted to know how the examination had gone. 'Okay,' I said, 'the doctor found a heart murmur, but ...' 'That won't help,' Wilfred interrupted brightly; 'they take people with murmurs.'

I found this remark immensely offensive and hurtful. (In fact, the examining physician had said he didn't think the murmur would be a problem but it could be, and if I wished he'd report it for a rejection; I asked him not to and he passed me.) Wilfred had certainly meant no harm and was only assuming that I shared his attitude, a very widespread one, toward enlistment; but it was just that assumption that upset me. The reasons were complex and not altogether clear, but at root they involved Jewishness: the sense that Jews had a special stake in this particular war and in the defeat of Nazism, that their tradition of avoiding combat service under the tsars was no guide now and that their behaviour in this war would profoundly affect their status in the future, that any effort to avoid military service or get into its low-risk branches (both Herb and Wilf ultimately served in the Ordnance Corps in Canada, for which their business experience equipped them well, but Wilf's younger brother, Edwin, enlisted in the artillery) would be closely monitored and unfavourably interpreted by a suspicious and often hostile population, among whom the antisemites had said from the beginning that the war was being fought for the sake of the Jews. There were other, more personal, elements in my extreme reaction: my three years of uneasiness about not yet having enlisted and my concern that this might have contributed to Bert's decision to enlist even before he'd reached the minimum age. Wilfred was our guest and I covered up as well as I could, but his remark shattered our relationship.

After passing my physical I entered the army as a private with the temporary rank of officer-cadet. I had to wear a uniform but, aside from occasional drills and parades, I would not be needed until my call to training camp came. The arrangement with the department had been that I would teach until I joined the army, but I was enjoying my teaching so much that I volunteered to continue until I was called to camp. I had enrolled in two graduate courses to meet the remaining requirements, but they had barely begun when my call came in late October; the school cancelled my registration and UC suspended my fellowship. We closed up our apartment, Lesley moved back to her parents' house to wait until I could send for her, and early in November, with Bissell and a few dozen others, I boarded a train for Three Rivers, Quebec.

CHAPTER FOUR

Canadian Army, 1942–1945

I

Three Rivers was about as bad an introduction to active service as a training camp could be. As if to symbolize what lay ahead of us, we were greeted at the station by a putrid stench and yellow fog; we learnt that they were from a pulp mill nearby, but the stench grew stronger as we neared the camp and after one or two meals it seemed to us to blend with the smell of the dirtiest mess-hall I have ever seen. The camp itself was an old fairground which we were told had been condemned by the provincial government and then acquired by the army, which adapted some of the buildings and added others; the work had not been completed in time for our arrival (we were the first intake). It took the onset of winter weather, which came soon enough, for the significance of this to be felt in the barracks huts, but in the mess-hall it was evident at our first meal: it was only dusk but the rats were already there, brought out by the rapidly filling drums of revolting slops that we discarded in disgust.

The sergeants and corporals of the directing staff assigned to supervise the first meal eyed our discomfiture with open glee: it confirmed their *a priori* view that as officer-cadets drawn from civilian life we were a pampered and unfairly privileged lot, and justified their plans to make us pay for it. Actually, this vindictiveness of those who saw themselves as unprivileged fit very well with the rationale of the camp. More officers were needed as the Canadian forces grew, but instead of simply enlarging the existing officer-training camps, which would have been the ordinary procedure, it had been decided to set up a new camp to impart a new tone to the training. Ever since the first Canadian troops had reached Britain, there had been British criticism of inadequate training and discipline; the Canadian experience at Hong Kong and Dieppe, and that of individual Canadian officers attached to British forces in Africa, had increased this criticism; and it was now decided to experiment with a more rigorous officer-training syllabus, emphasizing especially the physical aspects, and particularly endurance of hardship, where Canadian training was thought to have been weak. Accordingly, the camp at Three Rivers was set up, with Colonel William Mathers in charge. Mathers was a short, erect, strutting bantam of a man who affected distinguishing quiffs of dress and was said to have had desert-warfare experience. We learnt at once that he was a martinet: at our initial parade the morning after our arrival he set out the camp's aggressive rationale, saying that he believed fully in it and had assembled a directing staff which shared his belief and would carry it out relentlessly; any cadet who couldn't meet the demands of the new syllabus would be flunked out, which would save some future platoon or company from going into battle under an incompetent officer.

The idea of a more aggressive and demanding training program was reasonable enough, but for us this surface plausibility dwindled fast. As soon as the training started, with the sergeants and corporals constantly yelling at us and yapping at our heels, and almost never explaining or demonstrating anything, it became clear that for most of the directing staff this was an opportunity, not to build us up and fit us for command, but to humiliate and punish us for being privileged, a conclusion reinforced at every meal, when we continued to be confronted with putrid rations very unlike what the directing staff got in their own mess. As winter descended, opportunities for brutality increased, as the growing number of casualties witnessed. There was one more draft of cadets after us; then, despite the continuing and indeed increasing need for additional officers, the camp was closed, and I could only conclude that Headquarters had decided that the evil conditions there, which had become notorious, could not be corrected.

The camp was within walking distance of the town; I booked a room for Lesley at the Château de Blois and she arrived a few days later. On evenings when I was not on late duty I would join her, which meant getting up at five the next morning to arrive in my hut before reveille. In the Château dining-room Lesley observed with indignation the immense servings of roast beef and other foods strictly rationed in English Canada but brought daily to the tables of the advocates, priests, notaries, merchants, and other local notables. A number of other officer-cadets' wives stayed at the Château, and in the early evening they formed a sort of gallery in the hotel's mezzanine lounge, watching the entrance to see whether their husbands had been able to come, and observing from their vantage point who had the notorious 'Three Rivers Limp' (fractured heels resulting from being hurried over the camp's dangerously iced obstacle course). During the day they sometimes ventured into the town, but decreasingly; there was strong local antipathy to the army and *les maudits anglais*, and there were some ugly incidents.

Perhaps because I was Jewish I was for a time singled out by the non-commissioned officers of my company for gratuitous criticism, extra duties (especially latrine assignments), and punishment drills. Since I always carried out all assignments, kept up on route marches and distance runs, tried to be smart on parade, worked hard at battle drill and unarmed combat, scored among the first on the rifle range, prepared as well as I could the meagre theoretical and tactical lessons, and in general tried my best to be a good soldier, without effecting any diminution of this harassment, I concluded that further measures would be necessary to secure fair treatment. I took to asking hard questions of the NCOs in theoretical or tactical instruction when officers were present, always making sure that I knew enough to discern and rebut their frequently incorrect answers. After a time this had the desired effect, and although it may have increased their hostility, it improved their behaviour. Interestingly, a number of the other cadets, seeing what was going on, took to helping me on the obstacle course (which with their coaching I finally mastered), and sometimes asked for my help with theoretical problems. After a while even the

NCOs seemed to accept whatever it was about me that had originally annoyed them and we ceased troubling each other unnecessarily.

Tactical instruction was usually at the section and platoon, sometimes at the company, level; I cannot recall any instruction in battalion tactics. Although the objective of the camp was the modernization and reform of officer training, tactical instruction was still based on pre-war British army manuals. It took considerable self-restraint not to point out that these were often the tactics that had collapsed in *Blitzkrieg*, but by then I had realized that the best I could hope for from this camp was the training of my body and acclimatization to military life; I would have to look elsewhere for what more had to be learnt.

In January, Bert, now twenty and an air sergeant, stopped on his way overseas and spent his last two days of leave with us, and we were joined by Hilda, who came up from New York, and Sam Nitikman, in the east on a business trip. It was Lesley's first meeting with any of my family other than my father, and it went very well. We spent almost all our time talking; Bert was being very manly and optimistic about what lay ahead for him, and we all purported to be confident. In fact he had thirteen months to live, and I was the only one of the company, or of the family, who would see him again.

The course ended in mid-February, with those who passed being commissioned as second-lieutenants. I reported to the School of Instruction at the Infantry Training Centre at Camp Borden, near Barrie, Ontario, for a one-month training course. It was a huge camp, raw and ugly from continuous hurried expansion, but with an established core, settled routines, and a matter-of-fact approach to the trainees very welcome after the envious vindictiveness of Three Rivers. Training was quite hard but not punitive and no one worried much about flunking out.

Lesley was now back at her parents' house and we got together most weekends, either in Toronto or at a large guest-house in Barrie named 'Barrondale Hall' (some indication of money values at the time: a weekend for two in a very large and comfortable room, with lavish breakfasts, was $12.95). Ken McNaught was also stationed at Borden, with his wife, Beverly, in Toronto, and once we arranged a joint weekend. We ran into rank discrimination: Barrondale, the only good bed-and-breakfast available, accepted only officers and civilians; Ken was a sergeant in the Ordnance Corps. We solved this by making the reservations in my name and once we were inside, the operators, as we were sure they would, chose not to eject Ken. In England rank discrimination would prove harder to overcome.

When we completed our course in mid-March and became full lieutenants, few if any of us were immediately sent overseas; some were sent to battalions in Canada, but most were kept for some time in Borden or sent to other training centres. The Algonquin Regiment, to which I had been posted from the COTC, did not call for me and I was assigned for the time being to a platoon in Borden. This was a great step up from being a trainee – it meant that I could begin to take responsibility – but my satisfaction was immediately dimmed to find that two other new-minted lieutenants were assigned to the same platoon. Three weeks later, however, the company commander visited my platoon while I was teaching them map-reading, and afterwards he asked how I'd like to do the map-reading instruction for the whole company. I said I would like that, and seized the opportunity to ask to have the platoon to myself; he agreed on the spot. This allowed me to take an undivided responsibility, however limited, and while it would be an exaggeration to say that I enjoyed working with my platoon I did take some satisfaction in it.

In May I got my overseas furlough, a fortnight which we spent in Winnipeg and Winkler, where Lesley met most of the rest of my family. On my return to Borden there was still no indication of when I would be sent overseas, so I located a rental cottage at Minet's Point on Lake Simcoe; Lesley was alone there most of the time but I managed most weekends and occasional midweek evenings. My first platoon completed its training and I was given a new one, which interested me less, and I was glad of the break in routine when I was assigned to defend someone being court-martialled (although it turned out that he was an unpleasant man, guilty as charged). The bulletin-board in the officers' mess routinely carried notices of various training courses available, and when I saw one for an eleven-week Intelligence course at Royal Military College in Kingston, I asked my company commander to recommend me for it. He agreed, and at the end of June I was informed that I'd been accepted.

Accommodation, food, and facilities at RMC were good. We were introduced to the organization, weaponry, and tactics of the German army and to methods of gathering information, identification, reporting, etc., and while I suspected that the particulars would turn out to be obsolete by the time I got into the field, I was glad to be acquiring the rudiments of a skill that could give me a useful role in the war. Some of the exercises were even fun, such as mapping from a light observation plane with a removable bottom panel. I found a rooming-house for Lesley, and after a short while we found a rental cottage on Dead Man's Bay a mile or so from RMC. Friends had sent us a beautiful German shepherd puppy; Freya was wonderful company for Lesley in Dead Man's Bay but no great safeguard: one night there was an escape from Fort George, the nearby prisoner-of-war holding unit, and next morning one of the escapers was found in our hedge, where he'd spent the night without disturbing the sleep of either Lesley or Freya.

At the end of September I passed the course examination and was enrolled in the Canadian Military Intelligence Corps. Major Charles Krug, the director of Intelligence for RMC, offered me a job on staff with the promise of early promotion. Perhaps I was momentarily tempted: I had never been fearless; Bert, whose crew had finished training and gone operational at the beginning of the month, had urged me in every letter since his arrival in England not to hurry over; and I knew I was good at teaching. But the old issue was still dominant: as a Jew I should be in the dangerous shooting part of the war. I thanked Krug but declined and, after a flying visit to Winnipeg to take leave of my family, was sent to No. 1 Transit Camp at Windsor, Nova Scotia; Lesley returned to Toronto, her camp-following days over.

Windsor was another hurriedly laid-out and unfinished encampment, this one on clay, so that when it rained, as it did most of our time there, we slithered about in very sticky mud. There were two officers' messes, one for junior and one for senior officers; I never saw the latter, but the former was quite exceptionally bare and bleak; recreational facilities consisted of a chequer-board and a two-foot shelf of murder mysteries and westerns. An irony I greatly appreciated was that the officer in charge of the ad hoc training program was Mathers, returned to his permanent rank of major now that the Three Rivers experiment was ended, and on his way overseas; we recognized each other without any pretense of friendliness. I was called on to give a lecture on German army organization and tactics, and indeed most of the desultory training was given by one or other specialist among the trainees.

On 28 October we were at last sent to Halifax, where a motley convoy was assembled. My ship was a small freighter carrying thirty-two of us as supercargo. The first night out one of our number, ignoring black-out instructions, lit a cigarette on deck; at once a rifle-shot came from an escort vessel, aimed to miss but not by much. Security discipline on our ship was much improved for the rest of the long voyage. The convoy could move only at the speed of the slowest ship, and its route was deliberately indirect. The North Atlantic in November lived up to its stormy reputation and there was much seasickness; it was my first ocean voyage, but fortunately I was never sick. Despite the constant circling of the escort ships, the convoy lost several ships to torpedoes. With each loss the tension aboard our small ship grew, and we were very glad to sight landfall on the eleventh day.

Our train from Liverpool to London was late, and just as we arrived at the station the air-raid alert went. From the station platform we could see through the shattered roof the bursting anti-aircraft shells and hear the bombs, one of which, we learnt the next day, hit a crowded dance-hall and left many casualties. Because of the confusion there was no baggage party, but we managed to find our luggage, get it to another station, and load it onto a train there, arriving at Aldershot very tired and hungry in the middle of the night.

II

With some difficulty I got in touch with Bert, who was stationed at Harrogate, near York; I claimed my privilege leave and we spent two days walking the walls of the medieval city, visiting the Minster and the Shambles, drinking in what called itself the oldest continuing pub in England, and talking non-stop about home, the war, and the postwar world, about which he had stronger ideas than in the past. He had been promoted to flight-sergeant and was a little wry on his posting to the Royal Air Force; in the Royal Canadian Air Force, where many of his friends had been posted, his position as bomber-navigator would have carried a commission and the higher pay that went with it. But he was very devoted to his crew, and took me out to the station to meet them: English, Scots, a New Zealander, and one other Canadian, the Nova Scotian pilot. They welcomed me warmly, and after some drinks the pilot, saying there would just be room in his Halifax, invited me to go with them on their mission over Germany that night; Bert protested, I declined with thanks, and awaited Bert with some trepidation the next morning. We agreed to meet in London on his next leave, and I was able to write my father that Bert was well and in good spirits.

I got my first mail from home on 24 November, a letter written by Lesley on 7 November. When I left Canada Lesley had been several months' pregnant; by the time I arrived in England she had miscarried. It was a blow, bad enough for me, much worse for her; we did not know when or whether I could return to try again. Her letters were determinedly cheerful but in fact she was depressed for some time.

Aldershot did nothing to cheer me up. All of us in the Canadian General Reinforcement Unit were just waiting for a posting and could do nothing of any significance, and consequently morale drooped. I found opportunities to go to London, but the bombing had closed the places I most wanted to see: the British Museum, the National Gallery (except for a small section showing war art), and other museums. St Paul's was open, but it had been hit and seeing it was sad, as was seeing the ubiquitous wrecked houses and rubble. I enjoyed going to the Canadian Officers' Club run by Alice Massey, wife of the high commissioner, which was crowded with Canadians getting a hot lunch for two shillings, and there were one or two other agreeable gathering-places for Canadians. There was also the theatre, which included some quite wonderful classical productions and a lot of ordinary stuff of mixed quality. But although we had nothing of any significance to do in Aldershot, we weren't allowed out of camp often, and I ached for a genuine assignment.

Finally, on 10 December, I was sent to the Intelligence Section of First Canadian Army near Leatherhead, in Surrey, where I was glad to be assigned to room with Tom Fairley, Barker's son, whom I quickly came to like. The section was commanded by Lieutenant-Colonel Peter Wright, a Toronto lawyer; Operational Intelligence, to which I was assigned, was headed by Major William Broughall. Aside from the staff officers, the whole section, including Counter-Intelligence, worked in one large, unpartitioned general office, once the ballroom of a country mansion, with one of the G2s (General Staff Officer, second grade) perfunctorily supervising from a glass-walled office attached. There was plenty to do to prepare for the invasion of the Continent, but the inadequate supervision and the open work-area enabled the more irresponsible members of the group to make systematic work difficult. I foolishly attempted to quiet the disturbers, which naturally gave them an incentive to behave worse, and the tension carried over into the mess, where they were an aggressive minority.

In mid-December Bert, having completed one-third of a duty tour, got a week's leave. Since I wasn't due for leave I asked whether I could have him stay with me; the initial answer was yes, but when the mess captain took Bert's name and rank he said that officers' residences and messes could not accept NCOs as guests. Here there was no possibility of repeating the trick I'd used at Barrondale Hall in Canada; I traded weekends with another officer and joined Bert in London. Most of the missions he'd flown had been over Germany – several over Berlin – so he'd seen heavy action and took the danger seriously, but he was released from the tension of not knowing how he would respond to battle and he felt good about his crew. We were sitting in a pub talking about the war's progress and the heavy blows the Soviet armies were delivering (it was just at the time that the Germans were trying and failing to relieve their encircled Sixth Army at Stalingrad) when several American soldiers came in and were soon loudly assuring the bartender that now that their forces had become engaged the war would soon be over: 'Hitler can't take the kind of punches we're handing out for long.' Being well-disposed to the United States we squirmed with embarrassment, but a Cockney soldier sent the whole pub into fits of laughter by saying to his mate in a quiet but carrying voice, 'Lor', Bill, ain't it wunnerful what good English the Russians talk?' Bert respected the weight and the resolve of the U.S. Air Force in Britain, but he was not impressed by its level of training – hardly surprising in light of the speed with which the United States was trying to make up for its very late start.

In January I was sent on a week's Intelligence course at Cambridge. I was excited by my first visit to the great university and walked about the colleges whenever I had time, but with their walls and gates and suspicious porters they were rather forbidding to the outsider. However, a pleasant Englishman on the course had been an undergraduate at Jesus College and studied English under E.M.W. Tillyard, the well-known Miltonist; I told him that I admired Tillyard, and the consequence was that we dined in Hall as Tillyard's guests. It was my first experience of an Oxbridge High Table, and the beauty of the hall and elegance of the ritual made a vivid impression on me. I thought the claret excellent, but this was an opinion not shared by another diner, Sir Arthur Quiller-Couch, a literary institution, who complained that the wine was below the college's usual standard. Tillyard, who was the college master, attempted to defend the embarrassed cellarer by referring to the difficulties caused by the war, whereupon 'Q' launched into a diatribe about the havoc the war was wreaking in his Cornish village, where cigar-smoking American GIs in jeeps and lorries made the roads a danger to the residents. Accustomed to being the centre of attention, 'Q' set out to charm Tillyard's guests, and would have succeeded had he not first done his best to humiliate their host; it was a sad irony that the next year the old man was killed in Cornwall by an American military vehicle.

Tillyard, who expressed keen interest in my Milton work, asked me to look up a research student working on Milton under his supervision; it was Balachandra Rajan, who told me he was severely handicapped because certain recent American and Canadian books could not be got in wartime England, and he couldn't order them from North America because he couldn't get the foreign exchange. I therefore asked Lesley to get them for him, which she did; he paid me in sterling, and the books helped him complete his dissertation, later published as *'Paradise Lost' and the Seventeenth-Century Reader.* Years later, when I was graduate dean, he wrote from India to ask whether I could get him an appointment at Toronto, but Woodhouse wasn't interested; Rajan later was appointed to the University of Western Ontario, where Barker had gone, and the two added greatly to Western's strength.

After the Cambridge course I got a weekend, which I spent in London with Bert. One incident marred an otherwise enjoyable leave: we were sitting in the bar of a respectable hotel in Cromwell Road with a woman friend, when a large burly man in civilian dress came to our table and said something about kikes. Bert started to rise, but I restrained him; there had been some ugly incidents provoked by unjailed British Fascists and I didn't know how many friends the troublemaker had in the bar; in any case I didn't think we should be lured into a brawl at some antisemite's whim. I told the intruder that our appetites for fighting had been satisfied by getting into uniform, and perhaps his could be too. After another expression of distaste he went back to the bar, where he joined several other men, convincing even Bert that I'd been right and that he'd been sent to lure us into a fight in which we'd be badly outnumbered. That weekend was the last time I saw Bert.

In February my CO, Peter Wright, told me that a little regimental experience would be good for me and that he'd arranged for me to go to his regiment, the Royal Regiment of Canada, for a month's special duty. It was there that I learnt that Bert's plane had crashed on take-off for Stuttgart the night of 1 March; all the crew were killed, and buried at Harrogate on the 7th. I knew nothing of this until noon on the 7th. Bert's squadron wired me at once that he had been killed, and wired again on the 4th with details of the funeral, but the Canadian military censor intercepted the telegrams, although addressed by the RAF to a serving Canadian officer, then forwarded them to me by ordinary post without any attempt to let me know of them by phone; I got both of them in the regimental mail one hour after the time of the funeral. I was never able to learn who the censor was, or even at which level the intercept took place (my father in Canada received his telegrams without delay).

The regiment gave me immediate leave and I spent the next day at the cemetery and the squadron, going through Bert's effects and learning what I could from those who knew Bert or had seen the accident. I spent the evening writing very difficult letters to my father and sisters.

At the regiment I was treated sympathetically but given a good deal of work, in keeping with military psychology, which doesn't hold with much mourning. I had from the first been told that the regiment would expect me to 'do something,' and had brought along a lecture I'd given at Army HQ on the historical background of Germany's militarism, what we could expect from the civilian population after we'd won the war, and what we could do after the war to prevent a recurrence. I now revised it and gave it to the regiment's officers and a few guests brought in from the other units in the brigade (Peter Wright also came out from Army). The next day the CO, Lieutenant-Colonel Austin, had me in, told me that the regiment liked me and thought I might be useful to it in the coming action, and invited me to become a member while retaining my present posting. I had never been with the Algonquins and that affiliation had no significance for me, I felt that being in the Intelligence Corps without any relation to a forward unit was a little detached, and I liked the Royals and was flattered by the invitation; when I got back to HQ I consulted with Peter Wright, who said he'd known about and encouraged the invitation, and that accepting it would not jeopardize my Intelligence posting. I therefore accepted and shortly thereafter the transfer was approved.

A five-day Army exercise (or 'scheme,' as it was called) was to begin on 21 March, and I was allowed to postpone my return to HQ so that I could be with the regiment for it. Apparently HQ thought it went reasonably well, but I found it ominously confused, and I think the umpires were less satisfied than the generals. Viewed from company and battalion levels, control seemed uncertain and fragmented, and seen from Brigade HQ, operational

Intelligence was perfunctory. As for security, one small incident may illustrate its inadequacy. In the black-out one foggy night my driver lost his way and we came to a stop in a traffic jam; after some time a tall, angry man appeared on the passenger side of the jeep, leaned in, and shone his flashlight into my face; 'Who are you?' he demanded roughly. I identified myself and, a little irked by his belligerence, asked who he was. It was Lieutenant-Colonel C.M. Drury, CO, 4th Field Artillery, later to be a senior minister in the Canadian government; it was his guns which were blocking the road. 'What are you doing here and how did you get by the guard?' he wanted to know. I explained that we'd got lost but had seen no guard, not pointing out the obvious, that the route we'd unwittingly followed could have been taken by an 'enemy' planning to capture the guns.

A few days later I was sent on a special one-week course at Matlock, which was more closely related to operations than my earlier training and gave me some feel of reality. In addition to the usual British and Commonwealth mix there were several Poles and Czechs, from whom I learnt something about the politics and passions of exile. I walked a great deal; I had not expected the industrial Midlands to show the great natural beauty of Matlock, with its Heights of Abraham and the falls of the Derwent.

In mid-April the army went on another five-day exercise, this one involving, at least for me, a great deal of travel. Security was clearly improved, with guards posted in all the appropriate places. How much operational Intelligence had improved was less clear; I thought it had a little. Road control was better. It was hard to tell about the deployment of ground troops, but I chose to think it had improved. The exercises were doing their job; the question was whether they would achieve enough in time (there was, of course, the other question of why so much remained to be achieved at so late a date).

On 3 May Colonel Wright told me that I'd been appointed Intelligence Officer for the 2nd Canadian Infantry Division. I'd had no idea that I was being considered, since there were plenty of IOs with more seniority and experience than I had, but the appointment fitted in so neatly with his having sent me to the Royal Regiment (part of 2nd Division) and the regiment's adoption of me that I wondered how far back he'd thought of it. I was very pleased with the appointment; being an IO at Army was useful, certainly, but it was an office job, one officer among many, with little opportunity for initiative, whereas being IO of a division was a field job, where one would be personally responsible, under the G3(I) (General Staff Officer, third grade, Intelligence), for the operational side of Intelligence.

The next day I reported to 2nd Division, now bivouacked in the Dover area. I had much to learn and little time in which to do it. I had, of course, been given routine training instruction on how divisional Intelligence worked, and had had some glimpses of it in the various exercises, but that was a long way from knowing how to function in operations. After being briefed by the G3(I), Captain H.S.C. Archbold, and meeting the people at HQ with whom I would be working, I visited the brigades and battalions. At the 4th Infantry Brigade, which included the Royal Regiment, I was greeted warmly, and at the regiment itself I was in effect welcomed home. In the process of visiting the various units I came to know the Dover–Folkestone–Canterbury area fairly well and was able to spend some time in Canterbury Cathedral, though part of it was closed because of war damage.

During the evening of 5 June, air traffic grew very heavy and we could hear the distant sound of explosions across the Channel. It kept up all night, and in the morning we learnt that the assault had gone in over the Normandy beaches, and that the Canadian ground forces were the 3rd Infantry Division, 2nd Armoured Brigade, and 1st Parachute Battalion. By a kind of osmosis we came to understand that 2nd Division would be next and that we would move to our embarkation point in a day or two, as room was made for us in the beachhead. Of course that is not the way the battle developed; strong German defensive positions and fierce counterattacks constricted the beachhead, a violent gale virtually destroyed one of the two artificial harbours and seriously slowed supply operations, and it took almost three weeks for 2nd Division to get its call. They were weeks of suspense, for we knew very little of what was really happening on the beaches except that the fighting was heavy, as were Canadian casualties. To enliven the wait we had the first of Hitler's long-promised secret weapons, the V-1, or buzz bomb. These very noisy flying bombs presented no danger until the engine stopped; then the vehicle descended and exploded powerfully on impact. On several occasions I sat above the Dover cliffs watching the RAF intercept them over the Channel and shoot them down before they could reach land, but most nevertheless got through and wrought heavy damage. London and the shipping centres of the southeast were their main targets, but they were so inaccurate, especially at first, that their actual destinations were unpredictable, which many people found unnerving. When their engines flamed out overhead, all activity would cease until the explosion signalled that the danger, for those still alive and unhurt, was over for the time being.

During the third week after D-Day all our vehicles were waterproofed, which meant that they would overheat quickly and could be used only very sparingly, and on D+25 (which happened to be Dominion Day, as it was then called) the division moved to the 'hards,' or cobblestoned jetties, on the Thames Estuary. We spent all day loading our gear, and sailed early on the morning of D+26, 2 July. The convoy of tank and infantry landing-craft, escorted by several warships and intermittent flights of RAF fighters, made very slow progress; we were attacked a number of times by air and sea and took evasive action while our escort chased off the intruders, and I think little damage was incurred, but it was dusk before we made landfall in the Canadian sector of the bridgehead and much of the disembarkation was in the dark. The landing was carried out under artillery and mortar fire from the high ground inland, and occasional air attack, and there were casualties, but less confusion than might have been expected. We got off the beach and to our assembly area in traffic slowed by ground fire and air bombardment; when we arrived in our area we had several hours of work setting up temporary HQ, and by the time I was finished I was thoroughly exhausted and spent most of my first night under fire asleep. In the morning I found that my boots and kitbag had been holed by shrapnel: inexperienced and unthinking, I'd placed them on the edge of my cramped slit trench to get them out of the way.

III

The invasion plan called for the capture of Caen, about seven miles inland, on the first day. In fact it took thirty-three days of intense see-saw fighting to push the perimeter that far; finally, on 9 July, the city fell, and two days later 2nd Division went into the line in its ruins. Its citizenry, driven out by the battle and a heavy air attack that preceded the final push, began to drift back and sift through the rubble. We were told by the newspapers and the BBC that they were delighted to be rid of the Germans and welcomed their liberators enthusiastically, but I could detect little of this enthusiasm for what someone called their 'obliberation.' Of course, they could not be sure that we would make our invasion good, and a premature display of welcome might lead to reprisals if the Germans came back, but I got the impression that the coolness toward us was more than merely prudential. We later learnt that the Germans had established rest- and recreation-facilities in the area and had worked hard at local public relations, apparently to some effect. Perhaps for this reason, perhaps because of the intense and prolonged fighting on its soil, perhaps because of deeper political causes, Normandy as a whole seemed to me less welcoming of the Allies than were regions of France which we reached only after it was clear that the invasion was irreversible.

The contrast between the stalemate on the British–Canadian front and the significant advances on the American front was troubling, but General Montgomery insisted that we were achieving what we were supposed to: drawing some of the best enemy divisions to our front, thus enabling the Americans to break out of the Cherbourg peninsula and into the open country between the Loire and the Seine. Its first week in the line 2nd Division took a good deal of shelling and mortaring while preparing for Operation Goodwood, which was intended to push south from Caen, across the Orne River, and on to the high ground west of Route Nationale 158, the Falaise road. Goodwood started on 18 July with what the head of the RAF Bomber Command called 'the heaviest and most concentrated air attack in support of ground troops ever attempted.' It was a terrific display, and our high command assumed that it would utterly disorganize the enemy. It did in fact create enough confusion to enable our first wave to make good progress; in the Canadian sector 3rd Division secured the Orne crossings and the suburbs, and 2nd Division passed through, seized Louvigny at the junction of the Orne and Odon Rivers, and headed for the Verrières Ridge, about four miles south and just west of the Falaise road. But by this time the enemy, who had been well dug in and less hurt by the air attacks than had been supposed, was reorganized and ready for us. The ground here rises steadily to Falaise, and from the ridge there is perfect observation to the north, the direction from which we had to attack. It is *bocage* country, and behind every farmhouse or hedgerow there was a dug-in tank, gun, or machine-gun. The Germans had some of their best units here, and it was 2nd Division's first battle since Dieppe, of which there were very few veterans left in the division. Our battalions put in strong attacks and got onto the ridge, but could not hold against fierce counter-attacks from better positions with much better weapons; we suffered heavy casualties and, after two days of fighting held only the northern foot of the ridge.

Among the casualties was the IO of 4th Brigade. Instead of replacing him with an officer from within the brigade, according to established procedure, Brigadier Sherwood Lett asked the divisional commander to lend me to the brigade for the duration of the battle. I made my way forward on the morning of 19 July. The fighting was intense (by the end of the day the Essex Scottish Regiment alone had suffered more than three hundred casualties), and it was very clear that enemy strength was much greater than had been foreseen. I did my best to get better identifications on the brigade front; this allowed us to assess somewhat better the capabilities of the troops directly opposite, and it helped a little to clarify the enemy's general order of battle and capabilities. The battalion commanders were reluctant to risk further losses to get prisoners, but Brigadier Lett understood the need and ordered the necessary patrols.

After two days Goodwood ground to a halt and the enemy mounted a series of attacks to dislodge us from our new positions. 2nd Division was especially exposed, and all its brigades incurred heavy casualties. I had a narrow escape: one night three of us were working in a small tent when the area was strafed from the air; we got the light out and hit the ground in a row, with myself in the middle; when the attack was over, I found that machine-gun bullets had neatly stitched the canvas, killing the man on one side of me and wounding the one on the other, but leaving me unscathed.

On 24 July, during the preparations for the next phase of the break-out, Operation Spring, my divisional commander, Major-General Charles Foulkes, told me that he had received commendations of my work and was recommending me for a field promotion to captain. I was thrilled by this recognition, partly because it endorsed the aggressive line I was taking at Brigade and would help me maintain it, but partly also because it helped assuage my earlier doubts about whether I would be a good soldier under fire.

The strengthening of my confidence came at a good moment: the following day was, except for Dieppe, the costliest to Canada of the entire war; II Canadian Corps had more than 1,000 casualties, and the largest losses were in 2nd Division. With 3rd Division on our left, east of the Falaise road, we were once again sent against the Verrières Ridge and the area west and south of it. 4th Brigade made the best advance of the day, but this left us in an exposed salient, and the enemy tried very hard to cut us off. The afternoon attacks were beaten back with the help of tanks brought up from 7th British Armoured Division and tactical support from RAF Typhoons. A message about the latter came to Brigade a few minutes before the strike; on checking the map coordinates, I saw with horror that they were wrong and would send the planes onto a company position of the Royals. Severely pressed for time, I disobeyed regulations and spoke in the clear to Major Jack Anderson, now in temporary command of the Royals. Knowing that the enemy would be listening, I said, 'This is Ernest. The boys in blue will be visiting your Baker Company in ten minutes. Do you understand me?' I was enormously relieved to hear his calm voice replying, 'I understand you very well; thanks; over and out.' He got his troops out before the misdirected strike, which did no good, although several other strikes were helpful.

Brigadier Lett was wounded that day and had to be evacuated;

from late 25 to 27 July, the brigade was run by Lieutenant-Colonel Drury, the flashlight-wielding artillery officer whom I'd encountered on the exercise in England. I don't know whether he'd been appointed or had simply taken emergency command, but he and I worked in the HQ dugout throughout the night of the 25th, when there were several further counter-attacks and the brigade was seriously threatened with encirclement. I was able to provide rewarding targets for Drury's guns and the supporting British tanks.

We had made it through the night but, severely weakened and highly exposed, we didn't know whether we could beat off the renewed armoured attacks we expected in the morning. They didn't come. Simultaneously with Operation Spring, General Bradley had launched Operation Cobra on the American front, and by 26 July had made enough headway for the enemy to have to move some of his armour west – not enough to stop the Americans, but enough to reduce the pressure on us to a manageable level. We were swept with fire all day, and there were a number of limited thrusts which we were able to beat back; these intensified through the night, but in the morning we still held our positions. On 27 July, a colonel was flown in from a course in England to take temporary command of the brigade. He set out to visit the battalions and asked me to drive the jeep. When we arrived at the first battalion HQ, he climbed into the dugout and shut the trapdoor behind him, leaving me standing in a devastated field totally devoid of cover. Our approach had been observed, and soon the *Nebelwerfer* fire began (multibarrel mortars discharging a half-dozen shells at a crump). I hit the ground, but my reluctance to intrude kept me outside for several more minutes; finally, the mortars won: I opened the trapdoor and asked whether I could come in. The two colonels who had shut me out muttered apologies: they 'hadn't thought.'

The next day the Americans broke through at Coutances at the west end of the bridgehead. To keep the enemy from shifting too much strength to the American front, Montgomery, accepting that a further attack along the Falaise approach was for the time being impossible, ordered the British to attack at Caumont along the British–American border; First Canadian Army, whose headquarters had just gone operational, would carry out limited attacks in the eastern sector until the big move against Falaise could be mounted. By then I was no longer with 4th Brigade, nor for that matter with 2nd Division. During Operation Spring, 4th Canadian Armoured Division landed in France, and on 30 July it relieved 3rd Division in the line. A great deal had been learnt about the enemy in recent weeks, and someone decided that 4th Armoured should have an IO with recent experience; I was appointed. I was picked up at 4th Brigade on 31 July, given barely enough time to take my leave, and was driven – dirty, unshaven, and exhausted – to 4th Division HQ to report to the G3(I), Captain Arthur McMurrich, who eyed my condition with visible distaste.

On the way, I reflected on the change in my situation. I was losing the advantage of familiarity with Division and Brigade, and of having my own regiment nearby; I thought I had worked well with them all (I would receive the Order of the British Empire for my work there), and felt that in future operations with them my judgment would probably be trusted and my operational requests granted. Now I was going to a green division where I knew no one. On the other hand, I could make a contribution based on experience the division didn't have. Besides, I'd come in the past few weeks to a more vivid understanding than hitherto of the power of armour when confronting infantry, and thought it no bad thing to be on its side.

As the Americans advanced in the west, the Germans transferred some forces there from our front and made a renewed thrust to Falaise possible; the task was given to First Canadian Army, with some British divisions and the 1st Polish Armoured Division under command. Operation Totalize began just before midnight on 7 August; by morning it had gained the ground we'd attempted so long, including Verrières Ridge and Rocquancourt. To exploit this success, 4th Armoured and 1st Polish Armoured were to pass through, break the second line of defence about five miles farther on, and seize high ground around Falaise. To prepare for this, bombers of the U.S. Eighth Air Force attacked in strength. It was a calamity. Although it was shortly after noon, with perfect visibility, the bombing was again wild, much of it on our own troops. We suffered more than three hundred casualties, among them General

Keller of 3rd Division. Attempts to communicate with the bombers were fruitless, and as wave after wave came in, I saw some of our own guns open up on them. A kinsman of mine, Lieutenant Lawrence Cohen, also originally from Winkler, was killed in this day's battle. He was on loan to the Welsh Division, which was badly hurt by the misdirected bombs, and I've often wondered whether that was how Lawrence was killed. What began so badly continued not much better. We made some advances but at heavy cost, and once again our attack petered out well short of its objectives.

The Americans were now penetrating deeply in the German rear; the opportunity was at hand to envelop and destroy the German Seventh Army and Fifth Panzer Army, and Montgomery ordered First Canadian Army to take Falaise forthwith to close the pocket. Questionable tactics, inexperience, and bad luck on our side, and very determined resistance by the Germans, who were fighting hard to keep an escape route open, prevented us from closing the gap at Falaise. We were therefore directed on 16 August to swing wider and do it at Trun, some twelve miles southeast. Before daybreak on the 17th, while I was plotting enemy movements on the situation map, my phone rang: it was the divisional commander, Major-General Kitching, asking whether we were in Trun yet. I told him we weren't and reported the location of our leading elements. He acknowledged the information in a subdued tone. We got into Trun the next morning, but the gap was still not fully closed and I was not surprised when, on the morning of the 19th, General Simonds met his four divisional commanders at our divisional HQ. I supposed he was being stern, but I was not prepared for one of the results: on the 21st, General Kitching was replaced by Major-General H.W. Foster.

It was hard for me and impossible for the combat troops to think of the action of these days as a failure deserving punishment. For days before the gap was physically closed on the 21st all the forces in the area, ground and air, had been pouring fire on a fleeing enemy in a steadily shrinking space, and the slaughter was almost incomprehensible. Every road and path in the Falaise pocket was a carpet of bloated corpses, human and equine; the stench was unimaginable. Thousands of enemy soldiers had surrendered, and others trying to surrender had been shot by fanatics on their own side; after the closing of the gap, tens of thousands more gave up. The Seventh and Fifth Panzer Armies, the strongest and best equipped in the entire *Wehrmacht*, were destroyed, their remnants in retreat or on their way to prisoner-of-war cages. Nevertheless, despite this massive victory, there had been failure; the slowness to close the gap had allowed significant elements to escape, including much of the command structure, which was used to reorganize and strengthen the armies still in northern France, Belgium, and Holland, and which we would have to fight again at great cost later in the campaign.

One major factor in the enemy's ability to slow us up had been impressing itself upon us since we engaged him: his weaponry was greatly superior to ours. With our minds conditioned by the Allied propaganda touting our weapons as the best in the world, we were slow to realize the truth, but it was brought home sharply by our losses. Our tanks were no match for theirs: shells from the Sherman's 75mm gun would ricochet off the thick Tiger or Panther armour, while their high-velocity 88s and 75s could demolish the thin-skinned Sherman with a single shot. Our 2- and 3-inch mortars were laughable in comparison with their *Nebelwerfer*, which hurt our infantry more than any other weapon. Our light and medium machine-guns couldn't compare with their Spandau, whose rate of fire, 1,200 rounds per minute, quadrupled ours, and every German detachment, however small, had one of these killing machines. Our infantryman's anti-tank weapon, the PIAT, was effective only at very short and exposed range against light armour or vulnerable spots; their *Panzerfaust* could destroy any of our tanks at a range great enough to permit the operator some concealment.

At the time we could not understand why our weapons were so inferior. On reflection, reasons can be found. On the German side, war had been intended and prepared for at least since Hitler's accession to power in 1933; German technical and industrial skill had been mobilized early for it, weapons and equipment had been tested in the Spanish Civil War, and the improved versions tested and improved again in the invasion of Poland, the conquest of most of Europe, the war in the desert, and the invasion of the

Soviet Union; and arms and equipment factories had overriding priority for supplies and labour, including millions of slave labourers. On the Allied side, Britain did not begin seriously to prepare for war until Churchill became prime minister, and even then priority had to go to the air force; no real effort was made in Canada until after the fall of France, nor in the United States, the crucial industrial sector, until after Pearl Harbor. The result was that the goals of our armament industry were speed and quantity, and the factories had to rush out existing models of weapons and equipment, especially after the British Army lost almost everything at Dunkirk. Later, modification and redesign became possible, but by then the long supply lines were full, and those were the weapons and equipment we fought with.

Something much the same can be said of the armies. The Germans had been training intensively for years before their first military enterprises, had tried out and perfected their tactics and strategy over many campaigns, and had huge numbers of battle-hardened soldiers to whom war was a way of life, led by a professional officer corps and an almost equally professional non-commissioned-officer establishment. Now, with the Soviets advancing upon Germany from the east and the Allies thrusting at them in the west, this formidable army felt that it was truly fighting for the Fatherland, that defeat meant the end not only of German supremacy but also of their own families and homes. Not least, field discipline was very severe, and leaving one's post under fire or attempting to desert invited summary execution.

Canadians, on the other hand, had made no preparations for war, had only a small Permanent Force which no one took seriously until war actually came and which proved wholly inadequate to the dual task of forming the core of the mobilized units and training the mass of new recruits, with the result that very few officers or NCOs at the front were professional soldiers, most had only limited training, and only a handful had battle experience. The tactical doctrines with which we began the war were those of the First World War, superficially modified. Our long inaction in Britain had made the war seem abstract, and training had grown routine. The policy of voluntary overseas service made Canadians at the front feel that many at home were shirking and many others profiteering, and that the politicians were betraying the combat troops by failing to send needed reinforcements (in fact, many units were by now seriously understrength). This army, thrown green against crack German formations fighting from prepared positions, shocked by the reality and cost of combat and feeling betrayed by its inferior weaponry and lack of reinforcements, did not possess a spur equal to that motivating the enemy. After the battles of the bridgehead, Caen, and the initial attempts on Falaise, many of the troops felt that they had already made their contribution, and while they were willing to fight if necessary they did not seek out combat. Similarly, some officers and NCOs had become very sensitive to losses, especially since replacements were slow in coming and were often inadequately trained, and did not press their units very insistently.

IV

With the end of the Battle of Normandy we entered upon what was for me the third phase (for those who had been in the assault landing it was the fourth) of the Battle of Europe: after the break-out from the bridgehead and the envelopment and destruction of the Seventh and Fifth Panzer Armies, we now began the pursuit of their remnants and a drive toward Belgium and the Netherlands. First Canadian Army was on the left, next to the coast; Second British Army was on our right, and First and Third U.S. Armies were on its right. The 4th Armoured Division formed the right flank of First Canadian Army, and while 2nd and 3rd Divisions and the attached British divisions were to get across the lower Seine and go for the Channel ports and buzz-bomb sites, we and the Polish Armoured were to cross the Seine higher up and thrust northeast for the Somme and Belgium. On our right, Second British Army, unencumbered by the task Montgomery allotted to the Canadians of 'keeping the Normandy bottle securely corked,' got off early on a course parallel to ours, while on their right the Third and First U.S. Armies moved even earlier, reaching the Seine on 19 August.

The grisly task at Falaise was finished by the 21st, releasing the

2nd and 3rd Canadian Divisions; Trun and Chambois kept 4th Armoured and the Poles engaged until the 23rd. 2nd and 3rd Divisions and the British divisions under command encountered organized resistance, but on their right, coming after them, 4th Division got off lightly. For us the pattern on the way to the Seine was rapid forward movement led by squads of our reconnaissance regiment; when they drew fire, we would deploy a fighting force to reduce the position while the rest of the column went around it if possible; when its task was done the detail would catch up with the rest of the division. Bridges had been systematically destroyed, and it took time for the engineers to erect new ones or to raft tanks, guns, and motor transport across rivers. Another impediment was the vast numbers of prisoners of war, who had to be cleared off the road, guarded, fed, and taken to hastily constructed cages, where they could be interrogated by Army teams.

German officers now began coming in under white flags, offering to bring in their units provided they could keep their weapons and join with us to fight the Soviet armies advancing on Germany from the east. These people were brought to divisional HQ, where the G3(I), who didn't speak German, left them to me. I explained that the Soviets were our allies, the Germans our enemies, and the options available to them were to fight us, flee, or surrender. They always surrendered, some with great formality; I still have a ceremonial sword handed over by a battalion commander who wore it on his mission.

There was considerable resistance on our left crossing the Seine, where the reorganized Seventh Army had received reinforcements and was making a stand to cover the evacuation of its remaining heavy weapons and equipment, using ferries and pontoon bridges which were folded back against the banks by day. In 4th Division's sector resistance was not as strong; we reached the Seine and began crossing on rafts on 26 August, while the engineers erected a pontoon bridge; most of the division was across the next day and headed for the Somme, where we found only small units, which we quickly subdued. Farther up the Somme, at Amiens, the enemy had in effect no defences, and Second British Army swept through there in an epic if unimpeded march of over two hundred miles in four days, seizing Arras on 1 September, Brussels on the 3rd, and the grand prize of Antwerp, with its docks astonishingly intact, on the 4th.

This unexpected windfall, so uncharacteristic of the methodical German destruction of evacuated positions, dictated strategy for both sides. We needed to be able to use the great port for a main supply base in the north, and correspondingly the enemy needed to deny us its use. Accordingly, he withdrew his Fifteenth Army from the Pas de Calais and sent it, reinforced by what was left of Seventh and some divisions from Nineteenth, to defend the southern approaches to the Scheldt Estuary and occupy Walcheren Island and South Beveland, which constituted its north bank. Unfortunately the British, surprised by the quick evacuation of Antwerp, did not push north until the opportunity for a quick outflanking advance of the estuary was lost.

While the Canadian infantry divisions worked their way up the coast, seizing channel ports, we and the Poles were directed to the Scheldt. Resistance began to stiffen as we entered Belgium but we continued to move fast until 8 September, when we reached the Ghent Canal. We got a small force across but it could make no headway without reinforcement; after a pursuit lasting seventeen days and carrying us over 250 miles, 'the joyride is over for a while,' I said in a letter to Lesley on 9 September. It was not a view universally held, and it was some time before it was shared even in my own divisional HQ, let alone higher formations.

Farther left, on 9 September, one of our units reported entering St Michael's Hospital on the outskirts of Bruges, used by the Germans as a military post and hospital; all had fled save the Belgian medical staff and patients. Our troops, their security discipline grown slack through the easy days of the pursuit, had pushed on without leaving a guard, and the next day there were reports of the SS having returned at night and terrorized. I went with the reconnaissance section sent to investigate; there were no Germans there. We found an SS records and communications office with wireless and other equipment, a weapons storeroom, and a very extensive wine cellar. After bringing up a small guard for the hospital from Division, we loaded what we could of the wine cellar's treasures into our scout cars, and delivered our loads to the various messes (I was president of C Mess, for officers below staff grade), making them all participants in my first looting foray. The records left behind in the hospital enabled me to get in touch with the Bruges underground with unusual speed, which led to the formation of some friendships through which I received the kind of unverified but valuable information (e.g., the arrival or departure of units, weapons, supplies, or equipment, and local construction, demolition, or mining) that is sometimes given to forward units but rarely makes its way back to Division.

On 11 September the U.S. First Army crossed the Luxembourg border and entered Germany northwest of Trier. On the 12th British Second Army entered Holland south of Eindhoven. There was so little resistance that nearly everyone spoke of an end to the war before Christmas; in this mood of confidence Montgomery planned and Eisenhower approved the airborne drop on Arnhem; in the same mood we were ordered to cross the Leopold Canal and clear the south bank of the Scheldt. I had misgivings, partly based on what I was hearing from my Bruges friends, but I couldn't even get my own G3(I) to share them, and the Algonquin Regiment was ordered to establish a bridgehead across the double canal northeast of Bruges (here the Leopold and the Canal de Dérivation de la Lys run side by side for some miles). The Algonquins crossed on the 13th, met fierce resistance and suffered heavy casualties and, after hanging on for a day, withdrew across the canals on the 14th. I argued that this meant that the Leopold Canal was being organized as the forward defence line for the Scheldt, and McMurrich now gave enough credence to this view to allow me to put it into the daily Divisional Intelligence report as an opinion.

Corps found the opinion hard to credit, especially as the Poles on our right were having no trouble reaching and clearing the south bank of the Scheldt east of the Braakman Inlet, just beyond the Leopold. I argued that the enemy didn't need the south bank above the Braakman as long as he had the north bank and the Breskens pocket lower down on the south bank, and set out to prove that he was occupying the Breskens pocket in strength. I went to Lieutenant-Colonel Fred Wigle, the G1 of the division, and asked him whether I could speak to him without going through my G3(I). He drew a volume from the book shelf above his desk and consulted it briefly (I suppose it was a procedural manual); then, somewhat reluctantly, he agreed to hear me, his manner suggesting that the request had better be justified. I told him my view of the situation, adding that I thought we were no longer facing a ragtag of forces but rather a new formation brought in to deny us the use of the Antwerp facilities until winter closed in, giving the enemy time to reorganize his main defences. I had some civilian information, but to prove my case I needed solid identifications; could he arrange patrols across the canals to take prisoners? He looked indignant: 'Why should we risk casualties to satisfy your curiosity?' 'Because if I'm right the task of clearing to the Scheldt is unsuited to an armoured division; it will require a lot of infantry on the ground, fighting from polder to polder and across flooded terrain. But as of now the job is ours, and we'll take a lot of casualties before higher echelon sees that it's beyond our capacity. If we can show that the pocket is held by a strong formation with orders to stay put, we may be shifted to a more suitable assignment.' Wigle listened with increasing interest, was silent for a while, then said he'd think about it; as I got up to leave, he said he was glad I'd come to him, even though it was irregular.

In the next few days a number of prisoners were brought in and some new identifications emerged. We also began to get more widely based information from the Belgian underground as others besides the Bruges group told us what they were able to learn. Gradually, we put the bits together: the Fifteenth Army, with the remnants of the Seventh and Fifth Panzer, was withdrawing across Holland, leaving 64th and 70th Divisions and the coastal units to hold the Scheldt Estuary. What we'd encountered was the 64th, a very good division at full strength, well led and fully equipped, fighting from strongly prepared positions and backed by heavy coastal artillery at Flushing and Breskens. When Army accepted that this was indeed the enemy's order of battle, preparations were made for two infantry divisions to take over from us the reduction of the pocket, with another strong infantry force to take South Beveland and Walcheren. The two-front operation took a month of extremely nasty polder fighting, cost our side many thousands of casualties, and completely destroyed two full-strength German divisions and some garrison units. The 4th Division was required to clear to the start-line, which involved fighting across the Ghent Canal and north to the Leopold: dirty work but, unlike our original assignment, within our capability.

On 17 September, while we were engaged at the Leopold, the sky filled with aircraft passing very low overhead in a northeasterly direction – not the customary bombers, but Dakotas and other troop-carriers. After what seemed an endless parade, they were followed by other planes pulling gliders, making it even clearer that there was to be a large airborne assault. We didn't know the target, but we exulted in this show of strength and confidence, noting that there was a strong fighter escort but that the *Luftwaffe* didn't show up for what might be thought an inescapable confrontation. It was a heady sight, and even my usual caution concerning the enemy's continuing capability momentarily gave way to the general excitement. 'The last phase of the war in Europe has begun,' I wrote to Lesley that day, telling her of the sight; 'this round is the Battle of Germany.'

I should have known better. Over the next few days it became clear that the Battle of Arnhem was a severe and costly failure. It had been planned and mounted without real knowledge of what forces the enemy could bring to bear, a more extreme example of the same overconfidence that had ordered an armoured division to assault a fortified below-sea-level coastal area without stopping to secure real knowledge of the enemy's strength in the area. Fortunately, 4th Division's commitment across the Leopold had been limited; that at Arnhem, alas, was irreversible. The Arnhem defeat ended any prospect there might have been of bringing the war to a rapid conclusion. On our front it imposed a change of tactic: with 2nd Canadian Corps fully occupied in clearing the Scheldt, 4th Division was transferred to 1st British Corps, which now constituted the right flank of First Canadian Army and was to strike north from Antwerp to the Maas River. Before we left I got a twenty-four-hour leave in Bruges, where my friends from St Michael's Hospital took very good care of me. I saw Claude Bissell there; he had just been made IO of his battalion and wanted me to tell him all I could about the job.

On 4 October I got a cable from my sister Gertrude saying that my father had cancer of the bowel and would be operated on the next day. He had said he wanted me there and would wait until I could get leave for the purpose, but fortunately my surgeon brother-in-law had successfully insisted that there must be no postponement. Two or three days later I got another cable saying the operation had been successful but it was not known whether the malignancy had spread. I had at once applied for a ninety-day compassionate leave; the reply didn't come until 2 November: 'in view of the fact that this officer's father withstood the operation unusually well, his return to Canada is not thought to be warranted.' I didn't think the decision unjust but was disgusted with the length of time it took.

We moved from the Leopold about 20 October, passed through the virtually intact city of Antwerp (soon to become a prime target of buzz bombs and V-2 rockets), and were deployed on the left flank of the corps. There was some hard fighting, but on 27 October we took Bergen-op-Zoom, then pushed north to Steenbergen and the Rhine estuary. An improbable incident took place at the end of the St Philipsland peninsula; a small mixed force of our tanks and motorized infantry saw a group of four German naval craft in an island harbour a half-mile away; they engaged them with tank and mortar fire and managed to sink them. I was unable to resist the risible aspect of this action, and headed the next morning's daily Intrep 'HMCS Fourth Armoured Intrep No. 1'; the London *Daily Mirror* ran the story under a large headline reading; 'Monty's Men Sink German Fleet.'

By 9 November everything south of the Maas was clear. The 2nd Canadian Corps, having finished clearing the Scheldt Estuary, was moved east to hold the deep Nijmegen salient, the legacy of the Arnhem battle. The 4th Division was assigned the s'Hertogenbosch sector, and divisional HQ settled into Vught, with everyone in billets; I was placed with a well-fed and comfortable family, making me wonder what their relations with the Germans had been before we arrived.

The static situation yielded me a forty-eight-hour leave in Brussels – a long drive in an open jeep in November weather, but more than worth it. I was accompanied by John Gray of Macmillan of Canada, whom I'd known slightly in Toronto and who proved good company. The army had taken over the Atlanta Hotel for use as an Officers' Club. Except that the food was regulation army rations, it offered every luxury: real beds, hot water, wines in the restaurant and every kind of drink in the bar, a cocktail lounge and supper-dance room where civilian guests could be entertained, and a hostess service providing respectable female companions on request (who were driven home by the service at 10:45 P.M., a quarter-hour before curfew). I took full advantage of all these facilities, and for two days felt far from the war, surrounded though I was by scores of other officers equally intent on getting away from it. Once again I met Bissell and this time we were able to have a genuine conversation.

V

On 22 November Ted McMurrich, the G3(I), left for Canada to attend a staff course and I was told to assume his duties until a new appointment was made. I'd had no staff training, but that didn't worry me, as I'd worked closely with McMurrich and thought I could carry on. However, no one was brought in to do the IO's work, so that I had to do both jobs. The explanation offered me was that there was a shortage of trained Intelligence officers, and that since our front was quiet I should be able to manage for a while, perhaps getting some help from the Security officer. I knew this situation to be untenable but there was nothing I could do. Then, on 11 December, I was appointed G3(I). I was very pleased, not only to have the job (and the extra fifty cents a day that went with it) but because it was a joint appointment by Peter Wright at Army, Bill Broughall at Corps, and the GOC (general officer commanding) of my division, General Foster (this would have been on the advice of the G1, Fred Wigle). These were people whose good opinions I valued, and they'd made the decision knowing that I'd not had the staff training normal for a staff appointment.

About this time or a little later I was called in for a curious interview by the divisional personnel officer, who in addition to details of my personal background wanted to know about my role at the Leopold Canal and elsewhere. He was fairly new to the division, had a severe facial tic and a haggard nervous appearance, and said something at the end of the interview which, after half a century, I remember word for word: 'You do all right. Without the moustache nobody can tell what you are.' (I had recently ended a month-long experiment with a moustache.) What he meant was that without the moustache I'd worn when he joined the division I didn't look like his stereotype of a Jew. I learnt later that he'd been instructed to cite me for a decoration; unfortunately, among the choices available, the GOC, or more likely Wigle, had selected the MBE (Member of the Order of the British Empire), unaware that 2nd Division had already cited me for it; since the MBE, unlike some decorations, is not awarded twice, the 4th Division recommendation was unavailing.

One of the duties of the G3(I) was to attend the G1's morning conference, where each staff officer reported on the situation for his branch, and the G1, fresh from the GOC's morning Orders Group, finished the session with the day's instructions. On 30 November he walked in accompanied by a thick-set, florid, ginger-haired and moustachioed man, and introduced us to Major-General Chris Vokes, the new GOC. Most of us had not even known that the divisional command was being changed. Vokes made a short speech and left. This was something of a portent: Vokes was to be much more visible at HQ than his predecessor. He had come from the command of 1st Division in Italy, where operations were smaller, and apparently he liked being in fairly close personal touch with matters in his command. This was to have significant consequences. As G3(I) I attended the GOC's Orders Group to present the current enemy situation, and was able to observe Vokes's interaction with the brigade commanders, heads of support and service units, and his G1, and as time passed I thought I saw a growing unease in his relations with Wigle, who was accustomed to a looser rein under Foster. Later, when large-scale operations resumed, I thought I saw an analogous development with the operational commanders; Vokes was accustomed to terrain and scale favouring the deployment of task forces of limited size, while our division, except for special situations, was accustomed to being deployed as a whole, with the GOC at a corresponding distance from the units.

I was therefore not surprised at some command and staff changes in the following weeks and months. The first to affect me directly was Wigle's departure in mid-January to take command of the Argyll and Sutherland Highlanders, whose CO had, in the GOC's opinion, grown too cautious after the regiment had taken many casualties. Wigle claimed to be happy about the appointment, but he was a surprising choice, having been trained in armoured reconnaissance, not infantry, and never having held a line position in battle, so when the new G1, McKenzie Robinson, turned out to have been Vokes's G1 at 1st Division, most of us concluded that the GOC's primary motive had been discomfort with Wigle and a preference for his accustomed G1.

The next change was a new G2, whose surname I've forgotten. Herb, a short, brisk, dandyish major, also from the Italian theatre, arrived in the Ops Centre one evening and went from officer to officer being briefed on each one's role. He came to me last. I showed him my map of enemy dispositions and explained the structure and personnel of the Intelligence Section. He asked how he would be briefed to report on Intelligence. I said Intelligence was reported by the G3(I) directly to the GOC or the G1. This was new to him, or at any rate he said so: 'Do you mean I'm to be left out of the loop? Aren't you under my command?' I said that I was for internal and discipline matters but not for Intelligence, which by regulation had to be reported directly to the commander or chief of staff to minimize transmission error; I showed him a manual which said as much, and offered to brief him for his own information whenever he wished. He looked at me speculatively, said he'd sleep on the matter, and left. I could hardly believe that a relatively senior staff officer did not know the Intelligence reporting drill, thought it more likely that he wanted to gather all the operative power of the Ops Centre into his own hands, and prepared for a confrontation in the morning. Had Wigle still been there I'd not have worried, but I'd not yet come to know Robinson and thought there was a tendency for these transplanted Italian-theatre officers to stick together. I was nevertheless determined to hold my ground and calculated what help I could expect from Intelligence at Corps and Army. The next morning Herb said nothing about the matter, and it never surfaced again. Occasionally during an operation I'd ask him whether he'd like to see the enemy dispositions, but he was rarely interested.

When we settled into the s'Hertogenbosch area we had no idea that we would be there for about three months, but we did expect to be relatively inactive for some time. For one thing, we were overdue for rest and refit, with our tanks, guns, and transport all badly needing overhaul, to say nothing of the men's needs. Even more compelling was the supply shortage: it was 28 November before the first supply convoy arrived in Antwerp. Acknowledging the need for rehabilitation, Montgomery instituted a general program of leaves. Canadian Army established leave centres in Brussels and Ghent and made transit arrangements for officers who preferred to take their leaves in Britain.

In addition to the shortages common to all the Allies, Canadian formations had a further problem: because of higher-than-expected casualties and an acute shortage of reinforcements, most fighting units, and certainly all infantry units, were seriously under-strength. This had made it much harder and more costly than it should have been to carry out our assignments. Yet there were 60,000 trained conscripts serving in Canada under the National Resources Mobilization Act. They were not needed at home, but Prime Minister Mackenzie King refused to send them overseas, saying that 'would occasion the most serious controversy that could arise in Canada.' Refusing to send them where they were so badly needed also created serious controversy, with much ill feeling between the active forces and the home-service conscripts who refused to volunteer for General Service (whom the volunteers called 'zombies'). In the end the government had to change its policy. Colonel Ralston, the minister of defence, came overseas on a visit, became convinced that the situation was intolerable, and recommended that a number of NRMA troops be sent to the front as reinforcements for understrength units. King, having got General McNaughton, newly retired from the army, to agree that he would be willing to serve as minister of defence without demanding that conscripts be sent overseas, rejected Ralston's recommendation. Ralston resigned, McNaughton was appointed, a violent political controversy ensued, McNaughton's appeal to conscripts to volunteer for overseas service fell flat, and on 23 November King succumbed and agreed to send up to 16,000 NRMA troops overseas. They arrived in time to bring most units up to strength when the offensive resumed.

That had been planned for the beginning of the new year, but Hitler decreed otherwise. At his direct order, Rundstedt, on 16 December, launched his famous Ardennes offensive; on the first day, he tore a sixty-mile gap in the U.S. First Army front, through which he poured his armour and drove deep into the American position. Meanwhile, active patrolling and some cross-river raids for prisoners, together with civilian information, warned us of another planned thrust, this one against First Canadian Army's position, with Antwerp as target. Had these two attacks succeeded, the Allied forces in northwest Europe would have been divided and Canadian Army enveloped. To meet this sudden threat, 4th Division was pulled out of its position on Christmas Eve and hurried to Breda, where its armour would be ready to strike at the centre of the enemy's planned attack; meanwhile, Canadian Army HQ was pulled back from Holland to Belgium. On 26 December I suggested in my Intrep that the intended attack against Antwerp would depend on the Germans reaching the Meuse River in the Ardennes; this was confirmed after the surrender. In the event, the stubborn American resistance at Bastogne won time for other U.S. and British forces to arrive, and as their counter-attacks gained strength the logic of a second thrust from the north vanished, as I reasoned in an Intrep on the last day of the year.

At about the time this was being read, very early New Year's morning, the enemy seemed to mock my argument by mounting his largest air assault since the invasion. Allied pilots were sleeping off the previous night's celebrations, and the *Luftwaffe* destroyed a lot of planes on the ground, but then it spent too much time strafing the area, giving our pilots time to get into the air, where they destroyed a crippling number of enemy aircraft. The 4th Division, which was concentrated as a counter-attack force, offered an inviting target; we had some equipment losses but very few casualties.

After the defeat of the Ardennes offensive and the return to static warfare I tried to take my promised leave, but various divisional operations interfered, and then planning for the assault on the Rhine got under way. This was to begin in the north from the Nijmegen salient, with British and Canadian forces driving southeastward between the Maas and the Rhine (Operation Veritable), to be followed two days later by the Ninth U.S. Army striking northeastward from the Roer River to meet us west of the Rhine. Farther south three more U.S. armies and the First French Army would strike toward the Rhine when the northern hinge had been loosened.

The Battle of the Rhineland was very costly, in good part because of mismanagement on the Allied side. Jealousy and distrust between Britain and the United States, at both the political and the military level, led to endless jockeying for position, role, command, and supplies in what was expected to be the positioning battle for the final confrontation, and Eisenhower, subjected to these contrary forces, delayed and delayed his decision until 1 February. An operation planned for hard-frozen ground thus became highly vulnerable to an early thaw, which in fact came 4 February, followed by three days of incessant heavy rain, from 5 to 8 February. Almost as bad was the failure of First U.S. Army under General Hodges to take the Roer River dams on time, allowing the enemy to flood the valley and stall the Ninth U.S. Army's advance for two weeks; this in turn enabled the enemy to concentrate his powerful reserves against us instead of having to divide them between us and the Americans.

Montgomery, who had to penetrate the northern end of the famed Siegfried Line, assembled a very large ground force and laid on strong air support. The initial assault by infantry made good progress, but when the tanks tried to follow up they immediately bogged down in endless mud. On the left, the enemy had blown the dykes, and the Rhine, fed by thaw and heavy rain, flooded the ground to a depth of five feet. The whole area was prepared and fortified with German skill and thoroughness, and the fighting was at close quarters, hard, dirty, and bloody. The 4th Division was not yet involved; that would come only in the final phase of the operation, Blockbuster, when the earlier objectives of Veritable had been achieved.

At this point I was told that my turn for leave, already twice-postponed, had come up again and that it was my last chance, because with the resumption of offensive operations the leave program was being wound down. I felt guilty about leaving shortly before the division was to go into battle but I didn't intend to lose my leave, so I set off on 17 February on the long day's travel to London. I hadn't been able to get a hotel reservation by mail, but a servicemen's aid booth at the station arranged for two of us to share a room overnight in the old Pastoria Hotel in Leicester Square. As soon as I got there I undressed and ran a bath, only to find that the water was cold. There was no phone in the room, so I put on my boots and greatcoat and went down to the porter's desk to ask for some hot water. The truculent, ill-favoured porter eyed me and my Canada service flash disdainfully and replied, 'There's no hot water at this hour; don't you know there's a war on?' It was a question that had been addressed over the last few years by millions of Britons to one another and to perhaps as many foreigners, myself among them, but in the circumstances of the moment it was suddenly intolerable. I reached across the desk, seized his greasy serge lapels, drew him towards me, and said, 'Yes, I know there's a war on, and so will you unless you get me some hot water.' I suppose he could have called the police but he chose instead to get me a couple of buckets of nearly hot water. The next day we found a comfortable service flat in Jermyn Street, off Piccadilly.

London felt very different to me from my last visit. There were no more buzz bombs or air raids, no fires or sirens, some of the rubble had been cleared, and the blanket of fear had lifted; the only people still sleeping in the Underground stations were those with nowhere else to go. The whole city was thronged with servicemen on leave from or going to the front, and the entertainment and hospitality industries were going full tilt: hotels and restaurants overcrowded, theatre tickets being scalped, the prostitutes in Piccadilly and Mayfair working day and night. Mrs Massey's club and the unofficial Canadian club in the Haymarket were constantly crowded and full of the superficial gaiety that comes with a temporary release of tension and anxiety. I luxuriated in this overheated atmosphere for a week, going to such art museums as were open, buying a few books, seeing some films, and managing to get in to see Gielgud's *Hamlet*, which, except for Miles Malleson's wonderful Polonius, I did not much care for, finding Gielgud's febrile, high-pitched Hamlet alien to Shakespeare's.

VI

On 28 February I returned to the division, being driven the last few miles through country we'd been fighting over when I left. The devastation equalled the worst I'd seen since Falaise, but this time it was German and did not wring my heart. Operation Blockbuster began two days before my return; 4th Division had come in between 2nd and 3rd Divisions and struck for the Hochwald Layback, the third defence belt of the Siegfried Line. It had got as far as the gap between the Hochwald and the Balberger Wald, but at extremely heavy cost. We were now ordered to clear the gap.

General Crerar had told his two corps commanders, the Canadian Simonds in the north and the British General Horrocks in the south, that whichever first secured a good road for the attack on Xanten would have the bulk of the army placed under his command for the thrust to the Rhine. Simonds made the early capture of the Goch–Xanten railway, which runs through the Hochwald Gap and which he intended to cover over for road traffic, an absolute command to Vokes. This railway, built on an embankment, is fully open to observation and fire from all directions, and our two flanking infantry divisions had made little progress in clearing the two forests; nevertheless, Vokes split the division into a number of battle groups and kept hurling them in one after the other. The enemy had massed guns, tanks, mortars, and *Nebelwerfer* projectors; every possible position was preregistered, so that the fire was extremely accurate; and the whole length of the railway embankment and every road, path, and field was mined. It was slaughter, and probably avoidable: about three miles to the south there was a good road that would have allowed armour to be used properly. Without a race to be first, the forests could have been bypassed and then encircled.*

All three Canadian divisions in Blockbuster attacked almost without intermission until the morning of 4 March, when they found the enemy had withdrawn. On 6 March, 4th Division attacked Veen; it took three days of very costly fighting against this strongly prepared position before it fell, and another hard day for the nearby Winnenthal monastery. Robinson, the G1, asked me how an obviously defeated army could fight so long and hard, at such cost, for temporary possession of a piece of ground. He knew the tactical importance for the enemy of keeping the bridgehead open while he withdrew his forces across the Rhine, but how were the troops motivated? They couldn't all be Nazi fanatics. I explained that, in addition to zeal, the enemy had a uniquely persuasive discipline: he had long been shooting deserters, he was now shooting 'anybody about to surrender,' and he was letting everyone know of the enforcement of Himmler's almost unbelievable order of 10 September 1944 against the *families* of deserters: 'his ignominious behavior will entail the most severe consequences for his family. Upon examination of the circumstances they will be summarily shot.'†

By nightfall on 10 March, the enemy's remaining forces evacuated the bridgehead and blew the bridges. Farther south the Americans had also closed up to the Rhine or were rapidly doing so, seizing an intact bridge at Remagen. It was clear that the next phase would be mounted soon across the Rhine and, as then manned, my Intelligence section was inadequate to cope with mobile operations. We had taken very large numbers of prisoners in the Rhineland battle, and since I was the only one in the section

---

* For the account of operations during the ten days I was away from the division, I have relied mainly on W.D. Whitaker and Shelagh Whitaker, *Rhineland* (Toronto: Stoddart, 1989), pp. 219-35, 266.
† The document is quoted in Milton Shulman, *Defeat in the West* (London: Secker and Warburg, 1947), p. 218.

who could speak German I spent a lot of time doing initial interrogations, but I was also in charge of the section and of briefing the GOC; naturally, the work was not being well enough done. I consulted with the G1, who agreed to support me in a renewed demand for a German-speaking IO. At Corps I was told that none was available. I expected this answer, and asked permission to go to Army with my request; Broughall was hesitant, but agreed. When I put my case to Peter Wright he said he had no trained Intelligence officers available, and certainly no German speakers, but he'd been sent several officers with regimental or brigade experience who, for diverse reasons, were being posted to Intelligence; if I could find anyone among them who would be useful to me I could have him. On the list was Paul Corbett's name and I asked for him. Wright agreed, reminding me that Corbett had no German; I woke Paul, explained the situation to him, told him (against Wright's advice) that he had a choice, and went back to the division. Two days later Corbett arrived and was soon making a positive contribution to the HQ.

A little later, when the division was again taking many prisoners, Lieutenant Dave Wiens was detached from the Army prisoner-of-war cage and sent to help me. Wiens was a Winnipeg Mennonite whose first language was German, and he took on virtually all the work of interrogation, freeing me for my prescribed duties. There was at first an element of unease in our relationship: I had an image of Mennonites as opposed to the war and biased toward the German side, and I think he had a disagreeable stereotype of Jews. Working together diminished, although it did not eradicate, the stereotype I held, and I believe it must have done something similar with his; at any rate, we grew more comfortable with each other.

There was only token Canadian participation in the massive British assault across the Rhine at Wesel on 23 March. First Canadian Army, with all Canadian divisions together for the first time under a single command, crossed at Emmerich a week later against limited opposition. The 1st Corps, newly arrived from Italy, took the left sector toward west Holland, which it would liberate, while 2nd Corps went north and northeast toward the north coast and Germany, with 3rd Division on the corps' left, 2nd Division in the centre, and 4th Division on the right.

Our route took us back across the border into Holland. The first significant opposition the division encountered was at Almelo, which we captured on 5 April. The division then pushed on, but a bypassed enemy force west of the town counter-attacked and for some hours the situation was unclear. I knew that Almelo was a district Gestapo HQ and was eager to investigate; I therefore accepted perhaps too readily the company commander's assurance that the part of town I wanted to go to was clear, and my driver and I arrived in our jeep without any guard to find the office empty but with the feel of very recent abandonment. All the files in the main rooms were gone, but I found a closet (whose lock yielded to a couple of pistol shots) which contained not only a number of leftover Gestapo files but also a Dutch Fascist Party membership list. By this time some townspeople had gathered outside the office and they confirmed that this was also a regional HQ of the Dutch Fascist Party – and that the last of the occupants had left in a Gestapo car less than ten minutes before I arrived. The closet also yielded up a camera, a pair of binoculars, and a Luger pistol, which constituted my second and final appropriation of booty.

A little before this the Royal Navy, knowing that 4th Division was to strike northeast for the German coast and wanting to be early into the German naval base at Wilhelmshaven, sent a detachment under Lieutenant-Commander Antony Hugill to move with us until we got there. Hugill came to me to ask whether that would be acceptable; I made him welcome and took him to meet Major Clarence Campbell, the camp commandant (later head of the National Hockey League), who agreed to arrange the logistics. A day or two later Hugill, to express gratitude, asked whether there was anything he and his men could do for me. Being unaccustomed to such offers, I was at first nonplussed, then said the one thing I'd really like was a hot bath. He said to come to his billet in a small town south of Almelo the next evening, and be prepared to stay the night. Hugill's men found fuel and heated water; I had a long soak and slept in a bed. When I came down the next morning, the family and Hugill were at table waiting for me, and breakfast was fried K-ration from the modest store I'd brought; but the host was absent. When I said I had to get back to Division there was much pleading from the family, saying Father would be very upset if I left before his return; it then emerged that he was the town *Burgemeester*. I waited a little, then told them I could wait no longer; when I got out the door, however, I saw the *Burgemeester* half-way down the street, pulling a child's wagon at a trot, with its cargo being steadied by his young son: it was a case of Bols' Genever gin, which he presented to me with a little speech of gratitude for his town's liberation.

A few miles after Almelo we crossed back into Germany, where a huge peat bog confined vehicle movement to a single main road. We were opposed by 2nd Parachute Corps, which did not give ground easily; nevertheless, we didn't have a great deal of trouble crossing the Ems at Meppen on 8 April. In the next few days, however, two local battles took place whose aftermaths left me distinctly queasy. On 9 April we took the town of Sögel; after it was pronounced clear a squadron of divisional engineers, accompanied by a medical detachment and some signalmen, harboured in a field just outside the town. In the morning a mixed force of German paratroops and civilians suddenly attacked them, inflicting a number of casualties, some fatal. After help arrived and the enemy was driven off, neighbouring houses were found to contain large numbers of automatic weapons and quantities of ammunition. The engineers, enraged by the civilian participation, bulldozed the entire town, sparing only the church; officially the reason given was that 'to maintain the roads in reasonable condition 30,000 tons of rubble were needed immediately.' Then, on 14 April, the Argylls, after a stiff fight, had much of Friesoythe under control when a body of paratroops, again accompanied by civilians, attacked a house in which the CO, Lieutenant-Colonel Wigle, had established his temporary HQ, killing him. Again weapons were found in civilian houses and again the engineers, whose CO was a friend of Wigle's, bulldozed the town, this time 'to fill craters.'*

---

* The engineers' 'explanations' are given in a contemporary Corps of Engineers publication edited by M.O. Rollefson, *Green Route Up* (The Hague: Mouton, 1945), p. 86.

Although I too was upset by the death of Wigle, who had become my friend, I protested to the G1 that this kind of mass punishment for the actions of some was unjust; he said it had given a hostile population a necessary warning but that word would be put out not to do it again unless there were serious incidents.

On 12 April the U.S. president, Franklin Roosevelt, died. His death seems to have given the German forces opposite us new hope, and resistance at the next obstacle, the Kusten Canal, was fierce; it took us three days to bridge the canal and strike north. Resistance was lessening against both divisions on our flanks but remained stiff to the end on ours, perhaps to give the navy at the Wilhelmshaven base as much time as possible. We did not get into Bad Zwischenahn until 1 May, again after quite a struggle, and were on our way northeast when, at 1:00 P.M. on 4 May, we were told to cease offensive action in expectation of a surrender, confirmation of which came over the BBC that evening. We had known that it was bound to come soon, and the relief we felt when it came was enormous; nevertheless, there was a strange initial sense of dislocation, almost of loss: we were, for the time left us as a unit, an organism without a purpose.

Some weeks earlier I had responded to a request from Army for two volunteers to go to Ottawa to bring European battle experience to the Intelligence section of 6th Division, which was being formed to go to the Pacific (the prime minister had announced in the House of Commons on 4th April that all service in the Pacific would be strictly voluntary). In my application I'd stipulated that I would not leave 4th Division until the end of hostilities, and Robinson had drawn attention to this stipulation in approving it. Now, a few days after the German surrender, word arrived from Army that I'd been selected. Robinson tried to persuade me to stay, 'to enjoy the spoils of victory,' or, if I had no taste for that, he was sure that the GOC would recommend me for a senior post at Khaki College, which would be a good boost to my academic career. I explained that I wanted to get back to my wife and start again on raising a family, and that there could be no academic career until I'd finished my PhD. Then why did I want to go to the Pacific? I said that I didn't, but thought that, with Germany out of the war and the

United States able to concentrate entirely on the Pacific, Japan would be knocked out before the Canadian division could get there. He and Vokes recommended me for promotion to major, and this came through before I had to report for duty in Ottawa.

On 30 May I boarded the *Louis Pasteur*, then a hospital ship, and arrived in Halifax on 7 June. From there a special train got us to Toronto the next evening, where Lesley was waiting in a crush of people in the cavernous Queen Elizabeth Building in the Exhibition Grounds. We were to detrain at alphabetically designated stations, but when the train stopped the whole assembly surged forward. A certain wounded officer was expected at the 'S' door, and a crowd of his waiting friends pushed Lesley aside and formed an almost impenetrable semicircle there. I may have been a little physical pushing through to where Lesley was gesturing frantically, but I was too intent on reaching her to care: we had been married less than three years and separated almost two.

While in Toronto for a few days, I asked Woodhouse, now head of the English department, whether, if the war against Japan ended before the beginning of term and I was able to get out of the army, I could take up my suspended teaching fellowship while finishing my course requirements and taking the comprehensive examinations. He thought this a little ambitious but agreed. Then Lesley and I went to Winnipeg. I found my father a good deal aged, beginning to stoop, walking more slowly, hair almost white; he was only sixty-five, but Bert's death had hit him hard, and his subsequent anxiety for me, together with the cancer, had taken their toll as well. He was impatient to take us out to the farm, which was clearly a great source of support for him.

Walking around Winkler was instructive. People I met in the street, or who came to the store while I was there, usually felt they had to say something about some relative in the army (almost always a conscript) or the defeat of Germany, and their unease showed. Those who came to the house to greet me usually spoke about Bert's death and their relief that the war in Europe was over (the war against Japan meant little to them). No one mentioned the Canadian Nationalist Party, although a number of those I met on the street had been members or supporters; several people, watching me narrowly for my reaction, told me that Victor Unruh and Ed Penner (the 'Snake') had been drafted and Unruh killed (I did not ask how Jack Funk, still at home, had avoided conscription). Materially, the town had benefited from the war – strong markets for the countryside's produce and for labour – but there was much concern about future relations with the majority community (*die Englische*): the town had shown its hand when Germany's conquests were at their peak, and feared it would suffer in consequence.

After a few days in Toronto we went to Ottawa, where friends helped us find an apartment and I reported for duty at National Defence Headquarters. Within days, my suspicions about that place, shared by most men in the field, were confirmed: the number employed there was far greater than the volume of work warranted, ranks were inflated beyond reason, hours were short and energy output low. It was true that the war in Europe was over, but the occupation of Germany, the repatriation of surplus units, demobilization, and the dismantling of the huge forces apparatus were pressing matters, not to speak of the preparation of 6th Division for the Pacific; there was enough to keep a reasonable-sized staff busy, but the staff was not of reasonable size, and it worked at a pace that put me out of all patience.

My own task was never clearly defined. The 6th Division was to be part of a U.S. corps and organized to work in a U.S. framework, which seemed to limit the applicability of my field experience. Nevertheless, I spent my days going through reams of papers, some written with Army terseness but more with civil-service circumlocution and garrulity; I drew up memoranda of commentary or initiated my own suggestions, with less and less feeling that what I was doing had any reality. I'd been there only a month when, on 6 and 8 August, the atomic bombs were dropped; on the 10th, Japan sued for peace, and on the 14th hostilities ceased.

I at once applied for a discharge, asking that it be given in time for the beginning of the university year. Two or three weeks later Colonel W.W. Murray, the director of Military Intelligence, sent for me and suggested that I consider an alternative: my combination of field experience and academic training would qualify me for a very good career in the army, and he was prepared to recommend me for a senior position at Royal Military College. I thanked him but said I was a wartime soldier only and now that the war was over I wanted to get back as soon as possible to my interrupted academic career. I explained that University College had promised to reinstate my fellowship if I could get out for the beginning of term, and asked him to make it possible. In the end he agreed to expedite my discharge and, in the meanwhile, to post me to the Fort York barracks in Toronto with indefinite home leave; after reporting there I could go about my affairs, in uniform until the discharge came through. I thanked him warmly and left. I had won my gamble on an early end to the war in the Pacific.

CHAPTER FIVE

Toronto, 1945–1947

I resumed my teaching at University College as I had left it in 1942: in uniform. At that time my class had consisted largely of young women, with some youths under military age and a handful of males not subject to conscription; now it consisted entirely of demobilized service veterans, predominantly male. The administration and faculty of the university were very nervous about the advent of the 'returned men'; most professors had experienced or heard of the restlessness and indiscipline of the student veterans of the First World War, and fear of similar disruption was widespread. The Department of English decided to cope with this danger by streaming the veterans separately; perhaps it came to this decision because it had available two instructors who were themselves veterans, Murdo McKinnon and me. We were each assigned half of the total veteran enrolment in English, about 150, and warned about the dangers of permitting any kind of indiscipline.

These warnings reinforced my own concerns – I had heard a good deal about the veterans of 1918 at the University of Manitoba – and I entered my first class resolved to keep a tight rein. The uniform, and perhaps particularly the major's crown, created a palpable unease among these students recently released from the military hierarchy, which I tried to overcome by explaining that the uniform would go as soon as my demobilization came through, and I was, I think, given conditional exoneration. I had prepared a detailed schedule of lectures and assignments, and had been at least as painstaking in preparing my introductory lecture. By half-time I had the sense I wanted, that the class was interested and responding. A wonderful relief came over me: I'd been right to expedite my return from Germany, to decline Ottawa's offer of rank and position at RMC – this was what I was cut out for. I warmed to my work, buoyed by self-satisfaction; then a man in the front row yawned. It let some air out of my balloon, but I could detect no signs of boredom among the others and soon recovered my spirits; then he yawned again. This time I looked at him coldly but said nothing and finished the hour still satisfied with my first performance but robbed of the glow I'd had before the yawn.

At the second meeting the yawn was repeated several times. I was growing angry but restrained myself. At the third meeting I was tensed and waiting for it; when the yawn came I stopped, addressed the yawner, said I was sorry he was bored but his repeated yawning was disturbing me, and if he wasn't interested he was not to attend my class. The yawner flushed and looked down; there was an intense, almost breathless silence in the class. I resumed my lecture, aware of something unusual in the air. At the end of the hour the yawner came up and said he hadn't been bored – the yawn was an uncontrollable symptom of shell-shock.

I apologized to him, and the next day to the class, and the initial rapport was restored, aided a few days later by the retirement of the uniform. But I was troubled by the unwitting violence I'd done to a victim of war and took pains to tell the story in many places as a caution against too tight a rein and an antidote to the ubiquitous tales of post–First World War indiscipline.

Few members of faculty on overseas service had yet returned (some, like Bissell, spent the year in England teaching in the Army's Khaki College; Birney did broadcasts for the foreign service of the CBC). It may have been partly for this reason that the editors of *The University of Toronto Quarterly* selected me to review the first published history of the Canadian Army in the Second World War, Ross Munro's *Gauntlet to Overlord: The Story of the Canadian Army* (1945). Munro was a war correspondent who subsequently became editor and publisher of *The Winnipeg Tribune*; he had observed most of the operations he described, and my review credited him with an important and generally sound first account. But he had given inadequate treatment to some major operations and had been wrong about some others, and I set out to make up, at least in part, for some of these shortcomings; the result was a somewhat passionate eight-page review. I now wonder how the editors could afford me so much space, but I also recognize that that first review set a pattern which I followed with little deviation in many later reviews, usually copious and rarely detached, although as objective as I could make them. Certainly there was little detachment in my second review, or rather review article, also in the *UTQ*, and this time ten pages long, in which I set out to demolish the argument of Ralph Ingersoll's *Top Secret* (1946): that the British had played false with their allies in the war, deceiving, manipulating, and thwarting the Americans, who ultimately had to win the war despite the British.

In 1946 and 1947 I reviewed two more books about the war, this time in *The Canadian Forum*, and I began to feel that I was giving too much time to this, so I declined several further invitations, but I did agree to review Colonel C.P. Stacey's *The Canadian Army, 1939–1945* for *The International Journal* (1948). By that time I had left Canada, but Stacey was the head of the Army Historical Section, and although this was his personal book, published some years before he could bring out the Army's official history, I knew it would greatly influence the country's understanding of its participation in the war. It turned out to be a very good first report, and I treated it as such, but I was able from personal knowledge to correct the account of a few operations. I got a letter from Stacey expressing appreciation of the review and acceptance of the corrections, which he incorporated in the larger official history published a few years later.

The CBC invited me to be on a panel to discuss *Home-Made Banners*, a novel by Ralph Allen, a war correspondent who subsequently became editor of *Maclean's*. His was a novel with a theme: Canada's conscription law was unfair in that, until near the end, it required every conscript in effect to make a personal decision on whether to declare war, with devastating consequences to individuals and families, especially in Quebec. The panel would consist of Allen, Morley Callaghan, and myself. I was flattered to be on a panel with Callaghan, then one of the very few widely known Canadian authors, and accepted; I think the broadcast was reasonably successful.

There was some danger that I would spread myself too thin and I resolved not to be drawn into any further war-related enterprises. In particular, I determined not to participate in such organizations as the Intelligence Association or the Royal Regiment Association, although they offered the undeniable attraction of comradeship tested in battle; besides being time-consuming, they seemed to me to represent either some continuation of military commitment or the permanent backward look of those for whom the war would always be the big thing in their lives. I was strictly a wartime soldier, and I intended the gravamen of my life to lie in the future, not the past.

One event I did attend was an investiture of military honours conducted by the Governor General of Canada, Field-Marshal Lord Alexander, in Convocation Hall. I was summoned to receive the MBE, and after some reflection did a sentimental thing: instead of wearing uniform I wore a suit of Bert's. I was the only honours recipient in the Hall not in uniform and felt somewhat self-conscious about it. I observed the president of the university, Sidney Smith, in the gallery, beside the premier of Ontario, George Drew; Smith had known me in Manitoba, and after the ceremony he called me over and introduced me to the premier, who asked why I wasn't in uniform (he had been a colonel in the First World War). I explained that I felt that wearing my dead brother's suit gave him some role. The colonel was clearly unimpressed.

Besides teaching, I was taking two courses, preparing for my comprehensive examination and final language requirement, and getting my thesis restarted. One course was Knox's Drama to 1642, exclusive of Shakespeare. Since I had already taken Knox's Shakespeare course, I found little new in his approach, but the content of the course was largely new to me; I read avidly, did several seminar papers, and learnt a good deal.

The second course was J.R. MacGillivray's Keats and Shelley. MacGillivray was a shy, diffident man whom it was easy to overlook; I took his course because I had done no graduate work on the

Romantics. The course was as low-key as the man; the first fortnight was devoted entirely to bibliography and assignments, and even after his own presentations began MacGillivray seemed to expect the students to make the running. He was very patient and sympathetic during student papers, frequently offering bibliographical references but rarely personal opinions, and never displaying the sardonic wit which I encountered only when I became his colleague; a modest, gentle man, he kept his scholarship in reserve for suitable occasions.

I could get no useful advice on how to prepare for the comprehensive, other than to 'read a lot.' The exam would consist of two and a half days of written papers on all fields of English language and literature except the period of one's thesis, which was reserved for the thesis oral; each section would be set by one or more professors not identified to the candidate, and there were no copies available of earlier exams (there were, of course, some dark rumours); on the afternoon of the third day the examiners would go over with the candidate his or her answers, then determine the result. With no more to go on than this, I decided to cram Old and Middle English language, and for the rest simply to fill in the most important lacunae in my reading, so far as time allowed. I thought at the time that it was a very useful exercise in that I was deliberately trying, for an entire academic year, to relate every part of English literature to every other part and to the whole, and even today I think it was very educational.

But the actual questions showed an almost schizophrenic unevenness of approach, varying from broad questions drawing on one's general knowledge and understanding of a period, a movement, or an author, to questions of narrow detail such as might be suitable to test an undergraduate's alertness in reading a single prescribed text. At the time I attributed this variability to individual differences among the examiners, and doubtless that was an important factor, but as I study the papers now (some of them handwritten and identifiable) it seems to me that a more important factor was the lack of a common understanding in the department of what the exam was meant to discover; and this in turn derived from the department's failure to define the purpose of graduate work in English – something I did not fully realize until my return to the university many years later as graduate-dean designate, when I had to contend with this problem in many departments, among which English was prominent.

At the time, however, my displeasure about the exam I was given (as distinguished from the idea of the exam) was somewhat allayed by being told that I had done well, and I was further mollified by an invitation from Knox to a celebration at his house that evening, at which I found all the examiners. (It says something about the times that my wife wasn't invited, and indeed the only woman in sight was Mrs Knox, busy about refreshments.) I don't know why Knox gave this party for me; he had been the first chairman of the graduate committee of the department, but he had relinquished that position in 1944, and although PhD candidates in English came along pretty rarely at that time, it was not customary to celebrate their rites of passage. Knox had been in the First World War, and had been gassed; possibly my war service was a factor. At any rate, I was acutely aware of the honour and was enjoying it greatly, until F.E.L. Priestley said confidingly over a drink that he could have marked my paper more severely but had chosen not to. I asked him what was wrong with my paper, and he replied evasively in dog-Latin, 'hiati in scriptus,' which left me little the wiser.

Priestley had been appointed in 1944, while I was away, and at first there was an element of caution in our relations, largely overcome by a foolish incident. As a part-time instructor I'd been assigned a ground-floor office where the English staircase opened onto the cloister; there was heavy traffic in this part of the cloister because it led to the Junior Common Room, the cafeteria, and the path to Hart House. Students often stopped there, chatting just outside my window and disturbing my work, so after a while I put a card in my window reading, 'Please do not gather here, seminar in progress.' This had some effect, but one day two young men, presumably undergraduates, stood there talking rather loudly, as if in contempt of the sign. I went to the open window, pointed to the sign, and asked them to desist; they said something insulting; I whipped out of my office, burst out of the heavy door leading to the cloister, found the two had begun to run, and took out after them. At that time there was an iron fence on what is now the site of the Laidlaw Library; the youths jumped it and headed across the back campus, and I quit the pursuit. I have no idea what I'd have done had I caught the two strapping young men; it is true that I was in good physical shape and had been trained in unarmed combat, but I would certainly not have used such dangerous methods in this situation. Perhaps I would have demanded their student numbers in order to lodge a complaint, but they would have been unlikely to give them; in any case I had enough sense to be glad the fence gave me an opportunity to escape from a silly situation. When I turned to go back, I found Priestley standing in the cloister; he had witnessed the incident with delight, was enthusiastic about my aggressive response to provocation, and for weeks told everyone the story, suggesting that I be put in charge of student discipline or be made dean of residence. He told my children the story when we met at a road-house near Banff in the 1970s, and reminded me and others of it at the last UC Principal's Reception he attended shortly before his death, more than forty years after the incident took place.

When I asked the designated examiner in French, whose name I no longer recall, how to prepare for the exam, he recommended that I read La Fayette's *La Princesse de Clèves* and practise translating passages into English. On one of E.K. Brown's visits to Toronto, he suggested that I read the Bible in French. I spent many hours during the winter, after the day's other work was done, with these two books and the occasional journal article, taking a chance that I would remember enough grammar from my undergraduate French course to scrape by. The exam, while more formal than the one in German, turned out to be equally oriented toward potential scholarly use, and I did well enough.

My teaching took more time than a more experienced instructor would give. I was again assigned the first year of the Pass Course, a miscellany of literary texts drawn from most periods and covering most genres. It seemed to me thin gruel, particularly in comparison with the rich diet provided by the Honour Course, the university's special pride, and I was giving it to a class of veterans who seemed to me to deserve better; so I prepared a fairly extensive historical and critical introduction to each text, followed by as detailed an analysis of the text itself as the class schedule would allow. I was satisfied with the class's response, but dismayed at the amount of my time it took. When added to the time needed for the courses I was taking, and what I allowed in preparation for the comprehensive, it left very little for the thesis. I was able to identify a number of promising Puritan Revolution and Civil War pamphlets and get some of them in microfilm from American libraries (the war-disrupted British Museum would be unable to respond to such requests for some time yet), but I made little other progress during term.

On our return to Toronto at war's end Lesley and I had gone to live with her parents until we could find a place of our own. I joined in the search but couldn't give it much time, and the task fell largely to Lesley. She ran down what leads we could get, but for some time they all petered out. Finally she located an affordable apartment in a suitable building. The superintendent confirmed that it would fall vacant at the end of the month and agreed to hold it for her until evening, when I could see it. I liked it and said we would take it. The superintendent then peered at me very closely and asked whether I was Jewish. I said yes. 'We don't take Jews,' he said. I thought of the evening in the London pub when the thug had tried to lure Bert and me into a fight and what Bert had said afterward: that after the war he was never going to stand for anti-semitic shit. I thought of making an issue of it but couldn't see how to do so; it would be decades before anti-discrimination laws were adopted anywhere in Canada. We just walked away, feeling awful.

In the end we found a house on Alcina Avenue whose ground floor had been subdivided into two flats sharing a bathroom; despite that inconvenience, we took the apartment. The occupants of the back apartment were a clerical couple, he an Anglican priest and she a deaconess. We found that, when our alarm clock went off in the morning, they would rush into the bathroom before we could get there, and the wait upset my schedule until I devised a simple scheme: I set my alarm a half-hour early, listened to the clerics rush to do their ablutions, dozed off for another half-hour, then shaved at the time I'd intended. After some time the back-

apartment dwellers seemed to catch on and tried waiting a bit, but then I whipped in first. The game continued for some months, when they completed their academic program and departed. Robert F. McRae, an instructor in philosophy who, as an ex-POW, had also been returned to Canada early, was looking for an apartment; I showed him our set-up and he took the back apartment. There were no more contests for the bathroom.

Just down the block lived Professor E.T. Owen, of Classics, to whom Innis had introduced me at the Faculty Club. We had bought a second-hand car, and when I used it to go to work I often offered Owen a lift. We became quite friendly; his major interest was the Greek epic, and my interest in Milton gave us quite a lot in common. Of course he knew vastly more than I did, but occasionally he would ask something about English epic tradition.

Another man to whom Innis introduced me was Albert W. Trueman, who was visiting Toronto shortly after taking up appointment as president of the University of Manitoba. Innis thought Trueman could pick up useful information about Manitoba from me, and I did my best to be helpful. However, since Trueman 'resigned' the presidency three years later (in 1970 the man who had been chairman of the board of governors at Manitoba at the time boasted to me that he had fired Trueman), I have to conclude that our discussion didn't do much good. I've reflected since that both my luncheon companions that day would be my predecessors in one or other appointment.

I had a somewhat disillusioning exerience with Barker Fairley. He had during the war appointed as an instructor in German a middle-aged refugee German economist of socialist sympathies named Rudolf Coper. Coper was glad to teach German as a way to make a living in a new country, but he sought opportunity to do work in his own discipline, and was successful in getting B.K. Sandwell's *Saturday Night* to publish his articles from time to time. One of these articles was judged by somebody on the board of governors to be dangerously leftist, and Fairley was summoned to see the university president, Sidney Smith. He returned to tell Coper that he was hired as a language teacher and must not publish on economics or politics. Coper, alone in a strange land, had struck up an acquaintance with me and now asked my advice. I read the article and told him I thought it well within the bounds of public discussion in a free country, but that since he was in Canada as a refugee I hesitated to suggest resistance, whereupon he asked me whether I'd speak to Fairley on his behalf. I doubted the usefulness of this but couldn't refuse. Fairley, who may have felt vulnerable because of his own leftist position, said that there was nothing he could do: it was the president's decision. When I reported this to Coper he asked whether I'd speak to the president. This made me uncomfortable but again I didn't feel I could refuse, and after advising Fairley of my intention I got an appointment with Smith, who had only recently become president. He received me warmly enough, but when I stated my errand the temperature dropped. Ever the politician, he said something about the university's vulnerability and the need for the country's guests to observe limits. I was not surprised the next year when Coper told me he was moving to the United States.

I received an invitation from G.B. Harrison, the prominent Shakespeare editor then head of the Queen's University English department, to come for an interview, and another from the University of Western Ontario, where I was, I thought strangely, interviewed by the dean, not the department head. Both interviews led to job offers, which I reported to Woodhouse. It turned out that he already knew about them and was ready for me. He said that the department was pleased with my work as a teaching fellow and wanted to keep me; its starting salary for full-time instructors without the PhD was $2,000, but he had obtained the principal's approval to offer me $2,200, which he knew was not quite as much as Queen's would pay, but he thought I'd be better off here; he thought that in considering matters I ought to consult with Fulton Anderson, who had succeeded Brett as head of the Department of Philosophy. I didn't ask why but said I would.

When I went to see Anderson he too seemed ready for me. I told him the particulars and said I didn't know why Woodhouse had suggested I consult him. He didn't reply to this but after some other questions asked whether I was Jewish. When I said I was, he replied, 'That won't be a problem here, but it would be at

Queen's or Western.' I thanked him and, a day or two later, accepted Woodhouse's offer. I had always meant to stay in Toronto if I could, and the chief value for me of the other offers was to get the Toronto offer forward quickly. I didn't understand the reference to Anderson until I learnt later that he had just arranged to appoint a Jewish philosophy instructor at Harvard, David Savan, to his department; perhaps Woodhouse thought that Anderson would tell me this and that it would influence my decision: if I accepted the Toronto offer I might still be the sole Jewish member of a Canadian department of English, but I would not be the only Jewish faculty member of University College.

At a time when Jews have been freely accepted at all levels of Canadian universities, it may be hard to regain a sense of the difficulty of these first appointments, but it can be illustrated; among many examples, I give two told me by the persons involved and for which there is available evidence. When Leon Edel returned to Montreal with his Sorbonne doctorate, already well started on the Henry James studies which were to make him famous, he applied to the English department of every Canadian university but was unable to get a job and had to emigrate to the United States.* Bora Laskin, who would one day become the chief justice of the Supreme Court of Canada, tried for several years to gain appointment to the U of T Department of Law before succeeding in 1940, in wartime conditions. In a two-page handwritten letter whose tone and late date (21 September) indicate that it was in reply to presidential uneasiness, W.P.M. Kennedy, the department head, told President Cody that, at his demand, Laskin had '*categorically made*' a 'declaration' that he had no connection with communism or any subversive movement and 'repeated it in the presence of a witness.' Kennedy 'had made all the private inquiries possible' and was confident that 'Laskin is a loyal British subject and ... will not disgrace the University.'† There was no mention to me of a special loyalty declaration, possibly because of my war record, possibly because security didn't seem as important in Literature as in Law.

---

* Interview with Edel, *The Globe and Mail*, 11 May 1989
† U of T Archives A680006/046/03

I did not wait for my appointment to be approved before telling Woodhouse of my dissatisfaction with the Pass Course curriculum. I no longer recall the particulars of my complaint, but Woodhouse took it seriously enough to meet one evening at his house with Knox, MacGillivray, McKinnon, and me. I put forward my criticisms and suggestions for improvement; after some discussion of substance Woodhouse explained the complexities, especially that curricular change required approval not only by the UC department but also by the departments of the other colleges (the Combined Departments of English) and by the Faculty of Arts and Science, and suggested that perhaps the matter might be allowed to mature for a while. I was convinced, however, that my students were not getting a satisfactory introduction to literature, and pressed my point. Some slight agreement became discernible in the room, and in the end Woodhouse said he'd bring it before a departmental meeting. I was not as yet a member of the department but I was invited to attend and put my case; a portion of my proposed modification was recommended to the Combined Departments, and an even smaller portion was ultimately approved, and the next year I had the satisfaction of teaching a slightly improved course. It was not a very significant improvement, but the partial success may have reinforced my tendency to put forward my views even while aware of being junior in rank or new on the scene.

The department's planning for the following year assumed the return of Bissell but not of Birney, and I ventured to ask Woodhouse about this. He said that Birney wanted too much, that 'we can't compete with the CPR.' It was, of course, the CBC that Birney was working for, a very different matter, but I gathered from Woodhouse's tone that the issue was closed. Later, when Birney, then living in Montreal, visited Toronto, I asked him about this and he said the issue had been seniority as well as money. Woodhouse had proposed to rank him below Priestley, which he thought very unfair, since his initial appointment, in 1936, predated Priestley's by eight years, and when he had left the department in 1943 on active military service it was on the understanding, general at the time, that on his return he would not be put at disadvantage because of his enlistment. But that understanding had been reached with a different head of department, and Woodhouse, who said he was willing to have him back, insisted on Priestley's seniority. I was surprised that Birney, who was of a combative temperament, didn't appeal. Perhaps he did, unsuccessfully (there was a new principal, too, and a new president); possibly he really preferred an alternative career in broadcasting, although he told me he'd have returned to UC if his seniority had been respected. I have always understood Woodhouse's action to be based on several factors: I gathered that he had promised Priestley a certain place in the departmental establishment; he felt that Birney didn't fit the department he intended to fashion; and he disliked him personally. I was, however, a little surprised by his ruthlessness.

At the end of term, having met all other requirements, I was in the situation now generally known as 'ABD' (all but dissertation). I had, of course, to prepare to teach three courses beginning in September, but I thought I could make a significant start on my thesis. I found that it was slower work than I thought, chiefly because the paucity of library holdings made it take far longer than it should have for the pattern I was seeking to emerge.

Milton's first systematic use of the idea of natural law was in the divorce tracts (1643–5). The general Protestant view was that the Gospel restricted the grounds of divorce to adultery, the earlier permission of divorce for incompatibility having been part of the Mosaic judicial law abrogated by Christ. Milton's argument is that this permission is in fact part of the unabrogated moral law, having its source not in specifically Jewish circumstances but in universal equity. It is a consequence of the 'secondary law of nature' and is therefore applicable without exception to fallen man. (The 'primary law of nature' is the rule of perfection for man before the Fall; the 'secondary law of nature' is that part of the primary law still accessible to the reason of fallen man.) The use of this theory is not here primarily political, but Milton reminds his audience, generally supporters of the parliamentary side in the Civil War, that Parliament's position is that all civil affairs belong to the jurisdiction of natural law.

The Tenure of Kings and Magistrates (1649), written to support the deposition and execution of Charles I, makes the law of nature the basis of a theory of the origin of the state and the source, function, and responsibility of political authority. Originally, all men were naturally free. The consequences of the Fall, however, necessitated a social contract creating the community. The community, in turn, deputed one of its members to administer natural justice. Later, to restrict his abuse of this power, it promulgated laws defining justice and made the authority of the king conditional upon his observance of the law. It also created a number of subordinate magistrates to assist the king in administering the law and to prevent him from evading it. The authority of both principal and subordinate magistrates was and remains delegated and revocable; the inalienable natural rights of every member of the community reside in the community as a whole, and the people are therefore the ultimate sovereign power in the state, free, if they wish, to rewrite the laws and change the government.

The *Eikonoklastes* (later in 1649) repeats much of this argument, but introduces a new emphasis on the role of the subordinate magistrates (Parliament). Apparently because of its representative nature, Parliament is in effect the people, possessing absolute legislative supremacy and wielding the whole popular sovereignty. Alongside this thoroughly naturalistic conception of the state, however, there are a number of suggestions of a very different conception, which is clarified in the *Defence of the English People* (1651). In reply to the royalist defence of the right of the king, this document contains a complete and detailed reiteration of the naturalistic argument leading to the right of Parliament, but in reply to the more immediately damaging argument that it was not Parliament which had executed Charles but a minority disposing of the military power, the *Defence* introduces the doctrine that 'the sounder part,' the minority of the regenerate, possess the right to execute the will of God.

The Second Defence (1654) is based entirely on this theocratic conception of the state (the few reminiscences of the earlier conception are not pressed). But *Of Civil Power* (1659), whose object is the disestablishment of the church, returns to the naturalistic theory of the state, insisting that the magistrate's authority and duties are human, not Christian. There is some ambivalence on this subject in Milton's other pamphlets of that year, and more in *The Ready and Easy Way* (1660), whose analysis is precisely that of the first *Defence*. To oppose the right of the monarchy there is a secular view of the state leading from the law of nature to the supremacy of the majority of the House of Commons, but to justify the continuance of an unpopular Commonwealth there is a theocratic view of the state which asserts the supremacy of the minority of the House because they are the regenerate.

Barker, who was the first to analyse the inconsistencies of Milton's thought in something like this way, explained it in terms of confusion: Milton failed to recognize that the naturalistic view which he propounded in the days of his optimism could not be reconciled with his fundamental goal, 'a sovereign power which would ensure the establishment and protection of true religion as he saw it.'* In many conversations he described it to me as the inability or unwillingness of a great poet to deal with the mundane frustrations of politics. The very detailed argumentation of the political tracts did not read that way to me, and I turned to the other contemporary defenders of the Puritan Revolution to see whether a more likely explanation could be found.

During the first Civil War all the major component groups of the parliamentary coalition – Presbyterians, Erastians, and Independents or Congregationalists – based their political theory on the idea of natural law, in opposition to the divine-right theory propounded by the King. There was disagreement about certain particulars, but all agreed that the existing constitution must be interpreted in the light of the law of nature, and that that law placed sovereignty in the people and vested active supremacy in the Parliament.

After the end of the war, however, there emerged on the left of the victorious parliamentary coalition a group, known as 'the Levellers,' holding that the existing constitution deviated so far from the law of nature as to be wholly invalid, that the supremacy it

---

* Arthur Barker, *Milton and the Puritan Dilemma, 1641–1660* (Toronto: University of Toronto Press, 1942), p. 127

vested in the Parliament was as much a usurpation as was the prerogative of the King, and that a new constitution, which would respect the natural rights of all citizens, must be drawn from the law of nature by the sovereign people itself. A basis for cooperation between this radical group and the army was developed in the increasingly critical struggle between the predominantly Independent army with the predominantly Presbyterian Parliament. The army did not altogether repudiate the existing constitution (indeed, its last-moment refusal to do so, after having given its allies the impression of willingness, became the ground of its final break with the Levellers), but it several times coerced Parliament, justifying its actions by the argument that parliamentary supremacy was only a secondary consequence of the ultimate natural sovereignty of the people and became no more than a void form unless it subserved the primary dictate of the law of nature, common safety.

When the army leaders and their parliamentary allies had executed the King and established the Commonwealth, they found themselves hard-pressed to develop a rational defence against simultaneous attacks from right and left. The Presbyterians joined the defeated Anglicans in accusing them of violating the constitution; the government reply was, of course, based on the law of nature. But, retorted the Levellers and the even more radical Diggers, the natural sovereignty of the people can mean only rule by, or at least on behalf of, the majority, while the Commonwealth was manifestly opposed by the majority. To this the government could find no other reply than the theocratic doctrine of the 'sounder part.' Until the Restoration, government polemic was never able to recover from this extraordinary ambivalence. At the dictate of circumstance and tactics, government political theory alternated fairly regularly between a naturalistic constitutional conception of the state and a theocratic conception.

When I compared Milton's political theory with this new analysis of Puritan government polemic, I found a very close correspondence. During the first Civil War there is only incidental application to politics of his theory of natural law; such application is general, corresponds exactly to the theory shared by all the component elements of the parliamentary coalition, and stops short of those areas where differences among them exist. After these differences have grown great enough to be divisive, Milton supports (although sometimes with certain differences of theory) whichever group dominates the Revolution until the final dissolution of the Rump Parliament; he does this although it means that his political theory suffers from ambiguity, fundamental inner contradiction, and repeated reversal – weaknesses frequently and gleefully pointed out by the polemicists for the other side.

This suggested that the difficulties encountered in the analysis of Milton's use of the law of nature, which were not explicable in terms of development and which I thought could not be due to confusion, and which were the same ones as beset government polemic in general, were soluble in terms of tactics. I erected the hypothesis that Milton's use of the law of nature was determined by the ends he wished to serve, and that these ends were, first, that England should be Christian (as he understood that term) and, second, that England should, within the limits imposed by the primary end, be a free society. This made it possible to provide a reasonable and detailed explanation of the tortuous history of his political theory.

I did not, of course, get this far during the summer of 1946, but I had got far enough to be fairly confident of the pattern that was emerging. Therefore when E.K. Brown, on one of his visits, asked how my thesis was coming, I told him that, although very little was written, I thought I knew where it would go, and sketched in the pattern that I thought was emerging. On another visit the following year he asked again, and particularly wanted to know when I thought I could finish. By this time I was well launched into my first year of full-time teaching and could assess what free time I would have for the thesis, so I said I ought to finish after two more summers, that is, by the end of the summer of 1948. He then talked about the University of Chicago, where he had gone from Cornell, and asked me whether I'd be interested in seeing it. I knew very little about it except for its general reputation as a great academic centre which had abandoned football and was the home of the first nuclear reactor, the *Encyclopaedia Britannica,* the 'Great Books,' and

Robert M. Hutchins; and of course in my studies I'd used Manly's work on Chaucer, Hulbert's on Spenser, Williamson's on the Metaphysicals and T.S. Eliot, and Crane's on the eighteenth century; for me it was suffused in glamour, and I instantly said yes. A few weeks later, when the invitation to an interview arrived and I informed Woodhouse, he seemed, as usual, to be aware of it – not surprisingly, since Brown was his closest friend.

The University of Chicago made a strong if mixed first impression on me. The splendid Midway, a block-wide park-like strip almost a mile long inherited from the World's Columbian Exposition of 1893, marked what was then the southern border of the campus; fronting it was a long series of neo-Gothic buildings detailed like late-medieval fortresses; the Midway lawns being sunken, with steep slopes leading to the university buildings, the impression of a campus built to withstand siege was irresistible. (Later, particularly during the political witch-hunts of the 1950s, I came to think that impression quite appropriate.) The Gothic theme continued to the north, but here there was a scattered infill of buildings in various contemporary styles, yielding a somewhat risible effect and making me wonder whether it reflected the academic situation, for of course I'd heard the jibe that the University of Chicago was a place where Protestant students were taught Roman Catholic philosophy by Jewish professors.

The interviewing committee consisted of Ronald Crane, the chairman of the department; George Williamson, the senior seventeenth-century scholar; Napier Wilt, the senior person in American literature; and Brown. I thought it wonderful that four senior professors would be used to interview as junior a person as me; it was my first indication of the collegiality of decision making, as well as the seriousness of appointments, at the university. Crane started things off by asking me about my thesis, and displayed enough familiarity with the matters covered by it to ask good questions. Williamson put some very particular questions about the poetry of my period. Wilt asked about some eighteenth-century writers and, experimentally, some Americans. Brown waited until the others seemed finished and then asked when my thesis would be completed and whether some form of publication was likely. Throughout the interview I felt very comfortable and spoke in my own terms, making no effort to guess what the questioners wanted; indeed, I may have lectured a little, always a weakness of mine.

Afterward I was taken to the faculty club, called the Quadrangle Club, for lunch, where the conversation became very general. I recall being startled and impressed when Wilt said that there were four Nobel laureates eating at neighbouring tables; coming from Canada, where to that time only one Nobel prize had been awarded, I saw this as symbolizing the academic distance between Chicago and the universities I'd known. I also learnt that Hulbert would retire in a year, leaving no one in the department interested in teaching Spenser (whom he had, in any case, not taught recently), that Williamson no longer much liked teaching Milton, and that the recent departure to Princeton of Gerald E. Bentley left the department with no senior person in Renaissance drama.

I had a brief meeting with Clarence Faust, the dean of the undergraduate college; we had a pleasant but rather general conversation, during which he described the distinctive nature of the college but said little about its relation with the graduate divisions. I got the distinct impression that if there was a joint invitation the college would be going along with a departmental initiative and that the primary responsibility for future decisions about me would rest with the department. Brown later confirmed this view.

Not long after my visit I received a letter from Crane offering me a three-year appointment, once renewable, as assistant professor in the college and in the graduate Department of English, at a starting salary of $4,000. In the college I would teach the second year of Humanities, and in English I would offer courses of my own devising in the literature of the sixteenth and seventeenth centuries, including Milton.

This seemed like heaven to me and I wanted to accept at once (Lesley was in favour), but I knew it was not right to do so until I'd spoken to Woodhouse. Again, he knew what was coming and asked me to wait a day or two. The next day he said he'd received permission from the principal to offer me $2,600 instead of the $2,400 he'd had in his budget, and that Barker and Frye, with whom he shared the Spenser–Milton honours course, had agreed to make it a four-way split to include me; graduate work would come after I'd got the doctorate and had some publication. I appreciated his offer and thanked him for it, but pointed out that if Toronto wanted to keep me it was despite my field, in which it was very strong, whereas Chicago wanted me because of it, which made an enormous difference; I would be sad to leave Toronto and might one day want to return, but Chicago's invitation was too good to reject. He warned me that the Chicago appointment was perilous: if I wasn't promoted by the end of the second three-year period I'd be let go, whereas in Toronto I'd be secure. I thought that that was part of the trouble with Toronto: the stimulus of fear was lacking; but I said only that since there was an open field for me in Chicago and only a crowded one in Toronto I would go to Chicago.

I was at that time sharing an office with Bissell, who told Marshall McLuhan, newly arrived at the university, that I would be going to Chicago. McLuhan, whom I had barely met, arrived in my office and plumped a thick typescript down on my desk. 'Read that,' he commanded, 'and it will tell you why you shouldn't go to Chicago.' The previous summer he had visited the University of Chicago to help Cleanth Brooks, who had, after a stint there as visiting professor, been invited by Hutchins to tell him what needed change. McLuhan, who at Cambridge had studied the medieval and Renaissance traditions of education, wrote a report denouncing the deans at Chicago as 'dialecticians' and recommending that Hutchins hire him and some friends to reorganize the University to emphasize 'rhetoric and grammar.' He was blatantly preaching for a call; he didn't get it and was sore. 'Don't go,' he said; 'you'll be a humanist lost in a scholastic jungle.' I found his analysis of the Chicago curriculum divorced from actuality and his report self-serving, an early impression that helped insulate me from his more egregious assertions and demands in later years, when I had some responsibility for administering his work.

CHAPTER SIX

Chicago, 1947–1962

I

Almost the first thing I learnt on reaching Chicago in the fall of 1947 was that the department had changed chairmen; it was now Napier Wilt. I expressed some concern, since it had been Crane who appointed me, but Brown replied that the change was for the better – the department had become too cliquish and inbred under Crane. There were no negative implications for me, he said; Wilt had participated in the decision to invite me.

In the weeks that followed, I pieced together the story. Crane had made his initial reputation in the philological and bibliographic tradition, in which he had trained a generation of eighteenth-century scholars, some of whom he had given appointments in the department; two of them were now associate professors. But during the 1930s, in part because of the influences of Hutchins and the philosophers Mortimer Adler and Richard McKeon, Crane's interest shifted wholly to criticism, with Aristotle as his main guide. Thereafter he directed only critical dissertations, ensuring that all his advanced students also took courses from McKeon, and as these protégés took their degrees he gave some of them appointments in the department, aided by McKeon, who was dean of the Humanities Division; two were now associate professors and one an assistant professor. This group, together with some Crane–McKeon products appointed to the college and to other universities, constituted what was called the 'Chicago school' or the 'Neo-Aristotelian critics.'

The 'Aristotelians' were aggressive, and it was implied that the departures of Bentley and David Daiches were related to their increasing dominance. The rest of the department, including the earlier generation of Crane students, had decided against a further renewal of Crane's chairmanship and chose Wilt, who was not a publishing scholar but was a product of the department and a successful teacher not much embroiled in controversy. The department was left in an uneasy condition: a dethroned but still potent faction united by a common approach and personal ties, with the rest of the department distributed among many approaches and fields.

I found that I was one of an intake of five new assistant professors, the only one without a completed doctorate. One of the others provided a sobering note: he came to Chicago from Yale, which had let him go after two three-year terms. It was against the odds that all of us would be promoted six years hence, especially since two other assistant professors had been appointed in the previous two years.

In the college, which did not have a departmental structure, I learnt at my first interview with Russell Thomas, the chairman of Humanities II, that there was a weekly meeting of the staff to discuss how the successive texts should be taught. The idea was repellent to me and seemed wildly inconsistent with the complete freedom afforded by the English department, but I was assured by Thomas, an avuncular man without a departmental appointment, that the intent was not to prescribe a teaching method but only to achieve a common understanding of what each text was attempting, a common definition of its organizing principle, so that the students of the various sections could fairly be given a common examination. I was not much reassured, but there was nothing for it except to await the first meeting. Meanwhile, I was assigned office space in Cobb Hall, which I shared that year with another new appointee, William H. McNeill, and a visiting professor, Alan Tate. Tate was the first member of the 'Southern Renaissance' I'd met; I'd read some of his work and looked forward to his presence, but he didn't spend much time in the office and I never got to know him well.

McNeill, who was to become a leading historian of Western civilization, had a joint appointment with the Department of History, and we saw a good deal of each other. He was a protégé of Arnold Toynbee and had arrived from an extended stay at the Royal Institute of International Affairs, in London. I promptly told him of my reservations about the Spenglerian tone and the religious revivalism of Toynbee's *Study of History*, which he took in good part.

The English department did not assign office space to me because I was being given space in the college; like other joint appointments I was to use Wieboldt 101, the departmental meeting-room, for student interviews. There were many disadvantages to this arrangement for me, but one compensation was that it was where visiting creative writers did their interviewing; that term it was Nelson Algren, with whom I went out for coffee several times.

The Chicago degree program was unique: two years in the college after a Grade Twelve matriculation for the bachelor's, three years thereafter in one of the graduate divisions for the master's, and a minimum further residence of two years for the doctorate (students entering a graduate division with four-year bachelor's degrees from other universities spent three years for the doctorate). The calendar year was divided into four academic quarters, of which three constituted a normal load; this resulted in a much longer academic year than the Canadian but, since courses were ordinarily limited to a single quarter, much shorter courses.

I had two difficulties with this: I had trouble adjusting my notion of what should be covered in a course, and I would get a much shorter research period at the end of the year than in Toronto. In the department my first-quarter course was Spenser and Milton, and I assigned far too much work. Not many students enrolled for the course, and of those who did several dropped out after the first meeting when they saw the reading list. I was a little crestfallen but soldiered on, and was encouraged when two or three of the dropouts returned after a week. I was, however, slow to adapt, despite being unable to cover all the assigned material in the fall quarter; in the winter quarter, when I offered sixteenth- and seventeenth-century prose texts, I tried to cut down but again assigned more than could be managed in reasonable depth. Even in the spring quarter, when I offered non-Shakespearean Renaissance drama, I still assigned rather too many plays, although by then I had cut down severely on my list of secondary sources.

In the college, on the other hand, the syllabus was fixed and there was no assigned secondary reading; my problem was to fit into a program that proved much less congenial than I'd anticipated. On paper the college idea had looked very good: a two-year liberal education introducing students to the objectives and methods of all major branches of learning, after which those who wanted more depth in any field would enter a departmental program. The first staff meeting did not seem so bad; the opening text was to be Plato's *Symposium*, and the discussion seemed well suited to its analysis: what was Socrates attempting? what were his methods? how successful was he? My anxiety about the pursuit of a common approach receded somewhat and I enjoyed my first few weeks.

But when we moved from philosophy to history, fiction, and drama, the staff meetings grew more troublesome. It became apparent that for the core of the staff the questions which I had thought related specifically to Platonic dialogues were intended for all texts, and when I suggested more attention to the *matter* of Herodotus (the first of the history texts) they were aghast. There was little support for my opinion on that occasion, but similar discussions recurred with later texts and a few of the other joint appointments gave me modest support; together, we won a little leeway to introduce context.

My students, who were by and large pretty bright, seemed to accept these partial departures from college orthodoxy, but I think some of the more ideological staff members saw them in the light of the tension, about which I was at first ignorant, between the college and the graduate divisions. I only gradually learnt that the college program had been established by Hutchins and his supporters largely against the wishes of the departments, many of which remained sceptical of it. This distance was greatest in the hard sciences (Enrico Fermi was said to 'abhor' the college approach to teaching physics: 'they want to discuss how Galileo thought, but not teach what he thought about'),* least in the social sciences, and intermediate in the humanities. Joint appointments were consequently most frequent in the social sciences.

Another discomfort rose out of the continued need to teach translated texts which I could not read in the original. The theory of teaching in translation did not trouble me, but I felt inadequate when I couldn't ascertain the original meaning myself. It was said that Daiches had argued with one of the leading Neo-Aristotelians about the use to which the latter had put a key term of the *Poetics*, *catharsis*, but when he found that the Neo-Aristotelian relied entirely on translations Daiches said he couldn't argue the meaning with someone who knew no Greek. That was cited in the college as evidence of ridiculous pedantry, but it made good sense to me, since the dispute was about meaning. In a course intended as an introduction to the arts and sciences of Western civilization, many texts were in languages I couldn't read.

In the department, on the other hand, my discomfort was not with how things were taught – one learnt little about how others taught – but with what was not taught. The department didn't at that time offer courses in the history of English literature, nor did it require that candidates for advanced degrees cover the major fields within English. It seemed wrong to me that PhDs in English should not have general knowledge of the canon, and at a departmental meeting in which the curriculum was under discussion I raised the issue. The chairman explained that, when candidates proposed their lists for the seventy-five-book oral examination (which in Chicago served roughly the same purpose as the comprehensives in Toronto), the supervisor made an effort to secure reasonable distribution across fields. It was also suggested that coverage was an undergraduate responsibility, but when I argued that while that might be expected in other universities it didn't correspond at all to what was done in our college, and that the first two years of departmental work really were undergraduate, it became clear that the department had never fully clarified the curricular

---

* Edward Shils, *Remembering the University of Chicago* (Chicago: University of Chicago Press, 1991), p. 123

problems posed by admission from such very different preparations as that in our own college and conventional university programs. When I then suggested that, as we required students to have had or to take a course in Shakespeare, we expand that requirement to include one or two other writers of overwhelming importance, there was no support, and I desisted, but resolved to return to the issue on some later occasion.

For by that time I knew I wanted to stay. I no longer had much enthusiasm for the college and was increasingly troubled by its separateness from the graduate divisions, but I became steadily more appreciative of the department and the Humanities Division. Virtually everyone in the department, from established scholar to neophyte, was actively at work on some project intended for publication, usually with much shorter planned deadlines than prevailed in Toronto; the result was a livelier, more intense environment. It was also inevitably more competitive, since there were always more probationary appointments than tenured openings, whereas in Toronto initial appointments were usually made to meet long-term as well as immediate needs. This competitiveness led to tension and some sharp oppositions as junior members competed for tenure, middle ranks for promotion, seniors for influence, and all ranks for salary, but I thought the price worth paying for the greater intensity.

The department had lost a number of prominent scholars to death, retirement, and resignation, but there were still many men (at that time, the department had no women) of quality and reputation. Most important for me, of course, was Brown, in whose scholarship, critical acumen, and energy I had great faith, and whose friendship had brought me to the university. Hulbert was about to retire; of those continuing, Williamson's field was closest to mine and I knew his reputation to be fully deserved. Crane had formidable learning and an impressive intellect, and it seemed likely that his political setback would cause him to concentrate more fully on his critical writing. Another critic of wide reputation was Morton Zabel, still quite active. Wilt did not publish much, but he had built a reputation on attracting and supervising many excellent students of American literature, some of whom were actively publishing. Walter Blair, the other senior professor wholly in American literature, published a good deal and was a growing influence in the field.

At the associate-professor level, the two first-generation Crane products, Donald Bond and Arthur Friedman, were each well launched on important eighteenth-century editions, having given published evidence of their scholarly competence; and the two new-generation Craneites, Norman Maclean and Elder Olson, were aggressive and energetic, Olson with a national reputation as poet and critic, and Maclean with a growing, not entirely local, reputation as teacher and critic. One of the senior assistant professors, James Cunningham, was also a published poet and critic, as well as an aspiring Shakespearean; the other, Rea Keast, was another new-generation Craneite with some publication. The new intake were becoming assessable: James Sledd was a linguist and lexicographer of unquestionable credentials and great energy; Robert Streeter, in American literature, was doing sound and judicious scholarship; Theodore Silverstein, who had not been kept by Yale, claimed great medieval erudition and would probably publish; a fourth seemed out of his class; I was the fifth and intended to do my share.

What had become clear to me was that the *raison d'être* of the department was graduate teaching and research, but that this did not necessitate severance from undergraduate teaching. It was a very different environment from Toronto's, where the primary task and basis of appointment was clearly undergraduate teaching, with graduate teaching a burdensome reward for those who wanted it and had done some publishing. There were certainly people in the Toronto department who would have done very well at Chicago, but the academic climate there was markedly less strenuous. I wanted the more challenging environment.

Lesley also wanted to stay. Some initial misgivings soon gave way in the face of Chicago's much greater cultural resources (the Art Institute in particular was a revelation) and its more open and less formal social structure. We were rapidly forming friendships over a more diversified spectrum of interests and occupations than would have been likely in Toronto, and our perspectives were correspondingly broadening.

There was a negative factor we hadn't originally reckoned with: racial tension in the university precinct. Chicago's wartime and postwar industrial expansion had drawn in very large numbers of Afro-Americans from the southern states, most of whom settled in the near South Side. North of them was the commercial Loop and to the east was Lake Michigan; their expansion westward was blocked by ferocious ethnic resistance; so as their numbers continued to grow they moved steadily southward until they reached Hyde Park. There the administration of the university, whose faculty and students were still almost all white, was in covert alliance with the Hyde Park political and business establishment and the real-estate industry to preserve the white character of the neighbourhood. The resulting frustration of the black community not infrequently erupted in violence. Their southerly expansion had leap-frogged the university; it now seemed to some of their more radical spokesmen that a little pressure could squeeze the white filling out of this black sandwich, and there were frequent harassing incidents. At a married-students' residence on the south side of the Midway, just at the border between the university and the southern section of black settlement, white male residents carrying baseball bats patrolled nightly.

However, in our second year some university and local professional and business people, together with some Afro-American leaders, founded an organization dedicated to establishing a stable mixed community. Public meetings were held, support mobilized, and a number of houses were sold to middle-class blacks without being followed by the usual 'block-busting' phenomenon. It became possible for optimists who wanted to take a sanguine view to believe that the goal was feasible; we wanted to, and since we were then childless we easily accepted the risk of turbulence. In fact, during our fifteen years in Hyde Park, racial tensions increased and diminished in a rhythm influenced by both local and national factors, and relations with Afro-Americans were always sensitive. When we bought a house and engaged a black man named Leonard Spell to paint and repair it, we became friendly with him and his wife, a nurse, and when their first child was born they surprised us by asking us to be godparents. I explained that I was an atheist, but Leonard said that didn't matter, and we felt that to refuse would be a rebuff to the Spells' gesture of interracial solidarity. The baptism took place in a large church, and most of the all-black congregation lined up afterward to shake our hands and say something friendly. Leonard and I maintained a correspondence for many years after we left Chicago. On the other hand, when Ralph Ellison was a visiting writer at the university and several pleasant conversations I had with him led us to invite him and his wife for dinner, the evening was not very successful. The Ellisons came elegantly dressed, perhaps expecting a party, and the four-person conversation flagged; perhaps we unwittingly said or did something clumsy.

Having decided to stay, we looked about for an apartment of our own (we had spent the first year in a sublet). The university librarian was leaving to take up an appointment at Columbia and suggested we take his apartment on West 66th Street; it was well beyond walking distance from the university but otherwise suitable, and we seized it.

I was determined to finish my thesis during the summer. I had to take time out to do a review for *Modern Philology* of an unsound book on the composition of *Paradise Lost* by Allan H. Gilbert, a prominent Miltonist of the time, and another on Stacey's history of the Canadian Army in the war, but then I concentrated on the thesis. The university library provided some augmentation of the materials I had brought with me, as did the Newberry Library downtown, and I was both happy and relieved to find substantial confirmation of the pattern on which I had by now staked quite a lot. The Chicago heat in our third-floor walk-up was brutal, but I managed to finish the thesis before the next term began and, with Lesley's help, got the necessary three copies off to Woodhouse in September.

Despite Barker's hostility to the thrust of my argument, no revisions were called for and the exam was arranged for Friday afternoon, 17 December – the last departmental function before the Christmas break. The examining committee consisted of twelve professors, including Fulton Anderson, of Philosophy (replacing Brett, who had died) and D.J. McDougall, of History, a seventeenth-century specialist. After I had summarized the thesis and said that the analysis of Milton's inconsistencies and contradictions substantially agreed with Barker's but that the explanation was different, the proceedings took on something of the tone of a debate. Barker was not alone in feeling, without quite saying so, that attributing Milton's vagaries to a party line was virtually to accuse him of something dishonourable, while I defended such action on the ground that there had been a revolution in state and church, two civil wars, a regicide, the establishment of a commonwealth, and then the restoration of the monarchy and episcopacy: in such circumstances if one intended to be effective one had to take sides, which necessarily meant a party line; and I thought the evidence I'd presented that Milton's was a party line was incontestable.

Barker did not in fact contest it, but one or two others tried to ameliorate the impact. Frye, just then in a Hegelian phase, wondered whether there was a thesis–antithesis effect in Milton's thought, someone else whether the others who had fallen into these contradictions might not also be confused. I rejected both suggestions and insisted upon the evidence. McDougall made a different criticism, that I'd not used Hobbes; I explained that Hobbes's natural-law argument went in the opposite direction from Milton's and my purpose at this time was only to explain Milton's inconsistencies, but I promised that when I came to publish I'd take account of Hobbes and other royalist uses of the law of nature. Woodhouse then gave me an opportunity to state what I thought these were, which I was glad to do, and when the chairman brought the examination to an end I was almost sorry, having warmed to my work.

I was soon called in to be congratulated and it was suggested that when the thesis was ready to be published as a book it would be highly appropriate for it to come out in the 'University of Toronto Studies in English' series, of which Barker's book had been the first. Frye then invited us all to a celebration at his house that evening, about which he had said nothing to me in advance, perhaps thinking that it would be improper to appear to have presumed a successful exam. I appreciated the gesture very much, especially since Frye was not a party-giver, and was particularly glad to have a defusing drink with Barker.

II

Enrolment in my English courses was larger than in my first year. I had, with much effort and great misgivings, reduced my assignments, but I had still not conceived the quarter-course realistically, and one or two good students who had taken a course from me the previous year told me that others were inhibited from taking my courses because they were reputed to be exceptionally demanding. I checked with several faculty members and found the students were right about average course weights, whereupon I made yet another effort to approximate the mean, feeling uneasily that I was scanting my subject.

Teaching Spenser caused me to read him more closely than before and I found that Spenser scholarship, while copious, was not very rigorous, and anyway tended to concentrate on the obvious. This led in the next two years to two articles on Spenser and one on Spenser and Milton.

The university's Federated Theological Faculty had recently lost its specialist in the history of Puritanism to the Union Theological Seminary; his departure had orphaned a doctoral candidate who had now presented his dissertation to a faculty without expertise in the subject. The academic secretary of the faculty asked me whether I would read and help examine it. I told him that I didn't myself yet have the doctorate (it would be granted at Toronto's spring convocation), but he said that the only thing that mattered was my knowledge of the subject, so I agreed.

Unfortunately, the dissertation showed that it had been written without adequate supervision; when I reported this I was asked whether it could nevertheless proceed to examination, and I agreed. The examiners included professors from neighbouring institutions such as McCormack Theological Seminary, but none seemed very familiar with the subject; I wondered why the original supervisor had not been brought back for the occasion (just as I'd wondered why he hadn't been asked to read the dissertation) but forbore to ask. My questioning revealed very large errors in both the dissertation and the candidate's understanding of main matters, and the others left the decision largely to me. I suggested that the examination be adjourned until the dissertation had been revised, which was agreed. The academic secretary then asked whether I would help the candidate revise, and I reluctantly agreed. It cost me quite a lot of time, but when the revised dissertation was examined the reassembled examiners had no trouble passing it.

This incident had an amusing sequel. The morning after the successful exam the academic secretary phoned to ask whether I'd be willing to accept cross-appointment to the Theological Faculty. I told him I was an atheist, and was surprised by his reply that that didn't matter. I then thanked him but explained that I was already cross-appointed to the college and didn't want to attenuate my commitment to the department any further. When I later told this story as a joke to Brown he surprised me by saying that the faculty had a reputation for harbouring unbelievers.

There was also a more substantial consequence: Gerald Brauer, who taught Reformation church history in the Theological Faculty, came to see me to suggest that he and I join with Alan Simpson of the History department, who was working on a book on English and American Puritanism, to offer a joint seminar. I liked the idea and the three of us embarked on discussions about the shape and logistics of the potential seminar. From the outset it was clear that to attract students it would be necessary for them to get credit in their own departments; this was not easy, but after some persuasion the three departments, and subsequently the three divisions, agreed. (Later, in Toronto, I found this a useful precedent in setting up interdisciplinary centres.) For a title I suggested 'Milton and the Origin, Development, and Disintegration of the Puritan Revolution'; the others hesitantly accepted that, but after a year in operation we agreed that the title could read differently in the three calendars (another useful precedent).

While these arrangements for a true labour of love were being made, I was finding teaching in the college increasingly disagreeable. I had by this time come to understand why the staff meetings were so contentious: the core staff, those without joint appointments to the departments, would depend wholly on the college for tenure and promotion, and were therefore intent on dominating its procedures. Clarence Faust, the dean who had participated in my appointment, had left to manage the Ford Foundation; his successor, Champion Ward, was an agreeable man but not a strong administrator; the same was true of Russell Thomas, the chairman of Humanities II; and there appeared to be no one to bridle the ideological excesses that troubled me. I came to the conclusion, about mid-way through my second year, that I didn't want to teach in the college any more and would ask the department to take over the whole of my time.

When I told Brown of my decision he sympathized but pointed out the risk: what if the department couldn't or wouldn't absorb the other half of my time? I agreed that it was risky, but mentioned the opposite risk: if I remained a joint appointment, what if the dominant sect in the college prevented my promotion (they were under no illusion about my opposition to them)? And anyway I couldn't face the prospect of teaching indefinitely in the inbred and incestuous college environment, and if the department didn't want me full-time I would rather look for another job. My demand must have given the department some difficulty since, in addition to the budget implications, making me full-time would in some degree affect the tenure prospects of the other assistant professors, but it agreed that for the final year of my appointment I would be in the department full-time. Thomas expressed polite regret at losing me; so did Ward, somewhat more convincingly; and I taught my college section with an easier heart for the remainder of the year.

I had no difficulty making up a full teaching program in English for 1949–50. Williamson was helpful; he said that he didn't plan to teach Milton at the post-graduate level in the next year or two and would have no objection to my doing so. I asked Wilt whether I could also offer a Shakespeare course at the 300-level (there were already several) and he agreed. The sixth course would be the joint seminar. This meant that, while all my teaching would be in the graduate department, half the courses would be at what corresponded to the senior-undergraduate level in conventional programs and the other half at the graduate level. I now required office space in the department; Brown solved that problem by offering to let me share his office.

In the spring of 1949 I got a very surprising letter from Woodhouse asking whether I'd be willing to be nominated as editor of Volume II of the planned *Complete Prose Works of John Milton*, to be published by Yale University Press. I had understood that Woodhouse was to edit that volume, but he now said that he would be editing Volume V. That seemed a very poor exchange to me: the crucial pamphlets of 1643–5, in which Milton's ideas were still developing and changing, for the desperate ones of 1659–60, in which he fought a rearguard action against the restoration of the monarchy. It was only later that I came to recognize a Woodhouse pattern in this: he liked the idea of collaborative work but usually made his part in it await the completion of his individual projects, and therefore tended not to finish the collaboration. In 1934, when he and Watson Kirkconnell were both teaching in Winnipeg, he had suggested a collaborative work, from which after many years he withdrew, leaving Kirkconnell to publish his part separately. In the 1950s he and Douglas Bush were working on a collaborative project which Bush had to bring to completion alone. I think he surrendered Volume II for Volume V because he had made no progress and thought the later volume would give him more time; in the end he died with the work unfinished, and the pamphlets it was to have contained were published as Volume VII, edited by others.

Woodhouse's letter explained that if I agreed to the nomination it would go to the editorial board, which consisted of, besides himself, Don M. Wolfe, the chairman and general editor, and Douglas Bush, John Diekhoff, J. Milton French, Sir Herbert Grierson, Merritt Hughes, Maurice Kelley, and Alexander Witherspoon. No editors had been appointed for the individual tracts in the volume but there had been preliminary discussions with suitable persons and the board would be prepared to make recommendations, except for *Areopagitica*, which he supposed I would want to edit; the general historical and critical introduction would also be my responsibility. He recognized that such an undertaking would necessitate setting aside for some time the conversion of my thesis into a book, which would be regrettable, but thought that the thesis had put me into an exceptionally favourable position to do the volume introduction and that the opportunity to make a major contribution to what was likely to be the definitive edition of Milton's prose would more than compensate for the delay.

The editorial board, which was to have the advice and cooperation of James Holly Hanford and William Haller, constituted a substantial portion of the Milton establishment of the day; it included the other volume editors, and it was very flattering to a new PhD to be asked to work in that company. I had grave reservations about Wolfe, whose earlier books on Milton and on the Levellers had contained some new information but had shown a lack of percipience, an unsystematic mind, and some confusion of approach, but I thought that such a board would be a firm guide. I did not learn until much later that in addition to being chairman and general editor he was the *owner* of the edition (which was, however, also supported by grants from the Bollingen and Littauer Foundations); as such, he had the power of decision.

I wondered why Woodhouse had not offered the opportunity to Barker, whose published credentials so greatly exceeded mine, or if he had, whether the offer had been declined, and why; but when I mentioned these questions to Brown, who was at this time making frequent trips to Toronto and therefore seeing Woodhouse often, he said he thought Woodhouse now believed my analysis of Milton's thought to be more accurate than Barker's.

It was a big decision, and I tried to be deliberate about it. I knew it would mean a long delay of my planned book, for which there was assured publication in the respected Toronto series, and a need to work at considerable geographic distance with people I didn't know except through their publications. But the work and status of the board seemed a solid guarantee, and I had great faith in Woodhouse. I delayed my answer a respectable time but in fact I had effectively decided to accept the invitation on my first reading of Woodhouse's letter. I didn't dream that I would be entangled in that volume for a decade.

A month or so after I answered Woodhouse's letter I got one from Wolfe notifying me of my appointment and beginning the long process of collaboration. He proposed as editors Lowell Coolidge, of Wooster College, for *Doctrine and Discipline of Divorce* and *Colasterion*; Arnold Williams, of Michigan State, for *The Judgment of Martin Bucer* and *Tetrachordon*; and Donald Dorian, of Rutgers, for *Of Education*; as well as confirming me for *Areopagitica*. I knew none of these people but we arranged to meet and agreed to work together. We also agreed that the board's preliminary statement of editorial principles and procedures was seriously inadequate and that I should send in some proposed additions. For Volume II the most immediate problem was the presentation of *Doctrine and Discipline*, which had substantial changes of thought between editions, and Coolidge and I worked out a proposed treatment which would allow each edition to be read separately as well as compared with the other. I sent this and other textual suggestions to Wolfe, who replied after considerable delay, objecting to the cost and suggesting a cheaper procedure which entirely missed the point. I had to write several times (with blind copies to Woodhouse and several other board members) explaining the substantive changes in Milton's position between editions and the significance of the development for his thought before he would agree to put the matter to the board, which adopted a modified version of our suggested procedure. This was an early if mild indication of what working with him would be like.

Once I had committed myself to the project I knew I'd have to get to the British Museum, whose Thomason Collection of midcentury tracts was the one indispensable source for the detailed study of the Puritan Revolution, as soon as possible. I would not qualify for a sabbatical until 1953 (assuming I was kept on at Chicago), but I could take advantage of Chicago's quarter system to accumulate two quarters off by serving for six consecutive quarters. Accordingly I arranged to add the summer of 1950 to my teaching schedule, which would allow us to spend the summer and fall quarters of 1951 in England.

Almost as soon as I started work on the *Areopagitica* I reaped an unexpected dividend. Reading it word by word and having recently taught Spenser, I saw that Milton had made an error that had never been noticed, although the passage was often quoted: 'Spenser, whom I dare be known to think a better teacher than *Scotus* or *Aquinas*, ... brings [Guyon] in with his palmer through the cave of Mammon, and the bower of earthly bliss that he might see and know, and yet abstain.' In fact, while Guyon is accompanied by, and needs, the Palmer in the Bower of Bliss, Spenser very deliberately prevents the Palmer from entering the Cave of Mammon. Trying to account for this error led me to a fundamental difference, which Milton did not himself recognize, between his moral philosophy and that of his 'better teacher,' Spenser; I wrote this up in an article entitled 'Milton Revises *The Faerie Queene.*' Then, because the enquiry had sent me back to Aristotle's *Ethics*, I was able to discern a different and much more integral relation between that work and Spenser's epic than the one rather misleadingly proclaimed in the prefatory 'Letter to Raleigh,' which led the following year to a long article entitled '*The Faerie Queene*, Book II, and the *Nicomachean Ethics*,' showing that Book II is a poetic version, not as the 'Letter' claims, of the single virtue of Temperance, but rather of the whole of the *Ethics*, omitting the intellectual virtues other than practical wisdom.

Since I now taught entirely within the department I was meeting more, and more advanced, students, and could see that my 200-level courses were feeding into my new 300-level courses, which was a pleasant form of recognition. It was also gratifying that great epic poets like Spenser and Milton, who had, except for their lyric poems, virtually disappeared from the Chicago curriculum, were regaining some presence, as were the less dominant Elizabethan and Jacobean dramatists. The joint seminar with History and Church History got off to a promising start, although being experimental it presented a number of problems, one of which was the divergent levels of expectation among both instructors and students. I was put on several committees, took a more active part in departmental deliberations, and generally moved inward from the periphery toward the main body of the department.

The Humanities Division contained an invitational group called the 'Philological Society.' In my first year I had been invited to take part in a survey of books on the war, and had remained an interested member. Now an offshoot called the 'Epic Group' was created to do papers on epics of different cultures, partly to see whether any basic similarities could be discerned. I recall that

Thorkild Jacobsen, of Ancient Near Eastern, did a paper on the Gilgamesh epic; Richard Bruère, of Classics, on the *Aeneid*; and I on *Paradise Lost*. There were one or two others and there was some thought of publication but nothing came of it.

About the middle of my third academic year I was offered and accepted a second three-year appointment, with a modest increase in pay. I was also appointed, along with James Sledd, co-secretary of the department, Sledd to look after student affairs, I the rest; this appointment also carried a small stipend. Not long afterward a curious incident took place. Keast, whose appointment predated mine and whose reappointment had consequently come a year earlier, came into my office and told me that he had received an offer from another university; he didn't want to leave Chicago but he had a large family and couldn't take a chance on not being promoted two years hence. When I was slow to understand what this had to do with me, he explained that the decision on his promotion would have to take into account upcoming as well as immediate cases, and particularly, he hinted, mine. I realized he was right and that he was asking for something he didn't want to have to put into words. It was humiliating for him and I was embarrassed; I blurted out that I wouldn't consider his early promotion a threat to me. He thanked me and made a hurried exit, afraid, I think, that I would follow my concession with some caveats.

For a day or two I allowed myself to feel generous while resisting the suspicion that I'd been manipulated; then Brown confronted me with the closest approach to anger he ever showed me. Did I not realize that I'd played into the hands of the Crane faction? Earlier, Crane had argued in the Full Professors Committee that the department shouldn't reckon on me in its long-term planning because it was clear that I would be going back to a senior appointment in Toronto; now he was citing my concession to Keast as proof, since I would know that if Keast were promoted, either now or two years hence, it would reduce my chances. I had not known of Crane's ploy and was indignant, but I tried to defend my action: I'd been caught unawares, I couldn't stand the thought of all those children deprived because of me, Keast's field and mine didn't overlap very much, I thought that three years hence there would still be room for me in the department. 'Let's hope so,' was Brown's short reply.

I didn't really understand what else had been at stake until first Wilt and then Williamson also came to remonstrate with me, and then I gradually realized that I had been seen as one defence against a reconquest of the department by the Crane faction. I was contrite, blamed my lack of experience in university politics, and was partly forgiven, but reminded, at least by Wilt, that if the road was closed to me three years hence it would be my own fault. In the event their concern proved needless: the following year Keast took a more senior appointment at Cornell, where in due course he became dean and then vice-president before leaving for the presidency of Wayne State University.

There was another, much darker, reason why Brown needn't have concerned himself so much with the department's long-term planning. He was beginning to show signs of ill-health, tiring quickly, avoiding meetings, sometimes cancelling classes. Rumours went round. Since I was his friend and office-mate, I was frequently asked about his condition, but he had told me nothing. After some time Peggy Brown, who had maintained a loyal silence, came to our apartment, said she had to share the knowledge with someone, and told us that Edward had cancer and that the frequent visits to Toronto were to see a quack to whom he had turned when his doctors had told him there was no hope. He wanted no one to know and she asked us to keep secret what she'd told us, even from him. Meanwhile, he was struggling to complete his biography of Willa Cather.

I was appalled by the news. Edward had been my teacher, then a guide, and now my friend; he was just forty-five, and I was being told that he had only months to live, and those rendered even worse than they need be by his voluntary subjection to the torment and indignity of frequent long trips to a quack. Was there anything we could do? Her answer was, not unless he asked; meanwhile, to keep his secret, not let him know we knew, come to see him when she called, and let her come weekly to unburden herself. At her suggestion, Lesley painted her portrait during these visits.

Edward came less and less often to the university. Sometimes when he did meet his classes he would have to excuse himself partway through the hour and leave. The situation worsened; a delegation of his students came to see me, told me that his classes had become agony for them and presumably for him, and asked me to stop him from teaching; they must have thought me very strange when I said that I knew he was unwell but couldn't discuss it with him unless he broached the subject. I told Wilt the same thing when he came to see me about it, adding that as chairman he was in a better position to raise the subject than I was.

Peggy did call us fairly often to come for an evening, but Edward never referred to his condition, and our talk was much what it had always been: our work, university affairs, people we knew (he knew people everywhere), current writing, politics. Even on the last such occasion, during a heavy March snowstorm, there was no direct reference to his illness. Peggy took Lesley upstairs to leave Edward and me alone with each other; we talked very late into the night (I asked occasionally whether he was tired but he always denied it); the exchange of affection and the note of leave-taking were palpable, but the fact was left unspoken. He died on 23 April, 1951, and was buried in Mt Pleasant Cemetery in Toronto, being denied access to his family's parochial burial plot because he was a lapsed Catholic. I was a pallbearer, as were his friends Arthur Woodhouse, Ned Pratt, Alex Brady, and Harold Innis; he had told none of them he had cancer, although they knew he came to Toronto regularly for 'treatment.' I have never understood why he was so insistent about keeping his illness secret.

III

Some of the brightness went out of Chicago with Edward's death, for me and I think for some others, and I was glad to leave for England for my two quarters off. I had asked Tony Hugill, the Royal Navy officer who'd been attached to my Intelligence section during the final drive to the north German coast, to find us a six-month furnished sublet, and he had located one in Palace Gate, just off Kensington Gardens, which was something of a coup, since that was the summer of the Festival of Britain and space was hard to find. Decent cars were also hard to rent, so we took along our own. The ship, the SS *Europa*, turned out to be a wretched, smelly tub, which, after an uneasy voyage, dropped anchor in Plymouth harbour to offload by lighter, an extremely time-consuming operation. When we finally reached dock we found that the petrol pump had been closed for the night and we had to wait until morning, our car's tank having been drained for the voyage.

Our car, large by postwar British standards, became the cynosure for a gaggle of loitering youths, and we got a sudden revelation of the literacy level on the dock. The car was a Plymouth, with the name in large letters evenly spaced across the radiator grille; several youths, having examined the car's other parts, were puzzling out this legend; finally one hesitantly pronounced it as two words, 'ply mouth.' One of them asked me what this meant, and they all seemed astonished when I explained that the car was named after their own town of Plymouth.

We managed just before dawn to get a small amount of petrol and set out for London. As the sky lightened we were startled to see the fields alive with rabbits. We had earlier read that there was a plague of them on the Continent and that France had introduced the myxomytosis disease to control it, to much moralistic reprobation from uninvaded countries, especially Britain. After what we saw that early morning we were not surprised to read that Britain shortly afterward followed suit. Certainly when we stopped for more petrol at the first pump to open, the owner was vehement that it must be done.

At the British Museum I worked in the Thomason Collection throughout opening hours almost every day, slowly realizing the extreme complexity of the situation that I had undertaken to describe. I made copious notes, including copying passages in original spelling and punctuation (it was before the days of photocopying), but the more I found, the less prepared I thought I was to write, and I begrudged any time away from the library.

But I was in England for the first time as a civilian, Lesley for the first time since a pre-war Cook's Tour, and the Festival of Britain was on; there were some tourist things to do. As it happened, Claude and Christine Bissell and George and Pat Ford were there that summer, and we did some of those things together, such as staying late at the South Bank Fair, being unable to get a taxi, and, after walking over Waterloo Bridge, finding that the Underground and buses had also stopped running, under the still-curtailed postwar schedule. On another tourist outing I garnered the only material benefit I've ever had from my MBE: admission to the Tower, ordinarily sixpence, was waived for members of the order.

We made an early visit to Cambridge to discharge a mission Wilt had entrusted to me. H.S. Bennett, the medievalist, was to come to Chicago the following year for a quarter with the Committee of Social Thought, which he had visited before; Wilt had invited Bennett's wife, Joan, whose work on metaphysical poetry he admired, to come too, to teach creative writing in the department. She had declined, and Wilt wanted me to persuade her. The Bennetts invited us to stay for two or three days, which we were very happy to do. Joan explained her reluctance: she didn't know what teaching 'creative writing' meant, doubted her credentials for such work, and was uncertain about a university department that did such things. Stanley would have liked her to come with him but didn't know the department well and couldn't say much to reassure her. I explained that, unlike Iowa and some other universities, the department didn't have a program in creative writing but used the floating course as a means to give students access to writers, and while she had a recognized academic field, Wilt couldn't offer her an appointment in it because Williamson would be teaching it just then; Wilt had authorized me to say that she could do anything she liked in her course. Before our visit was over she had agreed; it turned out to be the first of several visits, and our two families became very good friends.

When we were leaving Cambridge we stopped for lunch at the Garden House Hotel. I remarked to Lesley that I was very pleased with our visit: in addition to persuading Joan to come to Chicago I had been introduced to Stanley's college, Emmanuel, seen the Trinity Milton Manuscript, visited Milton's college and the university library, met some interesting people, and had only one disappointment – that E.M. Forster had not been home when Stanley rang to see whether he could bring me to meet him. A little later a tall, thin man came to our table, said he hadn't meant to eavesdrop but couldn't help overhearing, and that he'd be glad to take us to see Forster, who was a friend of his. I thanked him, but fearing that it was someone whose unprepared entrance with a couple of strangers might be an unwelcome intrusion on the privacy Forster was known to guard, pretended that it was now too late for us – we had to be in London at a certain time. He said he was sorry, then, just as he turned to go, told us his name was Sassoon. I kicked myself; it was too late to call him back, but I'd have enjoyed talking with him as much as with Forster. In fact, I had a good visit with Forster on a later trip to England, but never had another opportunity to see Siegfried Sassoon.

Visits to art galleries and museums had perforce to be during library hours and therefore at the cost of my work, but theatre was after the library had closed, and a wonderful season had been mounted for the Festival. Olivier and a strong company alternated *Antony and Cleopatra* and *Caesar and Cleopatra*; Peter Brook directed Gielgud and Diana Wynyard in *The Winter's Tale*; Richardson, with Celia Johnson, Margaret Leighton, and Renee Asherson, did *Three Sisters*; John Clements and Kay Hammond did *Man and Superman* in its entirety; and there were many good contemporary plays. We didn't stint: best seats were a guinea and they ranged down to three shillings; even the Royal Ballet was only three or four pounds for middling seats.

In July we attended the unveiling by the Canadian high commissioner of the Stonefall Memorial Cross in the RAF cemetery at Harrogate. When I had first seen the cemetery the new graves were raw and the markers temporary; now all was in order, beautifully kept and landscaped. I took photographs, both for myself and for the rest of the family, noting that Bert's was by no means the only marker to bear a Star of David. We also went to York, where the Minster was still undergoing repair but the Book of Honour bearing the names of Commonwealth airmen killed in the war was on display under glass; I could not get the staff to turn the page to Bert's name.

We planned a few weeks on the Continent beginning about mid-September, so I felt constrained to write up the work I'd been doing, although I suspected it would need much altering when I'd read more. As the time approached I became concerned for the security of my laborious manuscript (before computers and photocopiers the academic culture was full of horror stories on this matter). We had become friendly with a Canadian couple in our building and I mentioned my concern; Lieutenant-Colonel Gil Turcot worked in the military section at Canada House and offered to keep it safe for me in the vault. He said he would mark it 'Intelligence Material: Secure,' which he said was okay since I'd been in Intelligence. Years later, when he was GOC Central Command, I wondered what he would do if his classification officer did something similar.

My return to the Continent six years after the end of the war stirred many grim memories; I didn't wallow in them, but we did visit one or two battlefields. What we had come for were the art museums, cathedrals, and theatres. Our inexperience led us to undertake far too much, but even a crammed exposure to the cultural treasures of France, Italy, and Switzerland was enriching and made us determined to return for more.

In our final months in London I accumulated as much additional material as I could, working flat out, but when it was time to leave I was confirmed in my view that it would require much more time with the Thomason Collection if I was to avoid the errors of oversimplification which marred the existing scholarship of the period.

We sailed on the *Queen Elizabeth* on 7 December, and returned to a subtly changed university. Hutchins had left to head the Ford Foundation; he had been somewhat withdrawn from the daily administration of the university for some time, but his actual departure meant the appointment of a new chancellor (Hutchins had thus retitled the chief executive). Lawrence Kimpton was a member of the Philosophy department but not an intellectual and certainly not an ideologue, and his succession led to a more pragmatic climate, one of whose results was some reduction of tension between the divisions and the college. The change of chancellors was the main theme of the 1952 Quadrangle Club Revels, the annual musical satire put on by the faculty, in which I was unexpectedly asked to play the role of Hutchins. It was a bit part but highly theatrical, and it led to my participating in several later Revels. In time I was elected to the club's governing board, where I met monthly with some of the university's most interesting members, including Leo Szilard, the progenitor of the Manhattan Project (the first self-sustained nuclear reaction), editor of the *Bulletin of the Atomic Sciences*, and inventor and keeper of its famous Doomsday Clock.

R.C. Bald had been brought in to fill the professorship made vacant by Brown's death, although their academic fields were quite different, Bald being a seventeenth-century specialist. He was given Brown's old office and I was put in with Crane, either at his initiative or at least with his acquiescence. Our relations had always been amicable; I admired his intellect and achievements, although I didn't share his critical position, and I had not brooded unduly upon his comments about my future: perhaps he really thought I intended to return to Toronto. He did me the courtesy of treating me as an intellectual equal, frequently asking my opinion about something he was writing; in particular I recall much discussion of a long article he was doing on Cleanth Brooks and the New Critics. He was the editor of *Modern Philology* and frequently asked me to do reviews; chary of my time, I agreed only seldom. I had become friendly with his critical disciples in the department; Elder Olson later did a volume for a critical series I edited with others; Norman Maclean and I became occasional golfing companions and good friends, and he often talked to me about fishing in Montana, his brother killed by rough associates, and a disastrous air-drop of firefighters: the subjects of the two very popular books he wrote after retirement, *A River Runs Through It* (which was made into a successful film) and *Young Men and Fire*.

I never doubted that I was learning from the discussions with Crane but they consumed much time, of which I had too little, and I asked Wilt to place me elsewhere for the following year; he moved me upstairs to share Donald Bond's office on the third floor.

I thought I was now in a somewhat better position to renew the attempt to get the history of literature into the curriculum, and after some preparatory lobbying I gave notice of a motion to that effect. This time the department accepted the idea of offering the courses but refused to make more than one of a four-quarter sequence (three in English and one in American) compulsory. I had hoped for more but was pleased to get anything, and for several years I taught in the program.

The tenure decision on James Cunningham was negative despite several publications. Objectively this probably improved my chances a year later, but I deeply regretted it, for we had become friends. I heard about the decision at the *kaffeeklatsch* regularly held in Jim's office; others were present and a hubbub ensued, during which I said nothing. Later that day I met Jim on campus and he confronted me: why had I not said anything about his termination? I knew I should have but explained that I'd been caught by surprise and then felt that anything I might say would have seemed hypocritical, since his departure must improve my chances. He accepted this and when the time came for him to leave Chicago we parted friends; fortunately, he got a good appointment at Brandeis University.

One of the best things about Chicago was the stream of distinguished visitors. T.S. Eliot came for a week or two in 1951 or 1952; George Williamson had been influential in establishing Eliot's early reputation, and his later studies continued to bolster it; perhaps that is why the Williamsons were able to invite some friends to meet Eliot at an evening party. There were not many of us; Williamson, a little mischievously, introduced me to Eliot as a Miltonist. Sitting somewhat magisterially alone on a chesterfield, Eliot immediately said that whenever anyone told him he'd read *Paradise Lost* he would ask what the function of the elephant was in Eden. Everyone listened, for I suspect that some others shared Eliot's proclaimed view that there could not really be a long poem; I replied that it was 'to make them sport,' and invited him to meet my class and put that and similar questions to them (I was less confident of their response than I pretended). Eliot said he'd consider it but his time was limited. I told him I'd done my graduating essay on *The Criterion* and had read all of it too, which he said surprised and pleased him; no one spoke to him about it any more. When I said that I not only taught both Milton and the metaphysicals, I also liked them both, he took this contradiction of his views in good part. He didn't come to my Milton class; I told them of the interchange and asked them about the function of the elephant; only one student knew.

Another high-profile visitor was Edith Sitwell. I was detailed to escort her to dinner at the Quadrangle Club and then to her lecture. There was a heavy snowstorm, and when it was time to go to Hutchison Commons, where her lecture was to take place, I led her to the side door of the club. She drew back, saying, 'I don't walk in snow.' I explained that we would only have to cross the street; she drew herself up to her full height, her famous Pre-Raphaelite costume dramatically setting off her indignation, and said, 'You don't understand: I don't walk in snow.' I led her to the front entrance of the club, asked Lesley to watch for our car, walked some distance to get it, picked them up at the curb, drove around the block on the one-way streets, let the women off at the curb facing the Commons, found another parking spot, and walked back. Sitwell seemed content, although she had had to walk approximately the same distance through snow as in a single crossing of the street.

Another visitor whom I was detailed to escort was A.L. Rowse. He gave his now familiar views on Shakespeare, and as the visit wound down became increasingly anxious to talk about a possible appointment. He alternated between what must have been an uncontrollable contempt for Americans and blatant flattery of the University of Chicago, and I was relieved when the visit ended.

When the Bennetts arrived, Joan found her work more congenial than she'd feared. She invited us to tea to meet one of her students; it was Philip Roth and the stories he was working on in Joan's class became *Goodbye, Columbus*. He was very intense and had pronounced views on the department; his wife seemed rather silent.

I was elected president of the Midwest Renaissance Conference and organized the 1952 meetings. One of the people I got into the program was Holly Hanford, then usually referred to as 'the dean of Miltonists,' retired and a visiting scholar at the Newberry. I liked him and invited him to meet my class, which he did with alacrity and success; sensing that he felt rather cut off, I brought him to the university fairly often. We talked a good deal about Milton scholarship; one day he asked me whether I'd share with him the task of revising his *Milton Handbook*, which his publisher wanted to bring up to date. I was flattered because this was the most widely-used aid to Milton studies, but said that he knew my time was committed far ahead. He asked me to think about it, and I was too cowardly to refuse, feeling the old man's vulnerability. I should simply have begged off, instead of leaving him to nurse his hope for a month.

My work on the Milton volume, as well as my Shakespeare course, had interested me in analytical bibliography; since Bald and Friedman were also interested, as was one of the librarians and a member of the University Press, we contrived to acquire and put into working condition a hand press, which we set up in a Press warehouse. There we taught ourselves to set and distribute type, pull and correct proofs, and finally to print some undemanding things. Fredson Bowers, then the leading bibliographer in the country, frequently taught in our summer quarter and sometimes joined the 'press gang;' under his influence we persuaded ourselves that we were growing more competent to trace the evolution of corrupted readings from state to state.

Among the things I sometimes printed were menus for a gourmet group, organized by Wilt, which met twice a year, once in the South Side, at one of the homes of its seven or eight university members, and once in the North Side, at the mansion of John Nuveen, a rich broker who had been a teetotaller until he was sent to Europe as a U.S. ambassador and developed a taste for expensive wines. When we met in the South Side, each of us would contribute one course of food and wine; in the North Side, Nuveen's household staff did everything. The dinners grew more and more ambitious, and on my turns to be host the burden of cooking fell largely and most unfairly on Lesley, who being a woman couldn't in those benighted and patriarchal days be a member of the group. My considerable interest in wine was further stimulated by these dinners and, with the help of a knowledgeable importer to whom Wilt introduced me, I built up a rather good cellar, the best parts of which I later brought to Canada.

Peggy Brown asked me to go through Edward's unfinished work on Cather to see whether it was publishable. I had to report that considerable work was needed. She sent my report to Edward's old friend Leon Edel, then in New York, who came to Chicago to look over the material. We had a long consultation, and much to my pleasure he agreed to do the work, which came out in 1953.

I had applied for a Guggenheim fellowship for the 1953–4 academic year, explaining that if it were awarded I would be able to take it up only if I got sabbatical leave. By the time the fellowships were announced, including one for me, my promotion had been approved; I was to become an associate professor with tenure from 1 July, with a worthwhile increase in salary. Silverstein, Sledd, and Streeter were also promoted; the fifth member of our intake was let go. My sabbatical was now assured. I wrote to Geoffrey Towse, the estate agent at Palace Gate, asking him to find us a twelve-month furnished sublet, and asked whether he could get our old flat, or something similar, for the Bonds, who were also going to be in London on sabbatical. He was able to meet both requests; we were to go into the upper floor of a house in Hamilton Terrace.

I had had another reason for being cautious about the Guggenheim: Lesley was pregnant. She had twice miscarried and we would not risk a third by travelling. In fact her doctor recommended prolonged bed-rest; for several months I prepared meals and did other housework. It was unavailing and she miscarried again. We began our year off in sombre mood.

To make matters worse, Wolfe's Volume I appeared, a massive tome of over a thousand large, closely printed pages. It was a sad beginning to an ambitious enterprise. The texts seemed acceptable, although there was almost no bibliographical apparatus, but the multitudinous footnotes were voluminous, often superfluous, not always accurate, and did not cover all the hard things that really needed explication. Worst was Wolfe's introduction. It declared itself to be 'historical and critical,' but this turned out to mean a miscellany of information and opinion of uncertain relevance to the prose works in the volume. I knew Wolfe intended to give a context for the tracts, but the connection with Milton was often extremely remote, and as a 'picture of the period' it was far inferior to existing historical scholarship. For me the introduction had only one good aspect: it was over two hundred pages in length, which meant that I too could have about a hundred thousand words. I was sure that the reviews, especially in England, would be severe, and wondered whether the edition would survive them. I was also determined not to do an introduction like Wolfe's, and wrote to Woodhouse and Bush to make that clear. They both reassured me that the board would not expect me to; Hanford, still in Chicago, said that, as an adviser, not a board member, he wasn't sure what the board would do.

We sailed on the *Île-de-France* in September. Hamilton Terrace is in St John's Wood; the house was handsome, with a fine garden, on a quiet street shaded by pollarded plane trees; it was conveniently near the Maida Vale Underground station, a fact of less importance than it would be now because the British Museum was still allowing users to park cars in its grounds (we had bought a British car on a twelve-month resale arrangement). In fact parking was manageable almost everywhere in central London, and we regularly drove to theatres, which in those days of open coal fires and the resultant heavy fogs could cause embarrassment: one particularly foggy night, when driving was very slow, we arrived late for *King John* at the Old Vic. Our seats were in the third row and we made our sheepish way to them while Richard Burton spoke the Bastard's first boisterous lines, eyeing us disapprovingly. He eyed us several times more because the intense fog crossing the river had got into Lesley's throat and for some time she couldn't stop coughing. Driving home was tortuous; I had to walk ahead of the car part of the way, shining a flashlight on the road while Lesley drove.

In preparation for my work I had brought from home a newly developed photocopying device whose name I cannot recall. At the BM I had to submit it for inspection by the engineering department, which decided that after it was adapted to the local electrical current I could use it, subject to the desk librarian's approval. The desk librarian in the North Library, the inner sanctum which housed the Thomason and other rare collections, was Angus Wilson, the novelist; our chemistries were not at that time compatible, and anyway he didn't like Americans, which he assumed me to be, so he found that several books I submitted were unsuited to photocopying. After some weeks, however, and after many staff members had come to see how the device worked, he relented and I was allowed to use my own discretion. In the 1960s, when he was on a North American tour, he dined with us in Toronto; by then he had achieved considerable fame (although not yet a knighthood) and was correspondingly less prickly, and the evening was remarkably pleasant.

I had brought with me the edited texts of all the tracts in my volume and was able to collate them with original copies. I was also able to run down many allusions for which Chicago libraries were inadequate. But most of my time went to the non-Miltonic pamphlets of 1643–5; I looked into almost all of them, skimmed many, and read many hundreds in detail, making copious notes but this time saved by my blessed copier from having to write out long passages full of eccentric spelling and punctuation. Every pamphlet I read did something to increase the particularity of the period for me, to loosen the hold on me of the generalizations in the received scholarship, until gradually I came to understand how, in the extreme fluidity of the political, religious, social, and military situations, parties which were partners on one issue could simultaneously be opponents on another.

At the next table to mine in the North Library sat the first PhD candidate to do a dissertation under my supervision. Barbara Lewalski had taken my Milton course and the joint seminar (where she met the history student she married), and was now fitting Milton's last pamphlets into the the final years of the Commonwealth; reading her draft chapters while working with the same method on the earlier period gave me a curious sense of chronological dislocation. At another table sat T.W. Baldwin, of Illinois, whose studies of sixteenth- and seventeenth-century curricula, and particularly of St Paul's School, had taught me much; we talked often, and I never failed to wonder what, besides the many illustrations he gave, was behind his bitter contempt for British scholarship.

Others whom I knew worked in the Reading Room, among them Don Allen, of Johns Hopkins, who would collect me occasionally for a pub lunch, at which he would gaily satirize the most sacrosanct academic conventions; and Douglas Grant, of Toronto, with whom I sometimes took sandwich lunches on the BM steps, often arguing about whether there was an American literature (he denied it but later came back to England from Toronto to teach it at Leeds); whether G.K. Chesterton, whom he admired, was an antisemite; or whether the war, the Holocaust, and the postwar world left any ground for religion. On one occasion I was reading *The Times* while eating my lunch; it contained the first joint report of the American Heart Association and the American Cancer Society on the health effects of tobacco; I ground out my cigarette and announced that I was quitting. He asked what I would do with the year's supply of cigarettes and pipe tobacco he knew I'd brought with me (post-war English tobacco was still very poor, scarce, and expensive); not having thought about it, I didn't know, whereupon he offered to buy it; I accepted his offer and have always felt a little guilty because he died young of a heart attack.

Olivier Lutaud of the Sorbonne was there working on Milton. When he found that I was engaged on the Yale Milton he said he did not much admire the published volume; he much preferred the work of the Toronto Miltonists. He grew more hopeful on learning that I had done my thesis under Woodhouse and Barker, and brightened even more to learn that I shared his reservations about Volume I. At his invitation I called on him when we went to Paris and was taken through the Sorbonne and the Bibliothèque Nationale. He later wrote very favourably in French journals about my work.

Geoffrey Tillotson, head of the English department at Birkbeck College, had visited Chicago and we had talked; he now suggested that his colleague Rosemary Freeman and I exchange places for a year. I knew that I would require another year in the BM, thought the idea worth pursuing, and discussed it with Dr Freeman, to whom Tillotson had already broached the subject. We agreed to explore the matter, and I did discuss it in Chicago, but in the end it did not work out.

The Bonds, who had our old flat in Palace Gate, asked us to tea with T.S. Eliot, with whom they'd established a relation in Chicago

(Judith was in charge of the university's Modern Poetry Library, and they were good Anglicans). We didn't at first talk about Milton; instead I said we'd just seen his new play, *The Confidential Clerk*. He asked what I'd thought of it; unfortunately, I didn't reflect that as a very occasional playwright he'd probably be more sensitive to criticism of his play than of his universally admired poems. I said that I thought the dramatic situation had been well introduced in the first act and well developed in the second, but I had some reservations about the denouement. He pressed me on the reservations, which produced a discussion that could not help being critical on my part and a little irritated on his. Later we got onto the seventeenth century and he said something about Cromwell's vandalism in Canterbury Cathedral. I said that was the other Cromwell, the sixteenth-century one; Oliver had enough to answer for at Ely. He said he was glad I cared. Thereafter the conversation was less controversial; when he rose to go I offered to drive him home; instead, he asked to be taken to see Wyndham Lewis, who was not well and to whom he sometimes read. En route there I reflected on the fact that Lewis was more overtly antisemitic than Eliot, but said nothing.

We saw a great deal of theatre on that visit. Both the Old Vic and the Stratford company had good seasons; Hammersmith also became a frequent destination, since both the King's and the Lyric there did a number of classical plays; there were a number of Elizabethan and Jacobean plays at commercial West End theatres; and we saw the first and perhaps the only professional production of *The Booke of Sir Thomas More* at the short-lived Theatre Centre; so that altogether we were able to see many Renaissance and Restoration plays which we would normally not encounter in North America, as well as many continental and contemporary plays. It was also a good opera and ballet season, of which we took advantage. Prices were still very favourable for visitors from North America: I bought a new set of the second edition of the *Oxford English Dictionary*, complete with the supplementary thirteenth volume, for forty-five pounds.

In February we drove to the Mediterranean, stopping for carnival in Nice and the Matisse chapel in Vence, spending some time in Florence and Rome, and then flying to Israel and Greece. In Israel we booked a three-day guided tour which turned out to have no other customers, so we had a car and driver to ourselves and saw a great deal of the country, then not fully emerged from its violent birth: the road from Tel Aviv to Jerusalem was littered with burnt-out tanks, the Western Wall of Solomon's Temple could not be approached from the Israeli side, and the *kibbutzim* all had defensive emplacements. In Athens we stayed at the American School. In Greece even more than Israel and western Europe, it was the right time to be a tourist. The Acropolis was still completely open and almost no one was there; we could examine anything we liked at leisure (I took particular note of the hill of Areopagus). Even downtown, where the agora was being excavated, one could see everything; we were lucky, because Homer Thomson, whom I'd known slightly in Toronto, was in charge of excavating the stoa and gave us a special tour. In Delphi there was only one other couple at the hotel; except for us the temple site was deserted all day (we lay on our backs at the temple of Apollo watching an eagle circle overhead). So was the temple site in Corinth. The agora there was being excavated under the general direction of Oscar Broneer, of the Chicago Classics department, the discoverer of the sanctuary of Poseidon; he was in Chicago at the time but had written ahead on our behalf, and the archaeologist in charge took me through the diggings (Lesley, who doesn't like tunnels, declined). At Mykene we were the only visitors at the excavation of the tombs of Aegisthus and Clytemnestra.

We returned to London in early April. I then got in another four months of work at the BM and other collections, chiefly the Bodleian, which had some pamphlets Thomason had missed, mostly royalist publications issued at Oxford during the first civil war. At the beginning of September we sailed on the *Liberté*, carting hundreds of index cards and photocopies, and moved into our new home, the upper two floors of a house on Blackstone within walking distance of the university, which Wilt had found for us.

Wilt was now dean of the division, and Walter Blair had succeeded him as chairman of English. With this change the joint secretaryship came to an end; I missed the stipend, but not as much as

I appreciated the freed time. I knew that several years would pass before my volume could appear and that I couldn't afford to drop out of sight for so long, so I resolved to publish at least one article and one review each year till then, which I did. Most of the articles were by-products of the research for my volume, and it was on that volume that I concentrated most of my attention. My teaching now consisted largely of courses I'd taught before and which therefore required less preparation, and I was able to devote several days a week to writing.

The pattern of the introduction had begun to emerge even while I was at the BM. The main issue in England during 1642 and the first half of 1643 was supremacy in the state, and while this was being contested by military force on the ground it was debated in terms of law in the explosively proliferating press. This led on the parliamentary side to the development of a natural-law theory of the state with which to oppose both Charles's divine-right theory and his propaganda alternative based on English positive law. From late 1643, when the precarious military balance began to shift toward Parliament, until well after the end of the first civil war in 1645, the main issue within the parliamentary coalition was church reformation. The Puritan right secured the establishment of the Westminster Assembly of Divines to formulate 'the one right discipline' for a uniform national church; the centre, after failing there to win 'an accommodation for tender consciences,' proposed a congregational structure within Calvinism; and the left demanded that all who based their beliefs on scripture be free to establish their own churches, or even to worship as individuals. This led to an escalating pamphlet war within Puritanism in which the centre and left developed and enlarged theories of Christian liberty.

These concepts of the natural-law state and Christian liberty were precisely the ones by means of which Milton broke from the Presbyterianism of his anti-prelatical tracts, with their demand for the immediate institution of 'the one right discipline,' and moved to, and then beyond, the centre of the Puritan spectrum with his divorce tracts and *Areopagitica*. I therefore organized my introduction by analysing the evolution of these central ideas, first in the pamphlet war, then in Milton's tracts, and showing how the latter related to, sometimes derived from, the former. I added a separate chapter on *Of Education*, freeing it from its reputed dependence on Comenianism and establishing its true provenience.

I sent my draft introduction to Wolfe early in 1955. The first reports from the board to reach me were from Woodhouse and Bush, who sent me copies. Both strongly supported the draft, with only limited suggestions. After some time, Hughes also sent me a copy of his report, which was generally supportive but raised a number of questions of detail. After a further delay I got a letter from Wolfe saying that the introduction, while very strong in what it did, didn't conform to the editorial principle of 'a historical and critical introduction,' and would need revision to take into account those aspects of the period not dealt with, on the pattern of Volume I.

I was not entirely surprised and wrote back, with copies to all members of the board, saying that his interpretation of the editorial principle of 'a historical and critical introduction' had not been explained to me at the outset, that I wouldn't have accepted the assignment if it had been, that I would not write that kind of introduction, and that I would like to meet with the board; I also asked that in advance of such a meeting I be sent the reports of individual board members. It took some time for me to hear from Wolfe, and when his reply finally came it called for me to attend a board meeting at the Harvard Club in New York that very Saturday. I was furious, but attended; to my dismay, Woodhouse couldn't on such short notice.

I repeated my position to the board, adding that there were numerous general histories of the period which I could not hope to better in a brief compass, that the reviews of Volume I had complained of a lack of focus and direct relevance to the pamphlets in the introduction, and that I conceived of my task as providing 'a historical and critical introduction' *to the tracts in my volume*, which aside from *Areopagitica* were not in the main thrust of revolutionary activity (Milton had described them as 'domestic,' as distinguished from 'religious and civil'). I had always expected to revise my first draft with the help of board criticisms, and would be glad to carry out all suggestions with which I agreed; however, I had seen only three board members' reports and would be glad to have the others. Wolfe stated his position, that the pattern for the edition as a whole had been set by Volume I, which the board had approved, and that succeeding volumes would have to conform. I reminded the board that this pattern had not been set when I was invited to participate almost six years earlier, and that it had not won strong support from the profession; I would not say with my author that I would ding a pupil-teacher's book a quoit's distance, but I would not write a book on a model foreign to me.

Bush said something diplomatic in my support; so did Diekhoff, more tentatively; then Hughes and Kelley said they had not fully understood the nature of the difference between Wolfe and me, and thought limited revision would be enough; even French, who was close to Wolfe, gave his position only limited support. I thought I had won my point; then Wolfe said that, although it appeared that the board might be divided in its views, as general editor and owner, and the person to whom the foundation grants were given, he had a responsibility to carry out the editorial principles as he understood them.

This was the first time I'd heard the word 'owner' in connection with the edition; I thought it a violation of the understanding implicit in having an editorial board, and I was outraged. I said that I'd entered the enterprise on the strength of the reputations of the members of the editorial board, but if their views were to be overridden by an 'owner,' I would have to protect my years of labour as best I could and try to secure publication elsewhere; I would leave it to others to contemplate the probable fate of the edition if that happened.

Wolfe went white, and there was a minute or more of complete silence. Then he asked me to withdraw while the board discussed the situation. I repaired to the bar, where I was soon joined by Hanford. He was mournful, knowing Wolfe's stubbornness, but I was carried along by the exhilaration of battle. Finally we were called in and Wolfe, his head slumping forward, said that the board had decided that each volume editor could interpret 'historical and critical introduction' for himself. He handed over the individual reports on my introduction.

Afterwards Bush and Diekhoff told me, out of Wolfe's hearing, that I'd saved the edition, and Woodhouse wrote the same. All the board members' reports were approving; several contained particular suggestions, some of which I carried out and to all of which I replied. Having won the right to construct the introduction as I'd planned, I was intent on improving it with anyone's help, and I wanted the board to understand this. Wherever I rejected a suggestion I gave my reasons, sending my reply to both Wolfe and the individual board member. In the end, however, these revisions amounted to relatively little, far less than those that grew out of the settling process as I continued to think about the introduction during the further year or so that it took to get final copy from my individual editors (now five in number as it had been decided not to have a separate volume for the private correspondence but, instead, to distribute it chronologically over all the volumes, and so Arthur and Alberta Turner had been added to my team).

IV

After Lesley's final miscarriage we had decided to adopt a child and had applied to The Cradle, a private agency in Evanston, just north of Chicago. In July 1955, shortly after my showdown with Wolfe, the child intended for us was born; we named him Robert, after my dead brother. We had allowed for his arrival in choosing our residence, but not long afterward Lesley became pregnant again, this time successfully, and we looked around for larger quarters. By this time it seemed that we would stay permanently in Chicago, so we decided to try to buy a house. The only one for sale in the university district was a three-storey house on Woodlawn which was larger than our needs and priced beyond our means. After waiting some time and searching elsewhere unavailingly, I went to see the owner, Professor William Ogburn, a leading sociologist who was retiring and moving east. I found him working in the garden, and after some conversation I named the figure I could pay. He said he hadn't had any other offers, didn't want to leave the house unsold when he moved, and accepted my offer.

It was an imposing house built by Ernest Burton, the third president of the university, and must have seemed pretentious for an associate professor on modest pay, but it had a third floor which would commodiously accommodate a live-in student sitter, needed if Lesley was not to be hopelessly tied down, a triple garage which could bring in some revenue, and a fenced garden and porch where the children could be put to play, in return for all of which we thought we could accept the obloquy that would come with owning such a house. We just had time to furnish it before our daughter, Katherine, was born on the last day of 1956.

All these indications of permanence, together with the U.S. presidential election of 1956, caused us to reconsider our position about citizenship. We had become eligible for American citizenship in 1952 but in those days it meant renouncing Canadian citizenship, which we were not then willing to do. By 1956, however, it had begun to seem unlikely that we would ever return to Canada, we felt increasingly involved in American affairs, and it began to feel quixotic to remain a resident alien reporting to the appropriate government office every six months, just to retain our Canadian citizenship; besides, we wanted to vote for Adlai Stevenson for president and Paul Douglas for senator.

The process of naturalization went along very smoothly until the question of my 'nationality' arose; I said it was Canadian by birth, but the officer then wanted to know where my father had been born; when I replied 'Russia,' he demanded that I swear a special affidavit of loyalty and jump through various bureaucratic hoops. I said I wouldn't; he said then I couldn't be naturalized; I demanded his name and particulars of office; he decided to consult his senior, who called me in and asked what 'race' my father was; I asked whether he meant 'ethnicity,' in which case it was Jewish. He then turned to his junior and said to proceed without the affidavit; Russian Jews were exempted; he didn't explain why, but that was the only occasion in my life when being identified as a Jew was an advantage. They also went behind Lesley's assertion of Canadian nationality, but when they found that her ancestors had emigrated from Scotland they were satisfied. The swearing-in ceremony was a little hard for us because we had to take an oath renouncing all previous allegiances.

I was now seeing some very good students in my classes. George Steiner's first essay for me was full of clever, high-flown assertion without demonstration; I marked it 'B for Flamboyance.' He came to see me, said he'd never got anything but A before, and asked what he could do; I said I would read and grade a revised and responsible essay. He delivered an excellent one and got an A. He took a second course from me, then asked my help in securing a Rhodes scholarship. Years later he was responsible for an invitation for me to be an Overseas Fellow at Churchill College, Cambridge, where he headed English, and in one of several visits to Toronto he told the audience of how I had forced him to write responsibly. George Starbuck also took several of my courses. I didn't know he was a poet, but he always got perfect marks in the short factual quizzes which I used weekly to ensure that students were reading the material. Many years later he sent me a poem to see whether I minded his publishing it; it was based on something I'd said in my Shakespeare class, and I had no objection. I was also directing several dissertations, some of which became influential books.

I had from the first taken an active role in the Divisional Council, and in the mid-1950s was elected chairman of its executive committee; this was time-consuming and sometimes abrasive, but it gradually taught me to relate policy abstractions to the personal situations affected, and thus was valuable preparation for my later administrative work.

The department decided to make a regular appointment in creative writing and brought in Richard Stern. By this time Bond had retired and Stern was given the empty desk. He was put in charge of the visiting-writers program, many of whom I therefore met. I recall vividly one Monday when Norman Mailer came into our office, threw his rolled-up raincoat on Stern's desk, and said, 'Dick, I've been on a high all weekend and have done everything there was to do on the West Side.' He looked it, too, and I uneasily recalled news reports of his actions while 'high.' It was also through Stern that I met Saul Bellow, a professor in the Committee on Social Thought and deliberately remote from the English department. Bellow was as contained and civil as Mailer was wild, and I was delighted to come to know him.

Our next-door neighbours gave frequent garden parties, and one of their usual guests was Milton Friedman. On some of these occasions I would be working in our garden, and Friedman and I, who had met on campus, would chat over the fence. I had understood him to be an ideological ultra-conservative, but found him to have surprisingly pragmatic and persuasive reasons for his positions. I had known Harry Johnson briefly in Toronto and came to know him better in Chicago, where he and Friedman constituted opposing poles of what was probably at the time the most productive Economics department in existence, several of whom would, like Friedman, win the Nobel prize. Friedrick Hayek, who would be one of the Nobel laureates, lunched frequently at the Quadrangle Club, seated with us at the Humanities table rather than with the social scientists, which symbolized his isolation within his own Economics department. He told me in 1960 that he was going to give a lecture at the University of Manitoba, so I wrote to my sister Gladys and she had a little party for him, which he reported he enjoyed very much, while my sister reported that he was very entertaining and drank vast quantities of brandy.

In October 1957, I received a letter from New York University, saying that William R. Parker, a leading Miltonist who had for some years combined the jobs of executive secretary of the Modern Languages Association and a professorship at NYU, was leaving, and Walter MacKellar, their Donne specialist, was retiring. They wanted someone to teach both Milton and Donne, and offered me a professorship at a negotiable salary, the minimum for the rank being $9,000. I didn't want to leave Chicago, but this was too important an opportunity to pass up silently, and I took it to Blair. This led to my promotion to professor, with a salary of $9,000. I thought I could have bargained for more from Chicago or got considerably more from NYU, but Chicago was the better university, I wanted to stay, and I didn't want to be difficult.

The university needed a new, larger library and I was put on the planning committee. Implementation had to await a benefactor, who was not found until after my departure, but the planning experience was later to stand me in good stead. The university also nominated me as one of its representatives to the Midwest Interlibrary Center, an organization of twelve universities formed to establish a co-operative library facility, and this experience was also useful later.

I would be eligible for a sabbatical in 1958, by which time I expected to have galley proofs of my volume; it was necessary to read these at the BM to ensure accurate rendering of Milton's texts and of the capricious spelling and punctuation of pamphlet quotations, and it was convenient to do other editorial chores in the same place. I therefore applied to the American Council of Learned Societies for a fellowship, which I received. By the spring of 1958, after many more tussles, not all of which I won, I had submitted my revised introduction and the edited tracts to Wolfe, and by May I had board approval, with a few final suggestions. In the following month or two I incorporated such of these as I agreed with, and Wolfe promised to send a first batch of galley proofs to me by October.

I had again written to Geoffrey Towse, a friend by now, this time requesting accommodation suitable for four for nine months; he got us the top two floors of a house in Glenloch Road, in Hampstead. At the beginning of September we flew to London on the British Airways turbo-prop Britannia, then a long journey with two small children.

I used the time before the arrival of the first galleys to verify references, which were legion. When the galleys arrived, not long after they were promised, I was able to check Milton's texts and pamphlet quotations against the originals. In those days of linotype printing one hesitated to make minor corrections because each one opened the way to new errors in the same line, or even page, but in this book there was no option: establishing a literal error-free text of Milton's prose was an essential part of our enterprise, and I wanted the quotations from other pamphlets to gain equal confidence ('modernized' quotation, even in 'accidentals' such as spelling and punctuation, has often transmitted an interpreter's imperfect understanding). The galleys arrived in batches; I returned them the same way and Wolfe had the corrected galleys set in page form as they came, so the page proofs would be ready soon after the last corrected galleys were returned.

It was tedious and demanding work, but we compensated in the evenings. The theatre season was very good, and the opera and ballet seasons even better. We were able to take advantage of these opportunities because there was room in our two-level apartment for an *au pair*. We began with Nita, a young Portuguese woman of wealthy family who was in England to learn the language; she was accustomed to many servants and it took a little tact to help her to adapt to our situation. Family complications drew her away after some months and we got Gerda, a young German woman who had a very possessive boyfriend at home but was a magnet for young men in London; she stayed with us until we left for home.

By the end of January I had sent off the last galleys and wouldn't receive page proofs for several weeks. I took off alone for a fortnight on the Continent (Lesley couldn't leave the children). I flew to Madrid on Air Iberia, the pilot giving a good imitation of a Calgary Stampeder; at the airport I tried unsuccessfully to arrange a drive to Toledo; two young Dutch women working for KLM at a neighbouring kiosk said they'd never been to Toledo, why was it important? When I explained its medieval and Renaissance glories they said they had the next day off and if I'd pay the expenses they'd take me. I agreed, then found that going fast on the mountain roads in the back seat of a Volkswagen was punishing. The cathedral and churches were very dark, but I had brought a flashlight; El Greco by flashlight is memorable. The Prado in Madrid had not yet been renovated; it was dark, cold, and drafty, but its collections were wonderful, especially since very few of the paintings had been reproduced and were therefore new to me. I stopped in Paris for a few days and checked some references at the Bibliothèque Nationale. I had booked a flight to Amsterdam, but it was fogged in and after much confusion I took a train there. After a few days in the Rijksmuseum, the Stedelijk Museum, and reference checking in various libraries, I spent an entire night at the airport waiting in vain for the fog to lift, then went back to London by sea.

New difficulties had risen with my volume. Hitherto I had screened all the criticisms of the work of the individual editors, arguing with Wolfe against those I disapproved and presenting in the most palatable form those I thought useful; even so, I'd had trouble placating my tract editors. Now Wolfe had the galleys in his hands and the excuse of my transatlantic distance, and he put new demands to the editors directly. This led to two kinds of difficulty. Williams rebelled, told Wolfe he wouldn't carry out his demands, and declared to me that he wouldn't add another word to his manuscript. Turner, on the other hand, now being given direct access to Wolfe, attempted to reverse a decision I'd made; and there were lesser problems with the other editors. It took an inordinate amount of time to mediate these positions by transatlantic mail, but at last all was agreed. Not long thereafter page proofs arrived, and the process of checking against both originals and galleys consumed many weeks. When at last I returned the corrected proofs, I was left with a post-parturition emptiness aggravated by my lack of confidence that the new corrections would be carried out without new errors.

I had never been in a Scandinavian country, despite their importance for both British and North American history and culture, so I flew to Copenhagen for a few days, Lesley again staying home with the children. Here the Glyptotek proved a modest attraction, with Tivoli Gardens and the working guilds, especially the silversmiths, a greater.

Before leaving for home in late June we attended the opening of the Mermaid Theatre in Puddle Dock, staging a Fielding play; it was the first new theatre opened in London for a very long time and was thought to portend a cultural revival of the East End, the London of Shakespeare's day. We also attended Glyndebourne for the first time.

V

The volume appeared in September and received a good deal of attention. All the English-language learned journals in the field, and some foreign ones, reviewed it, as did some in other disciplines, such as history and church history. One English and one or two American reviews treated it as if it were similar to Volume I, complaining about the number of footnotes, the length of the introduction, and the elaborate method of presenting *Doctrine and Discipline*, but most reviews were very favourable. Some were very extensive – *Seventeenth Century News* ran separate reviews of the volume's major parts in five successive issues – and the 1959 program of the Milton Society of America's annual conference described it as 'unquestionably the major event of the year in Milton studies.' I was at that time chairman of the Milton section of the Modern Languages Association, and although I naturally didn't put the volume on the conference program it was nevertheless discussed a good deal.

I received a number of job offers, all of which I declined without using them to bargain for more pay, thinking it imprudent to bring forward an offer unless one was prepared to accept it in the absence of an appropriate response from one's own university. One offer struck me forcefully, seeming to confirm the popular myth of Texas: Rice University, one of whose senior professors frequently taught at Chicago in the summer quarter and had come to know me, offered me an appointment; I sent a letter of polite refusal; shortly thereafter the Rice chairman telephoned to persuade me, and when I repeated my explanation that I was happy where I was he said, 'We can make you happier; we'll double the salary you're getting.'

I also received a number of invitations to lecture, most of which I declined, but one was from Toronto, and I neither could nor wished to decline that. Nor did I think it appropriate in that venue to rely entirely on material connected with the volume; there were to be three talks, of which one was based on my introduction, one on an article accepted but not yet published, '*Areopagitica* and a Forgotten Licensing Controversy,' and the third on an idea I'd been developing and would later publish as 'Milton's Idle Right Hand.' Milton's famous declaration in 1642 that, as soon as his currently necessary service in prose to church reformation was over, he would eagerly return to the service of God in poetry, had been much quoted and taken at face value; I showed, however, that there were substantial periods in the 1640s during which he wrote virtually nothing. To explain this I argued that, about 1637, he had renewed his dedication as God's poet rather than priest, this time giving a pledge of sacrificial celibacy in order to share the poetic inspiration of the 144,000 virgins of Revelation 14; but five years later, having performed what he thought good alternative service to God in the anti-prelatical tracts, he withdrew his pledge and married. The marriage was a disaster, and I argued that Milton felt he was being punished for violating his sacrificial pledge and that in consequence his poetic inspiration failed. When he does return to poetry, in *Paradise Lost*, he vehemently repudiates the 'hypocrites" doctrine of celibacy and adopts blindness as the symbol and source of his poetic inspiration.

In the course of this argument, I had to contest a number of what I thought wrong datings and interpretations of Milton's earlier poems, some by persons in my audience. Woodhouse's influential interpretation of 'Comus' had not taken account of the differences between the 1634 and 1637 versions, Barker had accepted and built upon a wrong reading of the 'Nativity Ode,' and both had been seduced by elaborate but demonstrably fallacious arguments in favour of an early date for *Samson Agonistes*; Frye had simply built upon what he thought agreed fact. There was, in consequence, an extremely lively debate after my presentation, greatly to the delight, I was told, of graduate students much in awe of these local titans. When I published the article the following year I added a lengthy appendix correcting the wrong datings, and the debate turned into an uproar, particularly since I had to demonstrate that the arguments of W.R. Parker and Allan H. Gilbert, which had held wide sway, were wholly indefensible. Parker promised an early reply, but it never appeared.

I arranged for Woodhouse to be given an honorary degree at the June convocation. He was delighted because he knew that Chicago, unlike other universities, gave such degrees only for intellectual achievement, and I strongly emphasized his in the citation. He was also delighted with the large party Lesley and I gave in his honour, partly because it included the president and many luminaries: Woodhouse was always a supporter of rank and hierarchy.

Claude Bissell had become president of the University of Toronto in 1958; he attended my lectures there and had previously read my volume and other publications. In October 1960 he spent a day with us in Chicago and spoke to me about returning to Toronto. Woodhouse was to retire in 1964, and both he and Bissell wanted me to succeed him as department head. I indicated my continuing affection for the U of T and the possibility that I might at that time be interested, but in the meantime I was happy at Chicago. In June 1961 he wrote to put the discussion on a different basis. Andrew Gordon, the dean of the School of Graduate Studies, would finish his decanal term in 1963; he would have another year before academic retirement but had indicated that he wouldn't ask for an extension of his decanal term. 'Finding a successor to Gordon,' he wrote, 'is, I think, my crucial administrative problem. The School of Graduate Studies is the fighting edge of the University, upon which its scholarly reputation principally depends ... I can see no natural successor here now.' He then suggested that I come in 1962 to have a year 'to get back into the Toronto way of things,' and become dean in 1963.

In follow-up telephone conversations he made a firm offer of $15,000 for 1962–3. When I reported this to my chairman he made a counter-offer, after consulting with the dean, of an immediate $3,000 raise, to $15,000, for 1961–2 if I agreed to stay on, a reduction in teaching hours from six to five, and a promise of a further raise for 1962–3. Bissell, writing from his summer home in Cape Breton, said 'I am delighted that Chicago is fighting for your services, and not in the least surprised,' and went up to $16,000 for 1962-63, with the assurance of a higher range when the decanal appointment came through.

We arranged that I should visit Toronto to meet the key academic administrators, which I did in September. There Bissell briefed me more fully on the general situation. The provincial government had belatedly become aware of rising post-secondary enrolment and had asked the province's universities for advice on how to meet the growing demand. The Committee of Presidents of Ontario Universities had established a research subcommittee under John Deutsch of Queen's, whose report projected continuing and steepening growth for many years and recommended the immediate expansion of undergraduate programs and the strengthening of graduate work in all disciplines in order to produce the required university teachers. Bissell had referred this report to a U of T planning committee, which accepted its findings and recommended that Toronto respond by establishing a number of new undergraduate colleges, some on the present campus and two in the suburbs, and that it also seize the opportunity to become the leader in the necessary expansion of graduate work in the province.

Work on the undergraduate expansion was in eager hands and well under way, but there was little enthusiasm for expansion of graduate work. The graduate dean, Andrew Gordon, a distinguished physical chemist of notoriously explosive temper, was concerned about the potential weakening of standards and was suspicious of government initiatives; he considered the graduate school's function as primarily to police the departments. He had not been supportive of a development that Bissell and Vincent Massey, the head of the Massey Foundation, had worked on, the founding of a graduate college, and lukewarm at best to another development Bissell was promoting, one very dear to his heart, a new library building. There was now a planning committee for this, but no firm decisions had been made and there would be ample room for a new dean to influence the plan. With respect to the proposed Massey College, it would be a residential graduate college offering facilities to the School of Graduate Studies and the academic departments but would have no academic functions of its own, and while it would report to the graduate dean, his responsibility would be very limited.

I asked about the school's constitution; its relation to the other faculties and the departments; its role in appointments and promotions, research, and university governance; its staff and budget; student housing; and many other matters. Bissell was able to answer most questions in a general way, which showed that his interest was more than abstract, and my own earlier experience of the school provided some context for his answers.

I then met individually with Gordon and with the deans of the faculties with significant graduate activity: Vincent Bladen of Arts and Science, Roland McLaughlin of Applied Science and Engineering, and J.A. MacFarlane of Medicine; also Moffatt Woodside, principal of University College, and Robert Blackburn, chief librarian. My interview with Gordon began rather like an oral examination, but apparently he was satisfied with my views on policies, standards, procedures, and strategy (and with my war record), for he ended up saying he hoped I would come. The other deans all professed an intense interest in graduate work and said it needed enlargement in Toronto; they all acknowledged that the school needed more influence in appointments, pledged to support such reforms, and urged me to come; Bladen added that, if I wanted to make a triumphal beginning and earn the gratitude of two large departments and his faculty, I should bring back with me Harry Johnson, of Economics, and a professor of psychology whose name I've forgotten, both Toronto graduates now at Chicago. Woodside was also very encouraging; he acknowledged that he had little to do with graduate work but recognized its growing importance, would welcome me on the college staff (the proposed appointment included a professorship of English in UC), and would help however he could if I came. Blackburn, who after a slow start began to view me as a potential ally, said he would welcome my participation in library planning.

Woodhouse confirmed that he would warmly welcome my appointment and would do all he could to help. I explained that if I came I'd be able to carry only a reduced load, to which he replied that something was better than nothing; this was not the way he had hoped to get me back but he was happy about it and would look in another direction for a successor as head.

I told Bissell that the attitudes of the major faculties, UC, and the English department seemed satisfactory, but library planning was on too limited a basis: it was predicated on a simple enlargement of present activities and did not allow for a development in the quality of activities, especially research; and it used a twenty-five-year planning horizon, which was half what it should be in a city campus where land was bound to become less available in twenty-five years. Another problem was that there was no plan to increase graduate-student support other than through Massey College, which would be on a limited scale. A further concern was that there was no provision for the school to influence appointments, and Gordon had confirmed (as had Innis, bitterly, before him) that he had no such influence.

Bissell's reply was that if I came I would be put on the library planning committee and he would support changes to the plan of the kind I'd suggested, and that discussion had begun with the province on graduate-student support and he thought it would be forthcoming. As for appointments, the place of the school in the university should be re-examined, but that would need new leadership; it was also tied in with my general role in the university, which he hoped would not be limited to the school: he needed help in the development and implementation of overall university policy.

We arranged that the Bissells would visit us in Chicago, which they did in November. Bissell brought a new suggestion: the term of the associate dean of Division I (Humanities and Social Sciences) of the school would be over at the end of June 1962; he proposed that I come as associate dean of the division and professor of English in University College, which would allow me to come to grips immediately with school matters.

The proposed arrangements, like the results of my Toronto reconnaissance, seemed satisfactory in themselves, and the U of T had a considerable emotional appeal for me, but I told Bissell that I was reluctant to forgo Chicago's academic superiority. He asked me to describe that, and as I analysed its elements we speculated on how far they could be emulated in Toronto. We talked far into the night, stimulating each other's sense of the possible, until we were both seized of a vision of the U of T transformed by research, graduate study, and new disciplines into a university of international quality.

Lesley had been part of the discussion from the beginning; after the Bissells left she and I tried to analyse the situation very deliberately. We were settled and happy in Chicago with many good friends, and my future at that great university was assured, with all the security of a tenured full professor and none of the turmoil of administration; I could write my book on Milton and the law of nature, and then another on *Paradise Lost*, teach my classes, and earn a quiet retirement. On the other side was the opportunity to help turn a good provincial university into something more, thereby giving a lead to other Canadian universities and affecting the whole Canadian educational system in a much-needed way; but this opportunity carried risks of a kind and extent we could not really foretell, and might result in an abrupt collapse; the prospect of a failed dean teaching in a resentful university was not attractive. Neither of us, however, really believed in such a failure, and the challenge of Toronto appealed almost as much to Lesley as to me. Besides, we had begun to wonder about Chicago as a place to bring up children and thought Toronto would be safer for them. We decided to go, and I wrote Bissell to accept his offer.

The next day I told Blair of my decision; soon Wilt came to my office and asked whether I'd see the president. I agreed on condition that there be no bargaining: I'd made my decision. George Beadle, who had succeeded Kimpton, was out of town, and I saw Pat Harrison, the second in command. He began by asking whether there was any use in offering inducements and I said no; he then asked my opinion of the university's condition, particularly of my department's, and ended by saying that if at any time I didn't like my new job I was to phone him and he'd see that I got my old one back. Beadle, when he returned, was very gracious; he too said Chicago would welcome me back at any time. Leaving a university one has come to love is wrenching, but these two interviews eased the pain.

The department set up a committee to consider a replacement for me, and I was, rather surprisingly, asked to chair it. When we got down to a short list of sixteenth- and seventeenth-century specialists, Williamson declared his willingness to resume teaching Milton (it was no longer thought incompatible with teaching Donne); this threw our emphasis onto the sixteenth century and we settled on William Ringler, of Washington University, whose edition of Sidney's poems Oxford was about to bring out. Blair, however, had personal reservations, and told Wilt that he preferred our second choice. They came to see me; Blair and I still disagreed, and Wilt said that he would have to endorse the recommendation of the department chairman but would arrange for me to see the new vice-president academic, Edward Levi.

I went to see Levi, whom I'd never met, and put forward the committee's reasons for recommending Ringler. He watched me closely from behind a large cigar; when I'd stated the committee's case, he asked, 'Why do you care?' I said that I had revived Spenser and Milton studies at Chicago and that, although the latter would be continued for the time being by Williamson, he would retire soon, and no one would carry on with Spenser if Blair's preference was followed; there were several dissertations being done under my supervision, one on Spenser, and there would be no one to supervise them; and that leaving the university didn't mean that I'd lost my feeling for it. He said he would think about it and I left. A few days later Wilt told me that Levi had instructed him to make an offer to Ringler, which was in due course accepted. Later, when I attended meetings of the Association of Graduate Schools, I several times met Levi, who represented Chicago but was not a graduate dean and, rather put off by their technical concerns, engaged me in talk about Chicago. When he became president of the university he invited me to attend his installation, where the celebratory dinner was made miserable by long, noisy demonstrations against the unwisely chosen main speaker, Robert McNamara, then National Security Adviser. Some years later, when I was president of the University of Manitoba, Levi asked me to help him secure for his university a deteriorated neighbourhood hotel owned by the insurance company headed by the chancellor of my university, which would be used for purposes harmful to his university if it fell into competing hands; I was very glad to be able to do this. Levi's tenure at Chicago was highly successful and he later became attorney general of the United States.

My departure put a formal end to the joint seminar, but it was really finished anyway. Brauer had become dean of Theology, Simpson of the college; my absence in England in 1958-9 had interrupted the seminar and we hadn't got around to restarting it, probably because it had stopped stimulating new thought. The experience taught me not only that a truly interdisciplinary course could be a responsible and rewarding academic enterprise but also that it might well have a natural life-cycle, and that in founding such an undertaking it would be wise to make provision for its termination when that cycle was complete, a lesson I carried with me to Toronto.

Another consequence of my impending departure was an invitation to participate in a new book series. Marshall McLuhan and Richard Schoeck, both of St Michael's College in the U of T, had proposed to the U of T Press a series of collections of critical essays on literary figures or movements; the Press, unable to contemplate the costs involved, had referred the project to the University of Chicago Press, with which it had working relations. The Chicago director, Roger Shugg, for whom I had read some manuscripts, knew I would be going to Toronto and told McLuhan and Schoeck that if I joined their editorial group he'd take on the series. Accordingly, they wrote to me, and on my next visit to Toronto we discussed the project and agreed to a series to be called 'Patterns of Literary Criticism,' each suggested volume to be agreed by the three of us and each to have a specialist editor who would write an original introduction and one original essay, the other essays being by several hands, usually reprints.

There was a somewhat disturbing outcome of Bladen's request that I 'bring' Harry Johnson and the psychology professor back to Toronto with me. I had said that if he made them offers I'd try to follow them up; in Chicago both told me they'd received offers, and Johnson came to discuss his with me. It was for barely more than his Chicago salary, but his main concern was that, as in previous offers it had made him, Toronto didn't seem to have any specific reason for hiring him in particular: 'they just want to add some laurels to their reputation.' I told him of Bissell's intention to build up Toronto's key departments, and he replied that, if Bissell personally could convince him that a serious strengthening of economics was in prospect, he'd consider the offer. I wrote to Bissell and a visit was arranged. It did not go well. Bladen and Tom Easterbrook, the department chairman, made it clear that they would not make the kinds of changes that would enable Johnson to effect serious improvement in the department, and his interview with Bissell was unhappy. Johnson told me that he'd given Bissell 'an earful,' and Bissell likened Johnson to 'an eastern potentate.' The psychologist's visit was also useless. I had persuaded two distinguished academics, one of them a friend, to undertake time-wasting and stressful trips on Bladen's urging; it taught me to exercise caution in my subsequent dealings with him. Before we left Chicago Johnson gave me a wood carving he had made for me (he pursued his hobby in classrooms and conferences worldwide); it consisted of one mule straining forward, linked to another mule straining backward, and was entitled 'Deaning.'

The housing market in Chicago was depressed in 1962 and we had difficulty selling our house; in the end it sold at a lower price than we'd expected, as a residence for Jesuits attending the U of C. In Toronto, on the contrary, the housing market was booming and it was difficult to find a suitable house. After several visits we found a three-storey turn-of-the-century house on Balmoral Avenue, just off Poplar Plains Road; it was expensive – almost twice the selling price of the Chicago house for about the same amount of space – but we bought it and moved to Toronto in June.

I was eager for the new challenge, but very regretful at leaving the university in which I'd come to professional maturity. My fifteen years there had been strenuous and competitive, which suited me well; I had met many people who were at the leading edge of their respective disciplines, in some cases getting to know them well and benefiting greatly from the exchange. It was an environment where excellence was assumed and the anti-intellectualism of much of North American society ignored, and I suspected that I would not again live in a comparable environment.

CHAPTER SEVEN

Toronto, 1962–1970

I

In the English department of University College, and in the college generally, there were many people who had known me before I left for Chicago, and there was in consequence considerable good will toward me personally and some optimism about my appointment; to a lesser extent this was also true of the federated colleges and of two or three 'University' departments. But to the rest of the university, where I was unknown, I was an outsider brought in by presidential fiat from an American university with predominant emphasis on graduate studies, to be associate dean and dean-designate of the School of Graduate Studies, presumably to reshape it in an American image, possibly with a separate graduate faculty, and with no commitment to, probably no knowledge of, Toronto traditions.

In an attempt to allay such suspicions I undertook to teach the Shakespeare course in the first year of the honours program as well as a graduate course in Milton, as a demonstration that I shared the Toronto view that members of the graduate faculty should also teach undergraduate work. These two courses amounted to two-thirds of a normal load in English, as against the half-load that Bissell and I had initially agreed on, but I thought it essential to make the tactical point. However, my sense of the training necessary for graduate students in English then led to a quixotic gesture. The department had no course in analytic and descriptive bibliography; there was only Endicott's non-credit course introducing undergraduates and graduates of other universities to the university library and to its main reference resources. I suggested to Woodhouse that the department needed a more advanced course for graduate students, and after some discussion he said, 'All right, if you'll teach it.' I didn't feel able to back out, but adding this to my two credit courses amounted to virtually a full teaching load, without considering my role in the graduate school.

The suspicion and resentment I'd anticipated did not take long to surface. At the first meeting of the Executive Committee of the school in the fall I sat next to Edward Sellers, head of Pharmacology, and across the table from Roger Myers, head of Psychology, the previous associate dean of Division I who had been denied a second term by my appointment. While we were waiting for the dean to arrive, and perhaps stimulated by sympathy for Myers (who was himself very civil and cooperative), Sellers turned to me and asked, rather brusquely, 'Do you know anything about the U of T?' I said yes, I'd taken two degrees and briefly taught here. Obviously surprised, he asked what is for Canadian academics fearful of American influence the test question: 'Where did you take your undergraduate degree?' When I said Manitoba, which is where he came from, he asked when, and it turned out that his wife and I had been classmates. Now much placated, he asked more questions, and when he found that I was born in Manitoba and had served in the Canadian Army overseas, he was ready to listen without prejudice to things I said, and in the ensuing years he became a strong and valued supporter of my policies. Something similar was true of a number of others whose initial hostility rose out of the fear that I would try to impose an alien system on them, but in some quarters it took years before I ceased to be regarded as a foreign ringer.

Shortly after arriving in Toronto, I met with Bora Laskin, whose report for the Canadian Association of University Teachers on the unjustified dismissal in 1958 of Professor Harry Crowe by United College in Winnipeg I admired, and who was the president of the U of T Association of the Teaching Staff. I asked him whether there were any deans or associate deans in the association; he said there weren't, and I asked why not. He supposed it was attitude; there was no prohibition in the ATS constitution. I said I was a member of the teaching staff giving three courses and wanted to belong to the association. He agreed at once and said that if I could encourage other deans to do the same it might have healthy consequences. I did get two or three deans to join, and for several years I attended meetings of the association, but as it became more like a union the other deans dropped out and I attended only rarely, although I retained my membership.

The School of Graduate Studies had been moved from Hoskin Avenue to the old bookstore next to the Observatory, and consisted of a general office housing the secretary, Jean Gordon, and two or three clerks, a meeting room, an office for the dean, and a smaller one for the two associate deans. The building, a classic 'temporary,' had no insulation, was crudely patched where sections of the inner wall had come away, leaked in heavy rains, was cold in winter and oven-like in summer, and generally symbolized the status of the school.

So did the school budget, which consisted of very limited fellowship funds, a meagre office-supply allowance, a small subvention to the federated colleges in consideration of their contribution to graduate work, salaries and stipends for the deans, and truly miserable wages for the office staff. I asked around and found that the pay scale for support staff in the other faculty offices was considerably higher, and resolved that the next budget would rectify this damaging injustice.

Long before budget time there was good news respecting graduate-student support. Bissell's prediction that the provincial government would make provision for this in anticipation of rapid expansion of undergraduate enrolment was borne out: a program of Province of Ontario Graduate Fellowships was announced for the 1963–4 session. It was to be confined to the humanities and social sciences, where the anticipated shortage of university teachers would be most acute and where other provision for student support was especially meagre, but otherwise it was virtually unrestricted: universities with graduate programs could recommend any number of awards for full-time graduate students; the stipend would be $1,500 for the regular session, with a $500 supplement for summer attendance; up to 20 per cent of the awards could go to non-residents.

The announcement had an immediate effect on attitudes. Faculty and administrators in Division I (Humanities and Social Sciences), thus for the first time assured that the provincial government valued their work, began to consider its expansion and prepare for increased enrolment, a few of them beginning to realize that the school could play more than a regulatory role. Division II (Physical and Biological Sciences), hitherto very conscious of being in a favoured position through National Research Council and Medical Research Council scholarships and faculty research grants carrying allowances for student assistants, suddenly felt aggrieved and demanded to be included in the POGF program, thus also becoming more aware of the school's potentialities (eventually we were able to persuade the government to include the sciences, but with a quota limitation).

In November 1962 Bissell held a retreat at the Guild Inn, consisting of the senior deans and central administrative officers plus myself. It was agreed that a second-in-command to the president was needed, to be called 'provost' (Moffat Woodside was appointed soon after), that the research office and the office of the registrar should be reorganized, and that a better method of negotiating with the Association of the Teaching Staff was needed. Then we turned to the library, which Bissell had prudently left to the end. It was indicative of the library's status that this crucial and determinative discussion took place without the chief librarian being present. Carl Williams, a psychologist who was head of the Extension department, was chairman of the Library Planning Committee, and Bissell asked him to summarize the planning to date. Then Bissell invited my comments.

I used the large-scale increase in graduate enrolment to be expected as a result of the POGF program to ask for a reconsideration of the basic assumptions. I suggested that we adopt a fifty-year planning horizon rather than twenty-five years, and that we aim at enabling all doctoral candidates at least to plan their research from our own resources, and a steadily increasing number to be able to carry it out here; this, I suggested, would mean an addition to our holdings closer to five million volumes than to the million being planned.

There was an incredulous silence in the room; even Bissell, who knew what I was going to suggest and had promised support, held his breath. The deans had all, to varying extents, been involved in earlier consideration of library expansion and thought themselves knowledgeable; for some of them the current plan to enlarge the Sigmund Samuel library building seemed over-ambitious, and they were all concerned that my proposal would divert capital spending to the library for years. The challenges were immediate, but I had been working with the enrolment projections on which the province had based its program, together with ratios I'd come to know while working on plans for a new library at the University of Chicago, and I was able to set forth my numbers for scrutiny. After they'd been examined and discussed there was some tendency toward agreement, but Williams was resentful. Addressing me directly, he said, 'Then you're changing the terms of reference?' It was, as he had intended, an embarrassing moment; I said I was recommending certain changes in those terms.

The minutes of the meeting read: 'The Library problem was discussed in terms of the strong recommendations of Dean Sirluck. We are thinking in terms of a Library that would have six million volumes in fifty years' time. It is agreed that this poses the problem somewhat differently, and that therefore the Library Building Committee under Dr Williams should meet immediately, with the addition of Dean Sirluck, to examine the function of the new Library, its size and its possible location.'

Later Williams went to Blackburn, the chief librarian, whom I had told what I was going to propose, and offered to resign from the committee but was persuaded to stay, and in the following months the committee, with his agreement, adopted my proposals. This would require a much larger site than was available in the old campus, and thoughts turned to the projected new campus west of St George Street.

The impending increase in Division I enrolment caused me to

think anew about the problem of quickly securing large numbers of new post-secondary teachers. In the humanities, and somewhat less in the social sciences, Toronto was notorious for the length of time its doctoral candidates took to complete their dissertations, and for the large number of ABD (all but dissertation) students who never finished. One problem was the scarcity of research materials, and work was now satisfactorily in train on that, but a different kind of problem was the one I'd encountered as a doctoral candidate: most departments in Division I had not really clarified the object of their doctoral programs. They all professed that the dissertation was to be an original contribution to knowledge, and in that sense it was a research degree; but they all also required two years of course work beyond the master's degree (three years beyond the four-year bachelor's), to which most added comprehensive examinations emphasizing coverage, which, taken together, made it almost impossible for the candidate to get a serious start on the research during the three years of residence; and thereafter lay full-time employment. A further problem was that the limited number of doctoral dissertations in most departments meant that few faculty members had much experience of supervision, and of course no training in such supervision had ever been contemplated: it was felt to be an art that came naturally with mastery of the subject-matter and membership in the guild.

This situation stood in urgent need of clarification on its own account, but meanwhile it seemed clear that the PhD in the humanities and some social sciences could not serve as a means for producing large numbers of new post-secondary teachers quickly, and I tried to work out an alternative. I thought that, throughout Canada, increasing demand for university places, municipal and regional ambitions, and economics would lead to the founding of new colleges with purely or mainly undergraduate mandates, and that such colleges would need teachers expert in their subject but not necessarily pursuing research careers. The MA did not seem enough to base a career on; would a master's degree of twice its weight be?

I worked out an outline for a two-year degree to be called 'Master of Philosophy' and put it before Dean Gordon, emphasizing that it would have to be structured so that it could not be mistaken for a failed PhD, and that departments should be free to decide whether they would use it or not. After a great deal of discussion, he said there might be merit in it but he was sure Division II would not use it. I then brought it to the Executive Committee, where debate was warm and protracted, with a final narrow decision to recommend it to the divisions, which met as half-councils because the council of the school, consisting of all members of the graduate faculty, was too unwieldy to operate without intermediate recommendation.

When I presented the proposal to Division I it received considerable support from the humanities, while some social science departments thought it would threaten the reputation of the PhD; it passed by a good majority. Jack Breckenridge, associate dean of Division II, presented the proposal there without recommendation and it was received very coolly. At the council of the whole school the proposal was approved with the notation that it was unlikely to be of interest to Division II. The final stage was in the senate, where the whole debate was repeated, and the proposal passed. The new degree came into effect in 1963 and was offered by a fair number of departments. It spoke to a need felt beyond Toronto, and a number of universities in Canada, the United States, and Britain, as well as the U.S. Office of Education, asked us to come and explain the degree; two or three Ontario universities and some others adopted it. At Cambridge and London, in England, and Waterloo, in Ontario, it was separate from the PhD and won respect, but at Yale it could be used as a consolation prize for not getting the PhD, and at Michigan it was given to mark the ABD stage of the PhD, and such uses naturally undermined its integrity and reputation. At Toronto it lasted about twenty years and was dropped when the academic market suffered a prolonged downturn and a surplus of PhDs became available.

Massey College would be fully functional in 1963–4, and Bissell, Gordon, and Robertson Davies, the first master, hoping to exploit its opening, had invited the Association of Graduate Schools to hold its annual conference in the new graduate college in 1963. The AGS consisted of the forty or so North American schools awarding the largest number of PhDs and included two Canadian members, Toronto and McGill; I accompanied Gordon to the 1962 conference, where he introduced me as his designated successor. Near the end of the conference we were asked to step outside while our invitation was considered. We went to the bar, where Peter Elder, of Harvard, that year's conference chairman, found us and asked Gordon whether he would still be dean the following year. The significance of the question was immediately clear: Gordon was a senior member of the association and a suitable host; the association did not know me. Gordon didn't reply at once; I made an instantaneous calculation of comparative benefits, then cut in and said, 'Yes, he will.' Elder asked Gordon whether that was right, and Gordon, barely audible, said yes. We then returned to the meeting, Gordon was elected vice-president of the association, and Toronto's invitation was accepted.

Afterwards Gordon asked how I thought Bissell would react; I said to leave that to me. When I told Bissell what had taken place he was not pleased, but I emphasized to him how much the university stood to gain by the exposure. He agreed but wanted to know whether all progress would be halted for an extra year; I assured him not, although I was not as confident of Gordon's co-operation as I pretended.

In fact, at budget time, I had a little difficulty with him. I asked him to let me see his budget request; he was accustomed to playing a very close hand and hesitated, but gave it to me. It showed disappointingly little change from the previous year's. I worked out large salary increases for Jean Gordon and her staff, together with provision for additional staff to handle the expected increase in enrolment, and fees for visiting examiners and thesis appraisers. He was shocked and I had to argue every item, the salaries by comparison with other faculties, of which he apparently knew nothing, the additional staff because of the larger administrative burden increased enrolment would bring, and the visitors because we needed to ensure that new courses met generally accepted standards, and this would give us an opening to encourage all departments to expose themselves to what other universities were doing. Finally he said that, although what I said made sense, the president would never approve such an increase. I replied with the same words I'd used a little earlier about extending his term: leave it to me. He sensed the echo and said I could try if I chose, but I'd have to sign the budget request – he wouldn't. I agreed, went to explain it to Bissell, and it was approved.

II

Interdisciplinary graduate work was in effect barred by the school's statute, which required that a candidate for a graduate degree pursue his or her work 'under the direction of one department.' This reflected the traditional ethos of the university, in which the departments were like separate medieval baronies. There were several research and service centres or institutes but none offering work for academic credit. I had spoken to Gordon and others about my experience in the joint seminar in Chicago and emphasized how the publications that came out of it were of a kind not readily achievable through a single discipline. Bertie Wilkinson, a distinguished medieval historian, responded with a proposal for a centre for medieval studies offering a degree program, and I thought it exactly right as an exemplar: a substantial and distinct field which offered ample opportunities for research requiring a combination of several clearly differentiated disciplines, with abundant local talent and adequate research materials. (Three independent church-related universities – Victoria, Trinity, and St Michael's – had long ago federated their arts colleges with the U of T; along with the university's own constituent college, University College, that had produced four separate teaching staffs in the 'college' subjects: English, French, German, Classics, Near Eastern, and Ethics. In addition, the church-related universities retained their separate theological faculties, which were an important resource for medieval studies, and later for the study of religion.)

I undertook a long process of persuasion. Fortunately, Gordon respected Wilkinson and some of those associated with the proposal, which inclined him to listen as I set forth argument after argument, including a demonstration that the combination of the federated structure of the university with the presence of the Pontifical Institute of Mediaeval Studies gave us the means to become the strongest force in medieval studies in North America. At last he consented to have the matter brought before the Executive Committee, where the statutory requirement of 'one department' became central to the discussion. I urged that it was a statute of the senate, which if it chose could either suspend it for a specific purpose or, as I would prefer, give the proposed centre the status of a graduate department, and the proposal was agreed. In Council and in Senate support came not only from the many faculty members in or near to medieval studies but also from some in other disciplines who saw in the innovation an opening for their own interests, and the Centre for Medieval Studies, with Wilkinson as director, was brought into existence in 1963 with all the powers of a graduate department, serving as an important precedent both locally and elsewhere.

The Linguistics Centre, also established in 1963, was a proposal of my own. All the language and literature departments, and some others like philosophy and those involved with computer studies, did linguistic work in the course of their other pursuits, but it was impossible to get a degree in linguistics itself at any level in the university. I thought there should be a regular Linguistics department at both undergraduate and graduate levels, but the overlapping departments were unwilling to surrender any of their turf. Finally, I concluded that the only way to make progress was to establish a purely graduate program in the school and hope that it would be fed from the various undergraduate sources long enough for an undergraduate program to emerge in Arts and Science. It was a hard struggle; every concerned department included someone willing to help and some others determined to obstruct. This was one of the many occasions when I benefited from my earlier period at Toronto: many senior people in the language and philosophy departments who were sceptical of the 'new' discipline were reluctant to oppose something I strongly believed in, and some even gave it limited support. It had a much rougher passage through Council and Senate than had Medieval Studies, but that program was a powerful precedent and the Centre for Linguistics was established in the same year. A problem was a director; it was agreed that an appointment from within would intensify turf wars, so we searched outside. Jaan Puhvel, of Berkeley, accepted the post but then changed his mind; finally we appointed Martin Joost, of Wisconsin, the first academic appointment other than the dean wholly on the budget of the school – another important precedent.

Computer science was in some respects analogous with linguistics; it was taught in many departments, such as mathematics and the pure and applied sciences, but the university had no degree program in it. There was a computation centre, but it was primarily a service organization; it was now proposed that an institute of computer science be established with a graduate degree program, again without an undergraduate counterpart. This time the opposition from the departments with vested interests was much less, partly because Linguistics had shown the way; and this time a director was very easy to choose from inside: all the recommendations made to me were for Calvin Gotlieb.

Two other, more modest, proposals that year did not fare so well. One, from Law, spearheaded by John Edwards, was for a centre for criminology which would offer a course that could be credited by any graduate department that approved it. Gordon refused to recognize criminology as a graduate subject and I advised Edwards to have the centre established within the Faculty of Law and then bring it forward to the school again in 1964. He was very reluctant to wait but could make no progress with Gordon and in the end took my advice; in 1964 we got him the limited graduate status he wanted.

The other proposal was from Marshall McLuhan for a centre of culture and technology. In *Halfway Up Parnassus*, Bissell tells how he and President John Kelly of St Michael's worked out an arrangement to keep McLuhan happy in Toronto, and it was with their backing that McLuhan made his proposal. Bissell writes: 'Andrew Gordon was the last person in the world to have any sympathy for McLuhan's unorthodox probes. Sirluck ... acted as intermediary. "The Dean suggests," wrote Sirluck, "that if the President would like to establish such a centre in the University at large, the School would have no objection." This was academese for saying that the graduate school would not give academic credit for work offered in such a centre. Sirluck added, conscious that he would be succeeding Gordon: "Next year we can try to thread him through the portals guarded by the Executive Committee of the School." The centre was so threaded and has had a tranquil and productive existence' (pp. 83–4).

It was not as easy as Bissell's account would suggest: Gordon was by no means alone in thinking that McLuhan was a charlatan, and I think my cautious support of his centre cost me some credibility. Nor was supervising his centre 'tranquil'; he frequently tried to get away with things contrary to regulation or instruction and, when checked, sent his old Manitoba friends, Jack Sword and Carl Williams, both members of his centre and vice-presidents of the university, to argue with me; to their credit, they valued legitimacy and didn't push matters. Of course, then he would go to the president, who sometimes eased him over the difficulty.

I was seeing McLuhan frequently in another context: he, Schoeck, and I met from time to time to plan volumes and procedures for our series, 'Patterns of Literary Criticism.' We would discuss possible volume topics and editors, submit several to the University of Chicago Press for approval, then one of us would be given responsibility for a particular volume, with approval by all three required before it could be published. My first suggestion was for my Chicago colleague Elder Olson to do a volume on Aristotle's *Poetics* and English literature; it was published in 1965 as the first in the series.

The senate, the academic governing body of the university, consisted of almost two hundred senior academic administrators, elected faculty members, and representatives of the alumni, the provincial school system, and the licensed professions of the province. Some people derided it as a useless talking shop, and Bissell thought it a block to progress, but I found it willing to entertain and respond to rational argument. I thought from the beginning that, because of its size and representative nature, its approval of any initiative would be a huge step toward its acceptance throughout the university, and I took my senate membership very seriously, participating in many debates that touched only remotely or not at all on the interests of the school. I was also on its Executive Committee, where policy could be discussed in a much smaller body. However, Bissell's scepticism about the efficacy of the senate caused him to divert many issues to special Presidential Advisory Committees, whose composition he determined and whose recommendations he could introduce to either the senate or the top governing body, the board of governors, where the final power lay.

I was put on many of these PACs; one was particularly significant, that on policy and planning. Most of my policy innovations were discussed there or in the successor body, the President's Council, before proceeding to the appropriate constitutional body. One proposal I made, which I knew would not be accepted but which I hoped would prepare for a more modest measure, was that the school be put on a trimester system. There had been much discussion in the press and in government circles of a twelve-month university year, to utilize the plant and personnel more fully. Everyone in the university knew that such a proposal would be fought tooth and nail, but I thought such a battle would threaten university autonomy, and I thought it could be avoided by a limited plan making greater use of the summer and achieving some needful ends.

I proposed that the graduate year be divided into three trimesters, any two of which would count as a full academic year for both students and faculty. Faculty members in departments choosing to use this plan could 'bank' credit for released time to be used when they wished it, to a prescribed maximum and in accord with the department's teaching needs. Formal graduate courses would for the first time be offered during summers, enabling full-time students to complete their residence requirements faster and giving new credit opportunities to teachers and others who could only attend in the summers, as well as increasing the opportunities for research guidance in the summer. To prevent faculty exhaustion and encourage released time to be used for research, summer teaching would not be for extra pay but only for time credit.

As I anticipated, this proposal drew fire from many directions, especially from Brough Macpherson, of the Department of Political Economy, who saw in it 'range after range of difficulties,' most rising from the linkage between the graduate and the undergraduate programs. As these difficulties were either met or acknowledged, the committee began to warm to the opportunities embedded in the idea, especially since from the outset I had taken the same tack as with the Master of Philosophy degree: that the plan would be for only those departments that wished to use it. The president, with whom I'd already discussed the matter, knew that released time would cost much more than the existing summer stipends, but agreed that the gain, both academic and political, was worth the cost, and the committee finally agreed to support the initiation along the lines I'd outlined of a formal summer session.

I brought the proposal to the school council, where all the difficulties were carefully examined with the help of the many members who were heads of both graduate and undergraduate departments, and it was agreed that the plan should be attempted. We settled on a fourteen-week term, to make it fully equivalent to half an academic year, and this, with the other arguments, satisfied Senate. The idea of bankable released time proved immensely attractive to faculty members, especially in library-oriented disciplines, and 28 courses were offered in the first summer session in 1964, with 175 students taking 228 courses for credit. Each year while I was at the U of T, the number of participating departments grew, and I had the satisfaction of seeing some people who had originally opposed the idea, including Macpherson, happily taking part; even greater satisfaction came from the increased faculty research and the expediting of student programs. Best of all was the evidence I was able to offer that the university's resources were really pretty fully used during the summer, which the deputy minister told me forestalled a move by the Department of Education to press for greater control of universities.

My course in bibliography led me to try to get a hand press for instructional purposes. Roy Gurney, of the U of T Press, was also interested in hand printing, and we were working on reconstructing a junked press of his when I read that Roy Thomson, the press baron, had purchased the Edinburgh *Scotsman* and was renovating its plant. I got Bissell to ask him whether there was a decommissioned hand press available, and Thomson sent us an Albion 48, hitherto used as a proof press and in good working condition. We set the press up in the disused key-room in the basement of UC and my students seemed to enjoy working with it; however, I turned the course over to someone else the next year, and the press eventually moved to Massey College, where the librarian, Douglas Lochhead, used it as the nucleus to build a considerable hand-press collection.

Social antisemitism in Toronto had diminished but had by no means disappeared. It was customary for some university functions to be held at the nearby York Club, which had a special reduced membership rate for senior U of T officers. After having been taken there for lunch several times by different persons, I was asked by Gordon whether I'd like to be a member; the special rate was manageable and I agreed, not knowing that the club didn't accept Jewish members. One day I found Neil McKinnon, head of the Canadian Imperial Bank of Commerce and member of the university's board of governors, waiting in Gordon's office to congratulate me on having been elected to membership the previous evening. They told me I'd be informed when the next vacancy occurred. Some time later I was lunching there as Bissell's guest when Leonard Brockington, then a famous figure in Canada, sat down with us; after we had chatted a little he asked, 'What is your background? Norwegian?' 'No,' I replied, 'Russian Jewish.' When he left, Bissell mentioned that he was chairman of the club's membership committee. I never heard from the club about my election to membership. Bissell later acknowledged that he knew the club excluded Jews and was deeply troubled by it but in his circumstances didn't know what to do about it. Later, shortly after I had been appointed graduate dean, the vice-chairman of the board, O.D. Vaughan, said worriedly to Bissell, 'Did you know that Sirluck is a Jew?' Bissell replied that he did, and no more was said. Gordon and Vaughan were very close friends; Gordon had earlier made antisemitic remarks in my presence but not after this; he never mentioned my Jewishness to me and the knowledge seemed not to affect our relationship.

In the summer of 1963 the Commonwealth Universities Association held its quinquennial congress in London. I was part of the Toronto delegation and Lesley came with me, the children being safely disposed at a closely supervised summer camp. There was a preliminary session at the University of Southampton, of interest to the conference for its new residences (where I came to know F.T. Prince, whose poetry I admired); then the main session at the University of London. Universities and governments everywhere were coping in diverse ways with a general post-secondary expansion, and it was instructive to see their different methods and results; in Britain the founding of new universities, and the upgrading of technical collegiate institutes into universities, were producing much tension between the new and the old universities and the new and the old curricula. As yet, few universities showed any concern that growing government grants would be followed by increasing governmental supervision, putting a touching faith in university-grants commissions.

It was surprising that the serious work of the congress could be sustained under the immense weight of hospitality. In the London sessions alone there were nine formal events, including a garden party at Buckingham Palace, receptions of incredible lavishness at Guildhall and Clothworkers Hall, somewhat more restrained but still abundant receptions at the University of London Senate House, Lancaster House, and (for Canadians) Macdonald House, and a dinner at the Grosvenor House hotel. The presence of the Queen and the Queen Mother (as chancellor of the University of London) at some of these events evoked some extraordinary behaviour on the receiving line, some people elbowing furiously to ensure they'd be presented. One entertainment was especially applauded: the prime minister, Harold Macmillan, was to toast the association; it was during the Profumo sex scandal, which threatened his government; with the Queen watching on his left, he tore up his prepared speech and talked about the personal problems of government, to the audience's delighted response.

After London the overseas members were divided among several university tours; Lesley and I went to Wales and Northern Ireland. In Belfast we encountered a special kind of myopia: the 'troubles' had for the moment subsided, and we were strongly assured by both Protestant and Roman Catholic members of the university that they were permanently over!

III

Enrolment in the school in the fall of 1963 amply fulfilled the expectations on which we had predicated so many initiatives. In 1962 there had been 552 full-time students in Division I and 673 in Division II, for a total of 1,225; in 1963 there were 778 in Division I and 867 in Division II, for a total of 1,645, an increase of 41 per cent in Division I, 29 per cent in Division II, and 34 per cent overall. This was a rate of increase even greater than projected in the Deutsch Report, which had alerted the province, and was evidence of a pent-up demand now unlocked by the POGFs and by certain federal initiatives. The staff of the school was hard-pressed to cope with the logistics of this intake, and even Gordon conceded that the extra appointments had been necessary. Fortunately, staff morale was high because of the salary increases and the school's rising status, and they were willing to work extended hours. The physical capacity of the ramshackle building was, however, stretched to its limits, and I told Bissell that we would need larger quarters for the following year. He supported this request, and after some negotiating with Buildings and Grounds I obtained a house at 65 St George Street, which was to be vacated by the Extension department at the end of the session. It was a handsome Victorian family home which had been divided into many cubicles, and I stipulated that it be restored to its original configuration. A couple of years later, to accommodate the school's continuing growth, we acquired in addition the larger adjacent Number 63, at various times the home of Sir John A. Macdonald and Sir Oliver Mowat.

Other Ontario universities with established graduate programs were also experiencing the stimulus of POGFs, although not in Toronto's proportions, and those without graduate programs or with very limited ones began to think of initiating or enlarging them. At the suggestion of several graduate deans, I convened a meeting of the representatives of all Ontario univerities offering graduate work to discuss the terms and administration of the POGF program and ways of maintaining the quality of graduate work in the province. It was a memorable meeting, held in the Round Room of Massey College. We began with the POGF program: would the government get agreed university advice in defining key terms, such as 'full-time attendance,' 'summer sessions,' 'qualifying disciplines'? would it leave administration of the program to the universities? or in these and similar matters, would the civil servants do as they chose?

It was moved that we form the Ontario Committee of Graduate Deans to make recommendations concerning the POGF program to the Committee of Presidents of Universities of Ontario. Several representatives thought this would be interference with the autonomy of individual universities. All were in various degrees suspicious of Toronto and resentful of its dominance, but some saw the need for joint action. The discussion went on and on, getting increasingly bitter. Finally, I intervened from the chair: no action would be successful unless it embraced all universities doing graduate work; in the absence of such action, the government would do as it saw fit; I thought that, if that happened, the University of Toronto would come out all right, but each representative would have to decide for himself how his university would do. It was a dangerous card to play: everyone who imagined that the ministry habitually did Toronto's bidding could see this as confirmation; but it worked. The motion was unanimously adopted and I was elected chairman of the new committee, a post I retained until I left the province. It was clear, however, that it would be unwise at this time to proceed to the other topic, maintenance of quality.

I reported this development to Bissell and asked him to put it on the agenda for the next meeting of CPUO, of which he was chairman; he did so and asked me to attend. Here the deans' discussion was in part repeated, at a lower level of intensity, but with a new twist: the universities without graduate programs had not been represented at the deans' meeting and feared they were being excluded from a growing field. They wanted all universities to be represented on the new committee, which would become an advisory subcommittee to CPUO. I thought that if universities without graduate programs were on the committee it would not be able to do the work intended, and pointed out that if it became an advisory subcommittee to CPUO all the presidents would have knowledge of and access to its work. That was accepted, and we became

CPUO's Subcommittee on Graduate Studies, the forerunner of similar subcommittees in specific fields, such as Arts and Science, Engineering, and Medicine.

CPUO accepted our particular recommendations on the POGF program and transmitted them to the government's Committee on University Affairs, of which J.R. McCarthy, the deputy minister of education, was secretary. He was glad to have them, and he took the opportunity to create a direct channel to the graduate deans by coming from time to time to discuss POGF problems with me. It soon became clear that he wanted to enlarge the area of discourse. The government had recently committed itself to a policy of access to universities for all who qualified, and was beginning to feel the resultant pressures. In May 1963 Premier Robarts had suggested in a speech that universities go on the trimester system in order to utilize their resources more fully, and this had been taken up and supported by all three Toronto daily papers, who of course thought that professors worked only seven months a year and should be required to work eleven. In November, McCarthy made a particularly ominous speech in Ottawa, saying that if universities didn't quickly solve their problems they would lose their autonomy. In fact, he would have welcomed such a development: he thought the universities should become a tertiary level under the Department of Education, with provincially determined curricula, admission standards, and supervision.

I had already realized that there would have to be some rationalization of effort in the provincial universities and that the government would be involved; I now felt that it must be a distinct branch of government, and along with others began to propagandize for a separate Department of University Affairs, preferably with a separate minister but certainly with a separate bureaucracy. This became a CPUO goal, and at a meeting it held with the minister of education, William H. Davis, to which I was invited, it achieved its minimum objective, a separate department. But Davis said he would 'for the time being' hold both ministries, and rejected CPUO's request for a separate secretariat. McCarthy held both deputy positions until 1967, when the bureaus were separated and he stayed with Education; Edward Stewart became deputy for University Affairs.

In 1964-5 there was a sudden proliferation of new universities and colleges in Ontario: Trent, Windsor, Laurentian, and Brock were founded, Scarborough became operational, and Erindale was not far behind. York, which had been developed under the U of T's aegis, became autonomous. (My overready mouth earned me some dislike in this: in Senate, Bissell said from the chair that the planned time for York to leave U of T had arrived, and would someone move to that effect? Everyone expected that York's president, Murray Ross, who was present, would make that motion, but he didn't, and an uncertain silence ensued. Finally I said, 'If it can be done without the appearance of unseemly haste, I will so move.' Ross didn't like the laugh that followed, and in my subsequent dealings with York I found that the story had spread.) All these institutions wanted to do graduate work. The graduate deans advised CPUO that this would be disastrous, and somewhat belatedly the mandates of Trent, Laurentian, and Brock were restricted to the baccalaureate. U of T's off-campus colleges were an internal problem, which we solved by cross-appointing their eligible members to the St George departments. York from the beginning was planned to include graduate work.

It was clear, however, that the new universities would not forever be content with their undergraduate limitation, and that more institutions would become universities. The problem had been temporarily contained but not solved, and CPUO decided, without consulting its Subcommittee on Graduate Studies, to suggest to OCUA that a commission be appointed to study the development of graduate programs in Ontario. I was informed of this after the fact, and the graduate deans were not asked to assist in drawing up the terms of reference or naming the commissioners (although I was personally consulted about one proposed name, someone I knew in the Association of Graduate Schools). The government, not surprisingly, jumped at the proposal, and in establishing the Spinks Commission in 1965, Davis used the key word 'planning': 'Of the many areas of higher education that require planning, the most important is that of graduate studies.'

This context enabled me to return to the Graduate Deans' agenda the matter too explosive to be pursued at our initial meeting, the maintenance of the quality of graduate programs, this time linked to the even more difficult issue of the orderly development of graduate studies. We had approached these subjects from time to time but without much progress. By now, however, we had developed some degree of common purpose, and the external pressures were more palpable. All the deans were now in favour of some qualitative test of graduate programs proposed by the new universities. The trouble came when I pointed out that to make this acceptable to the new universities, and therefore to CPUO, such appraisal would have to apply to all new graduate programs, including those proposed by established graduate schools.

Instantly the deans who had been so eager to thwart, like Juno, the birth of graduate programs by their upstart rivals, recoiled in wrath and vehemently attacked me. I was proposing a flagrant interference with their established institutions' autonomy. Strong doubts were expressed that I could secure agreement to my proposal on my own campus. I agreed that I wouldn't be able to, or want to, unless it were a common action applying to every institution, but pointed out again, and forcefully, that if we didn't achieve credible qualitative controls of our own it would be an invitation to the government to impose their controls, which were unlikely to be as valid. Gradually the logic of this position sank in, and over the course of several meetings it was accepted by all.

I was authorized to recommend to CPUO that we be reconstituted the Ontario Council on Graduate Studies, with a committee on appraisals, which would consider all proposals for new graduate programs solely from the point of view of academic adequacy, utilizing a standardized informational format and discipline experts from outside Ontario as appraisers, the cost to be defrayed by a charge on the university being appraised. At CPUO I emphasized that we were not now proposing that the question of need be considered, but that we might later be able to make some separate recommendations on that matter. CPUO was naturally very cautious, and the presidents without graduate programs were particularly uneasy. The question of enforcement rose early; I answered that I thought that, if the system came into effect, the Department of University Affairs would not finance new programs that had not been successfully appraised. To the question of what the deans would do if some universities refused to participate, I replied that the universities which favoured the proposal would operate it by themselves. When the objectors realized that their abstention would not prevent an appraisal system from being established, and that thereafter a government which had set up the Spinks Commission was unlikely to fund unappraised new programs, all the presidents decided to support the proposal.

The deans who had suggested that I wouldn't be able to gain acceptance of the scheme on my own campus were wrong: the Graduate Council debated the matter at length, many objections were voiced and some led to refinements in the scheme, but in the end Council voted overwhelmingly in favour, as did the senate. The extended discussion and widespread consultation proved exceptionally useful later, when the Ontario Confederation of University Faculty Associations protested the plan to both CPUO and the Department of University Affairs, because the U of T Association of the Teaching Staff, and some other faculty associations, dissented from their Confederation's position. Thus, when the executive committees of CPUO and OCGS met with the OCUFA executive to discuss its objections, the U of T members and some others had the immense advantage of our own faculty's support, and were able, through lengthy discussion, to persuade OCUFA to withdraw its objections. It was on this occasion that I first encountered Gerald Caplan, later a prominent New Democratic Party strategist; he proved a clever debater but amenable to reason.

The Appraisals Committee, which I chaired, became functional at the beginning of 1967. The Department of University Affairs did, as predicted, declare that only programs approved by the committee would receive government funds, which ensured that every proposed program came to the committee; by no means all were successful, and that not only inhibited the formulation of inadequate proposals but also assisted departments in getting the needs of their proposals recognized and supported by their own university administrations. Adequate staff, library, and laboratory resources, or at least authorized plans for their acquisition, were necessary to satisfy the first stage of the appraisals procedure, and in many universities librarians for the first time gained some budgetary influence.

Planning was naturally a much more difficult problem. To have introduced the question of the province's need for a proposed program into the appraisals procedure, as was often suggested, especially by government people, would have been to destroy a successful initiative. At first, every attempt to discuss planning or controlling the development of graduate studies was obstructed by the ambitions of the several institutions, intensified by the recognition that the U of T was unique in that it already was in all established fields and would expect to stay in them. The stimulus for a move forward was provided by a leaked chapter of the Spinks Report, which would not be published until November 1966 but whose most dramatic recommendation, for a University of Ontario on the California model, became known well in advance and shocked the presidents (although privately Bissell thought it not a bad idea). With this threat to their continued existence as independent institutions confronting them, and the fear that the government would adopt it, the universities were ready to discuss measures they had previously rejected out of hand, and it became possible for OCGS to agree in principle that we should pursue some division of responsibility for specific fields of graduate study and research.

This agreement in principle then allowed us to formulate a further proposal that we develop a provincial system of research libraries with acquisition responsibilities to correspond to the division of graduate responsibilities. I took this first to the Committee of Librarians of Ontario Universities, which after some hesitation endorsed the proposal. Working together, the two committees added recommendations that we develop a provincial bibliographical centre, an interlibrary-loan system with a transit and communication network, and liberalized access to one another's holdings.

There was as much initial dismay in CPUO as in OCGS about the planning proposal; indeed, at dinner, a well-lubricated president of a new university violently denounced the graduate dean who had accompanied me for this presentation for what he said was the intention of the latter's older institution to dominate their whole geographic area and suppress his own university's growth. But they all feared the impact of the recommendation for a University of Ontario and wanted to forestall it. They wanted to know how we would approach planning the division of responsibility. I said this had not yet been discussed by the deans but that personally I would favour a general meeting of all the presidents, graduate deans, faculty deans, department chairmen, and chief librarians in the province, leading to a compilation of an inventory of current activity and resources, and listings of planned initiatives, needs, and opportunities, and that we could then decide how to move forward on the basis of what that procedure revealed. Edward Sheffield, the executive director of CPUO, persuaded the presidents that this would be unworkable, and I didn't pursue the idea for the moment; what I wanted was approval in principle of the recommendations, and after a long day's discussion that was given. The librarians' committee was reconstituted as an affiliate of CPUO, the Ontario Council of University Librarians, and the Advisory Joint Council of Ontario Graduate Deans and Librarians was formed, of which I was alternately vice-chairman and chairman until I left Ontario.

In 1962, shortly after my return to Toronto, I helped found the Canadian Association of Graduate Schools, which became an affiliate of the Association of Universities and Colleges of Canada, and on whose executive I continued to serve while I remained a graduate dean. The role of CAGS was much more marginal than that of OCGS because education in Canada is a provincial responsibility and the federal government has only an indirect role; nevertheless, that role, rising out of its responsibility for labour-force training and research, is of great importance to higher education. The federal government was accustomed to receiving and considering advice from AUCC, and CAGS tried with considerable success to influence that advice, especially with respect to the budgets and policies of the federal granting agencies. The very rare occasions when CAGS communicated directly with government were unavailing, but it did develop useful direct communications with the federal research councils and some operating agencies, such as the National Library.

The clash of interests in CAGS was never as direct as in OCGS, but there were nevertheless strong differences, chiefly about the extent to which fellowships and research grants should be used to build on strength or to nurture beginnings; just beneath this theoretical question lay a familiar Canadian struggle, which frequently surfaced, between old and new, large and small, region and region. Toronto and McGill were the individual institutions most resented, partly because of their dominance but also because of a national study of some years earlier, led by Innis and Woodhouse, which recommended that all graduate work beyond the MA be concentrated in those two universities. 'Ontario' as a collective was, as in most Canadian gatherings of the time, the great bogeyman, although after the initial successes of OCGS its advice became more welcome.

In 1962 I was asked by the Canada Council to serve on its Final Review Committee for research grants, whose nominal function was to appraise the awards recommended by the discipline committees but whose real task was to reduce their number to a total corresponding to the money available. This was like a crash course in Canadian politics, more intense than that in CAGS. There was, first, the Quebec factor, not quite the same as the French–English factor, which also had to be considered; then other regional considerations; then the reverse-pecking-order or underdog factor, both as to institutions and as to disciplines (Toronto and McGill must not end up with too much, nor must English and history); finally, there were considerations of quality, feasibility, relevance, utility, relative value, and similar factors which the uninitiated might think determinative. Actually, the academic committee members, who were for the most part very good, were willing to give these factors primacy, but the Canada Council officials, without openly saying so, wanted them contained within their political framework.

In 1964 another somewhat similar chore was virtually imposed on me by the chancellor, Achille Jeanneret. He had served for some years on the Canadian Committee for Commonwealth Scholarships and Fellowships; he now intended to resign and wanted to recommend that I replace him. I asked what was involved, and he said two meetings a year in Ottawa. I really couldn't spare more time for committee work in Ottawa, but Jeanneret urged that Toronto, the largest single recipient of overseas scholars and fellows, should be represented, and pointed out that the fellows would be coming to the School of Graduate Studies, so I reluctantly agreed. At my first meeting I was dismayed by the procedure. There were eight or ten academics from across Canada and several staff members of the Canada Council, which administered the program; copies of the applicants' files were distributed, then the significant documents were read aloud by a staffer, after which there was leisurely discussion. By noon only a few decisions had been made and a formidable heap of files remained unopened. I asked when we would finish and was told the afternoon of the third day! I said I hadn't expected to stay more than a day but would arrange to stay one day longer, then suggested that in future the files be sent to us in advance and that we make it a one-day meeting. This caused shock – the council trembled at the work involved and the 'threat to confidentiality,' and the committee members apparently enjoyed these protracted expense-paid junkets. However, the procedure, if not the time limit, was agreed, and future meetings were a day and a half. I stuck it out for three years and then escaped.

I learnt a great deal about the Canadian university scene, and about Canada, during my four years of service on these two Canada Council committees; I also learnt a lot about the Council, and was ready, when the opportunity presented itself, to recommend the separation of the council's two very different functions, the support of the creative arts and the support of university research.

About the same time I accepted another, much less onerous, outside appointment. When I was at Chicago I had served as one of the university's representatives to the Midwest Interlibrary Center, at that time a consortium of twelve universities operating a cooperative library storage centre. It had since grown, and decided in 1962 to establish a category of non-voting associate members paying half-fees. Blackburn thought this would make it possible for us to join and asked what I'd think of the U of T becoming a member, without making clear that he meant associate membership. I said I'd support it, and he invited the director, Gordon Williams, to

Toronto, where Bissell and I joined them and we discussed the U of T library plans over lunch. Williams invited us to become the first associate member; this was news to me, and I said we ought to belong but would have nothing to do with second-class membership. He promptly changed the invitation, and in July 1963 we became a regular member of the centre; I was elected to its board of directors, along with Blackburn, but I never attended, sending one of my associates because I knew Blackburn always attended and would look after our interests.

IV

The graduate subvention to the federated colleges, under a formula developed in 1952, would have amounted to $53,000 in 1963-4, to which a supplement of $10,000 was added. Bissell called me to a meeting requested by the heads of the colleges – Arthur Moore of Victoria, John Kelly of St Michael's, and Derwent Owen of Trinity – to discuss the future of the subvention, which they thought inadequate. I suggested that the simultaneous growth of undergraduate and graduate enrolment gave them an opportunity to improve the quality, as well as to enlarge the size, of their faculties: if they took the needs of the graduate programs into account in making their new appointments, I would recommend that a new formula be devised which would reimburse them for a calculated portion of the salaries of those of their faculty giving graduate courses, rather than merely continuing the token subvention now paid. They would not require the prior agreement of the heads of graduate departments before making new appointments, but prior consultation would facilitate appointment to the graduate faculty and subsequent approval of graduate courses.

They were pleased by the offer, but they had an initial reservation: historically, the UC department heads had also been the heads of graduate departments; that was still the case, with the exception of Classics, where for very particular reasons George Grube, head of the Trinity department, had become the graduate head and was now coming to the end of his term. Would the graduate head always have to be from UC? No; I hoped that, as the federated-college departments strengthened in research and publication, they would be able to present suitable candidates. Who would succeed Grube? I didn't yet know, but I would chair a selection committee which would include representatives of all the colleges. With these assurances they all accepted the offer in principle. Payments were enlarged during the next two years, and when the new formula came into effect in 1966 it yielded $140,000; in 1968–9 it would have produced a little over $200,000, but was supplemented by another $100,000; and in 1969–70 another revision, this one containing the explicit proviso that the colleges would obtain the graduate dean's approval of all new appointments expected at once or later to offer graduate work, yielded about $500,000. These changes, in addition to encouraging high-quality appointments, were intended to establish a norm in the university: a graduate course was not to be tacked onto an ordinary teaching load, as had been the custom in many departments, but was to constitute at least a full third of a total load.

The appeal of the new arrangement was immediate. The faculties of the federated colleges stormed their graduate-department heads with proposals for new graduate courses, and the heads had to become very serious about selection. I had cautioned them that appointment to the graduate faculty would have to be on the basis of stated qualifications, which would be scrutinized, and that growth in the number of courses would have to be commensurate with growth in their student numbers. They all carried out this changed mandate scrupulously, which led to some disappointed applicants, but these now had a motive for qualifying, and increased publication soon resulted, along with a notable strengthening in the quality of appointments.

The appointment of a successor to Grube had a significance well beyond the Classics department. The school's statute provided that the head of a graduate department would be appointed by the president on the recommendation of the graduate dean, but this had always been a pure formality: the various faculties followed their own procedures, appointed heads of undergraduate departments, and then presented the graduate dean with a *fait accompli*; he could only concur. Gordon told me he'd never had any influence in the selection of graduate heads, any more than in the appointment of graduate faculty, and Innis had complained publicly and bitterly of the same lack of influence. The college subjects provided a strong opportunity to exemplify the differing mandates of graduate and undergraduate heads, and I used it. I chaired the committee to select a new head of the graduate Classics department and encouraged sentiment favouring Mary White, also of Trinity and not a department head. Her appointment, the first of a woman to head a graduate department at Toronto, constituted our first example of a graduate head who was not an undergraduate head, a distinction important for my purposes. The appointments of directors of centres and institutes also manifested the school's changing role, as did appointments in the Schools of Social Work and Business, neither of which had undergraduate structures. But this left the main mass of the university unaffected, and it was here that the gravamen of graduate work must lie.

I reminded Bissell that, during my initial reconnaissance of the position, his senior academic officers had promised to support the enhancement of the school's influence, especially in the selection of heads of departments, and he asked Bladen and Woodside to include the graduate dean or his representative on such selection committees. At first I was invited only to the final meetings, which made my presence ineffective, but after some pressure on my part the invitations took place at the initiating stage and worked well. But Bissell was reluctant to make the same request of the professional faculties, and this became one of the problems to be referred to a general examination of the purpose and organization of graduate studies, as was the wider problem of appointments to the graduate faculty.

Growth in the teaching staff naturally followed enrolment growth, but improvement was not automatic. The most urgent concern of heads of departments and deans of faculties was that their proliferating undergraduate classes be taught, and the easiest and cheapest way to ensure this was to make appointments at the junior level; furthermore, at a time when enrolments were expanding everywhere, the competition for new staff meant that it was easiest to appoint new or recent graduates of your own department, which had the added advantage of gratifying home egos. Then the same department head who had recommended the new appointees put them on the graduate faculty, which ensured graduate courses but also that they would largely be in the same mould as before. But knowledge was expanding at unprecedented rates in almost all disciplines and beyond the traditional disciplinary borders, and if the university did not use the expansion of its faculty to obtain footholds in these new areas it would lose the opportunity for a generation.

I felt that it was my responsibility to press for this more strenuous response to the need for new staff, and since the provincial grant was expanding Bissell agreed with this view. He also agreed that the constitution of the school needed revision, both to add authority in the matter of appointments and to make the structure more functional. He was aware, as I was, of certain centrifugal forces which were growing with the expansion of the school. Some of the science departments with outside research grants felt that they could run their own graduate enterprise without the participation of weaker departments or the supervision of a central school; this was also true of some departments even in fields where research money was less significant but where there was substantial external student-support money. Some budgetary deans saw the growth of the school's budget as competition and its growing influence as interference, and some weak departments feared that the school's new emphasis on research and publication would threaten their graduate ambitions.

I was convinced that internal considerations – the systematic advance in quality, the initiation of neglected disciplines and fields, the development of necessary academic support services, equal treatment across the university both of students and of staff, and the achievement of the influence and leadership within the university structure requisite to attain these goals – required the maintenance and strengthening of a unitary graduate school, and that because of external factors anything else would be disastrous. Growth in graduate enrolment and our capacity to cope with it were the direct results of government support, and with this growing investment would inevitably come growing informational and control demands which would necessitate a university-wide response. I was in no doubt about the government's ability and willingness to leap upon any variation of response within the university, such as would be inevitable in any but a unitary structure. Furthermore, all hope of coordinated action by the province's universities depended on Toronto's lead, and such a lead would disappear with the end of a unitary school. Bissell agreed with this view but could not ignore the centrifugal pressures; he also felt the growing challenge everywhere to traditional university hierarchy, with the concomitant decline in administrative authority just then making itself felt at Toronto, and he judged that he needed a presidential advisory committee to examine the academic, administrative, and financial structure of the school in the light of its new responsibilities, and to recommend necessary or desirable changes.

He chose the membership of the committee with the advice of the deans whose faculties would be most affected; of the eleven members, Bladen was allowed to nominate four, and Medicine, Engineering, Law, the federated colleges, and the graduate school each made nominations. The result was what Bissell calls 'the strongest internal committee in the history of the University of Toronto' (*Halfway Up Parnassus*, p. 80): John Cairns, of History; Harry Eastman, of Political Economy; Kenneth Fisher, of Zoology; Northrop Frye, of English and Victoria College; Archibald Hallett, of Physics; Charles Hanes, of Medical Biochemistry; Bora Laskin, of Law (chairman); Robert McRae, of Philosophy; John Polanyi, of Chemistry; William Winegard, of Metallurgy; and myself; Frances Ireland of the president's office served as secretary. The committee was appointed in December 1963, worked steadily for almost two years, held more than forty meetings, sent delegations to visit some twenty universities in the United States, six in Britain, and six in continental Europe, received seventy-eight group or individual submissions from within the university, and held numerous hearings on campus.

This process saw a remarkable evolution of opinion. Laskin put it judiciously in his report: 'It is worth comment that the Committee has arrived at recommendations in which all its members concur. The auguries for such a consensus were quite poor when the inquiry began.'* At the outset, only Eastman, Winegard, and I, all with administrative commitments to the school, were unequivocally in favour of a unitary school with a strong budgetary and appointments role; Fisher and Hanes, both department heads, favoured a vertical organization, with the individual department responsible for all graduate administration; Hallett and McRae thought the faculty or professional school the best base for graduate work; the others began with less defined views, but all bore certain home loyalties. In these circumstances I didn't think I could afford to miss a single meeting, and didn't.

I went on one of the expeditions to the United States, to California, with Laskin, Polanyi, and Hallett. We got to Berkeley at the height of the confrontation with the Free Speech Movement; as we stood in the midst of an excited throng, warmed up by Joan Baez and harangued by Mario Savio, watching the police carry the occupiers out of Sproule Hall, Laskin said loudly, 'As a *dean*, Ernest, what do you think of this?' He was delighted by the angry swivelling of heads. I also went to Britain with Laskin and Hanes, and on to Italy, Germany, France, and Holland with Laskin. Everywhere we found that, as it attracted greater numbers and government support, graduate work was becoming less informal and more organized, that policies, procedures, and administration were becoming standardized throughout the university. This tendency was most marked in the United States, somewhat less in Britain, and least but moving in the same direction on the Continent.

The committee began with what its report calls 'the threshold question': one graduate school or many? This was not soon settled, but the initial discussions brought out the various concerns of different constituencies. Then we moved to particular problems and looked for workable solutions. Gradually the uncommitted members began to lean toward a unitary school, then even those who had favoured competing models, and in the end the whole committee endorsed the unitary model. Before we got there we had settled upon answers to many particular questions, and in the end

---

* *Graduate Studies in the University of Toronto: Report of the President's Committee, 1964–1965* (Toronto: University of Toronto Press, 1965), p. vii

the report gave full endorsement to the whole of my program: restructuring to make the unitary school more effective; a strong role in the selection of deans, directors, and heads, and in the appointment of senior faculty; formal qualifications for appointment to the graduate faculty; interdisciplinary centres and institutes with degree-granting powers; clarification of the PhD as a research degree and support of the PhilM as an alternative; a central research library; special linkage with a research council; responsibility for graduate-student and postdoctoral support; the dean's membership on a university budget committee; graduate-student residences and a building for the Graduate Students Union; and many other constructive recommendations.

One recommendation had been overtaken by events. The president had already set up a research council, to which the school's links were comparable with those of other faculties. This had been a very contentious issue. At a meeting of the Laskin Committee in September 1964, Fisher had distributed a recommendation by the Presidential Advisory Committee on Research that university money for the support of graduate students in the sciences should be distributed through the Committee for Scientific Research. What infuriated me, aside from the naked threat to the integrity of the school, was that the recommendation was dated the previous October and I had never been told of it. I wrote a very hot letter to the president, saying among other vehement things that such action would end the concept of a unitary graduate school. Three weeks went by and I got no answer, although I did get a request from the president for my opinion on a quite different matter. Finally I asked for an appointment and met with him on 15 October. He had not seen my letter: the flow of mail now went through the provost and vice-provost, although he was still to receive 'crucial' letters, and it had been a mistake that mine went to Woodside for reply. Bissell read the copy I had brought and agreed with it: the proposal would not be considered (he didn't explain why I hadn't been told of it).

But two weeks later he told me he was appointing Gilbert Robinson to head the research office and proposed 'putting him in your bailiwick.' As he elaborated, it became clear that he didn't mean the school to have jurisdiction over the new office, just to give it an academic setting and some prestige. I said it would allow people to play Robinson and me off against each other and split the school; let him be housed in Simcoe Hall and report to the provost. Bissell was unhappy with my response, said I would have to guard against the charge of empire-building, but followed my suggestion. In the event, responding to the pressure of the science departments, he gave Robinson a vice-presidency; I think he feared that unless he gave them some of what they wanted they would unite against the research library, whose cost would divert a great share of capital construction from the sciences.

The Laskin Committee report was published late in 1965 and at once gave rise to widespread controversy. Several deans felt that their turf was being invaded; Bladen's reaction was particularly violent. He felt betrayed by his nominees, particularly by McRae, who was his associate dean (and who tells me that he was never forgiven). He drew up a petition against the committee's recommendations and got his other associate deans and the heads of all his departments except Zoology and Anthropology to sign, although I have reason to think that several wouldn't have done so had that been safe. Much excited discussion preceded a special meeting of the Graduate Council, augmented by deans, principals, and other interested administrators, which the president had called to receive the report. All over the campus, people were looking forward to what was being called 'the battle of the deans,' where it was expected that Bladen and I would fight it out. The Senate Chamber was crowded and people were sitting in the aisles; the atmosphere had something of a Roman holiday about it.

I came ready for battle and armed with facts and figures, but they weren't needed. Laskin presented an analysis of his report in a very thorough and persuasive manner. All members of the committee were there, most of them clearly ready to participate; the same readiness was not evident among the signatories of Bladen's petititon, who tried to make themselves invisible. Bladen did the prudent thing: he rose as soon as Laskin finished, declared that he was a wonderful advocate and had largely persuaded him (Laskin had in fact said nothing not already in the report), and that he would not oppose the report but thought that the particular recommendations should be discussed in smaller groups (which gave unintended support to my plan to make the Graduate Council smaller and elective). I immediately accepted this concession but asked that Council approve the report in principle, which led to a useful discussion, allowing several council members (among them Laskin's own dean, 'Caesar' Wright) to register their reservations without having to oppose the report itself.

Council's approval in principle was followed in February 1966, by two open symposia, both well attended, about which Bissell wrote in a letter to me while I was in England on a half-sabbatical: 'I get the impression that the heat generated just before your departure has now been dissipated.' This constructive discussion led to the establishment of two committees, one to examine in detail the feasibility of the Laskin recommendations and another to frame specific resolutions for Council to vote on. This work proceeded very satisfactorily, and in due course a series of resolutions incorporating most of what I'd been recommending was approved by Council. I returned in time to chair a committee to draft a new statute providing for a unitary school with a small elective council; four divisions (Humanities, Social Sciences, Physical Sciences, Biological Sciences), each with a comprehensive council; graduate departments, centres, and institutes whose heads and faculty were to be recommended by the graduate dean; and other good arrangements. This went through Council and Senate without any renewal of controversy, and it has remained substantially unchanged ever since.

V

In March 1964, I was appointed graduate dean with effect 1 July, at an initial salary of $21,000. I had too often had to cancel classes because of out-of-town missions to continue undergraduate teaching and now reduced my load to a graduate course, whose meetings could be rescheduled if I had to cancel because of a time conflict (but after two more years I had to drop it too). In addition to a growing external involvement, I was now serving on so many university bodies that it was clear that I would need help, and I asked for authorization to appoint an assistant dean; this was approved and I looked about for someone on the science side. After some consultation I settled on William Winegard, of Metallurgy, who agreed to come. A successor for me as associate dean of Division I was also needed; I consulted widely for this and then asked Harry Eastman, of Political Economy, already a member of the school's Executive Committee, who accepted the appointment.

In July we moved into 65 St George, restored to its original configuration, and found it excellent for our purposes. Its bare, newly painted walls were an opportunity; I asked William Withrow, director of the Art Gallery of Toronto (now the Art Gallery of Ontario), a recent graduate of ours, to lend the school a number of Canadian paintings so that the hundreds of faculty members and students meeting, examining, or passing through the school might acquire some sense that there was a Canadian art, not at that time a universal conviction. We walked together through the Canadian galleries while I pointed out some fifteen or so paintings I liked; some of these he sent, and for others he found counterparts in his vaults. I also asked Peter Swann, director of the Royal Ontario Museum, for some three-dimensional pieces, and he sent me two display cases full of splendid oriental artefacts and some Roman statuary. All this art work, distributed through the building, had a wonderfully civilizing effect; when I returned the art on my departure for Manitoba, the school environment was left bleaker.

Lesley liked the house and drew it for a Christmas card which I had printed and distributed to all members of the graduate faculty, thus beginning a practice which we kept up until my retirement. Lesley's scenes were so well-liked that several faculties asked her to do their buildings for covers for their calendars, and in Winnipeg the *Free Press* devoted an entire page to reproducing her University of Manitoba scenes when I retired.

In March 1964, Bissell took me to a meeting with the minister of education and Robert Jackson and some other staff members of the Ontario College of Education. Davis declared his intention to establish what became the Ontario Institute of Studies in Education to do graduate work and research in educational theory and practice, and asked whether it could grant U of T graduate degrees. I had been briefed by Bissell and shared his reluctance to see a free-standing institute capable of churning out limitless numbers of higher degrees without control, which would debase all Ontario graduate degrees; I knew the school's controls could only be partial but thought that better than nothing. I explained the route to graduate degrees at U of T and suggested that, for credit purposes, OISE could become the Graduate Department of Educational Theory within the school; the head of the department would have to be recommended by the dean to the president; our only control over staffing would be whether we would approve appointments to the graduate faculty; students would have to be admitted and degrees granted by school standards; and courses would have to be approved in the regular way by Council and Senate. I was asked whether I would recommend George Flower, who was present and whom I knew, as graduate head, and said yes. Jackson, who would be head of OISE, seemed satisfied, and Davis confirmed that affiliation with the U of T was the best choice.

However, by the time I informed the Graduate Council of what the government was planning, word had circulated of Davis's choice for chairman of the institute's board of governors: an official of one of the teachers' federations with little knowledge of universities. There was much concern in Council that, under him, the institute would be immersed in the politics of Ontario's many large and strong teachers' organizations and drag the school along; we needed someone whom the university community would trust. I shared this view and spoke to Jackson about it, who arranged for me to see Davis. I thought it would have been better for Bissell to go, but he declined.

Davis was very civil but for a long time unyielding, having to some degree committed himself. I conceded that he would have to be the judge of what was in OISE's interest, but I doubted that the Graduate Council would approve the Department of Educational Theory if the institute's board was headed by the person he'd chosen. 'Would you recommend it?' he asked. 'No.' Long silence. 'Well, whom would you suggest?' 'Bora Laskin.' Surprised, brightened countenance. 'Well, he'd be wonderful: he was my teacher;

but what makes you think he would accept?' 'I've asked him and he has said he would.' Davis was delighted; he realized the embarrassment to him and the blow to OISE of an initial confrontation with the graduate school, and he may also have been persuaded by my argument. I don't know how much difficulty withdrawing the original name caused him, but he agreed to appoint Laskin and we parted on good terms, after an interview that several times looked very threatening.

Laskin did in fact conduct the board with great regard for university concerns; nevertheless, Woodside and I, who were the U of T's representatives on the board, tried never to miss meetings, since OISE had a tremendous budget and a predilection for wild schemes, not all of which we were able to stop. It hired staff at a bewildering rate, brought in students on extremely fat fellowships, and proposed dissertation topics ranging from the respectable to the laughable, except that coping with them was no laughing matter: the school's battle against trivial topics and jargon-ridden dissertations never ended during my tenure. On balance, however, I think it was better for education in Ontario that OISE was not established as an autonomous degree-granting mill, and I have the impression that it has improved with time.

George Williamson was to retire from the University of Chicago in 1964, and I was asked to contribute to a *Festschrift* in his honour. I was not then pursuing literary scholarship but I couldn't decline this request, and decided to mine my doctoral dissertation. In the introduction to my volume of the Yale edition, I had fully worked up Milton's use of the law of nature in the prose of 1643-5, which was not directly political; I now showed how this natural-law theory of the state gave him the basis for his defence of the regicide and establishment of the Commonwealth in 1649, and how, in the works of the following five years, this secular theory became at first mixed with and then replaced by a contradictory theocratic theory. I then said that any explanation based on development or confusion was precluded by the precise repetition of this pattern in 1659-60, which I would show in a future study, and called the present article 'Milton's Political Thought: The First Cycle.'

Alas, I never wrote the promised follow-up, nor did I do anything further to utilize the unpublished thesis. I had become so immersed in the work of developing graduate studies, and more generally the U of T, that I could not take on serious literary scholarship, which like serious administration absorbs the whole mind. There was an immediate embarrassment: Woodhouse too would retire in 1964, and I was asked to contribute to a *Festschrift* planned for him, but by that time I had promised my piece to the Williamson book and had nothing else. I wish I had wrested myself free for long enough to write up the second cycle in the promise I never fulfilled, the more so as my absence from the Woodhouse volume caused him disappointment and gave rise to comment from others.

To add pain to embarrassment, there was a wretched exchange with Woodhouse about this time. He phoned me late one evening, in a manner reminiscent of my days as his graduate student, to discuss the departmental headship. He wanted Priestley to succeed him and wanted me to help bring it about. I tried to wiggle out: the UC headship was a matter for the principal, who would presumably set up a selection committee; the graduate headship would be decided later, certainly by a committee. He brushed all this aside and pressed his main point, which was for me to use my influence. I said that I liked Priestley and respected his scholarship, but that I didn't think the department would accept his somewhat authoritarian style. This painful discussion went on and on, becoming almost unendurable when he said, 'So you side with the Americans in the department against me.' I denied it, said I was siding with no one. 'Then whom do you want?' I said I had no candidate but was willing to make a suggestion: Clifford Leech. Leech was English and had been brought in two years earlier as a full professor; Woodhouse had taken special pleasure in appointing him; he was an excellent traditional scholar and critic, and was well liked. Woodhouse leapt at the suggestion: 'I never thought of him, but of course!' The conversation could thus be brought to a civil close, but Woodhouse's naked demand and my refusal could not be obliterated from memory, although the only reference we ever made to it was when I called him to say that the selection committee, on which I served, would recommend Leech. Sadly, Woodhouse died a few months after his retirement.

Another embarrassment had to do with the Yale *Milton*. After my volume was published some members of the editorial board had suggested that I be invited to join it, but Wolfe not surprisingly demurred. The critical reception of my volume, together with Woodhouse's withdrawal, led him to change his mind, and when I was invited I really had no decent option but to serve. Unfortunately, the first volume thereafter to be ready was Wolfe's Volume IV, published in two parts in 1964. I did what I could to modify Wolfe's excesses, but it didn't amount to much, and I felt uncomfortable to have my name on the flyleaf of his volume. Worse for me, but in a different way, was Volume V, which didn't appear until 1971 but on which trouble had started much earlier. Max Patrick, who was doing the state papers, got almost at once into a struggle with Wolfe, which he represented as parallel to mine and appealed for my help. It wasn't the same, but I felt obliged to help, which meant the renewal of the wearisome combat with Wolfe at the expense of much time and energy, after which I withdrew from the board, pleading the burdens of the Manitoba presidency.

In November 1964 I was the speaker at the first University of Manitoba Festival of the Arts, which meant three lectures. The first, which was on the university situation in Canada, took place the evening of the U.S. presidential election, and Lyndon Johnson beat me as thoroughly as he did Barry Goldwater: most of the expected audience stayed home to watch the election results. The next afternoon and evening, when I spoke on Milton, there were good audiences. It was my first substantial visit to the university since graduating; I had visited it for an hour or two many times during our years in Chicago and Toronto, but those visits were too brief to teach me much. I was now struck with the physical development of the campus but not greatly impressed by faculty morale. The pervasive depression that I had known had been overcome by relative prosperity, but seemed to have been replaced by a feeling of directionlessness, at least in the arts and science sector; what I saw of the professional faculties seemed predominantly vocational.

An outside commitment which took time but which I enjoyed and profited from was membership from 1964 to 1968 on the Woodrow Wilson Dissertation Fellowship Selection Committee. This recently established program addressed the ABD problem, and since that was acute at Toronto I was glad to be invited to participate. I did not set out to grab fellowships for Canada, but the committee approved a considerable number for Canadian applicants, of which many were for Toronto. At home I was able to utilize the resultant improved completion rate of our dissertation-fellowship holders to secure increased budget provision for a similar program which I had recently begun.

Another considerable outside commitment was with the Association of Graduate Schools. Its 1963 meeting in Massey College, the first in Canada, had been very successful, and I had come to know many of its members. When I succeeded Gordon as graduate dean I was appointed to its Committee on International Education, which entailed extra meetings but broadened my knowledge of educational systems outside North America. When my term on this committee ended in 1966, I was put on the Policy Committee, of which I became chairman in 1968. During that year the committee met in San Francisco; one of our issues was the student movement and I remember our noisy but instructive interviews with the leaders of the movement at Berkeley.

Bissell, partly through his membership in the parent body of the AGS, the American Association of Universities, and partly through other contacts, was also seeing something of the growing student movement in the United States, as well as a growing faculty movement, and his earlier concerns about 'the two solitudes' of Board and Senate were being reinforced by what he perceived as a growing gap between Senate and faculty. As a temporary measure to bridge these gaps he established, in May 1965, the President's Council, which was to consist of some members of the board, some academic and non-academic administrators, and some elected faculty members. The council, which superseded the Policy and Planning Committee, would be the principal agent for formulating policy, which he could then take to Board or Senate; beyond that, he hoped he could use it to work towards a new unified form of government for the university, which would embrace all its constituencies (which I called 'estates,' a name soon generally adopted). He consulted with me, as with others, beforehand; I supported the idea of an interim council, but entered strong reservations about an end to the academic senate. He accepted this in good part and I served on the council from its establishment until I left for Manitoba.

In the fall of 1966 Northrop Frye told me he'd received an extremely handsome invitation from Columbia: he mentioned a very high salary, a secretary, research assistants, a research fund, and graduate-student support. He had declined invitations from many universities, but this one had to be seriously considered. He didn't want to leave Toronto, but he was staggering under his load, with college administration (he was principal), undergraduate and graduate teaching, and a growing load of thesis supervisions; the vastly better working conditions were tempting, and the money was a factor. I said that the university would certainly want to keep him; what work would he like to drop? He said he'd want to keep his connection with Victoria but not the principalship, teach one undergraduate course there and one course in the graduate school which might not always be confined to the Department of English, and have a secretary and a place in which he could shelter from interruptions. I asked whether he'd prefer to speak with the president himself or have me do it, and he asked me to do it.

Bissell shared my determination to keep Frye, and accepted my suggestion that we create a new rank, University Professor, entitled to offer graduate work open to students throughout the university whose departments were willing to accept it for credit; that we give him an office and secretary in Massey College; and that we determine his total salary, letting Victoria pick up the portion it thought fit for his undergraduate course and carrying the rest, which we could set competitively, on the president's budget; Victoria would have to free him from the principalship. Bissell made the arrangements with Victoria and Massey, and Frye told me he was very happy with them. He declined Columbia's offer, and his continued presence was of enormous benefit to the school, the university, and the country.

Father John Kelly, the president of St Michael's, and Father Lawrence Shook, president of the Pontifical Institute of Mediaeval Studies, came to see me in a very sombre, almost desperate, mood.

The Pontifical Institute, they said, was in immediate danger of closing down; it didn't even have the funds to finish the academic year. The archdiocese had refused all aid; St Michael's had done all it could. I asked about the Vatican; they replied, rather bitterly, that all it had ever done was to charter the institute. The only source of income other than transfers from St Michael's was tuition fees, and these had fallen steeply because students, including priests, preferred PhDs to the private theological degrees the institute was able to give.

I asked how much they'd need to finish the academic year, already half over; they named a sum which I thought manageable and I said I would try to get it for them. A little of the weight seemed lifted from them. We turned to the long term. Shook recalled that in 1963 I'd arranged that, if institute staff were first cross-appointed to St Michael's, they could then be cross-appointed to the university's Centre for Medieval Studies, give graduate work, and qualify for the St Michael's graduate subvention; this had been the basis for St Michael's help to the institute and had in fact kept it going for two years. Now, he said, looking apprehensive, if we could go further and allow institute courses taught by such cross-appointed staff to count for credit toward U of T graduate degrees, students would have a strong incentive to register in the institute and their tuition fees would save it. Did he mean that students would be able to count the same course twice, once for the institute's theological degree and then again for the university's graduate degree? Looking pale and desperate, he said yes, acknowledging that it was against university policy but urging falteringly that credit would be given only once within the university.

I was perplexed. Such an exception to university policy would be very hard to justify or to limit to one area; I could imagine a similar request involving a Protestant seminary reaching the school through Victoria or Trinity, and if those were granted the way would be open to areas other than theology. I mentioned this concern but said that the prospect of losing the institute justified exceptional measures; I would consult with my colleagues and report to them. Meanwhile, would it help if the school told the archbishop how much it valued the institute? They were sceptical, but were glad to have me try, and arranged an interview.

Bishop Pocock, recently of Winnipeg, had been appointed acting archbishop of Toronto, and I thought he might consider my opinion seriously. For one thing, I was a Jew and had no axe to grind in the Roman Catholic Church. For another, my uncle Sam Nitikman had been chairman of Pocock's fund-raising campaign for the Misericordia Hospital in Winnipeg, which had exceeded its target, and had frequently mentioned Pocock to me. In fact, when I mentioned my uncle, Pocock's initial formality relaxed into warmth. He listened to my praise of both St Michael's and the institute, said he was glad to hear it, but the archdiocese was concentrating its attention on St Augustine's Seminary and he could do nothing.

It was clear that Shook's proposal was the institute's only hope. Steering it through Graduate Council and Senate was not easy and provoked some comment that had anti-clerical, even anti-Roman overtones. In the end, recognition of the uniqueness of the relation between the Medieval Institute and the university's Medieval Centre, and therefore of the probability that we could keep the arrangement unique, got it through, helped by Shook's scholarly reputation and Kelly's personal popularity. I think it also helped that, as a Jew and known by many to be an atheist, I was very unlikely to be pleading the institute's case out of personal bias.

Churchill College, Cambridge, where my old Chicago student George Steiner was director of English studies, invited me to be an Overseas Fellow, with some choice of when to take up the award. The stipend was reasonable and there were married fellows' apartments which would accommodate my family comfortably; the only formal duties were to give one public lecture and to dine at High Table a certain number of times. I felt a great need to regain connection with my discipline, which had been much attenuated by my utter immersion in administration. I had foreseen that this distancing from my subject would occur, and one of the conditions of coming to Toronto had been that I would have a sabbatical, and that my two final years at Chicago would be counted toward the qualifying period. I consulted with Bissell, who thought the

Churchill invitation great and was enthusiastic about establishing a precedent for administrative sabbaticals at Toronto, saying he might himself follow the precedent at the right time (in fact, he did, in 1967–8). However, we both doubted the wisdom of my being away for a whole year, and we agreed that the period from the beginning of January to the end of August, 1966, would be safe, thinking that by January the Laskin Report would have been adopted, the plans for the new library finalized, and the provincial graduate scene stabilized. Churchill College agreed to the shorter period.

At Churchill, and through visits to other colleges, I was able to get a sense of what was being done in England in Renaissance studies. I was also able to observe current practice in the organization and administration of graduate studies, especially in the way of residential accommodation, where I found the English, or at least Oxbridge, ahead of us. In Toronto I had received approval in principle for a large graduate residential development across St George Street from the planned research library, but real progress was infinitesimal (the university had bought an old apartment block at Bloor and St George as an interim graduate residence). In Cambridge, as I wrote to Bissell, a residential graduate college had been founded, and at least eight older colleges had already made residential provision for graduate and post-doctoral students; most others were planning such provision.

In preparation for writing my public lecture I read most current and recent criticism of *Paradise Lost*, and in reaction found myself writing a structural and thematic analysis of the poem, starting from Milton's stated intention and utilizing his prose to put that into context and interpret it. The college suggested that my lecture should be published and could form the first in a series to be entitled 'Churchill College Overseas Fellowship Lectures'; I agreed, and Heffer brought it out in 1967 as *Paradise Lost: A Deliberate Epic.*

We left Churchill a little early because my father fell gravely ill. In Winnipeg I found him lucid but very weak; he died after lingering another month, during which I commuted between Toronto and Winnipeg. The large funeral hall overflowed, and I was touched to see that there were many Winkler Mennonites there, even though he had moved to Winnipeg many years earlier. *Shiva* was a week of constant greetings.

VI

In the wake of the 1965 Bladen report, *Financing of Higher Education in Canada*, for which our school had prepared the brief of the Canadian Association of Graduate Schools, the provincial government was working toward a system of formula financing for universities, which the report had recommended as a method of making the grants predictable and equitable and of preserving the universities' budgets from detailed government scrutiny. In mid-October 1966, the federal government held a meeting in Ottawa of provincial ministers responsible for higher education, together with their advisers; Davis took along, among others, some of the university presidents, and I was one of those accompanying Bissell. We were happily expectant because another Bladen recommendation, which we understood was favourably received by the federal government, was that it greatly increase its per-capita payments to the universities. After a day spent on various problems, Davis called the Ontario people together and announced that Prime Minister Pearson wanted to shift all federal support to research and research training, making grants and re-apportioning tax points to enable the provinces to carry the full cost of the education component of universities. The Ontario civil servants thought the financial result would be favourable for Ontario; should he agree to the proposal?

We had very sketchy numbers to go by and very little time to form an opinion. From the standpoint of graduate studies, there seemed an advantage in having the federal government an overt partner, making us less dependent upon the whim of the provincial government alone; and the provincial civil servants in the crowded room were clearly keen on the new proposal. The U of T group said yes, then the other university representatives followed, and Davis went back to his meeting, which endorsed the plan. The President's Council asked Gilbert Robinson and me to analyse its import for Toronto, which confirmed that under current conditions the financial impact was favourable.

Serious doubts did not set in until we learnt some months later that Newfoundland would use some of its grant and transferred tax yield for road-building; we had been given the impression that the money could be used for higher education only, but it turned out that the federal government chose not to exercise its constraining power. In time, all provinces took the position that it was their money and they could use it as they chose, and the federal government conceded that. Manitoba took this view during my tenure there and it did harm to the University of Manitoba, making me realize more keenly than ever that universities had little power to enforce their interpretations of agreements on government.

Douglas Wright, the chairman of the Ontario Committee on University Affairs, invited the Committee of Presidents of Universities of Ontario to make suggestions on the weighting of the various categories of students for formula purposes. The U of T had recently established the Department of Institutional Research, under Bert Hansen; it was the only one in the province and naturally put us in the best position to make recommendations. Also, CPUO needed the help of the Ontario Council of Graduate Studies, which again put U of T at the centre of discussion. Wright and his colleague Edward Stewart, now deputy minister of the Department of University Affairs, spent considerable time in my office discussing the simulations Hansen had worked out for me of the results of various weightings, beginning with those suggested in the Bladen Report. I reported this to Bissell and Alex Corry of Queen's, who had succeeded him as chairman of CPUO, assuring them that I wasn't trying to bypass channels but that it would do the universities no good if I refused to work with Wright and Stewart, and they encouraged me to continue.

The greatest difficulty lay in persuading Wright and Stewart that the humanities and social sciences should receive the same weights as the hard sciences. Wright, as an engineer, understood the laboratory costs of scientific research, and Stewart was receptive to them, but neither understood the costs of research in the library-oriented disciplines. Computers were something of a bridge: social sciences were becoming dependent on them, and Wright reverenced computers and knew they were expensive; there might be some case for weighting doctoral candidates in computer-related fields the same as those in science. I explained that computers were moving into the humanities and would be increasingly important there, but pressed my case on the basis, first, of the tremendous costs of the libraries needed to make research in the humanities possible, especially from a late start, and, second, on the distorting effects of differential payments between disciplines.

When I finally got agreement to equal weights in all disciplines, I had difficulty persuading them to raise the weight for post-Masters students from the five units suggested by Bladen to the six I believed necessary (with a first-year pass student representing one, and increasing weights to more advanced students). Here new simulations designed by Hansen proved decisive. Wright and Stewart, persuaded at last of the validity of the proposed weighting, wanted to know how CPUO, with its many members doing only or mainly undergraduate work, would regard a formula heavily weighted toward graduate study; and if they were persuaded to accept it, would it induce them all to rush into graduate work the province didn't need? I told them that the Appraisals Committee would be in operation in January 1967, and that OCGS would soon renew its initiative regarding planning; all they had to do now to prevent the emergence of unqualified programs was to limit formula recognition of graduate students in new programs to those successfully appraised, and later, to prevent harmful duplication, to support the planning initiative when it matured. That was the clincher; they agreed to recommend the weights proposed.

The operating grants for 1967–8 were calculated in terms of basic income units; at U of T a huge and readily calculable portion of this derived from enrolment in the School of Graduate Studies. This greatly increased the school's leverage within the university, as became manifest in a showdown I had with the board while Bissell was away on a sabbatical year at Harvard. In September 1966, as part of the move to improve university government, the board had agreed to invite the President's Council to send three representatives to board meetings; it happened that at the March 1968 meeting of the board I was one of those representatives. The minutes of the previous meeting included the following from the report of the Executive Committee: 'The Chairman reported that in discussion with senior Government officials he had agreed that the university would be prepared to hold its capital requirements to a minimum. It was agreed that the Student Centre, Men's Athletic Building and the extension to Simcoe Hall would receive high priority.' A paper at the table listed the resulting proposed capital priorities; I saw with horror that the research library was Priority Eleven, with men's athletics as Priority One, a reversal of the priorities previously agreed. The explanation was that if the very costly library proceeded it would absorb all the capital available for some years and block everything else, whereas if it were postponed many needed projects could be carried out, after which it would be the library's turn.

Although I was a visitor, I got permission to speak. I pointed out that the great increase in graduate enrolment in the humanities and social sciences had been predicated on the promise of adequate library resources within a defined time, just as the heavy expenditures on library acquisitions over the past four years had presupposed a place where they could be housed and used; that without such working resources research was impossible and therefore the graduate degrees, especially the PhD, would be of unacceptable quality; that if the graduate departments in the library-oriented disciplines were told that there would be no start on the new library for many years they would no longer enroll large numbers of students, nor could I advise them to. The ensuing decline in basic income units would mean an immediate and precipitous fall in operating income and almost surely in capital grants as well.

There was a heavy silence. The captains of industry who constituted the board were not accustomed to hearing an employee speak in that manner; O.D. Vaughan, the vice-chairman of the board, could barely contain his indignation and I'm sure he thought the proper response was to fire me on the spot. However, Henry Borden, the chairman, asked me one or two clarifying questions, then said, 'You'll get your library, Dean Sirluck,' and instructed 'the proper officers of the university to prepare for the April 25 meeting of the Board a list of capital priorities.' Jack Sword, the acting president, referred this to the next meeting of the President's Council, on 22 April, when we rated the library first, the graduate complex fourth, and the men's athletics building eleventh. When we met again, on 6 May, we were advised that the Board had accepted our capital recommendation as a package, and on 30 May the board authorized a call for tenders for the library. In 1974, when I was in Toronto to receive an honourary degree and the new library was in operation, Borden, then retired from the board, said, 'I told you you'd get your library. It took some manoeuvring, but it was done.'

On my return from Churchill College in August 1966, I found that a speech Davis had given in February placing university autonomy in doubt, and the imminence of the Spinks Report's publication, with its known recommendation for a University of Ontario, were seriously agitating many universities. I was therefore able to get OCGS to come to grips again with the voluntary planning of graduate work as the only effective means of forestalling a governmental move toward the Spinks solution. This led to hard and bitter exchanges, but we kept at it doggedly throughout the fall, and in the end we agreed to recommend to CPUO the scheme I'd previously outlined to it for a general meeting of all the relevant representatives of the provincial universities. This time CPUO agreed, and the meeting was held on 11 May, 1968, in the Edward Johnson Theatre at the U of T. Some five hundred chairmen of departments, chief librarians, deans, and presidents came together, heard Principal Corry explain the situation and propose the method of their work, and spent the afternoon in a multitude of separate rooms, discipline by discipline, organizing themselves into working provincial bodies which would, over the following months, make inventories of the state of their respective disciplines in the province, of existing and planned graduate work by institutions, and of unnecessary duplications, unexploited opportunities, and possibilities for cooperation.

A fortnight later, at a Queen's convocation where I got my first honourary degree, I set forth the reasons for this voluntary rationalization and described its development, adding that discussion in OCGS 'began in an excited, not to say grim, mood, and for some time it appeared possible that relations between Ontario universities, never altogether easy, might suffer seriously. However, the threat of Government intervention was a prospect sufficiently daunting to furnish the incentives necessary for a start toward voluntary co-operation. The Council, in a series of really engaged meetings which took place during the first term of the 1966–67 academic session, may be said to have moved through, but not beyond, the first four of Touchstone's seven causes of a quarrel: the Retort Courteous, the Quip Modest, the Reply Churlish, and the Reproof Valiant. It never really reached the fifth cause, however, the Countercheck Quarrelsome, and so it was able to recover its way through a new frankness to an even newer harmony.' *Queen's Quarterly* immediately published my address, and CPUO ordered a special run of offprints which it distributed to all participants of the 11 May meeting and to many other interested groups, such as members of CAGS and AGS, and relevant members of government. Geoffrey Andrew, the executive director of AUCC, asked permission to publish large extracts in *University Affairs*, and it was extensively abstracted in *Sociological Abstracts* of New York. The Ontario effort was certainly widely watched from the outset; I remained in Ontario only long enough to participate in the formation of the Advisory Committee on Academic Planning and the preliminary phases of its operation, but that was enough to satisfy me that it had taken hold. I believe that ACAP has worked moderately well, and certainly the program accomplished its primary goal, to dissuade government from imposing a plan of its own.

VII

In 1962 the Canadian Association of University Teachers, under Laskin's presidency, and the Association of Universities and Colleges of Canada, under Bissell's chairmanship, had co-sponsored an inquiry into university government in Canada. Unfortunately, the resulting Duff/Berdahl Report was not published until 1966. It had been impatiently awaited by Bissell, who knew its thrust well in advance and hoped that it would help him with his local problem. It did, indeed, strongly recommend that faculty have an important role in governance at all levels, including governing boards, but by that time Bissell had lost all hope that the U of T board would ever accept faculty membership. At the September 1966 meeting of the President's Council he presented a 'Memorandum on University Government' arguing that the traditional idea of the university being divided into academic and financial realms, and having a corresponding two-tiered governing structure, was no longer workable, and proposing instead a single unified governing body which would incorporate all the interests now divided between Board and Senate.

I was less pessimistic about the board's ultimate posture, believing that it would do what the government told it to and thinking that, if we followed in the direction of Duff/Berdahl, we would be in the Canadian mainstream of university reform and, with the support of the Association of the Teaching Staff, would win government support. Also, I was very reluctant to lose the senate, which was always academic in orientation. I therefore suggested retaining the two-tier system, with faculty members of Senate elected to membership on the board, some board members on Senate, and the President's Council, which Duff/Berdahl had praised, continuing to act as a bridge between the two bodies. The board members present supported this approach and said they were authorized to invite the council to send three representatives to sit with the board, and also to establish a joint committee to discuss faculty membership of the board.

At the 17 October meeting, however, the council was reminded of the missing ingredient: the Students' Administrative Council had been invited to send a delegation, which laid out a large demand for full participation in university governance, with all meetings to be open to the public and all agenda and minutes to be published. They did not at this meeting spell out their demand for 'parity,' but it was not hard to detect it just below the surface. The students had accepted Council's invitation with the understanding that its proceedings were confidential; accordingly, the discussion was as free as usual. The next day, however, the students published their version of the meeting in *The Varsity*, attaching names to their versions of positions taken, making individual members out to be heroes and villains. When the adjourned meeting resumed on 31 October, the members of Council were indignant, the students unrepentant and adamant. This conflict over openness prevented the students from joining Council for two years, although they attended several times as guests to put forward particular demands. Precisely two years later, on 31 October, 1968, by which time the good order of the university was in jeopardy, seven students became members of Council; they had won their point about openness but had given up their demand that SAC have the power to appoint the student members, and were, as Council had insisted, elected for the specific purpose by the student body.

My own view about student involvement in policy making developed early, partly on philosophical grounds but more out of concern for the unnecessary handicaps many graduate students encountered in our own school, and the growing conviction that in some cases only the students themselves could show us how to overcome them. I put forward this view in the Laskin Committee, where it did not at first receive much support; indeed, in an article dated 23 January 1965, the *Globe Magazine* discussed early indications in Canada of student desire to be involved in university governance, and featured Laskin, still president of CAUT, and me on opposite sides of the issue. Working closely with the Graduate Students Union but within the limitations of the school statute, which made no provision for student membership, I invited them to elect four students to serve as assessors, or non-voting members, of the Graduate Council, which they did. By the time the report came to be written, the Laskin Committee had been persuaded, and the resultant revised statute provided for Council membership of four elected students. When the new council met on 14 February 1967, it was the first to include voting student members in the U of T, and I believe in any English-language university in Canada. (The second at the U of T was, on my motion, the Library Council.)

This readiness to give students a role in the governance of the school and library did not, however, earn me any credit with SAC. To begin with, the advance was made at my initiative, not as the result of confrontation, and was therefore not helpful – was indeed inimical – to SAC's ultimate end, which was, in their naïve sense of the term, 'revolution'; I had, in their jargon, 'co-opted' the GSU.

Later, they enlarged, and much more bitterly, on this charge: I was a 'splitist.' The story is very instructive. University regulations required every student to belong and pay a fee to SAC. The GSU complained to me several times that the services SAC supplied were useful only to undergraduates and that they could get nothing they wanted from SAC for their fees; they therefore wanted to be separated from SAC so they could use their fees for purposes of interest to graduate students, half of them married, many with children. Furthermore, GSU wanted to be able to deal directly with the school and the university, not through SAC, whose views were not always compatible with those of graduate students. I said that before I could contemplate supporting such action they would have to convince me that they'd seriously tried to negotiate with SAC, advising it that continued frustration would lead to a request for separation. They did so, but were met with blank refusal.

It is revealing that Steven Langdon, the SAC president and later a prominent NDP MP, who talked constantly of the right of students to change things that affected them, including statutes of the university, told the press (*Globe and Mail*, 23 October 1968) that he would oppose the right of the 5,500 graduate students to withdraw from SAC on the basis of 'legality,' i.e., his interpretation of the U of T Act and SAC's act of incorporation. I had, however, at the time of SAC's incorporation, sought assurance from the board that, if the GSU wanted to separate, their request would be considered. In September 1968, the GSU Executive, declaring that their attempts to negotiate with SAC had failed, formally petitioned that they be allowed to leave SAC. The school conducted a referendum of graduate students on this; the result was a 75 per cent majority for separation. I asked the board to amend the regulation so as to make it optional for graduate students to belong to SAC, and it did so. SAC and *The Varsity*, of course, accused me of plotting to split the student movement; since that had become extremely ideological and threatening, I was not sorry that SAC would no longer be able to pretend to speak for unwilling graduate students, but my motive was to help the GSU serve its members. I had already secured a capacious building for them, helped them acquire furnishings and equipment, and sponsored their application for a liquor licence; on the occasions when I visited their new Union, I was happy to see it well populated and active.

An important recommendation of the Laskin Committee had been that there be a central university budget committee, of which the graduate dean should be the only decanal member. During my absence in Churchill College, the President's Council agreed that there should be such a committee, but was divided on the graduate dean's membership. Winegard, who replaced me on the council during my sabbatical, unwisely pushed for a decision, which brought out the opinion, recorded in the minutes, that if I were on the committee I might, 'with his ... influence,' change the balance between graduate and undergraduate work, and in the end the Laskin recommendation was not supported.

If I'd been present I'd not have forced the issue but would have pursued the same objective by another route. As I wrote to Bissell, at every university where the attempt was made to give the graduate dean the influence on the distribution of resources needed to effect the desired reorganization of the university's original undergraduate and professional structure, it was met with accusations of empire-building; yet one by one the major American universities had found it necessary to do so, and I thought the task of making all faculties and schools in the U of T, to say nothing of central administration, responsive to graduate needs and opportunities would in the long run be impossible without such procedural influence (distinguishing between personal influence, which could not be counted on to continue, and the influence of the office). For some months after my return, Bissell was unwilling to act on this against the advice of the President's Council, but in February 1967, when budget making grew imminent and salary issues, divisional requests, library, laboratory, and computer allocations, student support, and all the other budget problems loomed, he decided the new budget committee needed the graduate dean and appointed me to it without further reference to the council.

I was careful not to intrude into the sphere of heads of divisions or unfairly to push the special interests of the school, but I saw to it that the graduate activities and plans of every division were clarified during its presentation and adequately considered in allocating resources, and I was active in discussing the salary briefs with the ATS. Afterward a number of divisions made it clear that they now welcomed the graduate dean's membership of the budget committee, and certainly the school found them much more responsive to the needs of graduate work, partly no doubt because they thought it might increase their allocation, but mostly, I think, because they became convinced that the university's commitment to graduate work was serious and lasting, and therefore their respective divisions could not afford to neglect this area.

In 1967 I completed the five years of residence then required to qualify for Canadian citizenship. It was not at that time possible to hold citizenship in Canada and the United States simultaneously, and I was reluctant to surrender the many advantages of American citizenship; nor was there any overt pressure on me to do so. But I thought that my role, both in the U of T and on the larger Ontario scene, really required a demonstration of commitment. I therefore resumed Canadian citizenship, which necessitated formal renunciation of American citizenship, the exact counterpart of my renunciation a decade earlier of my Canadian citizenship. I had enjoyed American hospitality as a resident alien and later exercised my rights as an American citizen, and it was with heavy heart that I had to sign and seal this renunciation, but I did. (Lesley was less ready, and didn't do it until two years later.)

Five years of residence was also the qualifying period for membership in the Royal Society of Canada, and I was approached by McGillivray and Priestley to permit my name to be put into nomination, which of course I was glad to do, and was elected.

The year 1967 being Canada's centennial, the AUCC held a Centennial Conference in Montreal on the role of universities in the nation's second century. The keynote speaker the first day was Robin Harris, who in a survey of higher education in Canada said that universities were placing an unhealthy emphasis on graduate work to the detriment of undergraduates, and that we ought to cut it back. Harris had been closely involved in U of T and Ontario universities planning and knew that the main reason for the graduate expansion he deplored was to get university teachers for the very increase of undergraduates he was supporting, and it angered me that he should speak so misleadingly to such an audience; fearing that unless his argument was instantly refuted it would find many supporters, I leapt up as soon as he finished, waved my papers to get the chairman's attention, and then went (one news account said 'rushed') to the podium. According to *The Toronto Daily Star* (2 November), which featured the story across the top of page one under a bold red headline, I asked, 'Does Professor Harris propose some measure to keep the great influx of undergraduates out of our universities? If the answer is yes, there is no problem. But if the answer is no, I would like to ask who is going to teach them?' Harris said that was a good question. *The Globe and Mail*, which also featured the story, reported that I then explained that in the past Canada had depended heavily for its university teachers on importing foreigners or reclaiming Canadians who'd done their graduate work in foreign universities, but that those sources were drying up and we had to produce our own.

As well, 1967 was the tercentenary of *Paradise Lost*, which the University of Alberta celebrated with a three-day conference in October, at which I was asked to give a paper. These were to be hour-long addresses by scholars from several countries, and there was no chance that I could find time to write a fresh one. My Churchill College lecture had just been published in Cambridge but had not yet reached Canadian libraries, and I asked the conference manager what he would think of my using it; he saw no impediment, and so for the only time in my life I gave the same paper twice.

About this time some members of the Hungarian-Canadian community came to ask me whether the university could sponsor a course of evening lectures on Hungarian literature by George Faludy, the recently arrived Hungarian poet. I knew that there were deep political divisions in their community, but when they told me that Faludy had been imprisoned first by the Nazis and then by the Communists because he criticized both in turn, and that although he was an outstanding poet he was penniless, I thought the university should help. I said we had no means to give credit for the course but we'd sponsor it as a public service on an experimental basis and give him a stipend, which delighted them.

A little later another group came to say that Faludy was a communist and we ought not to be helping him make propaganda; I had spoken to Faludy and been convinced of his integrity, so I replied that he would be talking about literature, not politics. They left muttering darkly, and before the first lecture we were told that if it proceeded it would be disrupted. I told the messenger that I would be at the lecture, fully prepared to call in the city police if needed; I said the same to Faludy, who was undaunted. There was no disturbance. In 1990, with the lifting of the Iron Curtain, Faludy returned to Hungary to great acclaim.

Also in 1967, the Science Council of Canada and the Canada Council jointly sponsored a comprehensive study of the role of the federal government in support of research in Canadian universities. John B. Macdonald, an academic dentist and microbiologist, had just resigned as president of the University of British Columbia and was made director of the study. He invited me to join the group; at first I thought it impossible, but he persuaded me that this was a singular opportunity to influence the future of research in the humanities; Bissell also encouraged me, and I agreed. The other members were Paul Dugal of Sherbrooke, a physiologist; Stefan Dupré of Toronto, a political scientist; Bruce Marshall of the National Research Council, a biologist; J. Gordon Parr of Windsor, an engineer; Guy Rocher of Montreal, a sociologist; and Eric Vogt of UBC, a physicist.

The task turned out to be enormous. We visited most Canadian universities and many departments and agencies of the federal government, received numerous briefs, conducted surveys, and collected a truly formidable amount of data, much of it for the first time, and had many meetings to plan what we would do next and digest what we'd learned. The English version of our report, published in May 1969, was about four hundred pages, including numerous tables and appendices, and presented seventy-seven recommendations, some of them highly controversial. We recommended that the mandate of the Canada Council to support research be terminated and a new humanities and social sciences council be established for this purpose, that the NRC be separated from its in-house laboratory role and have as its sole function the support of university research in the physical sciences and engineering, that the Medical Research Council be reconstituted as a comprehensive health sciences research council, that the National Library work with the universities and regional libraries to develop a machine-readable National Union Catalogue and an explicit acquisitions policy and then refrain from collecting in other fields, that the federal government greatly expand its support of university research, and many other far-reaching measures.

The officers of the Canada Council, one of our sponsors, were furious, issued rebutting statements, and worked politically to prevent our proposal from being implemented. They were able to delay it for several years, but the university world felt the results of the council's incompetence in research matters and in time our proposal was carried out: the Canada Council was limited to the support of the creative arts, and the Social Sciences and Humanities Research Council was established for research support. An irony is that after about two decades of the new structure's successful operation, Donald Mazankowski, minister of finance in the Mulroney government, proposed in his 1993 budget the abolition of the SSHRC and the return of university research to the Canada Council, on the purported ground of economy, although his department was unable to show that any savings would be achieved. A terrific howl went up from the universities, but party discipline got the bill through the House of Commons. For one of the very few times in history, the Senate earned its keep by defeating the bill by the narrowest of margins.

Not all of our recommendations were carried out (the NRC, for example, successfully resisted the severance of its laboratories), but during the following years the report had much influence both in government and in the universities. In particular, it stimulated and encouraged faculty members in universities not deeply engaged in graduate work and research, as did the study group's visits. Often we found in such universities that its researchers had been frustrated by the research councils' procedures and didn't know how to cut through them. This could also be true in the major universities; I recall that, at the University of Manitoba, Clarence Barber, a prominent economist, asked us what we would do in such-and-such a circumstance, narrating what was clearly an experience he'd had with the Canada Council. I said I would call so-and-so. 'Ah,' he interrupted bitterly, 'so you know his phone number.' This sense of being cut off from what should have been the central fostering agency of the federal government was very widespread outside of Ontario and Quebec, and contributed to our decision to recommend that research have a separate council.

I met a great many people during our university visits, which may have had something to do with some invitations I received. The most curious was a phone call late in 1967. The president of the Vancouver Club wanted me to come and speak to his club and 'an invited audience.' I asked, what about? Anything you choose. Now suspicious, I asked, why me? Oh, we've heard that you're doing interesting things. I said I'd think it over and call him back. That evening the penny dropped: Jack Macdonald had resigned as president of the University of British Columbia because of differences with the Social Credit government of Premier W.A.C. Bennett; did this club, which its president had described as 'close to the university,' want me to preach for a call? I called back and said it wouldn't be convenient to go out there now; perhaps another year. I later learnt that they'd brought out several willing aspirants; ultimately they chose Kenneth Hare, Master of Birkbeck College, London, who had a short and disastrous presidency, resigning almost at once (whereupon I helped to get him appointed professor of geography at U of T).

There were other, more dignified, approaches. John Spinks, president of the University of Saskatchewan, whom I'd met when he was doing his report on the development of graduate work in Ontario, phoned and said he was authorized to invite me to be principal of the Regina branch of the university. Patrick McTaggart-Cowan, the embattled president of Simon Fraser University, came to Toronto to tell me that a committee there had formulated a new structure of administration, under which a vice-president would virtually run the university, leaving the president to deal with the board and the public; he invited me to become the first vice-president. Chief Justice McLaurin, of Alberta, chancellor of the University of Calgary, who was chairman of a search committee for the presidency of that institution, came to ask me to visit the university and meet the committee.

There were two American overtures. A presidential search committee at Northern Illinois University asked for my *curriculum vitae* and bibliography; I was at the time a little unhappy about some gratuitous obstacles and therefore unwilling to rule this option out, so I sent what they asked. Later, when the chairman phoned to say I'd been short-listed and asked me to come down to meet the committee, I thought that would be getting in too deep and declined, much to his indignation. Ohio State sounded me out concerning their College for the Humanities.

I declined all these invitations or overtures without using them to improve my position at Toronto, observing my old rule of not putting forward a bargaining chip unless I was willing to play it. But in late December 1967 I was approached by Harry Thode, the president of McMaster University, whom I saw regularly at meetings of CPUO and respected. He told me that McMaster planned to regroup its faculties into three academic sectors, each to be headed by a vice-president. They wanted me to head the arts sector, which would include humanities, social sciences, and business, and which they intended greatly to improve and expand. He said he knew that there would have to be inducements to get me to come, and salary could be one of them. A few days later Arthur Bourns, the vice-president of McMaster, and Mel Preston, the graduate dean, came to tell me that they were aware of the discussion and wanted to encourage me to join McMaster.

Although I did not want to leave Toronto, I took this offer somewhat more seriously than the others for several reasons. Bissell, now on sabbatical at Harvard, had repeated during a Christmas visit an earlier hint that he was getting tired and might step down; I assumed that rotation would suggest that a successor be from the sciences, and I didn't know whether under a scientist the library project would survive the increasing attacks mounted against it. Nor did I know whether a new president would like working with me or would give my initiatives the support Bissell had. Besides, a new set of regulations had made academic administrative appointments, previously held at the president's pleasure, retroactively term-limited; I had no objection to a review before renewal, but the new arrangement demanded a search rather than a review. I would be fifty-three when my newly imposed term ended in 1971, nine years absent from a rapidly changing academic discipline and much less competitive in it than I had been; a search committee appointed by a new president might include persons who had not shared my priorities, and if student militants were on the committee they were unlikely to want their old antagonist back. Also, Toronto's salaries were as usual falling behind, partly because the board regarded us as employees and the central administration thought we were privileged to work for Toronto. By Toronto's standards I was well paid, but elsewhere my salary would have been thought low for the role I played; certainly the sums mentioned in the various approaches to me were higher.

I decided, therefore, to use the McMaster invitation and wrote to Bissell about it. He telephoned and I made the points noted above; he gave me certain assurances, then repeated them in a letter: he would not resign until certain projects, including the library and graduate complex, were assured, which he thought would take a minimum of three years; he felt the presidency needed to be reshaped to free himself for wider duties by diverting supervision of the areas now reporting directly to him (the graduate school, the library, Research Administration, the Press), and thought they should report to me as 'Vice-President Graduate Work and Research'; he would meet and surpass any salary offer. I then declined the McMaster offer with thanks; happily, it seemed not to impair my relations with Thode and his colleagues. Discussion with Bissell over the following year changed the plan somewhat; I didn't really want to relinquish the deanship at a critical juncture, and research couldn't have been brought into Bissell's scheme without friction, so it was decided that I should become vice-president and graduate dean, responsible for the school and the library; the appointment took effect 1 January 1969, with an initial salary of $35,000. I was accorded my wish to keep my office within the school rather than move to Simcoe Hall.

VIII

Beginning about 1967, the problem of maintaining order on the campus became increasingly acute. An important cause was the worsening of the war in Vietnam, whose slaughter was seen daily on Canadian as well as American television, combined with the termination, in February 1968, of the U.S. draft exemption for graduate students. This brought a renewed flood of draft evaders, as well as many army deserters, to such near-campus locations as Yorkville, and particularly to the violent, drug-saturated high-rise co-op, Rochdale 'College.' Other foreign influences contributed, such as the European student turmoil which culminated in the uprising in Paris in 1968 and the numerous violent disturbances in American universities.

But there were local causes as well. The university, under pressure from the provincial government, had expanded both its enrolment and its faculty very fast, with its facilities lagging badly behind and its programs, for the most part, unexamined in years. There were predictable and often justified complaints from alienated students of 'irrelevant' education and the 'impersonal multiversity.' But we began to hear new accusations, often brought by foreign, more politicized, students and faculty, particularly from Britain and the United States: the university was 'complicit' in the war machine and in the class structure of 'imperialist capitalist' society; it exercised 'repressive tolerance' as a means of smothering dissent; what was needed was an 'alternative' education for a 'truly democratic' society.

As we attempted to find and correct the weaknesses in our programs, we came up against a new attitude in the student leadership: it did not want improvements which would allow the 'system' to survive and renew itself; it wanted to exploit discontent to change the whole social system, of which the university seemed to it to be the heart and in any case was the nearest and most exposed part. Langdon put it very well in an article in *The Toronto Daily Star* (23 November 1968): 'the student left are not relativist and the university liberal cannot understand and accept this.' What he in turn may not have fully understood is that there were other absolutists farther to his left who did not share his distaste for violence and were very ready to exploit opportunities he created for them.

During his year at Harvard, Bissell became convinced, particularly by the disturbances at Columbia, that the danger of violence at the U of T was very real, a danger made more credible by mass physical confrontation on our campus in November 1967 over Dow Chemical's customary recruitment. Bissell distinguished among dissident students between 'radicals' and 'revolutionary saboteurs,' and decided that he must keep the former separate from the latter by winning their trust and bringing them into the government of the university. He therefore modified his plan for a single unified governing body so as to include students and, forgoing a Commonwealth Universities congress in Australia, spent the summer of 1968 working with the new student leaders.

This change did not take long to backfire. As modified by the inclusion of students, Bissell's proposed commission on university governance would have had equal representation from the faculty, the students, the board, and the administration (including the president), and lesser representation from the alumni. Now SAC changed its position: full membership should be limited to parity representation (four each) of students and faculty, with non-voting status for the president and two board representatives; there was to be no alumni representative. The President's Council proposed a compromise: four faculty, four students (one a graduate student), the president, two board members, one alumnus – all with voting rights – and a chairman from outside the university. The executive of the ATS supported this compromise and recommended it to a meeting of the association on 3 October 1968.

Bissell attended the meeting and spoke in support of the motion. Langdon and Bob Rae, the future NDP premier of Ontario, had been invited to present SAC's view and attacked the motion on the ground that there really were only two estates in the university, faculty and students. Kenneth McNaught, now a professor of history and with bitter experience of the board of United College in Winnipeg in the Crowe case, made an impassioned speech supporting the students and denying the legitimacy of the board; he then moved an amendment that the board representatives have no vote. The ensuing debate revealed the depth of the faculty's resentment of the board, which had rejected every request for faculty representation, and the amendment passed, 93 to 49. Another amendment stripped the alumni representative of a vote, leaving four faculty, four students, and the president as the voting members of the commission, with two non-voting board members. Bissell was seated in the front row; from near the back I watched him get up after the vote and, with a wan forced smile, walk the long narrow aisle of the Nursing Auditorium as if it were a ship's plank. I wanted to go to him but thought it unwise. My thoughts were not more comfortable because the blow had been delivered by my brother-in-law.

This was Thursday evening; Friday evening I was at an academic reception where people were speaking excitedly but uncertainly about the previous day's meeting, rather as if it were a hockey game in which the home team had for the first time beaten the outsiders. I asked John Leyerle, director of the Centre for Medieval Studies, whether he thought it would be good for the university if Bissell resigned at this juncture. He was alarmed and said it would be very harmful. In that case, I said, he might like to try to show Bissell that he hadn't lost the faculty's confidence. Leyerle said he would try, and went off to speak to some other professors. I gave the same message to two or three others, and went home.

On Saturday morning I was working alone in my office when Bissell rang: could we talk? I offered to come to his office, but he preferred mine, perhaps because there was less chance of being observed than in Simcoe Hall. He said that he felt the faculty had withdrawn its confidence from him and he thought he should resign. I said it wasn't a withdrawal of confidence from him but an expression of resentment against the board by a minority who had allowed emotion to blind them to consequences; I could attest that the mover of the amendment was favourable to his presidency, as were a number of other non-administrative professors I'd talked with on Friday. His resignation now would precipitate just the crisis he was working so hard to prevent: the saboteurs would embrace the issue and make common cause with the radicals, the faculty would be confused and divided, and the board would look to the leadership of its dinosaurs and do something which would provoke violence. The board, he said, would never accept the humiliating proposal of SAC and ATS, and the whole movement toward reform of the university's government would collapse. I said there were sensible men on the board who might put the good of the university ahead of their wounded pride, and that others might respond to a hint from government, which I thought might be forthcoming. If the board did reject the SAC-ATS proposal there would be a tremendous rallying of the campus to his support, which would present the board and government with a changed situation.

We talked for two hours; when he left he looked somewhat better and promised not to resign, at least until after his return from a Monday meeting in New York. On Tuesday a delegation of senior professors from all sectors of the university, brought together by Leyerle, met with him, assured him that he retained the confidence of the faculty, and asked him not to resign. He did not commit himself at that point, but told me and others a day or two later that he would not resign. On Saturday the story was all over the newspapers, with a fairly full and quite accurate account in *The Globe and Mail.* The publicity may have helped Bissell persuade the board to accept the SAC–ATS formula for the Commission on University Government, which it did.

The first meeting of the President's Council with students as full members took place on 31 October 1968; one of the seven students was Andy Wernick, a graduate student in sociology from England, whose application for a Commonwealth Fellowship I had supported. He never came to Council again; presumably, as leader of the revolutionary Toronto Student Movement, which he founded that winter, he didn't want to be involved with the 'regime.' At this first meeting, SAC concentrated on whether there was any military or otherwise secret or 'complicit' research in the university.

Shortly before the university was to make its annual submission to CUA, Bissell invited SAC to join our delegation. Langdon refused on the ground that it was a secret document which SAC had had no role in preparing; then, on 27 November, SAC called for a mass meeting for the 29th to decide on whether there should be a mass sit-in to protest the secrecy of the brief. Rae said the document 'might very well recommend that the U of T become a graduate campus, with undergraduates being shipped off to Sudbury ... the appointment of graduate dean Ernest Sirluck as vice-president earlier this month indicated something of the administration's bent' (*Globe and Mail,* 28 November 1968). The President's Council held a special meeting on the morning of the 29th and advised the president to go to the mass meeting that afternoon and say he would try to arrange publication of the brief and an open meeting to discuss it, which would require board approval and permission from CUA. Bissell entered the open meeting in Convocation Hall with this message and won a postponement of the sit-in, which had been intended for Monday, 2 December; he was now given a deadline of 6:00 P.M. Tuesday to make plans for a public meeting on the brief, or there would be a sit-in on Wednesday.

He got the permissions (some members of the board were opposed) and published the brief in the *Staff Bulletin,* and the special open meeting of the President's Council was held on Friday, 6 December. SAC representatives asked questions about and criticized the parts of the brief which most concerned them, and in this pattern John Winter, president of the GSU, asked constructively about facilities and accommodation for graduate students. Then Langdon, who acted as student moderator, took on the role of questioner and critic: was the projected increase in graduate enrolment and the request for graduate facilities an indication that the university was planning to increase its emphasis on graduate work to the detriment of undergraduates? did it aspire to become like some American universities, such as the University of Chicago, where the graduate school was central and the undergraduate college a minor appendage? why were so many American-style PhDs needed, and if they were, why not spread the task across all the province's universities?

I replied that the projected rate of increase in the school was smaller than the actual rate in the last two years because I had sought and obtained permission, for the first time in the school's history, to limit enrolment in crowded fields. The projected future enrolment looked to be an increasing proportion of the whole only if Scarborough and Erindale were ignored; when their wholly undergraduate enrolment projections were included, the ratio of graduate students to the whole remained constant at 1:3.5 over the entire forecast period. The expansion of graduate work, and the production of PhDs, which Langdon had criticized as 'Americanization,' was the only possible defence against Americanization: the swelling Canadian undergraduate enrolments necessitated enlarged teaching staffs; unless we produced enough Canadians equipped to do this work, Americans and other non-Canadians would have to be imported in large numbers. As for distributing graduate work across the province, this was feasible in many laboratory and practical disciplines where equipment could be economically provided, and was in fact happening, but research capacity in library-oriented disciplines took a long time to build and was extremely expensive, and duplication was against the government's wishes as well as being beyond its fiscal capacity; and graduate students in these disciplines would be very ill served without such research capacity.

As I spoke I could feel some of the air leaving the radicals' sails, and when I finished Langdon made me cringe by saying, 'I have to congratulate Dean Sirluck on his presentation.' Gary Webster, a graduate student from the United States but representing SAC, not the GSU, was a leading radical who would become co-chairman of CUG; he had come with a list of questions, but said he would not put them. I don't know why the students didn't point out that, while including the off-campus enrolments preserved the existing overall proportions, it wouldn't prevent the St George campus from becoming increasingly graduate; possibly they didn't see the point, but more likely it was because off-campus students vote in SAC elections. The questioning now turned to research; Gilbert Robinson repeatedly stated that all research in the university must be publishable and none was military, but the questioners were unconvinced, and I began to realize that they had not distinguished between research and consulting. This led to an issue we had not discussed in President's Council, one which we subsequently tried to deal with but never got satisfactorily resolved.

The meeting agreed that the brief to CUA needed revision and that a parity drafting committee of students and council members should be appointed by Bissell and Langdon jointly, to report to another open meeting on Monday, 8 December; I was made chairman. Lesley was in hospital undergoing surgery, the children had seen little of either parent during this week of crisis, and I felt that I must be with them over the weekend; I therefore said that I would accept the assignment if the committee would meet at our house, which it did, but without the other council members, who had weekend commitments and made their comments to me on the phone. The student delegation consisted of Rae and three others, and I recall that Rae tilted his chair and put his feet on the table, presumably to try to irritate me. We were able to reach agreement, which I was authorized to write up and present to the adjourned meeting. I said that if they wanted to see my report they could come back Sunday afternoon, but this prospect seemed to give them a sudden access of trust in me and they waived the inspection.

At the Monday meeting I presented our report. There was some discussion but the only objection was from Peter Russell, the new principal of Innis College: we had recommended that a building for Innis have 'a high priority' among still-to-be-rated capital projects, but he argued effectively that it should have 'the highest priority.' With that amendment our revision was adopted, including the recommendation that CUA adopt a more open procedure. When we met with it a week later Langdon and three other SAC respresentatives were part of our delegation and participated effectively. At the meeting of the President's Council immediately following I moved that our meetings be open to visitors, with provision for them to participate by advance arrangement; there was no dissent, repeated crises having taught their lessons.

I had no role other than spectator in the next crisis, on 5 February 1969. A lecture by Clark Kerr, who had been dismissed as president of the University of California by Governor Ronald Reagan for being too indulgent of student protest, was disrupted by Andy Wernick, Philip Resnick, and their Toronto Student Movement in a manner that seemed calculated to provoke police action, but after some guerrilla theatre and a minor scuffle, Bissell, who chaired the meeting, acting on a suggestion by Rae, was able to restore order.

The press demanded that the disrupters be expelled from the university and tried in criminal court, a view shared by some members of the board and some faculty, but nothing was done. On the same day there had been the second disruption in a week at McGill, and a few days later there was a violent disruption at Sir George Williams, in Montreal, with the trashing of the university's main computer. In April there were violent disturbances at Harvard and Cornell, and widespread unrest during the spring in universities throughout the free world. We had no further eruptions that term, but the public, the students, and especially the staff were puzzled by the administration's inaction in the face of disruptive or threatening behaviour and uncertain of the university's policy.

When I was asked to address the June convocation, I therefore decided to make an analysis of the year's events. As I worked through press reports and university and other documents, including Langdon's President's Report to SAC and some papers of the Canadian Union of Students, it became clear to me that the extremists who had captured the leadership of the CUS had decided that 1968–9 was to be the year to bring their 'revolution' to fruition, and that the U of T had been selected as the target, presumably with the concurrence of SAC. The important question then became why their plan had failed when so many universities had been brutally disrupted. I concluded that it was because of three factors. The least important was that the militants had used faulty tactics, underestimating the critical intelligence of the students and consequently pressing much too hard. The most important was that the university had genuinely accepted the need for extensive change – structural, educational, social, and parietal, all involving a broadening of the elements of democracy and consent – to bring itself into harmony with current conditions, and was moving in that direction with remarkable expedition. The third factor was that the university had been successful in persuading the student body at large of the reality and irreversibility of its commitment to these changes, and of the effectiveness of the methods it had chosen for achieving them. In all this I distinguished sharply between student leaders who genuinely wanted reform and the militants who were opposed to it as a barrier to 'revolution.'

My narrative and analysis added up to a very long speech on a very hot day in June, in a crowded hall without air conditioning. When I finished, Langdon, now an alumnus covering the convocation for a newspaper, rose from his seat in the balcony and at some length denounced all I had said as false and misleading. There was considerable stir in the platform party, several of them handing me scribbled notes of appreciation. Bissell quickly composed and handed me the following verses: 'Sirluck, stern advocate of truth / Rouses the ire of hot-blooded youth. / And Langdon, with slow-paced venom / (Who looks like Keats, but sounds like Stalin) / Shouted that what was was not / And then sank back in murky thought.' The downtown press paid a great deal of attention to the speech and *The Varsity* headlined its attack 'Sirluck Gets Bad Marks'; I got many complimentary letters from faculty members who said it had given them a better understanding of the situation.

I also got two letters of a different kind. William Harris, now vice-chairman of the board and a member of CUG, who felt close to SAC leaders and therefore able to understand the student position, wrote me a sorrowing letter hoping my speech would not harm the developing working relationship with students and explaining to me the necessity of their participation in university government. I replied that, so far from being opposed to such participation, I had been the first at U of T to introduce student members into divisional councils (the school and the library), and would support their membership on the central governing body of the university, but would not countenance disruption.

The other letter was from Bob Rae, who denounced my speech as 'a vicious, insulting, and completely inaccurate attack on the student movement as a whole ... an amazing collection of lies, half-truths, and innuendoes ... I am asking the President for a statement regarding your remarks and their status ... that makes it clear that your speech in no way represents administration or university policy, and indeed for a retraction of your attack. If unsuccessful I fear for the future of rational discussion. One cannot discuss menus with cannibals.' To his letter, which he had released to the press before I saw it, he pinned a note saying: 'I am reading this letter to the CUG.' The CUG minutes (24 June 1969) say that, after

Rae had distributed copies of this letter, 'a long discussion followed in which it became clear that Dr. Sirluck was speaking as an individual and not on the part of the University as a whole. This did not mean that the University was not committed to reform, as Dean Sirluck had pointed out.'

Bissell, who thought my narrative 'generally accurate,' wondered at the 'furiousness' of Langdon and Rae (*Halfway Up Parnassus*, p. 166), and attributed it to my assigning a 'heroic' role to the administration. I thought there were two further reasons. First, they knew I was right and feared, correctly, that this public depiction of the true situation would assist the university community to assess each of their demands in light of a general but controlled reformist commitment, rather than surrendering in confusion or panic to all demands as they rose; there had been moments when the militants might well have erected the banner that flew at the student occupation of the London School of Economics: 'If you concede all our demands, we'll think up some new ones tomorrow.' Second, they thought this was their chance to punish me for having secured for the GSU the right to separate from SAC. I later learnt of an additional reason: they had feared that I might succeed Bissell when he resigned from the presidency, which they knew he contemplated doing, and wanted to make sure that would not happen.

The fall term began badly with the disruption by the New Left Caucus of the annual UC freshman dinner on Thursday, 17 September. On Friday, by a masterpiece of mistiming, CPUO released a well-intentioned but very unfortunate paper entitled 'Order on the Campus,' which spoke of expulsion and arrest for violent disrupters. On the same day Caput, the university's disciplinary court, was summoned to consider the UC disruption, its first meeting since March 1968, when, feeling its own ineffectiveness and increasing irrelevance, it had established a subcommittee to revise its procedures. It now drew up a statement saying it would deal seriously with disruption; this was released on Saturday, and seen by SAC not only to reverse what it thought an understanding that Caput would confine itself to purely academic offences pending the long-awaited report of a faculty–student committee on discipline, but also to support the hard CPUO line.

On Wednesday, 23 September, the Caput subcommittee, which included faculty and students, met in the Debates Room of Hart House, with large numbers present wearing the red armband of the New Left Caucus. The SAC representatives demanded that Bissell, who was present, repudiate both the CPUO document, in which he had participated, and the Caput statement, which carried his signature as chairman; he refused, and in the unedifying scene that followed was called 'liar' and 'fascist.' SAC withdrew from the subcommittee, issued a series of demands, including the repudiation of the two statements on discipline, with a deadline of Wednesday, 1 October, and called a mass meeting in Convocation Hall for noon of that day; the clear implication was that if the answers were unsatisfactory the mass meeting would become a sit-in in adjoining Simcoe Hall.

Bissell secured hurried completion and publication of the Campbell Report on discipline, which was very conciliatory, proposing an interim parity student–staff tribunal until the full report could be implemented, and was sufficiently ambivalent on the main issue, violent disruption, to be acceptable to those who wanted to avoid that issue. Robin Ross, the vice-president and registrar, and I were summoned to the president's house Tuesday evening, 30 September, and worked with Bissell until midnight on a statement for his use at the mass meeting the following day. It embraced the Campbell Report, emphasized his own commitment to staff and student participation in discipline as in other matters, but reiterated the necessity for order; it was silent on the Caput statement and insisted that the CPUO statement was only a working paper and not the policy of the U of T. I thought it the best we could do, but didn't think we should rely only on words. In the morning I telephoned a number of faculty members, including two engineering professors, and suggested that they and perhaps some of their students might like to attend the mass meeting to give the president some support in a difficult situation.

I arrived at the mass meeting early, as I'd suggested that others do; already the hall was full. Some engineering professors had cancelled their classes so their students could attend, and they had strategically pre-empted the front rows. I spotted many of my friends in other faculties, looking appropriately resolute. New Left armbands were beginning to come in, their wearers looking bewildered at the unfamiliar crowd, and I was delighted that many were unable to find seats. The president of the Engineering Student Society was elected chairman of the meeting. Cheers greeted Bissell as he entered, and continued as he read his statement (of which copies were distributed); the radicals' speeches met groans and derisive laughs; a motion to accept the statement as an adequate response to SAC demands (which it had never mentioned) was overwhelmingly approved. Bissell, who entered feeling 'convinced of disaster' (*Halfway Up Parnassus*, p. 147), left greatly buoyed.

But the new discipline system, an improvement with regard to academic offences, was useless with regard to the real problem, disruption. Half a year later, on 25 March 1970, a very reasonable request for rehabilitation of a day-care centre housed in a university building was badly mishandled by middle management, which resulted in a mass demonstration outside Simcoe Hall, led by Lorrene Smith, of Philosophy, and Natalie Davis, of History. They demanded that Bissell meet with them; he ill-advisedly refused, and the angry crowd moved inside and occupied the Senate Chamber. There the original leaders lost control to the militants, the New Left Caucus and the even more extreme Worker–Student Alliance, and the red flag of socialism and the black flag of anarchism were quickly hung from the windows.

That evening Bissell again summoned Ross and me, together with three faculty members of the President's Council and the university solicitor, to the president's house; we were kept abreast by telephone of developments at Simcoe Hall, where food, mattresses, and marijuana were being brought into the Chamber. Views on what should be done varied greatly; one person suggested simple surrender. I suggested that we use the technique employed very effectively by Edward Levi, the new president of the University of Chicago: get a court injunction, protect essential services, wait out the occupation, then expel and prosecute the ringleaders; thereafter we could consider whether to grant the original request. Finally, Bissell proposed a statement: provided the occupation ceased he would pledge to get the money for renovations from the alumni fund. He would call a special meeting of the President's Council for the next afternoon for advice on what else to do.

Five board members attended that meeting, along with faculty and administrators, but no students. The board members wanted the occupation treated as a criminal act and the police sent in. I had advocated use of the law the previous evening, but nothing like this, and I spoke against it. Just then Dr Smith and Dr Davis returned with what they called a compromise proposal: the occupiers would accept Bissell's offer if he first gave his personal pledge to raise the money, but they feared that unless matters were settled quickly the extremists would take over. The council decided to accept this 'compromise,' and Bissell went to the Chamber to say this; I went with him, and saw on entering that the heavy tables and chairs were laid out on their sides according to a pattern I recognized from the army manual of house-to-house fighting – an indication, I thought, that U.S. army deserters were there. Smith and Davis had promised the council that its decision would not be allowed to look as if it were made under pressure, but as soon as Bissell said 'personal guarantee' there were great shouts of 'We won, we won!,' in which I thought Smith and Davis joined, and which were repeated in bold headlines in the next day's *Varsity* and the downtown press; *The Globe and Mail* lead editorial was headed: 'And who lost?'

I thought the university had, and I was heavy-hearted. I feared that the precedent of yielding under threat what had been denied before (although it should have been granted to begin with) would come back to haunt it. (Within days there were occupations at Ryerson, Laurentian, and McMaster in Ontario, and Simon Fraser in BC.) Bissell was putting his faith in the new unified governing body proposed by CUG, and I had supported him in this further than I originally said I would, but I feared that the disorder that was growing in the meantime would be hard to root out later, even if the new system of government commanded more support than the current one.

The CUG report was published in October 1969, very widely distributed, and discussed in an organized way during the next seven months. It proposed a 'communitarian' university with as many powers as possible decentralized to individual departments, each having a parity council to advise the chairman on all matters of policy and implementation, including appointments, tenure, promotions, and dismissals. There would be a central governing council to replace the board and senate, to consist of twenty students, twenty faculty, and twenty lay persons representing the public. I was for student participation in university government at all levels and for a formal means for considering their opinions about faculty members and departmental needs, but against the principle of student–staff parity and against direct student involvement in personnel matters. Because it had become clear that our present governing bodies could not be reformed, I was by now prepared to support a unicameral central governing body for the U of T, although I still did not like it; but I felt that a heavier lay presence was needed to shield the university from government intervention.

I told Bissell my views, adding that I thought they would be widely shared among the faculty, and he wrote to me on 27 October with a scheme to modify the impact at the departmental level, where individual faculty members would be most concerned. We discussed ways of getting faculty support for the general thrust of the report while acknowledging opposition to particular features, which could then be amended by the final conclave to formulate a university position. On Bissell's behalf, I invited a number of influential faculty members to meet with him in my office on 8 November (interestingly, Bissell suggested McNaught, whose amending motion on 3 October 1968 had almost caused his resignation). Bissell made an effective presentation, explaining why it had become necessary to establish CUG, how its composition had ensured that it would adopt the principle of student–staff parity, why a failure to produce an agreed-upon report would have been disastrous, and how the most dangerous effects might be controlled. I then gave my views. After vigorous discussion, it was agreed that the nonadministrative participants would introduce resolutions to the Arts and Science Council, the ATS, and other appropriate bodies, affirming support for the general thrust of the report but opposing parity, direct student participation in personnel matters, and what they thought the anti-faculty tone of the report. For two months discussion in the various councils concentrated on the objectionable features, but then turned toward support of a single governing council on which students would be represented but in smaller numbers than faculty.

In March, the President's Council recommended the election of a constituent assembly, to be called 'the University-Wide Committee,' to consist of forty students, forty faculty, forty administrators, twenty alumni, ten board members, and ten other university persons. Although my appointment to Manitoba had been announced, I was asked by a constituency committee to run; I'd intended to take some time off before taking on the new assignment but couldn't refuse a request made knowing I was leaving, and was elected. The assembly met for three days, 1–3 June. Many CUG recommendations, including the single Governing Council, were approved without significant dissent, aided by a good paper presented by the ATS. It was agreed that the structure of department councils was a matter for the Governing Council, and that body's composition became the real issue. There was much caucusing, including a meeting of the ATS delegates to which I was invited. A 3:2 ratio of faculty–student membership was all-important to the ATS, as parity was to the students; I was glad to support ATS in this, but got no support from it for a greater lay representation. The last day's debate was harsh, but there was almost no non-student support for parity, and a modified version of the ATS proposal, which preserved the 3:2 ratio, passed by a large majority. The students then endorsed the entire report, with the proviso that they would file a minority report favouring parity. There was a harmful delay of a year, due to political manoeuvring by the board and the students; then a modified version of the report, retaining the recommended proportions, became the basis of a new act.

IX

In the fall of 1969 Peter Curry, the chancellor of the University of Manitoba, came to see me. They were looking for a president to succeed to Hugh Saunderson, who would retire 31 August 1970. My name had been put forward by a number of people; he had consulted friends in a position to know something of my work, especially Neil McKinnon of the U of T board and John Deutsch of Queen's, and had received favourable reports. Would I be interested? I asked what Manitoba would want me to do and he said much the same thing I'd been doing in Toronto. Had they got down to a short list? No; they had finished accumulating names and he could direct the process of winnowing more intelligently if he knew whether I was a candidate. No, I was not a candidate; I was happy where I was and wouldn't jeopardize my standing by seeking a position elsewhere; if they chose to make me an offer I would consider it.

Early in the new year he came again to say that they were down to a short list of four: one inside candidate, Harry Duckworth, the vice-president academic, and three outside nominees, of whom I was one. Would I come to meet with the search committee? Again I stipulated that it must not be as a candidate, to which he agreed.

It was a large committee, including representatives of the board, the senate, the faculty association, the student union, the alumni association, and the 'public.' Every group had some prepared questions, usually rising out of some local situation but sometimes reflecting a Toronto situation; an example of the latter was a student question about whether there should be a single all-embracing student union or a separate graduate-student union, a clear indication that despite their pledge of confidentiality the students had consulted their U of T counterparts about me. I replied that a single union was preferable, provided the needs of the graduate students were met; that had not been the case at Toronto. Other questions ranged from the function of the university, through term appointments for the president, to condom-vending machines in the student centre, and suggested a university beginning to feel pressures already familiar in Toronto.

When the committee had no more questions I asked some. What did they want their president to do within the university? What should his relations be with government, with the community at large, with other Canadian universities? They did not have committee positions, but individual members put forward answers, sometimes supplemented by others, which I thought generally satisfactory, as I thought the tone of the meeting. In later years I wondered whether, if I'd been more specific in my probing, I could have got some sense of the traps awaiting the unwary appointee. I did get a troubling foretaste of one problem when, as the meeting broke up, the secretary of the committee, W.J. Condo, approached me, said he was the vice-president (business) and secretary of the board, liked what I stood for, and hinted that he could influence the committee's decision. I had a feeling of revulsion and recognized this as a positioning manoeuvre, but couldn't on the spur of the moment think of how to counter it; I muttered something and hurried away.

Not long afterward Curry and Maurice Arpin, the chairman of the board, came to Toronto, said the committee had voted overwhelmingly for me and the board had unanimously accepted their recommendation; they were now instructed to offer me the presidency. I asked whether all segments of the committee had concurred, and they said that the students had abstained but had said they would not oppose the decision; all others had concurred. They proposed a starting salary of $45,000, plus the use of a house and car. I knew the salary to be low (I was then drawing $38,000) and assumed they expected it to be bargained up, but I had my own priorities and said that if other things could be agreed the salary would not be a problem; if I took the job and they liked my work they would presumably want to recognize it.

The first matter was that the University of Manitoba Act, which had recently been revised, did not specify that, aside from the president's, all appointments, promotions, dismissals, and salary determinations were to be made by the board on recommendation of the president. They said that was in fact the practice but agreed that its omission from the statute could open the way to improper interference by the government and the board, and agreed to place such a clause in the contract.

My second point was that university presidencies were becoming a hazardous occupation, in recognition of which the AUCC had published recommendations concerning pension arrangements. If

I were appointed I would want those recommendations incorporated in my contract: a seven-year term, renewable for three more years unless either party objected; at the end of seven years I should have the option of retirement on an immediate pension (abated by Chicago and Toronto entitlements) of two-thirds of salary, three-quarters if I stayed the full ten years, and if I stayed less than seven years, a reduction of one-seventh for every year short. I would also require a professorial appointment, and at the end of my service a year's sabbatical on full salary and staff benefits. They said all that was reasonable and they would recommend it to the board.

I said I would give them my answer in a week, and invited them to our house for lunch, where they would meet Lesley. On the way I stopped the car and pointed to the huge excavation for the new library, with several cranes showing above the hoardings, and said that would be one of my chief difficulties in deciding: I had worked for a new library for eight years and now that it was being realized it would be hard to leave it.

There had in fact been a threatening episode in the summer of 1968. Stimulated by Toronto's plans, all the other Ontario universities entered requests for new libraries, totalling more than CUA wished to recommend. CUA told Toronto that our plans were proportionately more expensive than the others, and we had to work very fast to prove that their figures were wrong and that the small real differential was attributable to provincial requirements. About what followed I wrote in my report for 1967–8: 'The Department of University Affairs asked the universities of the province to clarify their commitment to the idea of a system of Ontario research libraries, and to describe their understanding of the place in that system of the proposed University of Toronto Library. This was a nervous moment, but the test showed that the thinking and planning in CPUO, OCGS, OCUL, and the Advisory Joint Council of OCGS/OCUL held up under pressure – to the satisfaction, but perhaps also to the surprise, of DUA and CUA.' In fact much anxious liaison preceded this success, and I was glad that at this critical moment I was chairman of the Advisory Joint Council.

Another potential threat came in December 1969, when the

Huron–Sussex Ratepayers and Residents Association organized resistance to the expropriation of land for the library. They demanded that Bissell meet with them, which he agreed to do but then asked me to substitute for him. I spoke of the educational needs of the country, province, and city, and the unique ability, and hence duty, of the U of T to answer those needs. When I had dampened the flames long enough, Alex Rankin, the vice-president (administration), and his colleagues gave particulars of timing and method of compensation, and the floor was thrown open. There were some very angry people; I was particularly concerned by the implied threats of Ron Thom, the architect of Massey College, who hinted at intervention by Vincent Massey. We had previously been told that Massey, who was still on the board of governors, was opposed to a high-rise building which would dwarf Massey College and cast a shadow over it during the latter part of the afternoon. However, Robertson Davies, who discussed it with him, told me that although Massey was unhappy he would take no action. The district alderman and the lawyer for the association also sounded menacing, but those threats also came to nothing.

Now the contracts were all signed, the construction towers in place, and the project far enough advanced that there was clearly no further danger of its abortion. (Indeed, Lesley had tied herself for a week to the catwalk on the seventh floor of the zoology building across the street to make a panoramic drawing of the construction for the last and most ambitious of our U of T campus Christmas cards.) Enrolment in the School of Graduate Studies, which had quadrupled in my eight years there, had according to plan begun to level off; the school was satisfactorily housed; the new school organization was working well, with the GSU satisfied to play an important but minority role in its elective council; the school's centres and institutes, now numbering almost twenty, were accepted as the best way to achieve interdisciplinary graduate work; the graduate dean's role in appointments and on the university's budget and other central committees had become firmly established and was fully accepted and supported by the new generation of faculty deans; and the university's increased attention to graduate studies and research was now unquestioned internally or externally. If I were to depart none of this would be jeopardized. On the provincial scene, the Ontario Council on Graduate Studies and the Ontario Council of University Librarians were established and functioning well; program appraisals were now accepted by all universities; program planning was under way, albeit painfully; interuniversity library cooperation was good, although acquisition planning could not get far without progress on program planning; I had done as much on that scene as I could, perhaps more than was politic, and even if I stayed it might be well to be less active there.

When I analysed it in this way, I realized that what I'd been doing of late was not so much building as helping to put out fires. In the meantime, a new system of governance was being built, which I had supported out of loyalty to Bissell and recognition that matters had reached a stage locally where the old system could no longer work, but without much affection for the system now emerging, or confidence that it would be fireproof or even defend educational standards (both the new discipline system and the new undergraduate curriculum seemed to me more intent on placating student radicals than serving real student interests).

In Manitoba, on the other hand, there was much to be done, and perhaps I could make a contribution there. The University of Manitoba had been expanding rapidly, but with no overall plan and very uneven results. A few sectors appeared to have used the opportunities afforded by growth to improve quality; others had not, and in some sectors growth had lowered quality. It had seemed to me on my visits that more committed leadership should be able to stimulate the weaker sectors to emulate the more ambitious and, given a few more years of expanding resources, propel the university as a whole to a higher qualitative level. I was deeply attached to the U of T, but Manitoba had a claim on me too: born, raised, and educated there, with some family remaining, I felt some sense of obligation to my old home. And I was tempted to extend my string of Jewish firsts: it would be interesting to become the first Jewish president of a Canadian university. (As it happened, Max Wyman, another Jew, was appointed acting president of the University of Alberta about the same time as Manitoba appointed me president-designate; during the summer Wyman was named president, and we took office about the same time.)

Lesley and I discussed all this, together with domestic factors, over several days. We wondered how disrupting a move would be for the children, but there were some difficulties in the school situation in Toronto, and we had been led to believe (mistakenly) that matters were under better control in Winnipeg. Finally Lesley said she thought I should accept the offer because, having spent eight years in senior administration, I would later regret it if I refused the challenge to accept final responsibility. I thought she was right; my own mind had been moving toward acceptance but I had not wanted to influence her because we would all be affected by the change. We decided to accept. When we told the children, they were thoughtful but, after discussion, said they were willing.

I had kept Bissell abreast of developments and now told him that I was likely to accept Manitoba's offer if forthcoming discussions worked out. He asked whether Toronto could do anything to keep me, saying it would meet any salary offer. I thanked him but said salary wasn't central; I was tempted to see what I could do, especially in my home university. He said that he would be resigning within a year or two and thought that if I stayed I'd be a likely choice to succeed him. I said that I didn't think SAC would permit that.

The whole family now went to Winnipeg for final discussions. I met with Saul Miller, the minister of colleges and universities affairs in the new NDP government, who said he'd been briefed about me and hoped I would come. The two years he had spent at the University of Manitoba before dropping out were the unhappiest of his life, but he wouldn't hold that against us now and hoped I could improve things. The Universities Grants Commission dealt with the three universities in the province on financial matters, but he would be available to me if I should want to talk with him. I met more briefly with the premier, Ed Schreyer, who had been a history instructor in the university and said he wished it well and hoped I would come; he would be accessible if needed.

We called on the Saundersons in the president's house on campus, who advised us not to live there: it was too exposed to student and staff demands and too far from town for the children to have friends of their own age. We had already decided against living on the isolated campus and had asked the university to suggest alternatives; it had lined up several available houses and said it would purchase whichever we wanted. We chose a large, old house on Kingsway that belonged to the Sellers family, and the design department of the university undertook to prepare a plan for renovation which would include furnishing the reception areas. The particulars of my contract were soon settled with Curry and Arpin, although Condo's written version contained ambiguities which made me wonder whether he lacked precision of mind or wanted to retain room for manipulation; it took some time and correspondence to get it right. The school situation seemed suitable and the children were caught up in the excitement. I accepted the offered appointment as president-designate from 1 July and as president from 1 September.

Back in Toronto I told Bissell that I would go to Manitoba. He asked again whether there was anything Toronto could do to keep me, and I said I'd already accepted Manitoba's offer. We were walking along Hoskin Avenue; he stopped and said, 'That decides it; I'll give my notice of resignation this year.' I said I was very sorry to precipitate his action; he replied that he had been considering when to resign and would have done it in a year or two anyway; my decision had just clarified matters. It was clear to me that the struggles of the past few years had worn him down and drained his job of any pleasure, and now that the library was secure, and the new unified form of governance virtually so, he felt free to get out.

My appointment was announced on 3 March and created considerable interest in both cities, and some elsewhere. Both Winnipeg dailies sent reporters to interview me; the student newspaper, *The Manitoban*, sent two. I received an astonishing flood of letters, some of which I found very moving, especially those from faculty members at the U of T which said they'd initially opposed both me and my policies but had come to be supporters and regretted my leaving; another I was glad to get was from the minister, William Davis, thanking me for what he termed my contribution to higher education in the province. There were resolutions in various official bodies, and a number of parties, gifts, and testimonials. On the other side, SAC sent a 'letter of condolence' to the U of M Student Union commiserating with them – 'Toronto's gain is Manitoba's loss' – and describing my 1969 convocation speech as 'Red-baiting.' *The Varsity* published a long denunciation of me, with a large drawing representing me guarding the closed door of a Gothic entrance with a sub-machine-gun (promptly reproduced in *The Manitoban*). W.L. Morton, who had written the history of the University of Manitoba, and some other Manitobans wrote exultantly that my appointment was a defeat for the Establishment. *The Manitoban* declared sorrowfully and often that my appointment was imposed by the Establishment.

CHAPTER EIGHT

Winnipeg, 1970–1976

I

When the time came for the move to Winnipeg, Robert, despite his earlier agreement, refused for a long time to get into the car. If I had been superstitious I might have taken that as an omen and saved us from a grievous mistake.

One didn't have to be superstitious to read another sign: the Winnipeg house, which was to have been ready for us by the beginning of June, was a mess. I spoke to W.J. Condo, the vice-president (business), and he assigned a special supervisor to expedite the job; weeks of cohabitation with the work went by and progress was maddeningly slow; finally I had Condo in and told him the incompetence must stop. He replaced the supervisor with another, put more men on the job, and came in himself every morning on his way to work; finally, months after the promised date, the work was finished. The impression of bad management and sloppy workmanship remained with me.

The purpose of bringing me in two months early as president-designate was to familiarize me with the university's situation before I had to assume responsibility. I was given a small office adjoining the president's, which should have made liaison easy, but Saunderson had virtually nothing to say to me. A few times during those months he came in with some trifle, but never brought up anything of substance. At first I tried asking him about potential problems, but his answers were usually to leave it to Condo. It became clear that he had no interest in preparing me for the takeover; he had groomed Harry Duckworth as his successor and I came to realize that he saw me as an intruder, resented my appointment, and regarded it as a defeat for himself.

Quite unsuspected by me, there were two urgent matters threatening the financial integrity, and even the autonomy, of the university; Saunderson never mentioned them. Neither did Condo, whom I saw frequently, or Duckworth, the vice-president (academic), with whom I had a number of briefing sessions. For that matter, neither did Maurice Arpin, the chairman of the board, or Peter Curry, the chancellor. It was not until October that I became aware of them, from an outside source.

My most immediate task was the construction of a new administrative team. During the preceding year or two there had been many recommendations, chiefly by the senate, for additional vice-presidencies: planning and analysis, health sciences, research, student affairs, development. In view of his impending retirement, Saunderson had left all this to his successor.

Duckworth had been given a sabbatical, to start 1 September; I asked him whether he would return to a vice-presidential post, and he asked to be given until November to decide. Keeping a post open for him made it very hard to proceed, but I knew that forcing an immediate decision on him would be seen as ungenerous by his supporters, so I agreed. He didn't give me his decision at the time arranged, and when I wrote to ask for it he asked for a further postponement until the end of the year; I granted this, but heard nothing. Finally, at the end of January, he sent me a postcard saying he had been appointed president of the University of Winnipeg, information I had read the day before in the newspaper.

William Sibley, the director of planning, had been in Hamilton on sabbatical when my appointment was announced, and had come to see me in Toronto. He described his mandate and said the senate had recommended it be upgraded to a vice-presidency; he would be happy to serve in that capacity if I wished, or he could return to his work as professor of philosophy. When I asked what he was doing in Hamilton he said he was visiting his brother, but had been ill and in hospital for some time, which made it harder for me to decide whether to give him a major administrative responsibility. But again, he had a following (he'd been dean of arts and science before becoming director of planning), he was intelligent and experienced, and in reply to a direct question he said the doctor had told him he was fully cured.

I didn't want a separation of staff and line duties at the vice-presidential level, having found that, like their respective army counterparts, purely staff vice-presidents become remote from the teaching and operating units, and purely line vice-presidents see their roles predominantly as the representation of their constituencies. I wanted a central academic administration each of whose members would be in close touch with the faculties while at the same time immediately concerned with all general university problems. Accordingly, I planned to have three vice-presidents in the academic area, each combining staff and line responsibilities. The first, in September, was Sibley, who became vice-president (planning and special assignments), with initial responsibility for supervising a considerable number of faculties in addition to the reorganized Planning Office. For the time being, until it became known that Duckworth would not return, the remaining faculties reported to me. Then, in February 1971, I appointed T.W. Fyles, the dean of medicine, as vice-president (health sciences), and in March, J.C. Gilson, the dean of graduate studies, as vice-president (research, graduate studies, and special assignments). In this way I was able to apportion seventeen of the eighteen faculties, together with the interdisciplinary centres, among the vice-presidents, but had to look after Science myself for another year, until Fyles could add it to his lot.

During the summer I responded to invitations to meet with the executives of the University of Manitoba Faculty Association and the University of Manitoba Students Union. The meeting with UMFA was not much more than a get-acquainted session; UMSU, however, had several particular problems to confront me with, especially concerning student participation in university governance. The University of Manitoba Act of 1968 had for the first time given students a formal position in university government, but in the following year UMSU had become convinced that the number of its seats on Board and Senate was too small for real influence. Its repeated efforts to secure enlarged student representation had always been met by the assertion that nothing could be done unless the provincial legislature changed the act, and it had seen no willingness to ask for such change. It had therefore boycotted Board and Senate, and relations with those bodies, and even more with the administration, had seriously deteriorated. What did I think of the situation?

I told them of the device I had used in the Graduate Council at Toronto, where I made provision for student assessors until the school statute could be changed to make them full members. Here the statutory change could be made only by the legislature, but it might be possible, as an interim measure, to secure the introduction of additional students as assessors on Senate and Board; such assessors would not be able to vote or make motions, but otherwise they could be accorded all the rights of members and would be able to represent the interests of their constituents. The conditions of my offer were that the assessors would have to be elected by academic constituencies, as the faculty members were, not appointed by UMSU, and the total number of students in Senate could not exceed one-quarter of the assembly, which would allow for an increase from six to twenty-eight; on the board, two assessors might be added to the single student member.

UMSU was clearly surprised by my proposal and uncertain about how to respond. Some were suspicious and, well-briefed by their U of T counterparts, asked about the first proposal the graduate-student assessors there had introduced, to abolish the ten-hour limit on paid outside work for full-time students, which had been unable to muster any support; didn't that indicate that assessors were helpless? I said the best answer was that when the assessors became full members they didn't reintroduce the proposal, having by then realized its necessity: without it, government tended to think graduate students should be self-supporting, with the result that they had to do too much paid work, did their course work as best they could but left their research for later, and all too often became ABDs. Indeed, we had pursuaded the Ontario government to incorporate the limit in its definition of 'full-time,' thus making both government fellowships and the universities' operating grants dependent upon its enforcement. The true question was how other proposals introduced by the assessors had fared, such as departmental councils with student membership, consultation with students on prerequisite requirements, space assignments, etc., in all of which students had initiated constructive change.

Several wanted to know why I would not accept parity of student and faculty representation, which was the students' right in a democratic society. I said they were being misled by a beautiful metaphor, the university as 'a community of scholars,' from which they had been taught to conclude that it should imitate the larger community in governance. But a real community is self-supporting, whereas the university depends upon government for about four-fifths of its revenue, given to it to perform certain services for society. It is thus a special-purpose institution which has evolved a structure and procedures designed to enable it to perform those functions. One major fault of its governance has been the absence of student participation, which we ought now to correct, but not from an invalid premise; the modified governance should be appropriate to an institution, not a community, and one whose special purpose was the preservation, advancement, and dissemination of knowledge, in which students had an important part but not one equal to all other parts together. Besides, there was the practical aspect: any demand for parity would immediately throw the faculty and administration (including myself) into a posture of opposition and nothing would be achieved, whereas a request for representation adequate to make the students a powerful factor in governance could probably be negotiated.

They turned to student discipline; it was administered by a committee consisting of senior administrators meeting in secret, and an ad hoc committee established a year earlier to review discipline procedures had got nowhere; what did I think about discipline? I thought it needed reconstruction and, if the senate had a large number of students, they could present their views effectively. For myself, I thought that jurisdictions should be defined and hearings open, and that students should have an equal voice with faculty in matters of academic discipline and be predominant in parietal discipline. The problem of disruption had to be tackled, not evaded as in Toronto. I would try to speed up the work of the review committee.

Could UMSU be incorporated so that it could own property and be responsible in law for its own affairs? Yes; if they sent me their formal request I'd recommend it to the board.

At the end of our first meeting the UMSU members were in a state of visible confusion, having expected a very different encounter. On the basis of the false picture of me given them by U of T's SAC, they had anticipated a stern rejection of all their demands and were preparing a response. I learnt later what they had envisioned: a referendum on whether to accept me as president, on the technical ground that the student members of the search committee had abstained from voting, and on the emotional basis of a campaign depicting me as a reactionary enemy of student rights. As a result of our first meeting, however, they abandoned that whole posture and decided to see what working with me would accomplish. Some members of the UMSU executive still harboured suspicions, but we did in fact work harmoniously to secure Senate and Board approval of my proposals.

There was an incident during the summer which neatly symbolized the difference in my relations with the students and with the old administration. As part of the province's celebration of its centennial, there was a royal visit, including a half-day at the university. Princess Anne was to arrive by helicopter at a temporary landing-pad on the outskirts of the campus, and Lesley and I were to be in the greeting party. We were awaiting the appointed time in my office when Saunderson came in and suggested that we go to the landing-pad with him and his wife so that there would be fewer cars crowding the parking area, which we did. By the time the helicopter arrived a strong wind had risen and a threatened downpour began; we stood, soaking and wind-blown, to see a grim-faced Anne emerge and, without acknowledging the drowned wretches waiting for her, head for the car indicated by her aides: Saunderson's. He drove off without a word to us, as did the other dignitaries, all scurrying to their cars to escape the rain and not noticing that we'd been stranded. We began the long walk back to the main campus, not aided by the weather or Lesley's shoe heels. We had gone only a few hundred yards when a beaten-up old car drew up beside us: it was the UMSU president and some of his executive, who had also been part of the welcoming party. We were very glad of the lift, which I thought revealing: stood up by Saunderson, picked up by UMSU. (When I was introduced to Prince Charles, who had arrived dry by car, I said I feared his sister had got wet and wind-blown, to which he replied, 'Do her the world of good.')

I became president on 1 September and took over Saunderson's office and secretary. I had wanted to invite my U of T secretary, Esmé Cummings, to come with me, but felt I owed it to the incumbent to let her show whether she would suit. It didn't take long to conclude that she wouldn't: she was willing but not up to the pace of the new administration. She was placed with the dean of medicine, and Esmé came to take charge of my office, where she combined calm efficiency with personal loyalty for the remainder of my tenure.

The fall term began with deceptive smoothness. The important first meetings with Senate and Board were constructive and agreeable. After careful discussion both accepted my proposals for student assessors. *The Manitoban* was very alarmed by this evidence of 'co-option' and advocated a boycott of the election for assessors, but there were good turn-outs in the various constituencies and very soon twenty-two additional students entered the senate, with two more entering the board. Both groups tested the limits of their role but soon settled down to constructive participation, although in the case of the board there were some warning signs that confidentiality would be a problem. At student initiative and with my support, Senate required all faculties to establish by-laws providing for student participation in both faculty and departmental governance. In fact, we never had serious difficulty with the students throughout my tenure; some UMSU executives and *The Manitoban* did try to stir up trouble, but the student officers at faculty and departmental levels, and the mass of students, proved sensible and stable. Lesley, accustomed to the grimmer Toronto radicals, thought the Manitobans 'sweet.'

Just before my arrival, the board had asked the planning office and the senate planning and priorities committee to study the implications of limiting enrolment to 18,000 full-time equivalents. I joined this effort during the summer and then asked the planning office to work with deans and directors to develop a plan for the achievement of such a target. The result was a tentative profile (by faculty and school, and by undergraduate and graduate levels) for a maximum enrolment of 18,000 FTE, with a tentative timetable for its realization. Simultaneously, we developed the methodology of a staffing policy. The first part of this would be the normative determination of the load carried by each faculty, expressed quantitatively as the sum of three factors: undergraduate teaching, graduate teaching, and extraordinary research or service missions. The second part would be a statement of the percentage of the load assessment to which the university would staff each unit, i.e., a statement of operating priorities.

The senate approved both the enrolment and the staffing policies for budgetary and planning purposes, subject to annual reassessment. The enrolment policy was presented to the board as a step necessitated by the absence of a provincial policy, to be taken in the hope that it would stimulate the other post-secondary institutions and the provincial government into joining with us in the development of an enrolment policy for the province as a whole; if that could be brought about we would regard our plan as an initial contribution to joint planning and would be ready to modify it if required for the general good. The board approved the policy and authorized me to pursue discussions with the relevant outside bodies. It also received the staffing policy for information, in the knowledge that it would underlie the annual budget proposal.

At the beginning of October *The Manitoban* published a substantial attack on the library administration, featuring photographs of a storeroom completely filled with unopened parcels of books, together with charges that the owner of the company engaged to computerize the book-ordering system also owned another company which had been given an exclusive contract to acquire books for the library. I called the director of libraries in, who acknowledged the facts as alleged but defended the ordering/purchasing arrangement as the best he could do with the limited staff at his disposal, and offered to resign. I told him that if he resigned while there were accusations of impropriety it would be assumed that he was culpable; if he was clean it would be better to stick it out while I had the Senate Library Committee investigate; meanwhile, could the ordering/purchasing contracts be terminated? He said they were about to run out but his staff didn't have the capability to take on the work itself. He agreed to set up a special task force to clean up the backlog. In February a subcommittee of the Library Committee leaked a preliminary report very critical of the library administration, but the main committee rejected it, and its report in March expressed confidence in the library administration, allowing the director to resign with dignity. This episode did not add to my optimism about the level of administrative competence I had inherited.

My formal installation, which took place on 5 November, had been timed to coincide with a meeting in Winnipeg of the AUCC to enable interested presidents of other universities to attend. Some thirty did, including almost all the Ontario and western presidents; most had brought their presidential robes and they made a colourful procession as they filed to the stage to deliver institutional greetings and personal congratulations. It was a long procession, since about sixty other institutions had nominated Winnipeg residents as their representatives. Altogether, the pomp and panoply were enough to satisfy the ambitions of the board, and even of Condo, who was deeply aggrieved at my refusal to permit an opening prayer; he had continually pestered me about it, suggesting that it could be a Hebrew prayer, but I said I was as firm an atheist in Hebrew as in English. I did ask the cooperation of the chairman of the Religion department, who gave an invocation which was without reference to any deity.

My inaugural address was an overlong analysis of the contradictions inherent in our eclectic North American idea of a university and of their partial realization in the struggles of the current scene, with a balancing of competing interests and a drawing of the line beyond which compromise could not go.* It was more

---
* *University of Manitoba Bulletin*, Fall 1970, 25–41

suited to a lecture hall or an academic conference than to so charged a ceremony, but the only person I saw fall asleep during the fifty minutes it took to deliver was Lesley, who had taken an unaccustomed tranquillizer to help her through the inaugural events, in which she had to play a prominent role.

II

Enrolment in the previous decade had grown rapidly, and had been projected to increase by 10 per cent in the fall of 1970. In the event, it increased by only 3.3 per cent, in line with similar slow-downs elsewhere. This meant a shortfall of $600,000 in fee income and $360,000 in associated forms of revenue. I knew this to be serious, but I did not yet know the context into which to fit it.

I learnt that late in October at a federal–provincial conference on university financing in Vancouver, where I met Scott Bateman, the chairman of the Universities Grants Commission of Manitoba. He was a long-time civil servant with what I was assured by my colleagues was a friendly and enlightened attitude towards universities, which made what he told me all the more shocking. He greeted me warmly, wished me all the luck in the world, and then said there were some things I ought to know but had probably not been told. First, the University of Manitoba had begun the current fiscal year with an accumulated deficit of about one and a quarter million dollars and with unbudgeted commitments of nearly another half-million. Sceptically, I said I had seen the 1969–70 comptroller's report, audited according to law by the provincial auditor, and there was no mention of anything like that, nor had Saunderson, Condo, or Arpin said anything about a deficit. He said that he was not surprised, but that if I looked into it I would find that he was right, and furthermore that there was no contingency fund to set against any of this. What was more, he would soon be telling all three Manitoba universities that the UGC thought their grant requests for the coming year heavily excessive and that, in the light of changing government priorities, he anticipated that future UGC budgets would be less expansionary than in recent years.

Bad as this was, Bateman's second piece of information was far worse. The university had developed a new pension plan, which the UGC had asked it not to implement until it had been able to study it. The university, however, had determined that the matter was within its statutory authority and had implemented the plan during the summer. The UGC and the government would not accept the plan because it required disproportionate contributions from the university and guaranteed unrealistic minimum pensions, all involving public funds, and he would confide in me that the government had been preparing a new act which would terminate the plan, put the faculty on the province's civil-service plan, and strip the university of its autonomy; it was almost ready and would be introduced in the current legislative session.

I could hardly credit what I was hearing. Why had Saul Miller, the minister, not told me of this when we met before I accepted appointment? Bateman didn't know; perhaps in February Miller thought the university would back off.

Could Bateman get the government to delay introduction of the bill until I could look into the matter? He couldn't promise but he would try.

When I got home I learnt that the university had begun work on the pension plan well before the establishment of the UGC in 1967, and although the UGC asked for postponement, the board, under the urging of UMFA, felt constrained after the lapse of so much time to put the plan into effect. In truth, Arpin, active in Conservative politics and appointed to the board by the previous Conservative government, told me that he had been glad to defy the new NDP government over the plan.

I told the board of the extreme imminent threat to the university and asked it to invite Bateman to tell us the detailed objections of the government. It did so, and Bateman presented a formidable list of particulars which taught the abruptly sobered board how reckless it had been. When he left I moved that it ask the Staff Benefits Committee to try to meet these objections; Arpin objected, but he was almost alone. I joined the committee in an urgent series of meetings, some with officers of the UGC; after much negotiation, during which the UGC very reluctantly gave some ground, we recommended to the board that it seek the consent of the staff for certain amendments to the plan which would reduce costs to the university and benefits to the staff.

In February I sent a notice to all participants in the plan explaining the situation and listing the needed amendments; then, in a series of open meetings with different sectors of the staff, I further explained the situation and asked their support; and late in March the staff ballotted. The result showed that the staff had understood the danger: despite the obvious reduction of benefits to each person, the response was massively affirmative. With this mandate the board implemented the changes on 1 April, 1971, the UGC having assured us that the plan was now acceptable to it and to the government. Both Bateman and Miller told me that the intended new act would be withheld, as in fact it was.

Simultaneously with the pension issue, I pursued the problem of the deficit, made worse by the revenue shortfall from lower- than- budgeted enrolment. The accumulated and prospective deficits aggregated over two and a half million dollars, a sum equal to almost 12 per cent of the provincial operating grant for 1969–70. To carry this forward with the prospect, now officially communicated to the three universities by the UGC, of less expansionary future grants would have been to court disaster. It proved impossible to get a clear picture of when and how the accumulated deficit was incurred other than that various divisions had been allowed to overspend, and after satisfying myself that there had been no fraud I settled for Condo's promise that his next report would say: 'An accumulated deficit from prior years' operations aggregated $958,130 as of April 1, 1970.' The other quarter-million dollars consisted of capital expenditures beyond project authorization, which, unless accepted as additional capital costs by the UGC, would become a charge against operating revenue, and the unbudgeted current commitments rose out of retroactive features of labour settlements.

I set up an advisory budget committee, explained the situation to the Board, Deans' Council, and Senate, and quickly developed a program of restraint on both expenditures and commitments. The purchase of supplies and equipment and the renovation of space and facilities were reduced or postponed, travel and optional activities were cut down, staff was allowed to shrink through attrition, and many local economies were effected. All this did some damage to the university's programs and plant, but it halted the developing threat. By 31 March, the end of the fiscal year, $850,000 had been recovered from the operating grant; to this was added $108,000, the accumulated revenue in the General Trust Account (ordinarily used for purposes not properly a charge against public funds); and the deficit accumulated as of 1 April, 1970 was thus amortized. The operating deficit for 1970–1 was held down to about $284,000, and against this was applied the year's revenue from the Trust Account, about $103,000. I was given hints that the UGC would accept some of the capital overruns for reimbursement, but meantime we had to show it in full, so that at the end of the fiscal year we had a net accumulated deficit of $430,000 – not comfortable, but a far cry from the $2.5 million which threatened us in the fall and early winter.

It is hard to see how I could have had a more unpopular start. I had barely arrived from hated Toronto when I snatched away a treasured new pension plan, cut staff, and imposed unfamiliar restraints on ordinary spending. At the time most people acknowledged that each measure was necessary, but some did not, and as time wore on and other reasons for displeaure emerged, even some of those who had originally recognized the need began to blame me for it. I had, however, earned some credit with the UGC and government, in token of which they accepted the capital-cost overruns as additional capital costs, further reducing our accumulated deficit.

This slight softening of the government's attitude towards the university did not prevent individual ministers from making unnecessary troubles for us. The labour minister, Russ Pauley, promised a banquet of the Service Employees International Union that he would 'investigate' their charge that the university had violated terms of the Manitoba Labour Relations Act. This was pretty rough behaviour. The union had written to the Labour Board, with a copy to the minister, complaining about occurrences in the past which it said discouraged employees from supporting the union, such as the formation of a staff council and a 'unilateral' salary increase when the union was attempting to organize the technicians in Engineering; the Labour Board had asked the university about these charges, and the board of governors had undertaken to look into them. The minister was aware of the state of the matter but nevertheless publicly attacked the university while the inquiry was in progress. It turned out that there had been no violations of the act, but there had been efforts to discourage the formation of a union, and these had contributed to the antagonism felt by the NDP government towards the university administration. On my motion the board resolved that such efforts would not be repeated.

The next bit of friction with the government was precipitated by an obscene special number of the student newspaper. When the inevitable fuss was raised I told the president of UMSU that the university would do nothing about it: the paper was owned and published by UMSU, now seeking incorporation and therefore to be held responsible for its own actions, and anyway the university would not act *in loco parentis* to adults. I said the same thing to the press, adding that I knew that many people had complained to the police and the attorney general, and it would be up to them whether charges were laid; the university was no sanctuary from the law (this was the phrase that appeared in the headlines).

Then Joe Borowski, the minister of transportation, phoned me, demanding that the culprits be expelled. I went through the argument with him, to no avail: 'why should university students be protected?' They shouldn't be; if they were charged the university would take no action on their behalf. When the legislature met a few days later, on 15 April, Borowski and Henry Einarson, an opposition member, vied with each other in denouncing the university for *The Manitoban*'s 'pornographic garbage' (which Borowski had reproduced and distributed to all members 'at public expense,' as he stated), and both demanded that I 'be called on the carpet and read the Riot Act,' Einarson suggesting that the university be closed for a year, which would have the added advantage of saving the government a lot of money. The press kept up the clamour for about a week (the lead editorial in the *Tribune* inviting 'mature and responsible citizens' to pick up duplicated copies of the offensive paper at its office), and the deputy attorney general and the director of prosecutions met with me, together with the president of UMSU and the editor of *The Manitoban*. No charges were laid, and the incident served to establish a new policy for the university, very different from the undefined and unpredictable parietal paternalism that had gone before.

The grant request to the UGC for 1971–2 had been developed under Saunderson. I had just become president when it was to be sent in, and thought it inflated ($43 million, as against the 1970–1 grant of $31 million, an increase of about 39 per cent), but of course it was politically impossible to begin my tenure by reducing the request. In February 1971 we were told what we'd get: $34 million, an increase of about $3 million, or just under 10 per cent. As against this, we were faced with non-discretionary cost increases rising from the opening of new facilities, sharply higher utilities rates and supply costs, and contracted wage increases for unionized support staff of about $2.6 million. In addition, the new pension plan, even after revision, would require a contribution increase of $600,000. Salary increases were essential because ours were substandard and inflation was strong, and some increased staff was needed for areas of growth, but money for all this would have to be found elsewhere than from the grant increase.

I therefore recommended, with the concurrence of Senate, a very stringent budget which terminated summer stipends for faculty research, reduced support for graduate students, and cut back library and computer appropriations and departmental supplies. There was some reduction in academic programs and in the number of low-enrolment courses, some services were terminated, and staff numbers in areas where growth had stopped were allowed to shrink through attrition. With the money thus saved, salaries for academic staff were increased an average of 7 per cent, non-unionized support staff an average of 8 per cent. But I had been shocked by the discrepancy, much larger than elsewhere, between junior and senior academic salaries, and pressed successfully for a bias in favour of the junior ranks, who were given an average increase substantially above 7 per cent, with the result that the average increase for senior academic ranks was somewhat below 7 per cent, which brought some complaints from senior faculty.

A very troublesome situation arose with respect to vice-presidential salaries. All except Condo had been newly promoted, and I recommended salary increases that would take this into account; I also recommended a 7 per cent increase for Condo, the average for administrative officers. The board approved all my recommendations, but a few days later Curry told me that Condo had been to see him to complain that he had not been given an increase commensurate with his 'promotion.' I said he hadn't been promoted; he had come to see me in midwinter to ask that his title be changed from 'Vice-President Business and Comptroller' to 'Vice-President (Administration),' and I had agreed, but there had been no change in responsibility except that he had eased his load by promoting the associate comptroller to comptroller. Curry accepted this, but a little later Arpin phoned and said, 'For reasons of my own, I'd like you to add $5,000 to Condo's salary.' I thought this utterly improper and replied, 'Fine, if I can add a comparable amount to each of the other v-ps and a proportionate amount to all other administrative officers and teaching ranks.' Recognizing this for a refusal, Arpin asked about the alleged unrewarded promotion, which I explained was no promotion. Then he said that Condo felt that as the 'senior' v-p he ought to have the highest salary; I strongly disagreed, saying that Condo was the highest-paid of any v-p except Fyles, who had to be compensated for surrendering physician's earnings; and anyway, academic and business administration were on different tracks. Arpin said that Condo had a lot of influence in the community and it would do me no good to make an enemy of him, to which I made no reply.

Finally Arpin desisted, but a month or two later he resigned from the board. In June, Justice Brian Dickson of the Manitoba Court of Appeal was elected board chairman. Condo never spoke to me about his salary, but he repeated his complaint to succeeding chairmen. What may have made an average raise harder for him to accept was that the board gave me a raise of $5,000, which amounted to about 11 per cent. That brought my salary to the level the board had expected to pay on my appointment but didn't because I hadn't bargained it up from the initial offer.

Condo's resort to the chancellor and the chairman to circumvent me strengthened my determination to have him removed as secretary of the board; at U of T, I had seen how the direct access of the vice-president (business) to the board chairman had handicapped and frustrated the president. I knew it was not going to be easy, for he had ingratiated himself with many board members, with whom he socialized at the establishment redoubt, the Manitoba Club. However, in 1972, when administrative tasks were increasing, I told the board that I needed Condo's full-time service as vice-president, and would like the board, whose work was also increasing, to have a full-time secretary. Behind the scenes Condo tried to persuade his friends on the board not to approve this action, but failed.

At our first regular convocation, in the spring of 1971, Lesley and I got a demonstration either of staff resentment of us as outsiders or of staff incompetence, perhaps both. At breakfast, Lesley asked me when she was due at the auditorium, and I said the ceremony was to begin at 10:00 A.M. but she'd have to ask the registrar's office, which opened at 8:30, when she was needed. When she phoned there was a silence, then: 'My God, Mrs Sirluck, didn't you get your kit?' She was supposed to be in place, in an ante-room, at 9 o'clock, to introduce the wives of the honorary graduands and the corresponding faculty representatives to each other, give them coffee, and lead them to their assigned places, nothing of which either of us had been told. She managed, against the odds and having broken the speed laws, to arrive on time and, with the aid of a list of names of people she'd never met, performed her task, but it left her disinclined to rely overmuch on University of Manitoba staff work.

We were invited by the American Council on Education to participate in a President's Institute in Key Biscayne, Florida, in June 1971. Since it was meant to help prepare new university presidents and their wives for their tasks, we accepted, and arrived in heat so intense that we spent virtually the whole week inside the air-conditioned hotel. We were the only Canadians in the group, and of course the curriculum reflected American conditions, which were more extreme than Canadian; for example, the session on student protest featured case histories of presidents and their families under elaborate electronic and human safeguard, with siege supplies and underground escape routes. Nevertheless the lectures, and particularly the discussions, were very informative, especially with regard to budgeting and collective bargaining. The positions put forward respecting academic governance seemed to me overly conservative, and I thought the discussions of financing and president–trustee relations had little Canadian application. The week began with a lecture by David Riesman on the current American culture within which the university operated, and ended with another by Max Lerner on the future outlook. The strongest impression the week made on me was that the university world was becoming a threatened and embattled special interest.

III

An embarrassing and damaging situation rose out of Bissell's resignation from the presidency of the University of Toronto. The chairman of the search committee to find a successor was the chancellor, Omand Solandt, with whom I was on friendly terms. One day in the spring of 1971 he called to say he knew I was going to be in Toronto the following week for a meeting; would I join his committee for lunch? I said no, I'd accepted the Manitoba presidency in good faith and couldn't abandon it so soon, so I wasn't a candidate for the Toronto office. He said that it would help his committee greatly if I'd meet with them, because I could tell them how certain Toronto situations had developed and in general brief them on problems facing university presidents; he would take it as a personal favour if I'd agree. Faced with this sort of request from my old university I could hardly say no, and said that, if he made it clear in advance to his committee that I wasn't a candidate, I'd come.

The first indication that my position had not been made clear to the committee was a letter from James Conacher, professor of history at U of T, whom I had known well on the Graduate Council and the President's Council; he said he was a Faculty Association representative on the search committee and would like to see me before I went to lunch; he would ring me at my hotel in the morning. There he told me that he and the two other faculty representatives were pushing to have me appointed and he thought they would prevail if I said I was available. This made it very hard for me to sustain my self-denying resolution. I loved the U of T, thought I knew its strengths and how to correct some wrong turns it had made, had a good working relation both with the provincial government and with the other Ontario universities, and thought if I were president I could press on with the project that had brought me there about nine years earlier: helping to develop a good provincial university into a university of international standing. After barely a year at the U of M I already knew that I would not develop much affection for it, and the prospect of raising it into a higher class had grown remote. I longed to tell Conacher that I would be available, but I thought it would be injurious to Manitoba if the new president left so soon. I explained this to Conacher and pointed out that I'd agreed to meet the committee only if it were clear that I wasn't a candidate.

At lunch I was asked many questions, some having to do with my actions and policies while at U of T, so that I felt constrained to say that, because of the newness of my Manitoba appointment, they must not think of me as a candidate. Unfortunately, the committee did not drop my name: in mid-June, Bill Harris, a member of the committee and acting chairman of the board of governors, held a press conference in which he said that the committee was down to three names: Fred Carrothers of Calgary, John Evans of McMaster, and me. I learnt of this when the Winnipeg media called me about it; I told them that I was not a candidate and would not leave Manitoba. Then I phoned Harris and asked him to issue a correction; I understood him to say he would, but none was forthcoming. When Senate met a day or two later, I began by stating that I had met with the U of T committee only to give them the information and advice the chairman had sought, that I had told them I wasn't a candidate, and that I was now formally announcing to my own university that I would not be leaving. Some time later the Toronto papers reported that the committee had voted for Carrothers; my name had been dropped because 'he had been in Winnipeg less than a year and U of T would make enemies by taking him so soon' (*Free Press*, 8 February 1972). (In the event, the negotiation with Carrothers broke down, and Evans was appointed.)

I heard no criticism of my role in this from Manitoba (there was some complaint from friends in Toronto), but it reinforced a widespread perception that, despite my Manitoba origin, I was really an outsider, that my orientation was to Toronto, and that my commitment to Manitoba was only to the task. There was some justice in this. It could have been otherwise: I had come ready to recover or develop a wider loyalty, but early events and the tone both on campus and in the city inhibited this, and those who closely watch a university president sensed it.

During our first year or so Lesley and I tried to give the presidency a substantial social dimension. We started our entertaining at senior academic and administrative levels, broadening to include other academics at post-convocation parties, but difficult and unpopular administrative measures affected the social atmosphere, and the task of entertaining grew less pleasant. After the first year we did very little faculty entertaining except for seven or eight post-convocation parties a year and an annual reception for new faculty. I think this remissness contributed to the distance that developed between me and much of the faculty.

As for the students, we gave a party in the fall of 1971 for members of UMSU and the senior elective officers of student councils; it went quite well until midnight, the leaving time specified in the invitation, when I recruited several obliging students to help get people out, but at 2:00 A.M. we were still coping with stragglers. *The Manitoban* devoted several pages to the event, describing it as a sybaritic, if not orgiastic, entertainment, in lavish surroundings, and we never tried it again. However, we went to an uncountable number of formal dinner-dances held by the graduating class of every faculty, school, college, and hall of residence, all crammed into the six weekends between mid-January and the end of February, when Winnipeg's winters are most intense and the banqueting halls of its hotels draftiest. Student budgets not being capacious, the middle-aged often found the food indigestible and the wine undrinkable, but it was clear that every group thought itself entitled to the president's presence, so we did our best to attend as many as possible. Each such occasion meant a speech by me, and I found it very difficult to make these increasingly empty routine speeches.

Peter Curry phoned me one day to ask me to stop in at his house on my way home from work to have a drink with him and Brian Dickson. There they said they'd been commissioned by the membership committee of the Manitoba Club to invite me to join. That club's policy of excluding Jews had been the subject of much discussion in the community over the years, and had, together with similar policies by other clubs, been the chief reason for the organization of a Jewish country club. I asked Curry and Dickson about that policy; they acknowledged it and said that the club executive wished to get away from it and thought I would be the ideal man with whom to start. I thanked them for their good opinion but said that the club's policy had been a long-time Winnipeg issue and ought to be resolved with long-time Winnipegers rather than with an outside ringer; if they recruited a dozen Winnipeg Jewish members and thereafter still wanted me, I'd be glad to join, but I didn't want to be the imported token Jew. They persisted, and I said I thought it wouldn't be good for the university; my election would become news, and they could imagine how *The Manitoban* would treat it. This was enough for Curry, but Dickson continued to urge the invitation, so I asked whether the club had provision for blackballing a nomination; he conceded that it did, whereupon I asked what would happen if I were nominated and blackballed. He replied that he would then feel obliged to resign from the club. How much good would it do the university, I asked, if the media were full of the story of the president being blackballed and the chairman of the board resigning from the club in consequence? This finally persuaded Dickson that it was useless to press the matter. When I left, Curry accompanied me to my car and said he thought I was right. Nevertheless, at one of our entertainments, a guest who turned out to be the club president tried to renew the discussion with me, but I stopped him; reform of the club's *Judenrein* policy would have been a civic good, but for me to be its agent would have engendered another divisive university issue. (I didn't join the Jewish country club either.)

An invitation that I declined with more regret came the following year. Curry invited me to a downtown dinner with several local business people and Gordon Fisher, the president of Southam Inc. There seemed no special purpose to the dinner, but it was a pleasant-enough evening, with some vigorous discussion in which I took part. A few days later, Curry phoned from out of town to say that he'd been commissioned to invite me to join the Southam board of directors, and suggested that I take a few days to consider it. I had never been approached by big business before, publishing was a field in which I could probably make a contribution, and I knew that such an appointment could be lucrative; I was tempted, but I had felt critical of other university presidents who'd accepted appointment to business boards, and I knew that if I accepted the invitation *The Manitoban* would play it up every time the local Southam paper, the *Tribune*, took a position they could criticize. Feeling that I was being quixotic, I declined with thanks and have had mixed feelings about it ever since.

In July 1971, the committee reviewing discipline procedures, which I'd urged to expedite its two-year-long deliberations, finally presented its report to the senate executive. Student participation in the committee had been thin and fitful, and the current UMSU asked for postponement until it could review the report. I agreed to a two-month postponement for review and revision, warning that I could not enter a second year with an unacceptable Star Chamber court, and urged UMSU to fill the empty student places on the committee, which it did. The reconstructed committee produced an excellent report, which the student members signed, and even UMSU had only one objection, that the new University Discipline Committee's powers were only delegated to it by the board, which retained ultimate responsibility. It was pointed out to UMSU that that was where the University Act lodged it, and that the board was most unlikely to intervene in a functioning discipline system, but it treasured its single ground of dissent. *The Manitoban* added a second criticism, that the new system provided for the disciplining of disruption! Senate and board quickly approved the report, and we promptly organized a discipline system in which elected students and faculty played the dominant roles and which functioned very well.

The only serious criticism, put forward both by UMSU and a number of divisional student officers, was that it did not provide for faculty discipline. In October I got board, Senate, UMFA, and UMSU to agree to a joint Committee on Faculty Responsibilities and Discipline, but it worked very slowly, and not much was achieved before faculty certification as a union necessitated a new start. Meanwhile I was left to direct faculty discipline without much guidance. This could be tricky. One example was in the matter of the cancellation of classes without notice; UMSU came to complain to me about that, and some inquiry made it clear that it took place on a fairly large scale. I raised the matter with the Deans' Council, which passed an appropriate resolution, but several deans said that, since the situation was of long standing, individual deans were not in a good position to act without an initial declaration of policy by the central administration. I therefore wrote a letter in November to all faculty members, acknowledging that probably 95 per cent of them either made alternative arrangements or at least gave advance notice when they had to cancel a class, but, since I did not know who the delinquent 5 per cent were, I had to address the whole faculty. I explained that the unreported cancellation of classes was not only unfair to students but also a breach of contract, as was the unauthorized cancellation of the final class of the term in order to get an early start on Christmas vacation. One faculty member of the board, Murray Donnelly, complained that the letter was unfair to the 95 per cent of the faculty who were conscientious about such matters, and UMFA said it would take the matter into consideration and respond soon (it didn't, but the media featured the story in hope of controversy).

At the opening of the 1971 fall term the new UMSU executive asked that the student assessors on board and Senate become regular members. I said that this would require a change in the legislation and that I was willing to recommend that the university ask for such a change if the minister would assure us that, once the act was opened up, he would not allow further changes. UMSU was unconvinced that opening the act was dangerous; indeed some of its more ideological members would have welcomed the increased government supervision of the university which I feared. It presented its request to Senate, which shared my misgivings about opening the act in the current political climate and was willing only to say that such a change was desirable when the act could be safely altered. This caused UMSU to withdraw from 'cooperation' with the senate and to ask student senators and assessors to withdraw; few of them, however, followed UMSU's wishes in this. At my suggestion the board authorized the chairman, the chancellor, and me, along with two UMSU representatives, to meet with the minister to seek assurance that, if we asked for the amendment the students wanted, no other changes would be permitted. Miller refused the assurance, which confirmed the university's decision not to ask for the change. By January 1972, however, he had changed his mind and gave the previously refused assurance; I don't know who worked on him but, as would soon become devastatingly clear, his was a particularly partisan ministry in a highly partisan government. With this assurance, both Senate and board made the request for the legislative change, which was enacted in July, whereupon all student assessors became full members.

One aspect of my job was membership in the Inter-Provincial Committee on University Rationalization. This consisted of the deputy ministers of university affairs, the chairmen of university-grants commissions, and the university presidents of the three Prairie provinces, and its task was to advise the Prairie Economic Council, consisting of the provincial premiers and treasurers, on the rationalization of current university activities and on the development of such new programs as might be needed in the region. The government of British Columbia was not part of either the committee or its parent council, but the BC universities participated by invitation in IPCUR's work. I began by taking this work seriously, seeing in it a parallel with the structure of rationalization I'd helped create in Ontario, although I was a little unhappy that the agenda seemed to reflect primarily governmental interests (the chairmanship was held by a deputy minister from Saskatchewan). My efforts to give more weight to university considerations may have been responsible for my election in the fall of 1971 as chairman.

During the next two years I increased the attention given to academic issues, but such recommendations got little response from governments. Typical problems put to IPCUR by governments were whether Saskatchewan should develop a dental college or continue to send its dental students to Manitoba, whether Alberta should develop a veterinary college or continue to rely on Ontario, whether Manitoba should develop an optometry college or continue to rely on Ontario: all significant questions, but ones the members of IPCUR had no particular qualifications to handle. As chairman I still had to devote considerable time to the committee, and as it met in different locales I visited a number of universities I'd not have seen otherwise (usually in the dead of a prairie winter), but I lost hope that I could make it an instrument of university advancement, and was not sorry when it ceased to exist in 1973.

Apart from the ministry of colleges and universities affairs itself, the provincial-government departments with the largest impact on the operation and financing of the university were those concerned with health and welfare. It therefore came as something of a shock to find that they did not intend to respect the integrity of the university. In late summer 1971, the government decided to establish community health clinics which would in part replace both hospitals and private practice, and the head of the interdepartmental committee which had recommended the policy, ignoring both the board and me, wrote directly to the deans and department heads of Medicine, Dentistry, Pharmacy, Nursing, Social Work, and Psychology, asking them among other things to define their objectives and priorities, identify programs to train people 'for service within integrated facilities such as the community health and social development centres which the government of Manitoba is committed to develop,' and explain 'what teaching relationship you envisage for integrated health and social service delivery systems,' and 'what use you see for [these centres] as educational facilities for teaching and research purposes' (*Tribune*, 23 September 71).

The first I heard of these letters was from Fyles, who had been consulted by one or two of his deans. I instructed all the recipients to acknowledge receipt of their letters and say that the university's reply would be coordinated by the president. I was angry but decided not to proclaim my anger; instead I wrote to the head of the interdepartmental committee, with copies to the ministers of health, welfare, and universities, saying that the various faculties and departments he had addressed were not autonomous bodies but parts of an integrated university and that the questions he had raised involved not only departmental but university policy. Some of them would have to be considered by Senate, some by the board, all by faculty councils; I would not make him wait for final decisions on all matters but would reply to various questions as became possible. I did not want to escalate the confrontation but I did want the premier to know of the issue, so I sent him a blind copy.

In due course and after much internal debate, we indicated to the government that we would cooperate with the proposed centres as far as was possible without jeopardizing our relations with the established teaching hospitals, which seemed to satisfy it. So far as I remember, the government initiative amounted, during my time in Winnipeg, to the establishment of one regional community hospital not affiliated with the university. But I insisted that all subsequent relations with the health-related departments be through my office, thus protecting both the individual faculties from the direct weight of government and the integrity of the university from divide-and-conquer tactics.

IV

In 1968 the university, at about the same time as many other Canadian universities, had adopted the tenure system of faculty appointments, but in Manitoba's case with an extraordinary by-law merely stipulating that in the absence of a negative decision within three and a half years from appointment to a tenure-track position a faculty member would automatically obtain tenure; it was silent about the goals and standards of tenure and the procedures to be followed in making tenure decisions. A committee had been established to make recommendations on the implementation of the by-law, but three years later, when in the fall of 1971 the time came for the first batch of tenure decisions, it had still not reported! I asked the deans what procedures they were following, and found they varied widely: some were planning to rely on their personal assessments, some on recommendations from their department heads, some had not given the matter any thought, and one or two, who were 'satisfied' with their staffs, had intended to do nothing and let the lapse of time confer tenure automatically.

I told them that the decision on tenure was among the most important a university could make and that it must be conferred as the result of a deliberate decision on academic merit made by qualified judges, never by default. In the absence of an approved procedure, I asked them to establish, in consultation with their respective vice-presidents, faculty or school committees to review and recommend action on all faculty members for whom tenure decisions were required; for multidepartmental faculties I asked that there also be committees at the departmental level. The primary criteria should be teaching and research, with some attention paid to departmental service; exceptional community service might be considered in marginal cases. In this first year the departments and faculties would have to determine how to apply these criteria.

There was a hurried scramble throughout the university to set up this temporary system. In some departments this was the first time the head had formally consulted his colleagues on personnel matters, and the tenure proceedings were therefore felt to be revolutionary. This feeling was intensified because the proceedings coincided with the adoption of a new policy on the appointment of deans, directors, and department heads, who had previously been selected by undefined methods and given indefinite appointments. There were now to be renewable term appointments with representative selection or review committees to advise the president.

Of 102 tenure cases, 96 recommendations were positive and 6 negative. One of the six left the university; the other five were granted special term appointments for one year. Three of those denied tenure appealed the decisions to the board, which had to establish a set of guidelines and a committee of appeal. In June 1972, this committee confirmed the termination of the probationary appointments of all three appellants but directed that two of them be considered again, by a new tenure committee, during their special term appointments. One of the two submitted his resignation; the other, an assistant professor of physics named W.N.R. Stevens, became the subject of an extremely protracted, irregular, and damaging procedure.

The university's difficult financial situation had put a considerable strain on its relations with UMFA, whose president told his general meeting in December 1971 that, 'as the economic situation deteriorates, the Faculty Association has diminishing leverage.' Since the same thing was happening throughout North America, many faculty associations were looking to unionization to restore their bargaining power. The Canadian Association of University Teachers adopted a policy of encouraging this trend, making it its top priority and devoting a good deal of time and money to it, and not unnaturally targeted universities in provinces with NDP governments to make a breakthrough in English Canada (there already were some faculty unions in Quebec).

Several elements made Manitoba particularly fertile ground for unionization at this time. In addition to the irritations and hardships of the unaccustomed budgetary constraints, coming as they did after the reversal on the pension plan, there was much anxiety about tenure. Enrolment had fallen well short of projections but it was very uneven; there was continued growth in some sectors, such as administrative studies and some of the professions, while it had begun to shrink in other sectors, such as arts, science, and engineering. This inevitably meant some shift of resources from the shrinking to the growing sectors. The planning office accordingly developed a load-related guide to tenure numbers to go with the staffing policy adopted the previous year; it was opposed in Senate by spokespersons for UMFA but adopted overwhelmingly. At the board in October 1972, an UMFA delegation, supported by several board members, opposed it, but it was seen as necessary by the majority. After the vote two of the government's recent highly political appointees walked out in protest: David Orlikow, an NDP federal MP from Winnipeg North, and J.D. Hughesman, an officer of the Canadian Union of Public Employees. Thus dramatized, the new policy was easily made to seem an immediate threat to untenured faculty in the static or shrinking sectors; in fact UMFA was using it to such effect that the policy had to be suspended the following year.

Another factor was that UMFA had very close relations with the NDP government; some UMFA leaders had important positions in the party. The government's stated policy was to encourage the formation of unions, and UMFA let it be known that it would call upon the government for such help. Faculty members opposed to unionization predicted that UMFA could not win a majority vote; those favouring unionization replied that the new Labour Relations Act which the government was preparing would take care of that, and indeed, when it came into force on 1 January 1973, it greatly lowered the requirement for certification and otherwise made unionization easier.

But this was by no means the only help the government gave UMFA in its drive for certification. UMFA had seized upon the Stevens tenure appeal as the needed means to polarize the campus; it found eager allies in UMSU and *The Manitoban*; and after all normal recourse had been exhausted, it would, supported by CAUT, find the government willing to use *force majeure* to impose yet another appeal procedure to protract the polarization until the exceptionally lengthy unionization process was completed. The departmental tenure committee and the departmental and faculty appeal committees had all been involved in the Stevens case, so to ensure that the 'new' committee would not be influenced by previous judgments, the board, which had in the interim established new tenure and appeals procedures, decided to go outside the university to secure a comparative ranking of Stevens and five other untenured members of the department, which was to help the new tenure committee in its fresh consideration of Stevens. This elaborate procedure, with which I had nothing to do, might have worked had the board not gone to the head of the Physics department to get a list of six 'internationally known physicists' outside the university, from which it selected three. This initial involvement of the man thought mainly responsible for the original denial of tenure made the whole process vulnerable to criticism from UMFA. The three prominent physicists came to Winnipeg, interviewed all the untenured physicists, and gave the faculty tenure committee their ranking. The committee then recommended against tenure for Stevens. In February 1973, Stevens appealed yet again, but the board, which had already heard one appeal from him and set up this special procedure in lieu of another, declined, by a vote of 10 to 7, to hear his further appeal.

This was UMFA's opportunity to bring CAUT openly into the struggle. At UMFA's request, but nothing loth, CAUT, in February 1973, set up a committee to investigate tenure procedures at the U of M. Donald Savage, the director of CAUT, said that, in addition to the Stevens case, there were 'a number of problems' but the major concern was 'the staffing policy which could limit the number of tenure positions' at the university. Because United College, the forerunner of the University of Winnipeg, had been blacklisted by the CAUT over the Crowe case, Winnipeg was very sensitive to the possibility of another blacklisting, and UMFA made sure that all the local media were aware of the 'danger' that the University of Manitoba would be similarly blacklisted. The members of the investigating committee were academics from Saskatchewan, Alberta, and British Columbia; the chairman, Leo Kristjanson, of Saskatchewan, visited the campus and interviewed Stevens, UMFA, the relevant persons in Science, and me. He came back to see me before he left and said he couldn't find anything to justify an inquiry and could only suppose it was part of the drive for unionization. CAUT did not publish its committee's report, nor did UMFA even acknowledge in its newsletter that the inquiry it had asked for was terminated.

In June, Orlikow wrote to the chancellor complaining that his motion to put the question of tenure for Stevens to an 'independent' committee had not been given serious consideration, and that therefore he would at the forthcoming board meeting move that the board give Stevens tenure forthwith. He recognized that this would be 'hard on the administration' but felt it had not been sufficiently 'flexible.' His motion was defeated, whereupon the matter was in effect taken out of the board's hands. On 1 August the chancellor and I were summoned to the minister's office (the chairman, now Peter Cain, lived in a mining town in the north and couldn't make the meeting) and confronted with an ultimatum: either we submit the matter of tenure for Stevens to a neutral committee of arbitration or Miller would do it himself; he had not looked at the act to see whether he had the power, but if he didn't he would change the legislation to get it. Meanwhile, he 'suggested' that Stevens be kept on until the arbitration was over. He explained that both UMFA and CAUT had asked him to set up an 'inquiry board' and determine tenure himself, but he thought it best to offer the university this opportunity to act itself; he would give us three days to decide. He then acknowledged wryly that he understood that the issue was '90 per cent unionization and 10 per cent Stevens,' but said that he 'had no alternative.'

We called an emergency meeting of the board for 3 August, at which Curry and I reported on our meeting with Miller, then gave it as our opinion that the university would suffer less from acting on his demand than from refusing, because, since the minister did not under the act have the power to give Stevens tenure he would, in order to get it, have to amend the act, which would make the university's loss of autonomy legislative and therefore probably permanent, whereas a surrender now to *force majeure* on a particular point could be recoverable, particularly if the arbitration went in our favour. The board agreed and I so notified the minister. At its first meeting in the fall, Senate considered a resolution from its executive committee expressing 'concern at possible interference in the academic affairs of the university.' This was strengthened by two amendments from the floor deploring 'recent interference' and 'giving notice that any future interference ... will be resisted strongly.' The UMFA assessor and some pro-UMFA members defended UMFA's and CAUT's role in the matter and Miller's action, but the amended resolution passed overwhelmingly. Miller, by now transferred to Urban Affairs, defended his action by alleging that the faculty was split into warring factions and a crisis was developing.

We tried to reach agreement on the method and terms of the arbitration, but Stevens and UMFA, and indeed CAUT, now had no incentive to come to an agreement, and every incentive to stall. Stevens, who had no university duties, was getting his salary, which might end with the arbitration. For UMFA and CAUT the advantage of delay was to postpone until after the certification vote the risk that the arbitration would show the hollowness of their stance. Their lawyer introduced numberless difficulties into the negotiation, even making an issue about the admissibility of evidence. However, once UMFA was safely certified, it became possible to make some, although very slow, progress, and on 20 June 1974 we reached tentative agreement on the terms of arbitration. Stevens, however, was not in a hurry, and it took months to conclude that we would not be able to agree on a chairman; we therefore agreed to ask the chief justice of the Supreme Court of Canada to name one, which he did: Bruce Dunlop, professor of law at U of T. Stevens named Professor Buckmaster at the University of Calgary as his nominee, and our Physics department named Professor Robert Bell at McGill. After further delay, the arbitration took place on 12–13 December, two and a half costly years after the failure of Stevens's first appeal, and led to a remarkable result: a *unanimous* decision against granting tenure. Neither UMFA nor CAUT ever announced the result, and in consideration of Stevens we confined our announcement to a small notice in the university bulletin, not picked up by the downtown or campus media. I wrote to Miller, no longer our minister, telling him of the result and emphasizing its unanimity; before I got his reply I correctly foretold it to Lesley: 'Justice has not only been done but has been seen to be done.' He didn't respond to my suggestion that the university be compensated for the heavy costs of his intervention.

V

I got an earlier indication of the government's interpretation of the relations between itself, the UGC, and the universities in February 1972, during the preparation of our 1972–3 budget. Bateman told me that in submitting its requests the UGC had included provision for seventy additional faculty members in the province, but this had been deleted by Management Committee; he had then argued for its reinstatement by cabinet, which had allowed provision for twenty-five on condition that he ensure that was the maximum. We would be secretly told what our portion of the twenty-five was; we were legally free to spend our grant as we saw fit, but if we exceeded the number of staff indicated it could be assumed that the following year the grant would be reduced without explanation. I asked whether, to prevent an internal clash over staffing numbers, I could tell Senate and board about this constraint; he considered this for a few days, then told me that it would be dangerous for univerity autonomy to do so: once a constraint had been imposed, it would be very tempting to government to enlarge upon it in future years. I replied that the constraint had already been imposed; the question was between an open and a secret one, the latter being the more damaging. The next day he said the constraint was by government, not by the UGC, and he couldn't permit any reference to it, although I could communicate it in strict confidence to Brian Dickson, the board chairman. This revealed a pattern: the government took actions not permitted under the UGC Act, then used the UGC to screen itself. A worse variant was still in store for me: the government promising action, then using the UGC to evade fulfilling its promise.

Ken Zaifman, the undergraduate member of the board, gave the 1972–3 budget, which he had accepted as a confidential document, to UMSU, which used it as the basis of the 1972 student handbook, entitled *Tales of Terror*. Published for the beginning of term, it listed the top sixty-four salaries in the university, all those above $25,000. Mine, which was $52,500, was made to appear higher by interpreting the provision for expense items for my office as personal benefits, and attracted enormous critical publicity. A frequent comparison was with the compensation of the prime minister of Canada and the premier of Manitoba, both of which it was said to exceed. The host of a local radio call-in show, Peter Warren, called to ask me to go on his program; Esmé didn't put the call through but came in to consult me about it, and unfortunately I told her to say no. It would have been better if I'd agreed to his request despite my distaste for that kind of publicity; at the very least I should have taken the call myself and explained to Warren why I couldn't agree. He began a campaign of criticism of me which lasted throughout the rest of my tenure; he called several more times during the following years, but by then going on his show would have looked like submission and I continued to refuse.

At the October meeting of the board, Hughesman demanded that my salary and contract be discussed at a meeting open to the public. This demand was rejected, although copies of my contract were given to board members in confidence. It was promptly leaked to the media, and the whole alarum was renewed with even greater intensity, particular attention being paid to the pension provision. So poisonous did the criticism become that the board reversed itself and held an open meeting on the matter in December. UMFA declared that the president ought to be the head of the faculty but that my contract had erected a barrier between me and them, since their pension plan guaranteed a smaller percentage of salary. Curry explained that the provisions of the contract followed the recommendations of the AUCC, but this did little to quiet the storm. The fact that their pensions were indexed to inflation and mine was not wasn't mentioned, nor were the hazards of a university presidency in those troubled times, the prospect of a radically shortened career, or the need for some compensation for giving up a happy and secure position in a very good university to undertake the task of trying to improve a mediocre one.

UMSU demanded that we publish the budget, which we refused to do, although I recommended and the board agreed that future budgets containing informatively aggregated information be public, with individual salaries remaining confidential. UMSU, however, had the current budget photocopied, distributed it at a press conference on 8 November, and sold copies for $12 to anyone interested.

The cumulative effect of the publication of the budget and of my contract predisposed the Winnipeg press, whose salaries were notoriously low, to credit the stories fed them by the unions and other adversary bargaining groups; besides, these made vivid copy and sold newspapers. UMFA and UMSU in particular became very skilful in cultivating and manipulating the press, growing steadily bolder as they saw that I would not counter-attack, limiting my own and university statements to assertions of fact and denials of distortions. I could see well enough that I was losing the public-relations battle, but I thought the harm to the university if I really struck back would be greater and longer lasting.

The new Labour Relations Act went into effect 1 January 1973. On the same day, UMFA asked the university to commence collective bargaining leading to a collective agreement for faculty and librarians, demanding a reply by the end of the month. Under the new act, agreeing to this would have constituted 'voluntary recognition' of UMFA as a union representing the entire full-time academic and library staff, without its having to take a vote, apply for certification, or distinguish between the bargaining unit and management. To agree would have meant denying the legal rights of hundreds of opposed faculty members and academic administrators and establishing a totally unworkable bargaining unit. The board refused UMFA's request but recognized that the University Act of 1968, by increasing the powers of the senate, had reduced the board's direct interaction with UMFA, and offered to recognize it as the representative of the academic staff on matters directly related to the economic welfare of the staff, and together to establish procedures for resolving issues on these matters. It was also prepared to discuss with UMFA other concerns beside the economic. Denouncing this reply, UMFA on 1 February applied to the Labour Board for certification as bargaining agent for the entire academic staff, including me, my academic vice-presidents, the deans, and the department heads, as well as those faculty members elected to the board by Senate.

A few days earlier, a new group, the Association of Employees Supporting Education Services, claiming to represent the twelve hundred non-academic employees not included in the many existing unions, had also applied for certification. It too felt the need to increase and solidify its support through polarization and contributed accordingly to the tumult. At the same time, UMSU and *The Manitoban* had been thrown into a frenzy by Senate's decision to hold elections for student senators, which UMSU had refused to do unless the university adopted UMSU's program of governance reform, and of course they attributed this action to me and renewed their violent clamour.

It was just at this inauspicious moment that my first presidential report was published (such a delay was not unusual for U of M annual reports because there was no proper information system). The day my report appeared, with its account of the accumulated deficit and the abortive pension plan, a special UMFA newsletter was distributed, obviously printed in advance and featuring a 'letter' to me from Saunderson which challenged my numbers and claimed that there had been no real deficit. All the media seized upon this 'battle of the presidents'; I naturally had to reply, my letter to Saunderson was published in the university *Bulletin*, and the campus was in the turmoil UMFA had desired. Curry asked me what lay behind Saunderson's outburst; I said I didn't know, and he said Saunderson would have to stop it unless 'he wants a complete break with me.' I didn't know what this implied, but the next day Saunderson, all smiles, was in my office, we shook hands, and he wrote to the newspapers saying that our 'misunderstanding' had been resolved. However, after Curry had left Winnipeg and the university was deeply embroiled in a struggle with the UGC and government about a deficit, Saunderson gave several interviews in which he said the university was living too richly and I was the problem.

During the 1971-2 academic year, the government set up the Task Force on Post-Secondary Education in Manitoba, with Michael Oliver, who had served as a senior officer of the federal NDP and had just been appointed president of Carleton, as chairman and the only academic member. The task force began by inviting comment on a list of topics from all interested persons and institutions, and the university took this invitation seriously. A broad-based presidential committee prepared a 154-page brief, which, after approval by Senate and Board, was submitted to the task force in June. Briefs were submitted by UMFA and UMSU, both recommending that 'administrators' be stripped of all authority, which would then be vested in committees of teaching staff, students, support staff, and 'the public.'

In January 1973, the task force published an interim report consisting of seven preliminary position papers, and invited comment. I had not been optimistic, but I was shocked by the actuality, a report not only marked by prejudice against the traditional structure of universities and in favour of the wildest of the current populist positions but also vitiated by a fundamental misunderstanding of the Manitoba system of financing universities. At the end of February I spoke to the Canadian Clubs of Winnipeg about the interim report. I commended it, faintly, for looking at the whole scene of post-secondary education and for attempting to clarify the roles of the three universities. But I severely criticized its proposal for a highly centralized system with a large governmental bureaucracy exercising vastly increased direction and control over the universities. I said that it had greatly exaggerated the degree to which the universities determined their own expenditures, confusing Manitoba's purported formula funding with Ontario's; the latter set a value for the basic income unit, counted units, and gave the resultant sum to the university, which spent it as it saw fit, whereas Manitoba universities had to explain their wishes to the UGC, which gave or withheld approval to specific proposals and allocated what it thought a suitable amount, expecting the universities to spend their grants as approved in these discussions. The UGC then expressed the grant in terms of the amount per student, but these 'formula' amounts for similar students varied widely among the universities. The task force's failure to understand the reality of the Manitoba system led to its most immediately damaging recommendation: that funding be by categories and non-transferable. Another error, that in the University of Manitoba the senate's powers were still, as they had been before 1968, limited to the academic, led to unneeded and unworkable proposals for changes of university governance. 'What appears to be desired,' I said, 'is the complete divorce of responsibility from authority: administrators are to be responsible to everyone and to have no authority, while committees are to be responsible to no one and are to have all authority.'

The speech attracted a good deal of attention. UMFA, many of whose suggestions had been adopted by the task force, naturally raged, although I had emphasized that my views were strictly personal and did not represent the university in any way. Oliver returned to Winnipeg to speak to the Rotary Club in defence of his report, indicating, however, that there would be some changes in the final report. In April Senate formulated its response along lines very similar to mine, and the board endorsed the senate statement and sent it to the task force; UMFA called it 'hasty and ill-considered,' and the UMFA assessor to the board was 'saddened but not surprised' to see the 'essence' of my speech included in the official university response.

When the final report was published in December, the only significant change was that funds should be transferable between categories; all the other destructive recommendations remained. At the end of January 1974, the board held a special meeting to discuss the report, at which I repeated my criticisms; another member pointed out that the only thing that prevented the government from exercising the control over the university desired by the task force was the failure of several of its twelve appointees to the twenty-three-person board to attend most meetings. Sentiment against the report was strengthened when the new minister, Ben Hanuschak, admitted in the legislature that the government committee to which he had sent the report for 'evaluation' was headed by the task force's research director, i.e., its primary author! At the beginning of March the board formulated its critical reply to the report, which was promptly adopted by Senate; UMFA called this university response 'arrogant,' but it met with a good deal of community support.

The minister spoke from time to time about preparations for implementing the report. His first specific action was in January 1975, when he announced that the University of Winnipeg would, as recommended by the task force, be permitted to offer certain MA courses in conjunction with the University of Manitoba, until then the sole graduate school in the province. In this he was usurping the statutory program-approval function of the UGC as well as impinging upon the autonomy of the U of M. He also announced that, in line with the task force recommendation, there would thenceforth be greater government involvement in university research planning. Virtually all university research in the province was done by the U of M, which had already been sensitized toward the existing government's attitude to research, partly through an incident early in 1973. The provincial Department of Mines and Resources had commissioned two professors in our Civil Engineering department to do an impact study of Manitoba Hydro's proposed northern development. They had formally completed only the first part of the study, which was to devise the methodology, but this already foreshadowed what later became tragically clear, that the development would drown much Native land and many villages. The mines minister, Sidney Green, abruptly announced that the rest of the study would be carried out by government employees and sent a truck to the campus to pick up the researchers' records, which he claimed were the government's property because it had paid for the research; he was only persuaded with difficulty not to persist in this claim. (Premier Schreyer, whose pet project the northern development was, later accused 'some professors' who opposed the project of 'extreme unreason.')

In February 1975, in further implementation of the task force report, Hanuschak asserted that society, not the universities, must dictate what universities teach. I knew what this meant; when I had conferred with him about the acute financial crisis in the university, he seized the occasion to request that the U of M take over as a credit course the government's 'Focus' program for northern Manitoba. This was a special instructional package on labour economics for remote-area industrial workers, developed at great cost using private consultants. The targeted consumers, however, were not interested unless they received university credit for the course, which Hanuschak now tried to arrange. I replied that we could teach or give credit only for courses developed by our own faculty and approved by Senate; we would, if he wished and would pay the cost, develop a course on labour economics and offer it in the north. He asked me whether a community didn't have the right to require whatever instruction it needed from its universities. I said no, only the kind of instruction appropriate to universities; the rest from its other institutions. He sucked at his pipe for some time, then said he would accept that, and got Red River Community College to give the course.

The saga of UMFA's certification unfolded with painful and damaging slowness. Immediately after UMFA's application to the Labour Board on 1 February 1973, the professors of the Faculty of Medicine applied for exclusion on professional grounds, and in another week five more faculties (Dentistry, Law, Agriculture, Engineering, and Science) asked for exclusion, a referendum, or both. The university filed no objection, not, as I explained, because it agreed with the application but because it believed that the faculty had the right to decide for itself; it did, however, file a list of 193 management persons whom it wanted excluded from the union if one was certified. In April the lawyer for some of the objecting professors challenged the legality of the procedure on a technicality and the Labour Board adjourned to await a court decision. The next month the court upheld the Labour Board's proceedings, but the objectors appealed, and the appellate court's decision upholding the original decision didn't come until October.

In the summer of 1973 the quinquennial congress of the Commonwealth Universities Association was held in Australia. I'd never been to Australia and had looked forward to the congress, as had others, but the university's straitened financial circumstances made me conclude that it should not undertake the cost of sending a delegation, and I so advised the board, which agreed. There was much disappointment among those who had been hoping to go, and some criticism by people who rightly complained that the university's visibility would be lowered, but I wanted the administration to set examples of thrift. About the same time I undertook to persuade the board of directors of the Association of Universities and Colleges of Canada, of which I was a member, to reduce the association's soaring costs and the consequent growth in member institutions' fees. This was hard work because, reflecting the Ottawa environment, the association had invited and undertaken to pay for student delegations to its meetings, had enlarged its staff, and in general expanded at every opportunity. I got it to reduce the number of meetings, but couldn't at first get it to reduce staff; I grew pertinacious, withheld Manitoba's assessed contribution, then told the next directors' meeting that the university would pay only a portion of our assessment unless it was substantially reduced. At home I told the board about this and created considerable unhappiness, but the association did in fact drop some activities and shrink its staff, and our next assessment was lower, whereupon I paid both it and the unpaid balance from the previous year.

We had entered the 1973–4 fiscal year on a precarious basis, without a final budget for the year because no salary settlements could legally be made. Negotiations with a number of existing support-staff unions were making little progress because our grant was very stringent, reflecting the premier's tough inflation-fighting line (he was urging the federal government to bring in wage-and-price controls). Salaries for academic staff and a large proportion of support staff were frozen by law because the applications for certification by UMFA and AESES were pending before the Labour Board. Accordingly, we presented a Phase One budget covering anticipated expenditures other than salary increases; it showed an estimated surplus of a little under $700,000, and we had a surplus of a little more than that from 1972–3, largely as a result of the salary freeze imposed by the Labour Act. I advised the board that, when negotiations were complete, the increases would use up these surpluses and leave us in deficit by more than half a million dollars, which we would have to ask the UGC to make up. The board accepted this procedure and agreed that I should advise the UGC. Bateman was at that time both chairman of the UGC and deputy minister of colleges and universities affairs; he agreed to accept my communication in both capacities, listened without apparent concern, and gave no warnings.

At the beginning of July the senate asked that the faculty be given a cost-of-living adjustment. We therefore asked the Labour Board to permit whichever of two defined increases UMFA preferred, a larger one which would be final for the year or a smaller across-the-board adjustment which would permit further negotiation after the decision on certification. At first UMFA rejected both options, asking that the latter be increased from 5 per cent to 6.6 per cent, but when the university held to its position UMFA accepted 5 per cent and the Labour Board permitted the adjustment.

VI

On 5 October, two days after the appeals court dismissed the dissenting professors' objection to the Labour Board's UMFA hearings, the Canadian Association of Industrial, Mechanical, and Allied Workers voted to strike. CAIMAW was a member of the new Confederation of Canadian Unions, had successfully raided the Service Employees International Union (CIO/AFL) in May, and was now intent on showing the five hundred tradesmen, caretakers, housekeepers, and maintenance and food workers it had won over that it could deliver more than their old union had. It had bargained rough, perhaps not wanting to succeed there, and on 11 October launched the first strike in the university's history. Knowing that we were inexperienced in strikes, and confident that we could be cowed (it kept reminding everyone that a similar strike at McGill a little earlier was won in four days), it announced that it would shut the university down in three days: the operating engineers and the powerhouse workers would come out in sympathy, and other unionized employees, Winnipeg bus drivers, and most faculty and students would not cross picket lines.

I had kept in close touch with the negotiations, was confident of the reasonableness of our final offer in view of our financial situation, and had seen to it that we did all we could to prepare for the strike. The powerhouse workers and operating engineers were reminded that, as essential workers, their contracts forbade sympathy strikes. When the strike was called, I announced that the university would continue its normal educational operations and as many support operations as was feasible. I said that all employees not on strike were expected to report for work according to their contracts of employment; they were legally entitled to cross picket lines. These lines were initially disorderly; all entrances to the campus were blocked, and traffic along Pembina Highway backed up for four miles, until the police arrived at 8:50 A.M. and cleared the entrances. UMFA advised its members not to perform work normally done by the strikers, and it sympathized with those professors who did not want to cross picket lines, but acknowledged that faculty members were bound by their individual contracts to perform their normal duties and pointed out that UMFA's position under the Labour Relations Act could be affected.

For some days it was touch and go whether we could continue to operate. There was vociferous support for the strikers from UMFA, *The Manitoban,* the Arts Council, and University College, but the other faculties and UMSU were divided. Nearly all professors took their classes as usual, and most of those who refused to cross picket lines met their classes elsewhere, usually at home. The student residents did their own housekeeping, with the cooking done by supervisory personnel. Buses did not cross picket lines, which meant that riders had to walk about three-quarters of a mile each way. There was a good deal of minor sabotage – plumbing jammed, garbage and dead rats brought in, then the provincial health inspectors called – and some intimidation, such as slashed tires and threatening phone calls (anonymous calls to our house were obscene and sometimes threatening, and the intermittent picketing of our house featured some very disagreeable placards). The media, presented with a novel situation (strikes were heavy in Manitoba that year, but this was the first in the university), were constantly after me with questions about how long we could keep going, and I apparently infuriated CAIMAW by saying that educational operations were nearly normal and we could probably keep functioning.

The turning-point came on 16 October, the fourth day of the strike. The Committee in Support of the Strike held a rally in the gymnasium, which was addressed, among others, by Pat McEvoy, CAIMAW's regional vice-president. He and others got the audience stirred up, and some five or six hundred people surged across the road to the Administration Building, shouting 'We want Sirluck.' Condo got to my office a second or two before the advance party, and couldn't conceal his glee when he told me of the demonstrators' demand. I went out onto the steps, which served as a platform; the demonstrators had brought along a loudspeaker, and, as they continued to chant 'We want Sirluck,' I said into the microphone, 'I'm glad somebody does.' This levity enraged some, who shouted abuse; a man on the steps called for silence so 'the Administration President' could be heard, then extended his hand to me; as I took it I asked who he was and he replied 'Pat McEvoy,' to laughter and cheers from the demonstrators. However, he did not stay, explaining that he had to go to the resumed negotiations.

At first the 'questions' were mere denunciation, and after coping as well as I could with them, I said to someone who kept reiterating distortions, 'You don't want answers; go to hell.' Immediately, I added, 'No, don't go to hell, come to me; I might be able to straighten you out.' This brought on some genuine questions from quieter members of the crowd, now increased by many who had come out to see what was going on; I replied with specific wage data and comparisons, and tried to set CAIMAW's demands in context. Some demonstrators tried to renew the initial line of 'questioning,' but after one such intervention someone in the audience called out, 'That man is only trying to make trouble.' The serious questions continued and broadened, I answered everything I could and, after a little more than an hour, when there were no more questions, was rewarded with applause and cheers. Two days later, when the UMSU executive unsuccessfully presented a resolution supporting the strike, '70 people who packed the students' union council chamber ... cheered particularly loudly when one student union member said a confrontation between university president Ernest Sirluck and about 500 students Wednesday destroyed student sympathy for the strike' (*Free Press*, 18 October 1973). On the same day, however, the Arts Council, with sixty professors present out of about three hundred, voted to support the strike.

We made a new offer, which CAIMAW rejected, and on 27 October there was another rally in support of the strike, this one in Campo, a large open space in the Student Centre. One of the organizers and a main speaker was Father Daniel Berrigan, a well-known American anti–Vietnam War activist who had been imprisoned in the United States for breaking-and-entering a government office and burning draft records. When the new head of our Religion department, without reference to the dean or me, invited him to come for a term as visiting professor of religion, there were objections both in our board and in the legislature. I was unhappy about the appointment, both on substantive and procedural grounds, but I defended it at the board on the basis of academic freedom, and indeed intervened with Canada Immigration (whose regional director was an old friend) to allow him into the country. Later, when he asked to see me about the strike, I gave him all the time he wanted, although I could ill afford it. Now he was predicting violence if the administration remained 'inflexible,' and calling for a one-day boycott of classes by faculty and students. Against my earlier intention, I went over to Campo and presented myself for questions. Berrigan asked none, those asked by others were largely factual, and I met none of the ideological barracking of the earlier rally.

There was sporadic pressure from the UGC and the government to settle, and of course much clamour in the legislature. We made the cost of CAIMAW's demands very clear to the UGC, adding that the settlement with them would inevitably determine those for the other support staff; finally the UGC indicated approximately how much of a deficit it would support. We made a new offer, and on 3 November, twenty-three days after the strike began, CAIMAW accepted it. It was much closer to our original position than to CAIMAW's, but still considerably more than we'd anticipated; but so was inflation.

Ten days later the Labour Board's hearings on the UMFA application resumed. UMFA had hoped that under the new act it would be certified without a faculty vote, and the chairman of the Labour Board, who would be an NDP candidate in the next provincial election, had given some indication of that happening, but 565 faculty members petitioned against this certification procedure and demanded that a vote be held. This was agreed, but 120 medical faculty were excluded from the vote because they would not be in the bargaining unit should a union be formed. The vote was held at the end of the month and was 562 to 415 in favour of a union.

Hearings were held 29–31 January 1974 to determine the scope of the bargaining unit. I was called as the first witness; Mel Meyers, UMFA's lawyer, started the questioning by asking whether it was true that I was a Milton specialist. 'Yes.' 'Would it be true to say that you regard the unionization of the faculty as Paradise Lost?'

Loud laughter from UMFA officers, appreciative giggles from the NDP members of the Labour Board. 'No, I never mistook the University of Manitoba for paradise.' Loud laughter from Roy Gallagher, the university's lawyer. I outlined the management functions of senior members of the central administration to only perfunctory questioning; there was much closer scrutiny of the role of deans, and the argument became intense over department chairmen, the new title for heads. After three days the hearings were adjourned because of a commissioner's illness and resumed 18–21 March. The decision was given 12 April: fourteen months after applying, UMFA was certified as a union representing academic staff and librarians below the rank of deans and directors.

The long delay had been extremely damaging. By freezing faculty salaries (except for a below-inflation cost-of-living adjustment), it had hurt faculty morale and contributed to the willingness to unionize; it had protracted the period during which UMFA and CAUT kept the Stevens case alive, in the end through direct government intervention, and thus continued its polarizing effect; it had paralysed the university's ability to make decisions touching in any way on terms and conditions of employment and reduced it to repeatedly petitioning the Labour Board for permission to enact specific changes; it had created an atmosphere in which a new and reckless union was able to raid an established one, and had made it more willing to strike; and it had made the unionization of the non-union majority of support staff inevitable, which was to bring an even worse strike the following year. It had for a long time given the otherwise fractious radicals on campus a common cause. It had seriously undermined the university's credibility with the public and the government. Not least damaging, it had forced the university to enter a second fiscal year with only a Phase One budget, since negotiations with UMFA could not begin until after it was certified.

Throughout fiscal 1973–4 we had kept the UGC fully informed of our financial position and deficit outlook, and Bateman hinted that it would probably be able to accommodate the deficit in our 1974–5 grant. The government's estimates were very late being tabled and we had to present an operating budget before our grant was announced, but the advance confidential advice showed that it would be another, even tighter year. Accordingly the budget committee recommended that we adopt another Phase One budget not inclusive of salary increases still to be negotiated. Before taking this to the board I asked that each member of the committee state whether he personally agreed with this recommendation; everyone, including Condo, said he did. In presenting this to the board on 9 April, I warned that without further help we would probably incur a deficit of about $4 million on the year's operations. I explained that the alternative involved major retrenchments, including firing a lot of staff, and Orlikow, who often reminded the board that he was very close to the government, said the university should not take such action: it was government legislation that had brought on unionization with its attendant limitations on the university's discretion, and if government wanted the university to lower quality it should say so. Others, particularly the academic members elected to the board by Senate, asked whether the budget as presented implied a lowering of quality, and when I said it did marginally, they successfully moved that the amount I'd requested for urgent allocations above the baseline be doubled, thus adding another half-million to the probable deficit. To judge by what he said later, this action particularly angered Condo.

The board approved the enriched budget, noting that other government-supported institutions such as the hospitals had been left to negotiate with their unions and then had their grants increased to cover the additional costs. It agreed that the chairman, now Peter Cain (Dickson had been translated to the Supreme Court of Canada) and I should advise the minister and get his reaction before implementing the Phase One budget.

The next morning Cain and I met with Bateman and his vice-chairman, Douglas Chevrier, and told them what we were planning to do, offering to give them any further information they wanted. In the afternoon we met with Hanuschak and explained the situation to him, giving him the size of the accumulated deficit and the probable size of the one that would be incurred during the year. He listened unperturbed, assured us that we were not unique, citing the case of the hospitals and mentioning other analogies, and said that 'if we have to go into deficit financing, we'll go into deficit financing.' Cain asked him whether he felt he'd fully apprehended our situation, and he confidently said he had. Cain then asked whether we ought not to meet with him and Schreyer to ensure that the premier agreed with the course being taken; Hanuschak said yes, and the three of us went together to the premier's office and arranged a meeting for 18 April. This meeting, for which we prepared very carefully, was subsequently cancelled, and repeated efforts to have it rescheduled failed. That was when my anxiety about our situation turned into alarm.

Nevertheless, an increase in academic salaries was necessary. Because negotiations for a first contract were bound to be protracted, UMFA asked for an interim increase of 6 per cent plus $700, the rest to be negotiated; this would have amounted to about 10 per cent of payroll, an unacceptably high starting-point for negotiations. The budget committee sought to avoid an interim increase and recommended that we propose a final increase amounting to 12.2 per cent of payroll (7 per cent plus $400 plus 2 per cent merit plus a sum for anomalies). In presenting this to the board, I acknowledged that it was higher than inflation but pressed the need to begin closing the gap with other universities, and the board agreed. UMFA at first refused to accept our offer; we administered it to the staff excluded from the bargaining unit, and UMFA reconsidered and accepted it, recognizing that there were plenty of other things to negotiate.

In June Lesley and I went to Toronto, where I was to receive an honorary degree. It was for me a splendid occasion. The evening before convocation, Sidney Hermant, a member of the old board of governors with whom I had served on the President's Council, took over the Faculty Club for a large dinner party for us where we saw many old friends (it was here that Henry Borden said, 'I told you you'd get your library'). At convocation the citation was read (and written) by Claude Bissell, and was as much a testament of friendship as a catalogue of achievements. Afterward there was a reception for us at the new Robarts Library, which Bob Blackburn put on as a substitute for the formal opening he'd been denied because the new president thought it might reincite campus turbulence.* My convocation address was published in large part in *The Globe and Mail* and in full in Canadian and British journals under the title 'Causes of Tightening Government Control of Universities,' a subject on which I had perforce become knowledgeable.

There were further planned celebrations, but the joy was not to continue: late at night we were wakened by a call from a surgeon in a Winnipeg hospital saying that our daughter, Kate, had been in a car accident; she was hurt but not in danger. Her mouth and jaw were wired shut for some time, and bits of glass kept emerging from her face and scalp for years, but she suffered no permanent disability.

At the end of June I embarked on a two-week visit to China arranged between Prime Minister Trudeau and Premier Chou En-lai. It was part of an educational exchange between the two countries and had been made feasible, despite Chinese suspicion of the West, by the fact that the leader of our team, Nathan Nemetz, chancellor of UBC and chief justice of the B.C. Supreme Court, had been host to Dr Norman Bethune, a great hero in Communist China, on his last day in Canada. The rest of our delegation consisted of the director of AAUC and eleven other university presidents, among them Oliver, which made for some initial tension.

The main foci of our visit were Canton, Shanghai, and Peking; for the most part we travelled by plane, with some rail and road travel; we were provided with guides, interpreters, and drivers, and wherever we went the universities and colleges made a great production of our interviews. Unfortunately, they almost all said the same things, and we gradually became aware that the officials and professors were terrified of speaking amiss. In the West we had had the impression that the Cultural Revolution had run its course, but we found that not to be true; most of the older academics and administrators had served periods of ideological purification and correction on collective farms, and were very fearful of being sent there again. At all our sessions there were a number of observers, many in army uniform, and when any of them began to write in his notebook whoever was speaking would turn pale. I had a stroke of

---

* For an account of the 1971-2 disturbances ostensibly concerning access to the research library and its stacks, see R.H. Blackburn, *Evolution of the Heart* (Toronto: University of Toronto Press, 1989), pp. 228-38.

luck: at Tsing-Hua University, in Peking, I was greeted by a professor who recognized me, having taken his Toronto doctorate while I was dean, and he risked some private conversation with me. His account of the all-out battles during the Cultural Revolution, the People's Trials and confessions, the punishments and re-education camps, revealed a far more drastic upheaval than had at that time been reported.

The work done in the universities was very disappointing. Our delegation included a considerable variety of disciplines; we would divide up and inspect sectors corresponding to our competencies, and each night we'd meet to receive sector reports. We almost never found anything which reached what we would consider university level; the one partial exception was a technical university in Shanghai, where an extremely brave principal organized the teaching of real rather than ideological science. In language departments, where English was by far the most important subject, very few of the students and not many instructors could follow spoken English, and similar situations prevailed in other subjects. One curiosity: everywhere our academic lawyer asked to be taken to a faculty of law, and everywhere the request was finessed. Finally a government official said there were no law faculties: revolutionary China practised justice, not law.

What was really exciting was the primary-school system, to which we were everywhere exposed, although it was not part of our mandate. In a nation which had always been predominantly illiterate, there were at that time 106 million children in primary schools and a further 30 million in middle schools, and so far as we were able to judge they were being well taught. Certainly they gave the impression of happy industry, and we became convinced that when the current regime had sobered or disappeared the universities would be transformed by the intake of such eager students.

We were exceptionally well treated throughout our visit. Museums and palaces which were normally closed were especially opened for us, and on one occasion when three of us expressed a wish to spend more time in one particularly wonderful museum, it was kept open an extra day. We could not, however, get into any temple; they were always mysteriously 'in unsafe condition,' and indeed it was unsafe for Chinese people to show interest in religion. The people were very curious about us, for very few had ever seen a Westerner; whenever we emerged from a building we'd find crowds waiting to see us, but although they often trailed us down the street, they were never really intrusive. We were allowed to go pretty well wherever we wanted to, and were the first visiting group to be shown Peking's underground shelter system. It had been built over the years as a defence against atomic attack and was still being extended; every evening, after finishing their regular work, people spent another hour digging. The system consisted of an integrated series of tunnels and service rooms stretching right across the city, with many hidden entry points (the one we entered was inside a shop). When we wondered at the enormous undertaking, our guide said atomic attack by the Soviet Union was a virtual certainty and such defensive works had been prepared in all Chinese cities. We didn't have the heart to point out that the ventilation system would bring in the radioactive fallout.

Near the end of our tour Nemetz gave an interview to the Peking correspondent of *The Globe and Mail* in which he said quite correctly that we hadn't seen Chou En-lai because he was in hospital, and then unfortunately added that he was thought to have had a heart attack. When we arrived back in Hong Kong we were met by a battery of reporters, and Nemetz had the embarrassing task of explaining that his remark, which had been reported around the world, was based on an incorrect rumour. In Hong Kong the delegation's final dinner fell apart over Canada's great linguistic divide: Paul Lacoste, of Montreal, one of two francophones, attacked the mission for being carried out entirely in English, and was particularly harsh about our Peking embassy, which had no francophone members and received us in English only. Roger Guindon, of Ottawa, tried to smooth things over by saying he hadn't encountered any Chinese who understood French, but Lacoste was not to be placated.

VII

Presumably because the university was in the process of unionization, the UGC told us not to bring forward an asking budget as usual; instead, we were to develop an estimate of expenditures not including the outcome of current negotiations. Meanwhile, Bateman worked with us during May and June to develop the information needed to justify our accumulated and prospective deficits; he clearly implied that the UGC would make representations to government to cover them, and he recognized the need to start the next year from a higher baseline. At the end of June, however, he retired, and although Chevrier, the acting chairman, continued the work, he was, as an interim official, less committed. Then, in July, Condo came in to tell me that he was resigning from the university as of the end of the year to become the new chairman of the UGC. Since he had been an active Conservative supporter, people thought his appointment by an NDP government must have a special reason, and speculated that it was because he would know all the soft spots in our budget and would be happy to bring pressure to bear on my administration.

The board set up a special committee on the financial situation. Richard Bowles, who had just finished a term as lieutenant-governor, had become chancellor in succession to Peter Curry, who had moved to Montreal; not having been involved in the board's earlier decisions, he expressed some uncertainty about the course we had followed. The other members repeated to him the arguments that had been used in April, told him of the minister's response, and stated their conviction that we should now return to the minister and ask for additional funding not only to cover the deficit but to enable us to maintain the competitive quality of the university; in this Orlikow, the member closest to the government, was the most emphatic. The board concurred with this view, and on 24 September the committee on the financial situation met with the minister and Chevrier. We began by recalling our April meeting with the minister, then showed that the deficit was developing as we'd predicted, and asked to have it covered and a higher baseline provided for the following year. Hanuschak didn't demur at our interpretation of his April response, accepted outline figures we'd prepared, asked some questions, particularly about whether any unfilled positions could be left open, and promised that he would give us guidance soon, recognizing that we needed it.

Ten days later he wrote to us saying, 'my feeling is that the proper avenue of approach for you is through the UGC'!

The board asked the UGC for an early meeting; at first Chevrier was cooperative, agreed that the information that had been developed during the summer and fall was appropriate and adequate, and a date was set. Then he began backtracking, asked for the information to be in a different form and for additional information, some of it for earlier years before our records were computerized, and suggested that the meeting be postponed until all that was complete. Under pressure he conceded that enough data had been received for the meeting to proceed, but then sent new questions: how had the current financial situation developed? what steps had the university taken to reduce expenditures? if additional support were not forthcoming, what were the university's contingency plans?

The budget committee, anxious to win the support of the UGC, proposed that we reiterate our position that further restraints would damage the university severely but add that, because of the crisis, we would halt replacements for unfilled positions and most other hiring until the answer to our request for additional funds was known. The board held a special meeting on 19 December, the day before the meeting with the UGC. Bowles argued that we should not on our own initiative take the first step away from our position; the minister had informally accepted our Phase One budget and the strategy it represented; if that consent was now withdrawn, let the UGC or government determine that leaving unfilled positions vacant was necessary. Many agreed, and Cain urged that we use the phrase dreaded by tenured staff, 'financial emergency.' I said that the budget committee, including myself, had hoped that the concession on appointments would help win UGC support, but since all board members who had spoken were against it and it was a board answer that was being formulated, I wouldn't argue further. The board replaced our suggested answer with: 'if government support is not forthcoming the university will be forced to declare a financial emergency and cut services.' Condo, who had remained silent during the discussion, looked grim.

The following day the board's committee on the financial situation, supported by the budget committee (including Condo), met with the UGC. Early in the meeting we were asked why we had not reduced our level of expenditure when it became clear we were facing a deficit; we replied by narrating the position taken on 10 April by the minister, whereupon the new deputy minister, Wesley Lorimer, expressed astonishment, as did his fellow commissioners other than Chevrier, who had been briefed before the April meeting and had been present at our second meeting with Hanuschak; however, he did not verify our statement. There was a large general discussion, during which I got the impression that the lay members of the commission were gaining more understanding and sympathy for the university's position, although Chevrier said that the federal government had adopted an increase ceiling of 15 per cent on its transfer payments to provinces and the Manitoba government had indicated that it would not increase its own transfers beyond that shared level. The commission agreed that we must have an early decision.

It was not until 5 February 1975, however, that I heard anything, and then I got a very aggressive letter from Condo, now chairman of the UGC, saying that the commission would be meeting on 17 February, and he would like, by 13 February, the answer to fourteen new questions. These were so threatening (e.g., what actions had we taken since the 20 December meeting to reduce expenditures, freeze hiring, block fund transfers, etc.) that the board held a special meeting on 10 February and approved the restraints it had rejected on 19 December, such as a near-freeze on hiring and expenditures. In the event, Condo delayed the meeting with the UGC, which at his demand was public, to 27 February. Then he read a prepared statement criticizing the board for not initiating the restraints earlier, rejecting salary comparisons with universities in 'more affluent' provinces (Manitoba's per-capita income at the time was fourth in the country), and declaring that 'this is an era in public financing when special pleadings in behalf of universities are unlikely to conscript public support.' He didn't acknowledge our difficult and much-publicized space shortage, simply announcing that there would be no capital grant for at least two years. As a rescue operation, the UGC would pick up one-half our deficit, provided we liquidated the other $2 million ourselves in five years and struck a balanced budget for 1975–6, which must be presented to the UGC no later than 1 June. He also declared that there should be no tuition fee increase, and then announced the operating grant for the coming year.

When we worked out the implications of this savage communication, we concluded that, without even starting on the liquidation of the remaining deficit, we would have to get $3.6 million out of the existing expenditure base before making provision for necessary salary and other increases. We tried to do it, with the result that the entire university was thrown into turmoil. The Board, Senate, Deans' Council, and Employee Relations Office were brought into the discussion at once, so that many different suggestions and even more rumours flew about. Everyone was fearful of something: staff feared for their jobs, promotions, pay, workload, or perquisites; students feared that there would be higher fees, fewer and more crowded courses, and worsened library, laboratory, and study conditions. Tension, already high between sectors that were still experiencing enrolment growth and those where enrolment was shrinking, heightened as the former demanded more space and resources and the latter resisted losing any.

An immediate result of the UGC's severity was that we were unable to come near meeting the demands of the half-dozen unions with whom we were in active negotiation. On 21 March AESES, comprising 1,200 technical, administrative, computer, secretarial, and clerical workers, went on strike. As before, I declared that the university would continue its educational operations, and put as our first priority the completion of courses and the evaluation of student work, whether by conventional examinations or alternative means. Again the Winnipeg buses stopped at the picket lines; again there were no sympathy strikes, and most non-striking staff came to work. UMSU was split, some supporting the strikers and some the university; UMFA declared itself in support of the strike but did not urge its members to stay away. Vandalism at first was fairly light, but grew as the strike wore on, and by the end of March we had our first strike-related fire, with considerable damage to the print shop. An especially nasty act was the setting of one or more attack dogs into a sheep pen, killing some and mangling more.

We made repeated efforts to negotiate, but AESES was a new and inexperienced union and the leaders could not distinguish between flexibility and surrender; all our offers were rejected, including binding arbitration. UMFA, whose own negotiations with us were stalled, held a pro-strike teach-in; with some misgivings, I went there, made a statement, and submitted to questions, which were reasonably civil. I was, of course, under intense personal attack from the striking union and the others negotiating with us, as well as most of the media (on 10 April, Peter Warren devoted his show to the university's situation, beginning by declaring me 'the sole person responsible' for the strike, the deficit, and all the unhappiness). On 12 April we had our worst vandalism: arson destroyed the operations and maintenance building and all the equipment in it, with damage running to well over a half-million dollars. In reply to questions in the legislature suggesting that the strike was being prolonged because the university didn't have the money to meet the union's demands, Hanuschak said, 'I don't know if the university has the money or not. I have received no notice from the University of Manitoba that it has no money.' I was in regular communication with the UGC and asked Condo about this; he agreed to speak to Hanuschak about it and later reported that the minister had promised to correct this statement, but he never did.

Exams began on schedule on 14 April, with several departments, principally in Arts, conducting alternative evaluations. The strike leaders' control of their membership was steadily weakening and more and more union members were returning to work; instead of making the leaders more amenable to negotiation, this made them step up their campaign of harassment and intimidation, and the newspapers carried a number of letters reporting such tactics. Letters also began to be published criticizing the government for underfunding while allowing it to appear that the university administration was alone responsible for the situation; one was to the premier from the Alumni Association, signed by its president, Gary Filmon, who would himself become premier. Some faculty members familiar with Schreyer asked me why I didn't go to him; I explained that if at my own initiative I went over the heads of Condo and Hanuschak, there was a real danger of retaliation in later years; however, if they could get Schreyer to call me I'd be very happy to see him. Finally, on 22 April, Schreyer's assistant called to invite me to lunch in his office on the 25th. On the 24th Schreyer called to ask if I preferred Hanuschak to be present or not; I said present, and asked to bring John Hunt, the board vice-chairman, Cain not being available; in the event, I found Condo there too. During our meeting there was a large demonstration of strikers and sympathizers outside the legislature demanding that Schreyer intervene to settle the strike; they'd been expected, and Paulley, the minister of labour, went out to speak to them.

Schreyer began by talking about the need for a 'rational approach to university financing,' perhaps through using a percentage of gross provincial product, and of his impression that by that measure Manitoba did as well as other provinces. I showed him the comparisons I'd prepared of higher-education percentages of gross provincial product, as well as some other comparisons, and he grew uncomfortable at the cumulative evidence that, by comparison with other institutions of a like nature in Canada, we were substantially underfunded. I also explained the depth of our deficit by recalling that on 10 April 1974 we had shown Hanuschak our Phase One budget and estimated deficit, to which he had said, 'If we have to go into deficit financing, we'll go into deficit financing.' It was apparent that Schreyer had not really understood our situation; he now became quite sympathetic, agreeing that the remaining $2 million of accumulated deficit would somehow have to be absorbed by government.

At this point Condo, clearly worried that the onus for our situation was shifting toward the minister and the UGC, protested that despite the time elapsed since the meeting on 27 February we hadn't given the UGC any response for its consideration. I explained that to meet his conditions we had to get $3.6 million out of the base, which proved impossible and led us round and round in circles without making real progress. If we were allowed a substantial shortfall, we might, despite the strike, have a document for him in about three weeks. Schreyer then suggested that getting $1.5–2 million out would be 'a good-faith demonstration of our intent to cooperate.' This would lead to an operating deficit of $1.8–2 million and enable us to settle the strike without direct government intervention.

Hanuschak questioned whether university financing should be settled directly with the premier, and Condo said that constitutionally the level of financing must be recommended by the UGC. Schreyer instantly backed off, leaving us where we began. I said that if the situation remained that we couldn't go to the UGC except with a balanced budget, and thereafter beg for relief, untold damage would result in the interval. Schreyer then said we mustn't be trapped in a vicious circle by a constitutional theory; all levels (university, UGC, minister, premier) were now in one room and could reach common understanding. He would await the UGC's recommendation, but if it recommended, as he hoped it would, a supplement of $1.5–2 million, he would support it and recommend it to cabinet. Hanuschak said he would too. Condo was silent. I then asked him if he agreed that the situation was that the board would be coming to the UGC with a budget proposal showing a deficit of about the magnitude indicated by the premier, and he very reluctantly said yes, the UGC 'would then consider it.'

This enabled us to make a new offer to AESES, but the strike leaders, under the mistaken impression that the government was compelling us to give in to them, insisted that they could not reduce further than they already had their ridiculously inflated demands. The strike continued, but more people were returning to work, and exams continued to be carried out.

The understanding with Schreyer also helped me to deal with a new emergency. Led chiefly by Don McCarthy, the dean of arts, and thoroughly upset by the budget exercise by which we'd been attempting to meet the UGC's hostile conditions, the deans and directors had signed a letter 'inviting' me to meet with them on 30 April to discuss the university's financial situation, how it had arisen, what the university's priorities were, how the envisaged cuts were being administered, and other similar questions. (McCarthy delivered the letter to our house on a Friday evening when I was out of town and said to Lesley that he 'feared this would distress Dr Sirluck.') I knew that this was the way more than one university president had recently been forced to resign; one of them had answered my letter of condolence by saying that he knew what needed to be done in his university and how to do it, but that he had come to the conclusion that with the deans aligned against him he would not be able to carry out the needed actions. He had been succeeded by one of the rebellious deans, and I wondered whether any of the U of M deans were emulating that rebel. I received word from one or two of the signatories that they had signed because they did not want to be cut off from the other deans, but this looked like very cold comfort. The vice-presidents reported that their deans had suddenly grown much less communicative than usual, and some of the v-ps themselves showed signs of running for cover. After my meeting with Schreyer most were strengthened.

The meeting with the deans, which began at 7:00 P.M. and which the v-ps and I left at 11:30, was very tense. It was chaired by Robin Connor, dean of science, who had joined McCarthy in initiating the affair, and who opened the proceedings with a long, elaborately diplomatic, statement of the matters that were particularly troubling the deans, ending with the declaration that there was 'no element of confrontation here.' On the intervention of Arnold Naimark, dean of medicine, I was then invited to make a statement; I began by reporting in confidence the meeting with Schreyer, Hanuschak, and Condo, and the resulting permission to budget for approximately a $2-million deficit for 1975–6. This would change the nature as well as the severity of our budget-cutting exercise, allowing us to begin with judgment calls in each unit, rather than, as we had been doing, with the determination of what cuts were legally possible under our multitudinous regulations. We would start with the administrative and centrally administered units, where we expected to be able to cut the base about 8 per cent (I had already begun with myself and my office, cutting much deeper than that); we would then turn to the academic units, where the cuts would vary but aggregate, we thought, about 5 per cent.

McCarthy led the questioning: what were the reasons for the initial 1974-5 Phase One budget, with its implied deficit, what were the university's priorities and on what principles were they based, how could we tell whether the senior administration cost too much, and so forth. I said that the Deans' Council had not only concurred a year earlier in the idea of a Phase One budget but had recommended that its contemplated deficit be increased, after which the board had increased it again; I could not write a statement of principle on which to base priorities other than to say this was an academic institution, not an institution for support staff or administration; my budget colleagues and I were guided by judgment based on function and need. Martin Wedepohl, who had recently come from England to be dean of engineering, surprised me by asking (possibly reflecting discussions at recent deans' meetings) who would decide on the size of the deficit if we could not agree among ourselves on the budget. I said the responsibility for the budget was the president's; there would be no effort at a consensus budget; I expected the cooperation of the deans in working toward the budget proposal, but the recommendation would be mine and the decision the board's.

McCarthy reiterated his initial line of questioning, but several deans expressed satisfaction about the changed circumstances, and as the discussion wore on it became increasingly clear that it was the strain of the strike, already forty days old, the fears that had been engendered by the UGC's harshness, the agitation and pressure they were feeling from their department heads and which they were passing around to each other during our desperate efforts to forge a workable budget, rather than a wish to unseat me, that had caused them to sign the 'invitation' to me. Sensing the shift of mood, Connor, who may have been uncomfortable about his part in bringing on this 'non-confrontation,' declared that a great deal had been accomplished and he was now much more hopeful about the formation of the budget than before, and thought the same was true of the others. There was what appeared to be majority assent, and the budget committee and I were thanked, apparently sincerely, when we left.

In the following days the budget committee restructured the

exercise to aim for a $1.9-million deficit, and the vice-presidents got better cooperation from their deans. But we were making no headway with the strike. Thinking that we could not put the non-unionized employees to further distress, we gave them all, some five hundred excluded academics and support staff, a retroactive salary increase. At the same time we made a new offer to AESES, which their bargaining team refused to endorse but put to the membership, where it was turned down by a 3–2 margin. However, this caused more AESES members to return to work, and a few days later the union made a new proposal, dropping some of its more extreme demands but still asking far more than we could afford. By 7 May the newspapers estimated that 20 per cent of AESES members were back at work, and we were getting increasing indications that there would be a mass return almost at once.

That evening I was visited by my cousin Leon Mitchell, whom I'd seen only rarely since he left Winkler when I was still in school. He was now a labour lawyer, a committed partisan with close ties to the unions and the NDP government. 'What would you give,' he asked, 'to settle the strike?' 'A hundred thousand dollars.' 'You know you don't have to give anything? You've got it beat.' 'I know that, but I don't want to destroy the union and have the university plagued for years by hatred. I'll cede enough to save the leadership's face.' 'How do you want the hundred thousand distributed?' 'More or less as the union wishes, as long as it doesn't create new disparities.' 'May I use your phone? You can be there and listen in.' 'I don't want to listen in.' He came back to say the deal was agreed, provided I would myself meet the next day with the union leadership, since it didn't trust my bargaining team.

The next morning the union leaders Allen Yost and Rance Petty, all smiles, met with Don Wells, whom I'd appointed to succeed Condo, and me. I asked whether they'd been in touch with Mitchell; they had. I asked what their revised demands were, and Yost repeated their previous proposal, which we'd rejected. I said that was not my understanding of what they'd agreed to on the phone with Mitchell, and I thought it best to adjourn until they could talk with him again. Then I called him and told him what had happened. He said something in exasperation and promised to get back to me, which he did, saying it was straightened out, and Yost and Petty would be back in my office that afternoon. When they returned there were no smiles but they had a diminished schedule of demands which added about $200,000 to our last offer. I said, 'Reduce that to the agreed $100,000, please, or I withdraw from the negotiation.' Yost took the paper and made the corrections; I handed it to Wells, who confirmed that the distribution would create no new anomalies. I then asked Yost and Petty to confirm that their bargaining committee would recommend the settlement to their membership, which they did. I asked when the membership would be back at work, and they said beginning the next day, and the vote would be on the weekend. I said it was a deal and shook hands. Shortly thereafter Mitchell was appointed to fill one of the government vacancies on the board of governors.

Thus after fifty-one days this immensely damaging strike ended. In its final fortnight there were renewed rallies and demonstrations; media attacks on the administration for refusing to settle had never abated; but toward the end there were also a number of statements blaming the government for the inadequate funding which made the university unable to meet worker demands, and the opposition politicians used these to attack the government in the legislature. Hanuschak told the legislature that the UGC had seen 'no evidence that would enable it to recommend changes in the level of support' (Hansard, 3 May 1975), Condo told the press that the university was properly funded, and even Schreyer defended the level of grants. All this criticism caused the board, on 5 May, to issue a statement that the deficit was not a mistake but resulted from a plan made known in advance to both government and UGC, that it was not a true deficit but a shortfall in funding, and expressing confidence in me and my administration.

VIII

Negotiations with UMFA had stalled, not only over money issues but over its demand to participate in management, and we were in conciliation, which was also proving useless. On 8 May, before it became known that the AESES strike was ending and when it could reasonably be thought that a little more pressure would bring the administration down, an UMFA meeting narrowly rejected an executive motion expressing lack of confidence in me, but approved a second motion demanding that I adopt a policy of 'openness,' create new channels of communication, and meet with UMFA within a month, or resign. Clare Pentland, a senate representative on the board and UMFA's most vociferous champion there, demanded at a board meeting that I resign forthwith ('There's a stalemate; do something: resign'), but the board declared UMFA's demands unacceptable, again expressed its confidence in me, and instructed me not to meet with UMFA as demanded; it requested me to study the improvement of communications, but added that 'members of the university and the public at large have received an unprecedented quantity of meaningful information on the university budget and related matters.'

Somebody with access to confidential negotiating documents must have decided that honouring negotiating confidentiality while UMFA misrepresented both its position and ours was costing the university too much, and sent copies of our team's analysis of the cost of UMFA's demands to the press. The front pages headlined 'Profs Demand $9 Million': salary costs alone would increase 47.7 per cent. UMFA cried foul and denounced our analysis as 'misrepresentation,' but the unaccustomed adverse publicity, combined with the board's firmness, had an effect: in its next newsletter UMFA found reasons to believe that the administration was growing more 'open' and that it would therefore be 'inappropriate' to push now for my resignation.

We were now making good progress with the formation of a budget, and on 14 May I reported to Senate on our financial situation, speaking guardedly about a possibility that the UGC's conditions for the 1975-6 budget might be eased. On 22 May the board approved my budget proposal, which assumed a $1.9-million deficit. The UGC arranged another open meeting, this time in a hotel ballroom, for 18 June. Our role, as I interpreted it, was to give the UGC a public face-saving basis for changing its position; I therefore arranged for a number of deans and chairmen to set forth the damage that would result in their respective sectors from the cuts needed to obtain a balanced budget. I then argued that such overall damage was unacceptable and irrecoverable; the alternative was the elimination of whole faculties or schools, but since that would directly affect the ability of the province to meet its needs it was not a decision the university should make without government involvement, and asked that, if we must indeed balance our budget, the UGC get the government to tell us which faculties it would be willing to see us eliminate. On the other hand, a budget deficit of the size we proposed would enable us to work down more gradually to an expenditure level acceptable to the UGC and government; our proposed budget, in addition to other harsh measures, already eliminated eighty-eight full-time-equivalent staff positions, to be achieved through attrition.

The next day Condo phoned to tell me that the commission was 'suggesting' to the minister that we be permitted to proceed with our deficit budget on the understanding that there would be a supplementary grant, not to exceed $1.9 million; also, that we be given ten years rather than five to liquidate the 1975 deficit.

This was the victory I needed, for both the university and myself. I had long wanted to leave, ever since it became clear that government financial policies would make impossible the major improvement of the university I had hoped to achieve; but by that time I was deeply involved in struggle and was loth to leave under attack. As the battle intensified and the attacks became increasingly personal and poisonous, my family feared for my health and urged me to resign; I in turn was concerned for the effect on them as well as on me and longed to get out, but would not do so in circumstances which could look like an acknowledgment of responsibility for harming the university. Now the UGC's reversal of its punitive 27 February position, and the government's concurrence, constituted something like a public acknowledgment that our position was in some unrevealed way right. Within the university there was a massive sense of relief as well as a general recognition that we must have had the consent of government for the deficit budgeting of the previous year. I felt vindicated and therefore free to go.

Even this was not without its difficulties. I held to the old-fashioned convention that a university president who chooses to resign before the end of his term owes his institution a full year's notice to enable it to carry out a proper search for his successor, negotiate his appointment, allow him in turn to give decent notice to his institution, and enable the departing president to brief his successor fully. I had contemplated the circumstances of my resignation for so long that the twelve-month period had acquired a talismanic quality in my mind. Now changes in the board threatened it. Cain had moved to Ontario, and therefore had left the board, on 31 May; Hunt, as vice-chairman, had become acting chairman and was expected to become chairman at the next board meeting, 26 June. Instead, he announced his resignation from the board on the ground that the increasing involvement of government and struggles with unions threatened the appearance of political independence and impartiality necessary for a judge. He made a point, both in his public statement and in a letter to Schreyer, of saying that he had no differences with me and my administration, which he praised handsomely. Sol Kanee, a recent government appointee to the board, was elected chairman. That seemed to give me four days to meet my self-imposed deadline.

I arranged a meeting with Kanee that weekend and told him that I'd served five of the seven years of my contract, which made provision for early retirement; I was now going to announce my retirement as of one year hence. He tried to talk me out of it, thinking I was just reacting to the extraordinary pressures of the past year. I told him that I had become convinced that there was little more I could contribute to the U of M because, in the course of doing what was necessary, I had myself become a source of friction; I thought a sound base for the future had been built, but it was now time for new leadership. He then said that he thought I ought to speak to the chancellor. I went to see Bowles the same day; he too tried to dissuade me, and when he couldn't, asked me to delay my announcement for 'a while' for unexplained reasons. I explained my twelve-month fixation, and he asked me to wait at least until the next board meeting, saying that I'd met my deadline by speaking to him and the chairman. I was worried by this because, in the university's unsettled condition, another great public alarum could occur at any moment and spoil my plan to make my announcement during a rare moment of triumph, but I didn't want to be obdurate; anyway, the board executive would meet in a fortnight, and the board a few days later.

At the executive I was asked whether there was any chance of reconsideration; I said no. My great moment of release came at the board meeting on 16 July; I made my statement, carefully describing my action as retirement as of 30 June 1976 under the terms of my contract, not resignation. I pointed out that this gave the board twelve months to find and appoint my successor, then emphasized that I would not be a caretaker president in the intervening year but would remain fully seized of the office's responsibilities.

There were expressions of regret and suggestions of reconsideration; those of the new president of UMFA surprised me by seeming genuine. Indeed, the reaction in the university to my announcement made it expedient for UMFA to write to the papers to deny that it had ever called for my resignation, and to add that 'the faculty association, whatever its past disagreements with Dr. Sirluck, looks forward optimistically to helping him make his final year in office an effective and pleasant one' (*Tribune*, 19 July 1975). In press interviews immediately after my announcement I had speculated that I might be able to serve the university better in the coming year now that there could be no suspicion that I was trying to enhance my own powers, and in fact this turned out to be correct, particularly in three matters: negotiations with UMFA, a study of priorities which the board and senate undertook on my recommendation, and a management consultant's study of our 'budget process' which Condo imposed on us to accompany the rescue package.

There was now a flurry of resignations. Sibley announced that he would leave in August to become vice-president of Mt Allison; I decided to reassign his duties rather than appoint a new vice-president in our inflamed condition. Then Gilson said he would like to give up administration and asked when I'd prefer him to do it; I asked him to stay for my final year, he agreed, and made his announcement at the end of August. The most dramatic resignation was that of Kanee. As a businessman with scarcely any experience on the board, he took a much more literal view of government and UGC statements of restraint than was warranted. There was some hint that either Schreyer or Hanuschak had spoken to him and encouraged him to take drastic action to reduce our expenditures; at any rate, in July, he introduced for initial consideration an outline plan which thoroughly alarmed the academic members. Afterward I urged him to await the results of the priorities study, which I promised to push as fast as possible, and he seemed willing to be persuaded if the board committed itself in advance to serious reductions, but at the next board meeting the elected academic members launched a strong attack on his plan, which was not defended by anyone; he took umbrage and on 28 August announced his resignation from the board. He was replaced by Ray McQuade, an alumni representative on the board, the sixth chairman or acting chairman of my tenure.

At the time of my announcement there were six union contracts under negotiation, and of course a settlement in one would set a floor for all. The most difficult as well as important was with UMFA, which we had been negotiating since UMFA's certification in April 1974. It had already accused the 'administration bargaining team' of refusing to negotiate in good faith and had unsuccessfully demanded a meeting with the board itself. It now applied for conciliation, and its propaganda increasingly centred on 'the faculty's right to participate in university governance.' My position was that the faculty's right was uncontested and actively exercised, but vested in department and faculty councils and Senate, as well as Senate's elective representation on the board (which never in my time rejected Senate's advice); we could not wrest faculty rights away from where the statute placed them and lodge them in a labour union whose primary role must be to look after the economic interests of its members, not the health of the whole. A particular point of contention was that UMFA insisted on writing tenure decisions into the contract. Our concern was that if tenure became a matter of management–union negotiation it would cease to be one of academic judgment, and might one day be negotiated away in favour of some other system of job security.

On 2 July the presidents of UMFA and CAUT, together with their senior colleagues, came to see me. They included some very skilful rhetoricians, and the great phrases were duly deployed: as an academic I must surely believe in faculty participation, collegiality, tenure, academic freedom, and so forth. I agreed with all these abstractions but persisted in distinguishing between 'the faculty' and the union, tenure and job security, collegiality and a contract under the Labour Relations Act. I was prepared to include a definition of tenure procedures as they had evolved in the university, but I would not agree to move tenure decisions from their established train and lodge them in negotiating committees; I would also agree to a definition of academic freedom, provided it was accompanied by one of academic responsibility; and I raised but did not press the question they would have preferred to avoid – conflict of interest when union members sit on bodies making the employer's decisions. In the end I told them what I later reported to the board: I didn't discern a clash of principle; I saw difficulties which I thought could be overcome with mutual goodwill, and would labour to help overcome them.

I think the meeting had a good effect; it helped define the area in which negotiation would be fruitful and that in which it wouldn't. On 29 August we reached agreement in principle, and on 26 September we signed the first collective agreement between an English-speaking Canadian university and a faculty union. One of the main reasons the negotiations were so difficult and protracted – seventeen months of formal negotiation after a fourteen-month certification process – was that both sides, but especially CAUT, were very conscious that this contract would set a precedent in Canada, which increased the significance of every contested decision. Indeed, throughout our negotiations and for some time after their conclusion, I was regularly called by presidents of other universities for advice on their negotiations, as I know UMFA was called on to advise other faculty unions or associations.

The International Association of Universities was holding its quinquennial conference in Moscow in August. I wasn't sure whether, in our straitened circumstances, it would be good public relations for me to attend, and referred the question to the board, which decided I should. Universities from all over the world were represented, but the majority of papers were from the Warsaw Pact countries and had a deadening sameness. Most of the problems they dealt with had little relevance to the U of M; the West Europeans spoke more to our situation. For me the high point of the conference was a luncheon given for a dozen presidents by the Soviet Academy of Sciences, all of whom spoke some English. I was seated next to a fascinating woman who had been in Leningrad throughout the terrible German siege, and her account of how she and her family had survived made that dreadful ordeal very real to me.

While I was listening to a conference paper two men sat down next to me and engaged me in conversation. They knew who I was and something of the U of M, and asked whether I'd be interested in meeting the Soviet minister of education. I agreed, and shortly thereafter they returned escorting a very heavy, formidable-looking woman, whom they introduced as the minister. We had some amiable conversation, and then she asked whether there was anything she or her ministry could do for me; at first I said I didn't think so, but she pressed and finally I asked whether it would be possible to trace my family's roots; they came from Teofopil' and Vishgorod in Ukraine. She didn't know the towns but assured me it would be easy; her assistants would take all the details, and if the municipal records were lost, the information could be recovered from church records. I said that wouldn't help: I was Jewish. Her smile didn't quite vanish, but it froze; she soon swept away, and the assistants went through the motions of taking details but without conviction; then they too left. They had my home address but I never heard from them.

The conference ended with a state reception in St George's Hall in the Kremlin. The huge gilded hall with dozens of chandeliers and scores of tables, but no chairs, was packed full; the speeches, mostly in languages I didn't understand, went on for a long time. By the time the toasts were drunk we were ready for the extraordinary viands set out in uniform patterns on the tables; I concentrated on the great heaps of black caviar, taken with Georgian wine. This and the Academy of Sciences luncheon were the only occasions in my ten days in the Soviet Union when the food was other than badly prepared and unappetizingly presented.

Some sightseeing was arranged for us, including the major tourist attractions in and near Moscow. Very few churches were open, but those who asked were taken to the monastery at Zagorsk, an hour's drive out of Moscow. It was so packed with Russian worshippers that we vistors had to push our way in a few at a time and could see little of the historic treasures, but the smell and the almost desperate worship made a very strong impression. After the conference I went on my own to Leningrad (as it then was) for three days, most of which I spent in the Hermitage Museum, which was much better and less crowded than the Tretyakov in Moscow. I took a half-day to go to Petrodvorets, Peter the Great's version of Versailles; half-way there the hydrofoil lost its elevation and went on as an ordinary boat. I half-expected the Aeroflot planes too to lose their elevation, they shook and clattered so much.

IX

On 22 August the UGC consultant's report on our budgetary procedures was released. It showed no recognition whatsoever of the difference between a university and a business; rather, it took the deficit of 1975 and the expected deficit of 1976, together with the lateness of these two budgets, as *a priori* proof that our administrative procedure was faulty and needed radical change, totally ignoring the real reasons: a government prepared to impose unionization but not to pay for it, the board's reluctance to do damage to the university, its recourse to the minister and his initial encouragement of the deficit course taken, then his and the UGC's effort to escape the financial consequences. The consultants interviewed mostly persons opposed to the administration, speaking to few responsible officers (they paid me a brief formal visit, asking the kind of questions found in an elementary textbook). In consequence, the report was riddled with errors of fact, on which it built its recommendations. It ignored completely the major problems of budgeting when the grant was not known until almost the start of the fiscal year but union negotiations had to be completed in a timely fashion to prevent strikes, and where half the members of Senate were also members of a bargaining unit with which the university had to negotiate, and several members of the board, although temporarily excluded from the bargaining unit, would return to it when their terms on the board ended. It appeared to us that the main object of the exercise was not to assist the university in its difficult task of finding its way through unmapped territory but to prepare the way for the assumption of greater control by the UGC and government.

We quickly prepared a critical analysis for the next board meeting. A number of board members, particularly some new ones, had been shaken by the report and the support for it by some media people; they were further confused when our analysis was attacked by McCarthy and the group he led in the board. After much wrangling it was agreed that the senior consultant would be brought back to Winnipeg to meet with the board. It was an evening meeting with a full board turn-out; after the consultant's presentation I put a series of questions to him about his report which he found increasingly difficult to answer. After he left McCarthy adopted a new line: just because some things in the report were silly (this was the first time he'd conceded that), we must not ignore the need for essential reform. He was a much better logician than the consultant, but he couldn't be much more specific than to point to our difficult situation and complain that administration was too expensive.

The answer to this, and one the board was willing to accept, lay in the study it had set up of priorities. An important merit of this Board–Senate committee was that it had representation from most sectors of the university: lay members of the board, elected academic members of Senate, representatives of UMFA, UMSU, and administration. This meant that a lot of persons who'd had easy solutions for our financial crisis received an elementary education in university administration and experienced the clash between abstract justice and practical policy. There were endless meetings, all of which I attended, where I was able to press the administration view the more persuasively because my retirement had been announced and it couldn't be thought that I was defending my own future prerogative. In the end we produced a much soberer report than the composition and temper of the committee might initially have suggested; the recommendations were not radical, but many of them were useful, and the whole process taught the sponsoring bodies that there were no hidden riches and budget balance would have to be achieved through universal austerity.

On 12 September the UGC issued guidelines for all Manitoba universities for 1976–7: grants would not exceed a 15 per cent increase over 1975–6; no deficits; no funds for additional staff; no individual salary increase of more than $2,800. In much of this it merely anticipated Trudeau's federal wage-and-price controls, which Schreyer soon applied retroactively to the whole public sector; the special hardship for the university was that the commission, despite our repeated representations, refused to count the supplementary grant of $1.9 million as part of our 1975–6 base. This meant that we had to get that money out of the base before striking the new budget. I put immediate further restraints on hiring and spending, and asked the Deans' Council to elect representatives to work with the budget committee to develop a method to reduce the base, and in December we presented a working paper to the board, which authorized us to proceed with advance preparations based on it. This allowed the deans and directors to work down over a longer period than would otherwise have been available, and when the grant was announced in February 1976, and proved to be what had been foretold, we were already well launched on the needed second downsizing. This time we eliminated 94 full-time-equivalent positions (40 of them academic), making a total of 182 over two years.

The priorities committee, in the hope of avoiding what it referred to as 'misunderstandings,' recommended that the university hold regular joint meetings with the UGC and the government. No longer so intent on keeping any hint of criticism of the UGC out of the media, I told the board that both the government and the UGC would dislike the proposal: the UGC had been resentful of any direct contact between the university and the government, and had in fact acted less as a buffer to protect the university from political interference than as a screen to prevent access to government, which in turn wanted the screen in order to evade responsibility. When this was reported in the press one heading was 'Sirluck Raps UGC for Role in Talks' (*Tribune*, 22 March 1976), which would have worried me earlier, but it was now too late for the UGC to punish the university on my account.

Although I'd given my notice before the end of June, the presidential search committee was not set up until October. Since I knew many of the nominees and applicants not known locally, the board asked me to help the committee chairman. As the committee narrowed its list, the inevitable media leak showed three internal names, Deans Connor, McCarthy, and Naimark; when interviewed, Connor and Naimark were noncommittal, but McCarthy acknowledged that he was a candidate. When the committee was nearing its short-list of three, the chairman asked me about Ralph Campbell, principal of Scarborough College in the U of T, whom I had worked with at Toronto; I gave him a favourable report, and the committee placed him on its short-list: McCarthy and Naimark from within the university, and Campbell.

On 25 February the board met to receive the committee's report, and I was asked for my opinion, especially of the external candidate. I reported rather fully on Campbell's achievements and strengths, emphasizing particularly his penchant for flexibility and compromise, knowing that some board members thought that was especially what my administration had lacked. One thing that troubled several board members was that Campbell had no PhD; how important was that? I was anxiously asked. Swallowing hard, I said that its importance was greatest at the outset of an academic career, but that after adequate research achievements the formal credential shrank in importance; Campbell, I said, had made contributions to his field and would be accepted as a peer in academic circles. Campbell was chosen, and his appointment was announced at the end of February.

Immediately thereafter, presumably in order to compare the terms of his appointment with mine, the media rediscovered my pension arrangements and went into a renewed frenzy about them. The matter was again raised in the legislature, where Hanuschak denied knowledge of the details but said he would 'investigate' and Schreyer couldn't comment because 'I am left somewhat speechless by the magnitudes involved'; both invoked university autonomy (Hansard, 3 March 1976). The *Tribune* ran numerous columns with headings like 'Size of Prize Depends on Punch in the Crunch,' 'The Rich Get Richer, the Poor Stay Poor,' and 'Sirluck's Pension Has Adam Steaming.' Among the many pieces in *The Manitoban* was one headed 'Insult Added to Injury,' demanding that students demonstrate 'to pressure Sirluck and demand that he not accept' the pension.

All this didn't reduce our eagerness to leave, and I was troubled to learn that Campbell had said he might not be able to hand over at Scarborough until the following January. I had very foolishly succumbed to pressure from Bowles and Kanee the previous summer and said that, if a new president could not be in place by the end of my term, I would, if wanted, stay on for a short while; now I feared that situation might arise. I was to meet with Campbell in Toronto the following week and pressed him on timing; he explained that it would depend on when the central administration could appoint his replacement. I called John Evans, the president of U of T, who promised to help; Campbell was replaced quickly and did arrive on time, and Lesley and I were able to leave Winnipeg on the last day of my term, 30 June.

There were the usual rituals and ceremonies of departure, at which the usual complimentary things were said. I was not foolish enough to take them at face value, but some things pleased me. At a dinner given by the deans who had the previous year invited me to the 'non-confrontation,' several speakers said that we had survived the abrupt reduction in real-dollar funding better than if we had not risked the deficit strategy. The senate's resolution of appreciation, while a little flowery, was satisfying because I had devoted a great deal of time and energy, not to speak of endurance, to it and its committees. I regarded Senate as the institutional meeting place of faculty, students, and administration, the true as well as legal academic governing body, and never in my six-year tenure missed a single meeting. At a general reception I was surprised and pleased by a plaque the new UMSU executive had had made for me, presented with unexpected words of appreciation; even *The Manitoban* ran an editorial suggesting that the criticism of me over the years might have been unfair. One thing really touched me; at a dinner given by the board, McQuade, after denouncing 'the unbridled and unwarranted criticism' that had been levelled at me, said that I had made the necessary unpopular decisions, then made myself 'the target upon which criticism was focused in order to deflect it from those' who were implementing them. I had not realized that anyone had understood this strategy, which I'd adopted in some bitterness; it reversed what I'd practised at U of T, where I'd taken care to deflect as much criticism from the president as possible.

I did not take leave of Condo or Hanuschak, but I did of Schreyer. In reply to my request for an appointment, he arranged lunch at a disconcertingly dark restaurant where, accompanied by an aide, he seemed to anticipate that I would be asking something for myself. I told him I was leaving Manitoba the following day and wanted to talk to him only about the university. I explained the ways in which its troubles were aggravated by matters within his control, such as the increasing tardiness of the announcement of the annual grant, the failure to fill government vacancies on the board and the lack of interest in the university of some government-appointed board members, the UGC's growing determination to prevent access by the university to the government, and the tendency of some operating ministries to try to make deals directly with individual departments rather than through the university. I reminded him that, before there was a ministry of colleges and universities affairs, and when there was only one university, the government's relation to it was through the premier's office, and while that was no longer feasible it remained true that unless the premier set the government's tone there would be a growing tendency to treat the university as an importunate but toothless nuisance, rather than as one of the province's most important assets. My request, therefore, was that he be seen to interest himself in the university. He said that he could see that he could have done more and promised to do what I'd asked. I don't know to what extent he carried out his promise.

When interviewers asked what I thought were the main achievements of my administration I said I'd leave that to others to say. To myself I acknowledged that they were not as visible nor as satisfying as I would like, nor could I be sure they would be lasting. The most comprehensive was managing the traumatic transition from a period of headlong expansion and rapidly rising expectations to one of ever more severe financial constraint despite soaring inflation – a protracted situation which brought an endless stream of problems and robbed the presidency of all joy.

The most important single achievement was defensive: the preservation of as much as possible of the university's autonomy from the incursions of a government philosophically opposed to such autonomy and hoping to organize higher and other postsecondary education into a tertiary level of a centrally administered provincial education system. The university's foolhardy and defiant pension plan that confronted me on arrival had given the government its opportunity; I had pre-empted the planned legislation by amending the pension plan, but at great cost to my popularity within the university. The government's next overt intervention was in the Stevens case; again I had bent to irresistible force, but we had won that case in so overwhelming a manner as to make another such intervention unlikely. I had successfully rejected the minister's 'request' that we accredit his Focus program. We had fought, with considerable if incomplete success, both the government's Task Force Report and the UGC consultants' report, and severely limited their proposed infringements of our autonomy. We had with fair success resisted both the overt and the inadvertent threats to our unity, coherence, and autonomy from the various operating departments of government. By the end of my term the government and UGC had developed the habit of citing our autonomy as a means of deflecting criticism, while infringing upon it only at the edges.

I think my next most important achievement was constitutional: replacing personal governance by the president and his cronies with a system of defined procedures for nearly all appointments and most major decisions. Elected departmental committees now nominated chairpersons, faculty and school committees nominated deans and directors; only vice-presidents remained the choice of the president, who himself was selected by a committee following a defined procedure. Students now constituted a quarter of Senate and faculty and school councils, and their participation was in consequence serious and productive. A comprehensive student discipline system, commanding general student and faculty support and with heavy student participation, was in successful operation, and the first faculty reponsibility code was in place. Senate's role had been significantly enhanced, and in addition to its dominance in academic matters, it had acquired real influence in financial affairs. Tenure procedures were now fully defined and, as a result of the Stevens case and other appeals, standards had become clarified and were seriously applied, with a resultant noticeable improvement in the quality of faculty and the amount and quality of productive scholarship and research.

Administration had been made more rational and responsible by the development of a proper information system, together with a major upgrading of the computer centre. This made possible, among other things, the development of a staffing policy, a space policy, and policies for the allocation of other resources, enabling us to cope with the imbalances of growing enrolment in some sectors and declining enrolment in others. Other administrative advances were the revision and enlargement of the sabbatical leaves policy and a salary-equity program for women. We had fought one strike to a draw and defeated a second (then an unprecedented feat in Canadian universities), thus ensuring that, even at a time of rampant inflation, our unions would bargain within the limits of possibility.

There were too few educational achievements. Graduate studies and research were strengthened, as was the woefully weak library system. Some new academic programs and interdisciplinary centres and institutes were established despite the financial constraints. Academic standards in several weak divisions were strengthened. A program to improve teaching had achieved some success.

It had been, I thought, a needed contribution, but not one which compensated my family and me for the misery of those six years or for the abbreviation of my academic career.

CHAPTER NINE

Toronto, 1976–

I

We moved back to Toronto and settled gratefully into a private life. Kate had found us a small apartment on Rosedale Valley Road; she was then an undergraduate at the U of T and had her own living arrangements, and Robert had chosen to stay in Winnipeg, so we were on our own. There was no space in the apartment for a studio; Lesley rented one downtown, where she did a series of highly therapeutic satirical paintings of the Manitoba situation, which had in some ways been even harder on her than on me because she had no direct way of fighting back.

I made no attempt to find work. I'd been out of the classroom a dozen years and away from research in English even longer, and by the time my sabbatical was over I'd be fifty-nine years old; no department needed such a professor. As for administrative employment, I knew that ex-presidents, especially controversial ones, are untouchables. Some additional financial provision was therefore necessary; despite the hullabaloo in Winnipeg over the size of my pension, I knew that inflation would soon render it inadequate. I had some savings and decided to build them up through a cautious program of investing, relying primarily on a close reading of political, economic, and business news. By the time the real value of my unindexed pension had shrunk below our modest needs I was able to supplement it with some investment income.

I had leisure to think how I might have managed the Manitoba situation better. Perhaps I could have avoided the whole problem by carrying out a more rigorous initial investigation; I could not have found all the booby-traps on my own but I could probably have uncovered the tenure mess, and if I'd asked to see the chairman of the UGC he might possibly have told me of the hidden deficit and the pension challenge to government (but not, I was sure, of government's confidential planned response). Any one of these discoveries would have been enough to make me decline the Manitoba invitation with thanks.

But having failed to probe hard enough in the first place, and having accepted the job, could I have done it better? My most obvious shortcoming, I thought, was in public relations. There was a special irony in this because at the University of Toronto and on the wider Ontario scene I had got along rather well with all the constituencies for which, or to which, I was responsible, but in Manitoba I became saddled with a reputation for remoteness. I had not intended to be withdrawn, but I was immediately confronted with a mountain of unattended but inherently urgent problems that kept me at my desk all day, so during the crucial first months I would eat a sandwich at my desk instead of going to the faculty club for lunch – a sad error whose consequences I was never able to overcome. Similarly, although I made initial visits to all faculties and schools and some departments, I failed to continue them, appearing only for cause instead of managing a flow of casual appearances. We didn't do enough home entertaining (my fault: Lesley several times suggested we do more); and as members of the university had fewer occasions to think of the president's house as a university resource, more and more of them thought it too large and expensive just for the president's family.

I put too little effort into relations with the general community and the highly ideological and partisan government. During my initial months I had to decline most of the many invitations to speak (including a strongly urged one from the minister of colleges and universities affairs to address his *shul*). I joined very few public associations and attended almost none of their meetings, and I declined all invitations to join private clubs. We attended the theatre, the ballet, and occasionally the symphony, but didn't join their associated societies. Lesley enrolled in an art institute and painted there once a week, but I did nothing comparable. I answered all questions put by the media but did not cultivate them, and infuriated one hot-line host by repeatedly refusing to go on his show.

Thus, when the diminishing flow of resources in the university turned the permanent contest for shares into grim struggle, I could readily be demonized as secluded, aloof, invisible, hence presumably harbouring secret intentions; and the media, with varying relish, gave this line some play.

Another mistake was in making my initial report too confrontational. I was so intent on presenting the university, the government, and the public with a clear account of the situation I found, and why my measures of budgetary restraint and pension-plan curtailment were necessary, that I accepted the risk of implying unspoken criticism of my predecessor's administration. This turned him and his close associates, already hostile, into active enemies just at the moment when a polarizing fight best suited the purposes of those attempting to achieve union certification.

I had also failed to understand an underlying cause of uneasiness in the Faculty Association and the Students Union. The University Act had been revised two years before my arrival and had substantially increased the powers and the elective faculty membership of the senate, thus displacing the association as the faculty's chief representative. It had also placed a few students on the senate and one on the board, to some extent displacing the Students Union and creating rival student spokespersons. Consequently both UMFA and UMSU were feeling marginalized and threatened. Had I realized this soon enough (or been briefed on it) I might have been able to work with them to develop constructive roles to fit the new circumstances.

There were doubtless other mistakes, but after much reflection I concluded that in the end avoiding them would have made little difference to the outcome. The university had for some years expanded headlong in all directions, stimulated by growing enrolment demand and fed by steadily enlarged government grants. There had been little planning and little effective concern for the quality of appointments. An atmosphere had been created in which all staff felt entitled to annual salary increases greater than inflation and to regular promotions, and teaching staff to automatic tenure, which is what the extraordinary tenure by-law and the absence of tenure procedures virtually presupposed. In any circumstances I could never have agreed to tenure by default, and given the qualitative situation, permitting tenure by perfunctory judgment would have been a betrayal of principle and dereliction of duty. Ensuring responsible judgments which weeded out weak appointments would have put me in conflict with UMFA whatever our initial relations. Later, when both the demand for student places and the real level of government support began to decline, and limits to the size of faculty and support staff had consequently to be planned, the inevitable staff response was defensive mobilization; given the policies of the provincial government, this meant seeking unionization, which in turn required polarization. Had I courted popularity I might have been a slightly less inviting target and that might have meant less personal stress for my family and me, but it is most unlikely that it would have affected the result for the university.

For a time after my departure some U of M people wrote or called with bits of information they thought would interest me, sometimes with requests for advice or help. One whom I'd not have expected to call was McCarthy, who phoned several times with bulletins on how some matter I'd set in train was progressing. Some things he said made me wonder whether he was trying to stir up opposition to Campbell's administration, particularly when he sent me a copy of a letter he wrote to the board for its January 1977 meeting. Campbell had urged that a scheduled review of the UGC consultants' 1975 recommendations was unnecessary because of new budget procedures and a better financial situation, and McCarthy was resisting the implication that the new administration had wrought the improvement; on the contrary, 'the present improved situation must in justice be attributed to the Sirluck Administration ... I feel that as one who harassed the previous President last April until he showed more clearly how he had worked to produce a balanced budget I have a serious obligation to give his administration virtually full credit for success if that is achieved; I hope others on the board, especially those who also pressed Dr. Sirluck so hard at the time, will feel the same obligation.' I thought all this was true, but I was not going to be part of any opposition to my successor.

II

The U of T Department of English invited me to be a visiting professor (part-time) for 1977–8, to give one course in sixteenth- and seventeenth-century literature. This struck me as a good opportunity to regain contact with my subject and with the academic side of the university world; I accepted, and returned to teaching with something of the old excitement, but mixed now with considerable unease, for which my own rustiness was the main but not sole reason. The course I was to give had been designed for third- and fourth-year students, but there were now no prerequisites: the old honours program had been abolished, and the 'specialist' program which had replaced it was not structured to ensure that students would know the antecedents of what they were studying. I had been warned of this and overcompensated: I prepared a series of lectures on the Renaissance which I meant as an introduction while the students got a solid start on their reading, but which seems to have persuaded much of the class that this would be a lecture course in which they could sit passively while I did all the work.

One of my students asked me whether I was aware that my name didn't appear in the University Library catalogue. I was incredulous but he insisted, then told me to look under 'L.' That is where I found my entries: the computer had been programmed to cope with honourific prefixes by treating them as suffixes, and some glitch had caused it to treat the first three letters of my name as a prefix. Many years later *The New Yorker* magazine reported the incident: 'the program not only moved all the stand-alone 'Sir's but bestowed involuntary knighthood on writers like Ernest Sirluck ... turning him into 'Luck, Ernest Sir' (4 April 1994, p. 82). This article gave rise to considerable jesting, and the incident did have its amusing aspects, but it had led to my disappearance from the catalogue for several years, and since the U of T Library was the source of much bibliographical information for other libraries, doubtless also from other catalogues. What made this more poignant was that as vice-president I had encouraged the computerization of the U of T catalogue, very expensive because it was the first by a major university library.

I was given an office in my old staircase at University College, but UC was no longer a real teaching college: a consolidation of the colleges' teaching departments, which may have been necessary, had been poorly designed and badly executed, stripping the old colleges of their historic roles and leaving UC in particular without a clear academic function. Some of the members of the consolidated University Department of English were cross-appointed to UC and gave their classes there, but they didn't constitute a department, and although this UC contingent made me welcome I didn't participate in their meetings or in those of the department itself, then an enormous body of well over a hundred. I was invited to teach my course a second year and agreed, but enjoyed it less. The initial reconnection with my academic subject had been achieved, so there was less to offset the negative aspects of teaching a class of such mixed preparation. If I spoke to suit the needs of those with least familiarity with the necessary background I would bore those who had some knowledge of the period, but if I addressed the latter group the others would simply flounder. I became convinced that this cafeteria-style curriculum could only be effective with the help of strong, even authoritative, counselling, where students were also guided by long-term course reputations. I decided I didn't want a further year, and it turned out that the department no longer needed an extra course. When I surrendered my office UC gave me a desk in the emeritus professors' room, at that time the site of the college faculty's morning *kaffeeklatsch*, which has remained for me one weekly window on the university, a second being lunch the same day at the Long Table of the Faculty Club, where a permanent unofficial seminar of many disciplines convenes daily.

I also had some opportunity to observe changes and developments outside Toronto. I visited a number of universities to participate in conferences, receive honourary degrees, or address the Royal Society, and I have a mediated link with the University of British Columbia, where Kate teaches. These glimpses of university developments have not given me an insider's knowledge – I would no longer be able to describe the university situation in detail – but they have given me a general sense of what is going on.

The most jarring change I found on my return to the U of T was the revival of overt antisemitism. For some years after the war, as the horrors of the Holocaust became known, and with the successful establishment and defence of the state of Israel, antisemitism had declined in much of the world. In Canada the decline was assisted by remorse, or at least shame, for the country's exceptional severity in denying pre-war and wartime refuge to Jews, many of whom perished in consequence.* Another favourable influence was the declaration of the Second Vatican Council that Jews were not guilty of the death of Jesus. Antisemitism in these years was certainly not extirpated in Canada, but it gradually ceased to be fashionable. In universities its decline began earlier and went farther than in the general society: Jews gained virtually open access in the major Canadian secular universities and became prominent in faculty and administration (it is no longer unusual for a university to have a Jewish president). Somewhat more slowly the larger society too opened to Jews; indeed, the rate of intermarriage alarmed some Jewish organizations who feared that assimilation would threaten the continuance of the Jewish community.

They needn't have worried: some time in the late 1960s and early 1970s the decline in antisemitism was arrested and a reversal set in. To some extent this was part of the global revival of racism and ethnic nationalism engendered by mass migrations, furthered in the case of Jews by a generational resentment of the burden of Holocaust guilt. In Canada there was special stimulus for a revival of antisemitism because of heavy immigration from countries where it had historically been overt and violent; some of these

---

* The policy is described in Irving Abella and Harold Troper, *None Is Too Many* (Toronto: Lester & Orpen Dennys, 1982), *passim*.

immigrants acted as conduits and agents for the flow of money and materials from their home countries for the organization of antisemitic and anti-Israeli activities.

At the U of M, and in Winnipeg generally, I had seen little evidence of this development, although I was aware of it through news reports; perhaps the change came more slowly in Manitoba than in Toronto, where almost half of all Canadian Jews are concentrated, or perhaps I was somewhat insulated from it. But it thrust itself on me the moment I stepped onto the U of T campus: vicious graffiti, hate-filled articles and letters in the student press, active recruitment by various openly racist and antisemitic organizations. The depth and extent of the new or revived antisemitism were, however, difficult to measure. I saw none of it among the students in my class or the faculty members with whom I associated. It was the same in the wider community: much antisemitic propaganda and many criminal acts, but I rarely encountered antisemitism myself. When the Arts and Letters Club of Toronto made me its first Jewish president, I could not discern that the fact of my Jewishness troubled the membership.

It may be that the revival of antisemitism in universities has peaked; certainly its outward manifestations have diminished in both number and intensity at the U of T, and so far as I can tell at other universities as well. It is not clear whether the same is true in the broader community; the number of reported antisemitic incidents in Canada in 1994 was up sharply (to 290), and in 1995 a spokesman for the Metropolitan Toronto Police's Hate Crime Unit said that 'blacks and members of the Jewish faith were the two most victimized groups.' The scandal of the Airborne Regiment in Somalia would seem to suggest that hate and intolerance remain high, for racism and antisemitism in the Armed Forces always derive from the general society; but the level in the army may be a lagging indicator – immediately intensified by the general revival of racism and antisemitism but slow to reflect any subsidence.

Whether this particular recrudescence of antisemitism is waning or not, it should have served to remind yet another generation of an old and bitter truth: millennia of religious preaching and political agitation against Jews have left an enormous reservoir of actual or potential antipathy in all cultures deriving from Europe and the Middle East, a reservoir which may at any time be drawn on and exploited by any group whose interest is to inflame or destabilize.

III

A year back in Toronto confirmed our view that it was where we should settle permanently. We bought a house on Strathallan Boulevard and sent for Robert, who was by then glad to leave Winnipeg, to redecorate it. He made his own living arrangements, however, and Kate, who had finished her bachelor's and master's degrees at the U of T, was pursuing her PhD in Renaissance drama at the University of London; there was therefore room in a modest house for a studio for Lesley and a study for me.

I rejoined the Arts and Letters Club, to which I had belonged before leaving for Winnipeg. I respected its history and tradition (it was founded in 1908 and had been an artistic and cultural stronghold) and valued the talents it continued to embrace, but didn't at first take an active role; in the interval since I'd belonged in the 1960s I'd become sensitized to the exclusion of women from many organizations and found myself increasingly uneasy about the idea of a club for men only. This seemed particularly reprehensible in an arts and letters club, since so many of the best writers, visual artists, and performers were women. A number of other members felt the same, but for several years all attempts to open the club to women were defeated. I contemplated resigning, but decided instead to make another effort; I joined the executive and became much more active in the club. Some others did the same, and in 1985 the membership voted to admit women. Fortunately, the first few admitted were professional artists, performers, writers, and educators who strengthened the arts orientation of the club, rather than emphasizing the social, as some had feared would happen. Lesley joined a few years later. She had exhibited in various settings since our return to Toronto but didn't wish to conform to the fashions of the art market; at the club she has exhibited frequently in its juried shows, where she is able to reach a more independent audience.

The building in which the club had rented space since 1920 was put up for sale; the club bought it, borrowing money for the purpose. With the admission of women the club's activities soon overflowed the space it had retained for itself and it decided to take over the whole of the century-old building and renovate it; it was a time of great economic and financial exuberance and the membership was confident of its ability to carry the new, much larger, mortgage.

By the time the plans were ready to go to tender I had become president. Just at that point, in the early summer of 1990, recession hit Canada, with Toronto experiencing the sharpest downturn. This was especially hard on our membership, which depended heavily on the art and culture markets, notoriously sensitive to economic conditions; at the same time, interest rates continued to go up because the Bank of Canada thought it still detected inflation in other parts of the country. The renovation was very successful (it won an award from the City of Toronto), but I was soon in an unhappily familiar situation: in charge of an organization facing a large deficit. Our operating costs were excessive; we hired a professional manager, changed the staff, and increased occasional rental revenue. But while this brought our actual operations into the black, the cost of servicing the debt kept us heavily in the red overall.

We had one really saleable asset, even in the depressed art market, a Lawren Harris painting we'd owned since the Group of Seven were key members. I knew that a proposal to sell this would be hotly resented by many members, and I too deplored the necessity, but I was convinced that unless we substantially reduced our debt the club would go under, as some others had. The proposal created much initial controversy, but by the time of the general meeting called to consider it the membership had come to understand the gravity of the situation, and the debate, while prolonged and emotional, never grew really divisive; the vote in favour of selling was overwhelming, and in an otherwise flat auction the Harris brought a good price. Together with a number of member donations and a substantial bequest, this reduced our debt by more than half, and I had the pleasure of handing over to my successor a club whose finances were no longer threatening.

IV

At the time of the U of T's sesquicentennial in 1976–7 I gave a lecture entitled 'University Presidents and the Politicians.'* Based on my experience in Manitoba, I presented what many people then thought an overly pessimistic view of the future relationship of universities and governments. Unfortunately, it was not; since that time governments have become much more intrusive into university affairs, while steadily reducing the real value of grants in relation to enrolment. At the time of writing (1994), new interventions are being proposed or discussed by many provincial governments, such as a suggested 'purchase of service system' of university funding (Ontario), a government-mandated merger of universities (Nova Scotia), a government-mandated renegotiation of collective agreements to provide for termination on fiscal grounds of tenured appointments (Alberta), an overt government 'challenge to its postsecondary institutions to re-engineer and redesign the education enterprise,' failing which 'government will become more involved' (Manitoba), and other interventions. Economy is certainly a motive in these initiatives, but they all demonstrate a growing unwillingness to trust universities to effect necessary economies themselves.

It is true that universities have found it hard to cut costs. In part this is because of objective factors, such as growing and more diversified enrolments, increased sophistication of equipment and materials, higher costs of necessary services, and so forth. But seen from the increasingly unsympathetic perspective of government, several other factors predominate: the university's values, its efficiency, its will.

There are many clashes of value between universities and government, the most important concerning the balance between research and teaching. In theory universities value them equally, but it is evident that in appointments, tenure, promotion, and pay, research has for about three decades been far more important and, governments believe, more expensive; they also think its ben-

---

* *The Canadian Journal of Higher Education*, 1977, 1–12

efits accrue more to the professor than to his or her students or the community, and are increasingly determined to push teaching higher in the universities' priorities.

In assessing a university's efficiency, governments tend to use such criteria as cost-per-student, and while they have generally acknowledged that undergraduate, graduate, and professional student costs must be separately weighted, they usually insist that within these major categories costs should be comparable, and they focus particularly on teacher–student and square foot–student ratios. This makes them very critical of the tendency of most universities to retain small-enrolment courses in unfashionable disciplines, which they cite as a prime example of university inefficiency. Governments also complain that universities are unwilling to 'rationalize' within a provincial post-secondary system, insisting on continuing all their operations when it would be much cheaper and more efficient to divide the educational task up between the several institutions in a province. From government's viewpoint, all that is lacking to rationalize university operations both internally and as parts of a provincial system is will. Governments are therefore moving more and more aggressively to effect what they think necessary changes through external pressure.

Universities often have important academic reasons for resisting the changes urged on them by governments, but there is also some truth in the charge that they lack the will to effect difficult change themselves. One reason is that the distribution of real power in the vastly expanded and diversified contemporary university has made contested decisions hazardous to administrators' careers. The old governing hierarchy survives in most universities, at least in form, but it has lost confidence in its own legitimacy and in its power to make its decisions accepted.

Governing boards, which now usually include faculty and student representatives, know that faculty and student organizations, support-staff unions, alumni groups, and sometimes others, often go directly to government and are listened to roughly in proportion to their political influence, which makes boards very chary of taking firm stands. Administrations, thus uncertain of board backing in a dispute, and now more dependent for reappointment upon those they administer than on those above them in the hierarchy, display varying degrees of administrative paralysis. Fear of opposition from affected interests leads to endless proliferation of committees whose true function is to postpone needed but contested decisions until they are no longer divisive (i.e., have been overtaken by events). In the face of resource restraint, and lacking the discipline of resolute authority, the university's mix of interests quickly becomes a clash of interests, and healthy competition for new resources turns into harsh battles for survival.

The thrust toward research and scholarship is both natural and highly desirable. Anyone genuinely interested in his or her discipline will want to explore its frontiers and contribute to its advancement, and this redounds immediately to the benefit of both the institution and its students. Conversely, a professor who does not participate in research and scholarship is very likely to lose touch with the advancing edge of his or her discipline, which all too soon harms the institution and its students.

But research and scholarship necessarily imply specialization, and active specialists want to teach their specialties. The natural place to do this is in graduate studies, where it suits the needs of the student as well as those of the instructor. But specialization has now entered deeply into the undergraduate curriculum as well, where it is the subject of much complaint by students confronted with a menu of narrow specialized offerings. It is the duty of the academic branch of the university hierarchy – departmental committees, faculty councils, the senate – to ensure the educational quality and appropriateness of the university's programs, but consisting as it does predominantly of professors, it is naturally very responsive to professorial concerns; and most professors have not wanted to limit the growth of specialized courses. Partly this is a matter of enthusiasm for their specialties, but it is also a matter of fundamental self-interest. To have a competitive place in their disciplines, research and publication are essential; without such recognition professors have no market for their labour other than their present university, and an employee without an alternative is in a weak bargaining position. Consequently there is unrelenting pressure to increase specialization, and internal efforts to return to a broader, more liberal, curriculum have generally been thwarted, putting in question what ought to be a self-evident proposition, that research and teaching benefit each other.

The university's reluctance to terminate small-enrolment courses can be defended on theoretical, experiential, and pragmatic grounds. The deletion of an academic discipline which has for a long time been an integral part of the evolution of knowledge would leave a gaping hole in the universe of discourse, and some of the loss might never be recovered. And fashion is fickle: a quarter-century ago, for example, governments were pressing universities to discontinue Classics, for which there was then very little student demand. Today Classics, taken to include ancient history and often taught in translation, is very popular; how could the current demand have been met if universities had closed their Classics departments when pressed to do so? Besides, the savings anticipated from closings would probably not materialize: the professors in the unfashionable discipline probably have tenure, cannot be reassigned to subjects in which they have no competence, and cannot be terminated without immense and costly turmoil. There are also good arguments against rationalization among universities. A university should preserve the universe of knowledge, whose constituent parts should develop together and cross-fertilize one another; a university deprived of a major discipline cannot develop normally. Good students will not go to a university which they perceive to be artificially stunted. Local demand should be met locally. Graduates of the affected program will be orphaned and badly hurt.

But the charge of inefficient use of public money carries great weight with government, which perceives self-interest behind what it thinks stubborn retention of unneeded offerings and unnecessary duplication between universities dependent upon a common purse, just as it does behind what it thinks the excessive emphasis on research to the detriment of teaching. As pressure on heavily indebted governments to reduce spending increases, so will government pressure on universities, and in a struggle with government universities cannot win unaided. Their best hope to escape serious mutilation lies in two kinds of action, fortunately closely related: to enlist public support (government quickly responds to voter opinion), and to persuade government that they are themselves taking action to meet government complaints.

The first step in regaining public approval, and simultaneously meeting one of government's most exigent demands, is to redress the balance between teaching and research in tenure and promotions. This would make it feasible to reinstate broader, more liberal undergraduate curricula; a possible program might be two years of general education followed by two years within a single discipline or group of cognate disciplines. Graduate studies should remain predominantly specialized and emphasize research training. A second step would be to examine *objectively* which small-enrolment undergraduate courses are genuinely necessary to the integrity and continuity of a discipline, and prepare others for phasing out as staff and other considerations permit. The third step, even more difficult than the first two, is to work out a genuine, functional division of responsibilities and assets among the universities in a province or region. This will encounter every kind of opposition from affected interests both within and outside the universities, but failure to do it will invite governments to act on their own, which will mean decision by civil servants and management consultants. More than tradition and comfort is at stake: the university's autonomy is.

In the 1960s the government of Ontario was growing pessimistic about the prospects of an unenforced solution to the problem of balancing, within the limits of responsible financing, the internal interests of its proliferating universities with the interests of higher education in the province as a whole, and began moving toward an imposed solution through integrating all its universities into a University of Ontario. The Spinks Report, which recommended such a step, alarmed the Ontario universities and made them realize that their choice lay between voluntary restraint and cooperation, on the one hand, and absorption into a mega-university, on the other. They chose the former, and the government backed off.

The current threat, manifest in most provinces, takes different forms but rises from the same fundamental problem: balancing, but now within tightening financial limitations, the internal interests of self-governing universities with the interests of higher education as a whole. One unpromising difference from the 1960s is that university governance is now more fragmented, less effective, and far less willing to take unpopular measures. Nevertheless, the hope for a solution consistent with the universities' continued autonomy is the same: voluntary restraint and cooperation.

V

In writing my life I realize yet again how large an influence the farm has been. I live a long way from it, and it is many years since I last visited it; indeed, most of my adult life has been spent far from it. Nevertheless, it has remained something of an anchor for me and my family. My father left it in equal parts to my sisters and me; we pooled the parts, with Gertrude, who lives in Winnipeg, managing the joint operation; it now belongs to the next generation, one of whom manages it, and for them it continues to be a common interest, scattered though they are in four cities and two countries. There is little prospect that any of my descendants or my sisters' will ever work the farm again, but we have not discussed selling it.

In the embattled years of my University of Manitoba presidency Lesley and I would, at particularly stressful times, drive to the farm on a Saturday morning and spend a few hours there. For my father and grandfather this farm represented the fulfilment of an impossible dream: after centuries of huddling on the margins of a constantly threatening society, with no greater security of tenancy than a hostile landlord's whim, they now, in their new country – not a friendly one, but not threatening – actually owned what in the old country had been the forbidden symbol of security, land. It came with problems, but problems were what they expected of life. I had been born into the legal security of Canada, with the material security of the farm added shortly thereafter, and had never known the helpless fear of waiting for a gathering pogrom. But we had watched from a distance the European pogroms grow more organized and deadly, and the Canadian society begin to reflect this temper and grow more threatening. For my forebears in Russia the only defensive action available had been flight. My brother and I had a better option; it cost Bert his life, but we had needed to have a part in pushing the threat back.

Walking the fields I'd so often as a boy walked with my father when he was struggling to make a go of them, unconsciously imitating him as I scooped the soil to test its frangibility or winnowed ears of grain to check their fulness, I sometimes wondered what he would have thought of my current life as a university president. He had received the news of my initial move into administration with marked reserve: scholarship and teaching were of such worth to him that he had not really objected to my declining the management of the farm and his other business for their sakes, and he had felt that my work at the University of Chicago justified the choice; but he didn't see administration yielding comparable values. I thought if he had lived he would have taken pleasure in the Manitoba appointment, but only fleetingly; he'd have thought the incessant and debilitating battles unavailing and an inordinate expenditure of spirit. He would have agreed that the universities were fundamental to the civilization of the country, but would have been sceptical of my view that, having been invited to do so, I ought to accept responsibility for the management and defence of the University of Manitoba Jews, he'd have thought, had trouble enough; there was no need to look for more.

I had come soon enough to agree that there had been no need to answer this particular call, but retained a different view of administration. If you lived in a university you ought to share its burdens as well as its advantages; from that it followed that your share should be determined at least as much by the institution as by your own preferences. If your university called you to an administrative role its health and future became your obligation, taking precedence over all other academic considerations; your former universities also had some, though diminished, claim. In favourable circumstances an administrative role might enable you to help build the university's strength and raise its standards; I'd had such an opportunity at Toronto, and the satisfaction of that experience compensated for the cost to my scholarship and teaching. My error had been in thinking that because the University of Manitoba was my Alma Mater, and Manitoba the province in which my family had found refuge and built a stable life, I had some obligation to accept that university's call and would be able to repeat there in some measure the constructive work at Toronto; but recognition of the error did nothing to diminish the obligation I'd assumed, and in this at least I thought my father would have agreed. He'd also have understood that I couldn't withdraw from it except at a victorious moment. The debate could thus be suspended, if not resolved; meanwhile, the benign influence of the fields would have restored my sense of proportion and put the battles of the day into perspective.

It is generally said that one mellows with age. I am not sure that 'mellows' is the right word; perhaps one just grows less certain about one's judgments and opinions, and, if retired, less engaged. I have been told that I've mellowed, and I frequently feel the generous glow that comes from acknowledging that someone else's opinion or judgment has as much chance of being right as my own. But I suspect that the generosity comes largely from not being responsible, not having to decide what is right in a contested situation. At my age it is not hard to be relativistic about distant matters, but in writing these pages and thus reliving earlier struggles I find myself as committed as before. Many decisions are between better and worse, and there compromise is often a good, allowing persons of somewhat varying judgments to work together for the common benefit. Some decisions, however, are between right and wrong, where compromise is simply bad. These are situations in which it is right to grow embattled, if necessary paying the price. I do not regret having made some such decisions, although I've sometimes regretted the price.

Index

Abella, Irving, 46n
Adamson, Alan H., 33–4, 41, 47, 54–5, 64, 92–3
Alberta, University of, 275, 300–1
Aldershot, 105–6
Alexander, Field-Marshal Lord Harold, 148
Alexander, W.J., 71; Lectures, 87
Algonquin Regiment, 97, 103, 110, 125
Algren, Nelson, 167
Allen, Don C., 195
Allen, Ralph, 147–8
Almelo, 139–40
American Council of Learned Societies fellowship, 206
American Council on Education, 320–1
Anderson, Bill, 65
Anderson, Fulton, 88, 154–5, 173
Anderson, Major Jack, 116
antisemitism, 8–9, 15–17, 20–4, 32–3, 35–6, 39, 46, 50, 52, 59–61, 64, 68, 93, 97, 101, 109, 130, 138, 152, 154–5, 196–7, 233, 324, 372, 387–9, 396–7
Antwerp, 124, 126, 128, 132–3
Archbold, Captain H.S.C., 112
Argue, Fletcher, 49

Arnhem, 127–8
Arpin, Maurice, 297, 302, 305, 313–14, 319–20
Arts and Letters Club of Toronto, 388–90
Association of Graduate Schools (U.S.), 216, 225–6, 238, 259, 269
Association of Universities and Colleges of Canada, 242, 269, 274, 297–8, 312, 337, 343–4, 352
Austin, Lieutenant-Colonel, 110
autonomy, university, 231–2, 236–7, 239, 264, 268–9, 294, 305, 314, 327, 329, 332–6, 340–2, 352, 372, 374, 379, 387–9, 391–6

Bad Zwischenan, 141
Bald, R.C., 189, 192
Baldwin, T.W., 195
Barber, Clarence, 277–8
Barker, Arthur, 74–6, 79, 83, 86–7, 92, 96, 109, 159, 163, 173–4, 179, 196, 210
Bateman, Scott, 313–15, 335–6, 344, 349–50, 355
Beadle, George, 215
Bellow, Saul, 204

Bennett, Joan and Stanley, 186, 191
Bentley, Gerald E., 163, 166
Bergen-op-Zoom, 128
Berrigan, Daniel, 347–8
Birney, Earle, 48, 76, 83–4, 90–1, 96, 146, 156–7
Bissell, Christine, 185–6, 214
Bissell, Claude, 70, 77, 91–2, 95, 98, 127–9, 146, 156, 164, 185–6, 210–303 *passim*, 321, 351
Blackburn, Robert, 213, 223, 244–5, 351–2
Bladen, Vincent, 212–13, 217–18, 247, 249, 252–3, 264, 266
Blair, F.C., 16
Blair, Walter, 171, 198, 205, 211, 215–16
Bodleian Library, Oxford, 198
Boeschenstein, Hermann, 78, 88
Bond, Donald, 171, 189, 192, 193, 196–7, 204
Borden, Henry, 267–8, 351
Borowski, Joe, 317
Bourns, Arthur, 279–80
Bowers, Fredson, 192
Bowles, Richard, 355–6, 368, 377
Brauer, Gerald, 176, 216
Breda, 133–4
Breskens, 125–7
Brett, G.S., 83, 85–6, 88
British Columbia, University of, 48, 276, 278, 327, 387
British Empire, Order of, 118, 130, 148, 186
British Museum, 106, 180, 185, 188, 194–6, 198
Brockington, Leonard, 233
Broneer, Oscar, 198
Broughall, Major William, 107, 129, 138

Brown, E.K., 40–1, 66, 70–2, 76, 78–9, 151, 161–3, 165, 170, 177, 179, 182–4, 189, 193
Brown, Margaret, 40, 183–4, 193
Bruges, 124–5, 127
Bruser, Bert, ix
Bruser, Fredelle, 57
Brussels, 129, 132
Buckingham Palace, 44, 234
Bueckert, Peter, 22, 26
Buller, A.H.R., 34–5
Burton, Ernest, 202–3
Burton, Richard, 194
Bürzle, Anton, 35–6, 78
Bush, Douglas, 178, 194, 200–2

Caen, 114
Cain, Peter, 334, 350–1, 356, 368
Calgary, University of, 279
Callaghan, Morley, 147–8
Cambridge University, 108–9, 186–7, 262–3
Campbell, Major Clarence, 139
Campbell, Ralph, 376–7, 384–5; Campbell Report, 291
Camp Borden, 102–3
Canada Council, 243–4, 276–8
Canadian Army, 99–144
Canadian Association of Graduate Schools, 242–3, 264, 269
Canadian Association of University Teachers, 220, 269, 331–5, 349, 370–1
Canadian Clubs, 340–1
Canadian Forum, 147
Canadian Jewish Congress, 46
Canadian Military Headquarters, 143–4
Canadian Military Intelligence Corps, 104

Canadian Nationalist Party, 21–2, 52, 142
Canadian Officers Training Corps, 63, 68–70, 80, 83, 91–2, 95–6
Canadian Pacific Railway, 4, 12, 23
Canadian Union of Students, 288
Caplan, Gerald, 240
Carrothers, Fred, 322–3
Chamberlain, Neville, 53–5, 62
Chevrier, Douglas, 44, 350, 355–7
'Chicago school,' 165–6
Chicago, University of, 161–218, 223, 227, 230, 262, 285, 292, 397; College, 163, 166–9, 176–7; Department of English, 162–218; Humanities Division, 170, 204; Press, 217, 230; Theological Faculty, 175–6
Chortitz, 12–13, 16
Chou En-lai, 352, 354
Churchill College, Cambridge, 204, 262–3, 273, 275
Clawson, W.H., 76, 83–4, 91
Cochrane, Charles, 88
Cody, Canon H.J., 79, 88, 155
Cohen, Aaron, 4, 5
Cohen, Lawrence, 119
Commonwealth Scholarships and Fellowships Committee, 243, 284
Commonwealth Universities Association, 44, 233–4, 343
Conacher, James, 321–2
Condo, W.J., 297, 302, 304–5, 312–13, 315, 319–20, 346, 350, 355–62, 365–9, 378
Connor, Robin, 362–3, 376
Coolidge, Lowell, 179–80
Coper, Rudolf, 153–4
Corbett, Paul, 70, 80, 91, 138
Corry, Alex, 265, 268
Coulton, G.G., 84

Council of Ontario Universities. *See* Ontario Universities, Council of
Crane, Ronald, 162–3, 165–6, 170–1, 182–3, 189
Crerar, General Harry, 136
Crowe, Harry, 220, 282, 333
Cummings, Esmé, 310, 336
Cunningham, James V., 171, 190
Curry, Peter, 295–8, 302, 305, 319–20, 324–5, 327, 334, 337, 339, 355

Dafoe, John W., 57
Daiches, David, 166, 169
Daniells, Roy, 47–8, 56, 58, 64, 78
Davidson, Reverend John, 95
Davies, Robertson, 225, 299
Davis, Herbert, 87–8
Davis, Natalie, 292–3
Davis, William H., 237–8, 254–6, 264, 268, 302
Depression, Great, 18–24, 29, 30, 46, 52
Deutsch, John, 211, 235, 296
Dickson, Brian, 319, 324, 327, 336, 350
Diekhoff, John, 178, 201–2
Djwa, Sandra, 96
Doerksen, Peter, 17
Donnelly, Murray, 326
Dorian, Donald, 180
Dover, 112–13
Drew, George, 148
Drury, Lieutenant-Colonel C.M., 111, 117
Duckworth, Harry, 296, 305–6
Duff/Berdahl Report, 269–70

Eastman, Harry, 249, 254
Edel, Leon, 155, 193
Edgar, Pelham, 76–7

Edwards, John, 229
Einarson, Henry, 317
Eisenhower, General Dwight D., 125, 134
Elder, Peter, 226
Eliot, T.S., 64, 82–3, 190–1, 196–7; *Criterion*, 64, 76, 82–3, 190
Ellison, Ralph, 173
Endicott, Norman, 71, 75–6, 220
Evans, John, 322–3, 377

Fairley, Barker, 77–8, 88, 153–4
Fairley, Tom, 107
Falaise, 114–15, 118–20, 122
Faludy, George, 275–6
Faust, Clarence, 163, 177
Fermi, Enrico, 168–9
Fieldhouse, Noel, 41–3
Filmon, Gary, 359
First Canadian Army, 107–11, 117–18, 122, 126, 132–3, 138; Intelligence Section, 107
Fisher, Gordon, 325
Fisher, Kenneth, 249, 251
Flower, George, 255
Focus program, Manitoba, 342, 379
Forster, E.M., 186–7
Foster, Major-General H.W., 119, 129–30
Foulkes, Major-General Charles, 116
Fourth Canadian Armoured Division, 118–42
Fourth Canadian Infantry Brigade, 112, 115–18
Freedman, Sam, 25
Freeman, Rosemary, 196
French, J. Milton, 178, 201
Friedman, Arthur, 171, 192
Friedman, Milton, 205
Friesoythe, 140–1

Frye, Northrop, 76–7, 96, 163, 174, 210, 249, 260
Funk, Jack, 21–2, 53, 143
Funk, Nelson, 14–15, 22, 23, 53
Fyles, T.W., 306, 319, 329

Ghent, 132; Canal, 124, 127
Gilbert, Allan H., 173, 210
Gilson, J.C., 306, 369
Globe and Mail, 272, 275, 284–5, 293, 352, 354
Gordon, Andrew, 211–17, 224–5, 229, 233, 235, 246
Gordon, Jean, 221, 226
Gotlieb, Calvin, 229
Grant, Douglas, 196
Gray, John, 89, 129
'Great Defalcation,' 30
Grube, George, 246–7
Guggenheim fellowship, 193
Guindon, Roger, 354
Gurney, Roy, 232

Hanes, Charles, 249–50
Hanford, James Holly, 179, 191–2, 194, 201
Hansen, Bert, 265–6
Hanuschak, Ben, 341–2, 350–1, 355–62, 365, 370, 373, 376, 378
Hare, Kenneth, 278
Harris, Robin, 274–5
Harris, William, 289, 322
Harrison, Pat, 215
Harrogate Cemetery, 109, 187
Hart, Steve, 91
Hayek, Friedrick, 205
Heinzelman, J.H., 35
'Herb' (Major), 131–2
Hermant, Sidney, 351
Hiebert, Paul, 41

Himmler, Heinrich, 137
Hitler, Adolf, 21, 39, 51-3, 62-7, 113, 120, 133
Hochwald Gap, 136-7
Howe, Joseph, 36
Hughes, Merritt, 178, 200-1
Hughesman, J.R., 332, 337
Hugill, Lieutenant-Commander Antony, 139-40, 184
Hulbert, James, 162-3, 170
Hunt, John, 360, 368
Huron-Sussex Ratepayers and Residents Association, 299
Hutchins, Robert M., 162, 164-5, 168, 188-9

Ingersoll, Ralph, 147
Innis, Harold, 86, 153, 184, 214, 243, 247; Innis College, 287
International Association of Universities, 371-3
Inter-Provincial Committee on University Rationalization, 327-8

Jackson, Robert, 254-5
Jackson, Stan, 61
Jeanneret, Achille, 243-4
Jesus College, Cambridge, 108-9
Johnson, Harry, 205, 213, 217-18
Jones, Meredith, 60
Joost, Martin, 229

Kanee, Sol, 368-70, 377
Keast, Rea, 171, 182-3
Kelley, Maurice, 178, 201
Kellough, Harold, 14, 53
Kelly, John, 229, 245-6, 260-2
Kennedy, W.P.M., 155
Kerr, Clark, 287
Kimpton, Lawrence, 188

King, Mackenzie, 54, 63, 79, 132, 141
Kirkconnell, Watson, 178
Kitching, Major-General George, 119
Knox, R.S., 76, 83-5, 89, 148, 150, 156
Kremlin, 372
Kristjanson, Leo, 333
Krug, Major Charles, 104
Kusten Canal, 141

Lacoste, Paul, 354
Langdon, Steven, 272, 281-7, 288-90
Laskin, Bora, 155, 220, 249-50, 252-3, 255-6, 269, 271, 335
Laskin Committee, 249-53, 263, 271, 273
Leatherhead, 107
Leech, Clifford, 257
Leonard, R.W., fellowship and Foundation, 81-2
Leopold and Dérivation canals, 125-8, 130
Lett, Brigadier Sherwood, 115-16
Levi, Edward, 215-16, 292
Lewalski, Barbara, 195
Lewis, Wyndham, 197
Leyerle, John, 283-4
Lochhead, Douglas, 233
Lodge, Rupert C., 43, 50, 55-6
Long, Marcus, 50
Lower, Arthur, 60
Lutaud, Olivier, 196

McCallum, Reid, 88
McCarthy, Don, 361-3, 374, 376, 384-5
McCarthy, J.R., 232, 237
Macdonald, John B., 276, 278; Macdonald Committee, 276-8
McDougall, D.J., 173-4
McEvoy, Pat, 346-7
MacFarlane, J.A., 212

MacFarlane, R.O., 49–50
McGill University, 42, 226, 243, 288, 345
McGillivray, J.R., 76, 148–9, 156, 274
Machray, J.A., 30
McKeon, Richard, 165
McKinnon, Murdoch, 84, 145, 156
McKinnon, Neil, 233, 296
McLaughlin, Roland, 212
Maclean, Norman, 171, 189
McLuhan, Marshall, 42, 59, 164, 217, 229–30
McMaster University, 279–80, 293
Macmillan, Harold, 234
McMurrich, Captain Arthur, 118, 125, 129
McNaught, Beverly, 102–3
McNaught, Carlton and Eleanor, 94–5, 152
McNaught, Kenneth, 70, 77, 80, 89, 102–3, 282–3, 294
McNaughton, General Andrew, 133
McNeill, William H., 166–7
MacPherson, Brough, 91, 231–2
McQuade, Ray, 370, 377–8
McQueen, Robert, 58–9
McRae, Robert, 153, 249, 252
Mailer, Norman, 204
Manitoba Arts Review, 57, 64–5
Manitoba Club, 320, 324–5
Manitoba, Government of, 301–80 *passim*; Departments of Colleges and Universities Affairs, *see* Hanuschak, Miller, Schreyer; Health, 328–9; Labour, 316–17, 360; Mines and Resources, 342; Welfare, 328–9
Manitoba Labour Board and Labour Relations Act, 316–17, 332, 338, 343–5, 348–9, 371

Manitoba Task Force on Post-Secondary Education, 339–42, 379
Manitoba Universities Grants Commission, 301, 313–18, 335–6, 339–41, 344, 348–9, 354–67, 369–70, 373–6, 382; consultant's report, 369, 373, 379, 384; *see also* Bateman, Chevrier, Condo
Manitoba, University of, 30–66, 145, 153, 258, 265, 277–8, 295–8, 300–80, 382–5, 388, 396–8; Act, 297, 306, 325–7, 338–9, 383; Alumni Association, 296, 359; Arts Students Council, 38, 50, 57, 65; Association of Employees Supporting Educational Services, 338, 344, 358–61, 364–5; Board, 296, 307–80 *passim*; Board Committee on the Financial Situation, 355–7; Board-Senate Committee on Priorities, 374–5; budget committee, 315, 356–7, 363–4, 375; Canadian Association of Industrial, Mechanical, and Allied Workers, 345–8, 380; Dean's Council, 315, 326, 358, 361–3, 375, 377; discipline committees, 325–6, 380; Faculty Association, 296, 306–80 *passim*, 383–4; installation, 312–13; library, 311–12; *Manitoban*, 56, 302–3, 310–11, 317–18, 323–5, 332, 338, 346, 377; pension plan, 314–16, 318, 379; planned deficits, 344, 349–51, 354–76; planning office, 306, 311, 331–2; Senate, 296, 307–80 *passim*; strikes, 345–8, 358–65, 380; Students Union, 38, 50, 296, 303–80 *passim*, 383; tenure and tenure by-law, 329–35, 370–1, 380, 382, 384
Massey, Alice, 106, 136

Massey, Vincent, 106, 212, 299
Mathers, Colonel William, 100, 105
Mazankowski, Donald, 277
Medical Research Council, 222, 277
Meek, Theophile, 89
Mennonites, 3–29 *passim*, 52, 263
Menorah Society, 32, 37
Midwest Interlibrary Center, 205, 244–5
Miller, Saul, 301, 314–15, 327, 334–5, 382
Milton, John, 74, 79, 86–7, 108, 157–61, 163, 167, 173–81, 186, 190–4, 199–202, 205–10, 216, 219, 256, 258, 263, 348–9; *Areopagitica*, 178, 180–1, 200, 209; *Complete Prose Works*, 178–81, 193–4, 196, 199–202, 206–9, 258; MA thesis on, 75, 79; *Paradise Lost*, 210, 263, 275; PhD dissertation on, 83, 85–7, 96, 152, 157–61, 173–4
Milton Society of America, 209
Mitchell, Leon, 364–5
Mitchell, Shlomo, 32
Modern Languages Association, 36, 209
Modern Philology, 173, 189
Monson, Rabbi David, 95
Montagnes, Ian, ix
Montgomery, General Bernard, 114, 117, 119, 122, 125, 132, 134
Moore, Mavor, 80, 85
Morons, The (University of Manitoba English Club), 41, 50
Morton, William L., 56, 303
Mulock, Sir William, 79
Munro, Ross, 146–7
Murray, Colonel W.W., 143–4
Myers, Roger, 219

Naimark, Arnold, 362, 376

National Defence Headquarters, 143–4
National Library, 277
National Research Council, 222, 276–7
National Resources Mobilization Act, 80, 90, 132–3
Nemetz, Nathan, 352, 354
Newberry Library, 173, 191; Conference (orig. Midwest Renaissance Conf.), 191
New Left Caucus, 291–2
New York University, 205
New Yorker magazine, 385
Niemberg, 12
Nijmegen, 128
Nitikman, Aaron and Annie, 6, 12, 16, 29, 31
Nitikman, Arke, 4
Nitikman, Herb, 8, 16, 31, 97
Nitikman, Sam, 32, 45, 94, 102, 262
Nitikman, Yosel and Freyda (grandparents), 5–6, 12, 16, 31–2, 38–9, 45, 93–4
Nitikmans Sirluck Company, 6
Norwood, Gilbert, 88
Nuveen, John, 192

Ogburn, William, 202
Oliver, Michael, 339–42, 352
Olson, Elder, 171, 189, 230
Ontario Committee on University Affairs, 237, 265, 284–7, 298
Ontario Confederation of University Faculty Associations, 240
Ontario Council of University Librarians, 241–2, 298, 300
Ontario Council on Graduate Studies (orig. Ontario Committee of Graduate Deans), 235–42, 265–6, 268–9, 298, 300; Advisory Committee on

406 Index

Planning, 241, 266, 266, 269, 300; Advisory Joint Council of Ontario Graduate Deans and Librarians, 242, 298; Committee on Appraisals, 239–41, 266, 300
Ontario Department of University Affairs, 237, 239–40, 265, 298
Ontario Graduate Fellowship Program (POGFs), 221–2, 235–7
Ontario Institute for Studies in Education, 254–6
Ontario Universities, Council of (orig. Committee of Presidents of Universities of Ontario), 211, 236–40, 265–6, 268–9, 290–1, 298
Ontario, University of (proposed), 241–2, 268
Orlikow, David, 332–4, 350, 355
Owen, E.T., 153

Parker, William R., 205, 210
Patrick, Max, 258
Patterns of Literary Criticism, 217, 230
Pauley, Russ, 316–17, 360
Penner, Ed, 21, 143
Penner (teacher), 10
Pentland, Clare, 366
Perry, Aaron J., 48–9, 84
Petty, Rance, 364–5
Phelps, Arthur, 60
PhilM program, 223–5, 232, 251
Pocock, Bishop, 262
Polanyi, John, 249–50
Pontifical Institute of Mediaeval Studies, 227–8, 260–2
Pratt, E.J., 76–7, 84, 96, 184
Preston, Mel, 279
Priestley, F.E.L., 150–1, 156–7, 257, 274
Prince, F.T., 234

Quadrangle Club, 163, 188–9, 191, 205
Queen's University, 154–5, 268–9; *Queen's Quarterly*, 269
Quiller-Couch, Sir Arthur, 108

Rae, Bob, 282, 284–7, 289–90
Rajan, Balachandra, 108–9
Ralston, Colonel J.L., 132–3
Rankin, Alex, 299
Rhineland, Battle of, 134–7
Rice University, 209
Ringler, William, 215–16
Robarts, John, 237
Robarts Library. *See* University of Toronto Research Library
Robinson, Gilbert, 251–2, 264, 286
Robinson, Lieutenant-Colonel McKenzie, 131–2, 137, 141–2
Robson, John M., ix
Ross, Murray, 238
Ross, Robin, 291–2
Roth, Philip, 191
Rowse, A.L., 191
Royal Air Force, Harrogate station, 105–6
Royal Military College, 103–4, 144
Royal Regiment of Canada, 109–12, 116
Royal Society of Canada, 274, 387
Russell, Peter, 287

St Philipsland, 128
Saskatchewan, University of, 278
Sassoon, Siegfried, 186–7
Saunders, Doris, 49
Saunderson, Hugh, 296, 301, 304–5, 309–10, 313, 318, 339, 383
Savage, Donald, 333
Savan, David, 155
Scheldt River and Estuary, 124–7

Schoeck, Richard, 217, 230
Schreyer, Ed, 301, 329, 342, 344, 351, 360-2, 365, 368, 370, 375-6, 378
Science Council of Canada, 276
Second Canadian Corps, 116, 128, 132, 138
Second Canadian Infantry Division, 111-18
Second World War, 62-3, 65-8, 80-1, 99-144; declared, 62; German aggression beforehand, 51-3, 62
Sellers, Edward, 220, 302
Seventeenth-Century News, 209
Sheffield, Edward, 242
s'Hertogenbosch, 128, 132
Shook, Lawrence, 260-2
Shugg, Roger, 217
Sibley, William, 305-6, 369
Siegfried Line, 134, 136-7
Siemens, P.H., 10-11
Sigma Alpha Mu Fraternity, 32, 37, 39, 44, 51, 58
Silver, Edwin, 97
Silver, Hannah, 13, 32
Silver, Wilfred, 13, 19, 44, 97-8
Silverstein, Theodore, 171, 193
Simon Fraser University, 278, 293, 327
Simonds, Lieutenant-General Guy, 119, 136-7
Simpson, Alan, 176, 216
Sirluck, Bert, 9, 15, 18, 38-9, 45-6, 52, 60-1, 80, 97, 102, 104-10, 142, 148, 152, 187, 202, 396-7
Sirluck, Gertrude (later Mitchell), 6, 32, 45, 48, 93-4, 128, 396
Sirluck, Gladys (later Bruser), 6, 45, 48, 57, 205, 396
Sirluck, Hilda (later Sturc), 6, 45, 48, 102, 396
Sirluck, Isaac (father), 4-6, 12-19, 23-4, 29, 32, 38-9, 44-5, 60-1, 80, 93-5, 110, 128, 142, 203, 263-4, 396-8
Sirluck, Katherine Ann, ix, 203, 287, 301, 352, 381, 387, 389
Sirluck, Lesley McNaught, ix, 89-90, 93-5, 97-8, 101-4, 106, 109, 124, 127, 142, 152, 163, 171, 173, 183-6, 191-4, 198, 202-3, 207-8, 210, 214-15, 233-4, 254, 274, 287, 298-9, 301, 309-10, 313, 320, 323-4, 335, 351-2, 362, 377, 381-3, 389, 396
Sirluck, Oudie Chasanoff, 44-6, 94
Sirluck, Robert McNaught, ix, 25, 202, 287, 301, 304, 381, 389
Sirluck, Ruchel (Rose) Nitikman (mother), 4-6, 17-19, 32, 38-9
Sirluck, Usher Zelig and Bella (grandparents), 5-6, 12, 16, 396
Sitwell, Edith, 191
Sixth Canadian Division, 141, 143-4
Sledd, James, 171, 182, 193
Smith, A.J.M., 91-2
Smith, Lorrene, 292-3
Smith, Sidney, 65, 148, 153-4
Social Sciences and Humanities Research Council, 277
Sögel, 140
Solandt, Omand, 321-2
Southam Inc., 325
Soviet Academy of Sciences, 372
Soviet Minister of Education, 372
Spell, Leonard, 172-3
Spenser, Edmund, 162-3, 167, 175, 180-1, 216
Spinks, John, 278
Spinks Commission, 238, 240; Report, 241, 268, 395
Stacey, Colonel C.P., 147, 173
Star, Toronto Daily, 275, 281

Starbuck, George, 204
Steiner, George, 204, 262
Stern, Richard, 204
Stevens, W.N.R., 331–5, 349, 379–80
Stewart, Edward, 237, 265–6
Streeter, Robert, 171, 193
Swann, Peter, 254
Sword, Jack, 230, 267
Szilard, Leo, 189

Tate, Alan, 166
Thode, Harry, 279–80
Thom, Ron, 299
Thomas, Russell, 166, 177
Thomson, Homer, 198
Thomson, Roy, 232
Three Rivers Officers Training Camp, 98–102, 105
Tillotson, Geoffrey, 196
Tillyard, E.M.W., 108
Toronto Student Movement, 284, 287
Toronto, University of, 66, 67–99, 145–64, 209–14, 219–303, 321, 385–8, 391, 397–8; Archives, ix; Association of the Teaching Staff (later Faculty Association), 220–2, 240, 270, 274, 282–4, 294–5, 322; Board, 266–8, 270, 282–4, 295; Budget Committee, 273–4; Caput, 290; centres and institutes, 227–9, 261–2, 283, 299; Commission on University Governance, 282, 289–90, 293–5; Committee for Scientific Research, 251–2; Department of English, 67–99, 145–64, 213, 219, 385–6; Faculty Club, 85, 386; federated colleges, 217, 219, 221, 227, 229, 245–6, 249, 260–2; Graduate English Club, 76, 87–8; Graduate Students Union, 271–3, 285, 290, 299, 307; Massey College, 212, 225, 233, 235, 259–60, 299; Presidential Advisory Committees: Policy and Planning (later President's Council), 231–2, 259, 264, 266–8, 270–1, 273, 282–95, 322; Press, 217; released time from, 231–2; Scarborough and Erindale colleges, 238, 285–6; School of Graduate Studies, 70, 81–2, 85, 98, 211–14, 219–303, 307, 322; Senate, 228, 230–2, 259–60, 270; Students Administrative Council, 270–2, 282–95, 303, 309; Summer Session, 231–2; University College, 59, 71, 88, 98, 145, 213, 219, 227, 245, 290, 386; *U of T Quarterly*, 146–7; *Varsity*, 270, 272, 289, 293, 303

Towse, Geoffrey, 193, 206
Toynbee, Arnold, 77, 167
Trudeau, Pierre E., 264, 352, 375
Trueman, Albert W., 153
Trun, 119, 123
Turcot, Lieutenant-Colonel Gil, 188
Turner, Arthur and Alberta, 202, 208
Turner, Ogden, 33–4, 39, 41, 44, 47, 55

Uhrich, Bill, 27–9, 53
Underhill, Frank, 77
United College (later U of Winnipeg), 60, 220, 282, 305, 333, 341
university autonomy. *See* autonomy, university
Unruh, Victor, 17, 143

Vancouver Club, 278
Vaughan, O.D., 233, 267
V-1, 113; V-2, 128
Veen, 137

Verrières Ridge and Rocquancourt, 115–16, 118
Vokes, Major-General Chris, 130–1, 136–7, 142
Vught, 128

Waines, W.J., 43–4
Walcheren Island, 124–7
Wallace, Malcolm, 71, 76, 90, 92
Wallace, Stewart, 86
Wallace, William, 92
Ward, Champion, 177
Warren, Peter, 336–7, 359, 383
weaponry, army, 120–1
Wedepohl, Martin, 363
Wells, Don, 364–5
Wernick, Andy, 284, 287
Wheeler, A. Lloyd, 37, 41, 48, 50, 56, 59–60, 64
Whitaker, William, 21–2, 52
White, Mary, 247
Wiebe, Dr C.W., 25, 61
Wiens, Isaac, 4, 11
Wiens, Lieutenant David, 138
Wigle, Lieutenant-Colonel Fred, 125–6, 129–30, 140–1
Wilkinson, Bertie, 227–8
Williams, Arnold, 180, 208
Williams, Carl, 222–3, 230
Williams, Gordon, 244–5
Williamson, George, 162–3, 170, 177, 183, 186, 190, 215, 256
Wilson, Angus, 194–5
Wilt, Napier, 162–3, 165–6, 170, 177, 183–4, 186, 192, 198, 211, 215–16
Windsor Transit Camp, 104–5
Winegard, William, 249, 254, 273

Winkler, Manitoba, 3–29, 31, 34, 39, 45–6, 52, 60–1, 66–7, 80–1, 103, 119, 142–3, 263, 364
Winkler, Valentine, 4, 11
Winnipeg, 30–66, 103–4, 142, 263, 300–3, 304–80
Winnipeg Free Press, 57, 254, 323, 337–8, 347
Winnipeg Tribune, 146, 317, 325, 328, 337–8, 369, 375–7
Winter, John, 285
Withrow, William, 254
Wolfe, Don M., 178–80, 193–4, 200–2, 206–8, 258
Woodbury, Leonard, 56–7
Woodhouse, A.S.P., 70–5, 79, 81, 83, 86–7, 90, 96, 109, 142, 154, 156–7, 162–4, 173–4, 178–9, 184, 194, 196, 200, 202, 210, 213, 220, 243, 257–8
Woodrow Wilson Dissertation Fellowship Selection Committee, 258–9
Woodside, Moffatt, 212–13, 222, 247, 251, 256
Worker–Student Alliance, 292
Wright, Douglas, 265–6
Wright, H.W., 43
Wright, Lieutenant-Colonel Peter, 107, 109–11, 129, 138
Wyman, Max, 300–1

York, 105–6, 187
York Club, 76, 233
York University, 238
Yost, Allen, 364–5

Zabel, Morton, 170
Zaifman, Ken, 336

www.ingramcontent.com/pod-product-compliance
Lightning Source LLC
Chambersburg PA
CBHW020348080526

44584CB00014B/939